The American Society of International Law

STUDIES IN FOREIGN INVESTMENT
AND
ECONOMIC DEVELOPMENT

Previously published

Foreign Enterprise in India: Laws and Policies by Matthew J. Kust
Foreign Enterprise in Colombia: Laws and Policies by Seymour W. Wurfel
Foreign Enterprise in Nigeria: Laws and Policies by Paul O. Proehl

FOREIGN ENTERPRISE IN MEXICO

Laws and Policies

FOREIGN ENTERPRISE

IN MEXICO

Laws and Policies

By HARRY K. WRIGHT

THE UNIVERSITY OF NORTH CAROLINA PRESS · CHAPEL HILL

Copyright © 1971 by

THE UNIVERSITY OF NORTH CAROLINA PRESS

All rights reserved

Manufactured in the United States of America

PRINTED BY THE SEEMAN PRINTERY, DURHAM, N. C.

ISBN 0-8078-1151-3

Library of Congress Catalog Card Number 76-97020

Foreword

Harry K. Wright's study of *Foreign Enterprise in Mexico* is the fourth of a series of studies, commissioned by the American Society of International Law, of the legal environment for foreign investment in selected countries. Earlier monographs on India, Colombia, and Nigeria were published by The University of North Carolina Press; and a fifth, final study, that of *Foreign Enterprise in Japan,* is in preparation.

The aim of the series is to describe and analyze the legal institutions and practices that govern the participation of foreign capital and technology in economic development, through thorough consideration of the experience of five key countries. Three are developing; a fourth, Mexico, has been developing at an especially notable rate; and the fifth, Japan, is a phenomenon of economic upsurge all its own.

The factors that affect foreign private investment are not, or may not be, primarily "legal." Yet important policies of an economic, social, and ideological kind are often crystallized in legal form. The adequacy or inadequacy of the legal framework for investment may markedly influence the potential foreign investor in his decision to invest or not to invest. Moreover, the practice of governments in dealing with foreign investment is part of the raw material of international law; it is of great importance in the shaping of a law that has its impact upon, and reflects the impact of, the policies of governments, corporations, and lending institutions, national and international.

The committee of the Society that planned the series was under the chairmanship of The Honorable John R. Stevenson, then of the firm of Sullivan & Cromwell in New York, now The Legal Adviser of the U. S. Department of State. Mr. Stevenson; Professor Covey T. Oliver of the University of Pennsylvania Law School (who subsequently served as U. S. Ambassador to Colombia and Assistant Secretary of State for Inter-American Affairs); Professor Myres S. McDougal of Yale Law School; Lester Nurick, Deputy General Counsel of the International Bank for Reconstruction and Development; and Walter Sterling Surrey, of the firm of Surrey, Karasik, Greene & Hill of Washington, D.C., assisted by the Society's staff, drew up the "guidelines" that have served as a general outline of contents for each book in the series.

In this series of country studies, each research fellow has been assisted by an interdisciplinary advisory committee. Those who have counseled Professor Wright, formerly of The University of Texas School of Law and now Area Counsel for Latin America of Texaco Inc., are: Dillon Anderson, of Baker, Botts, Shepherd & Coates; Elting Arnold, General Counsel, Inter-American Development Bank; William S. Barnes, Fletcher School of Law and Diplomacy; Rodolfo Batiza, Tulane University School of Law; Paul W. Carrington, of Carrington, Johnson & Stephens; Richard Frank, formerly of the Department of State; Robert D. Hayton, Hunter College of the City University of New York; George Kalmanoff, International Bank for Reconstruction and Development; John G. Laylin, of Covington & Burling; Mark Massell, Washington, D.C.; Robert F. Meagher, Fletcher School of Law and Diplomacy; Covey T. Oliver, University of Pennsylvania Law School; Albert J. Parreno, of Curtis, Mallet-Prevost, Colt & Mosle; William D. Rogers, of Arnold & Porter; Seymour J. Rubin, of Surrey, Karasik, Greene & Hill; and Edmund A. Schaffzin, I.B.M. World Trade Corporation.

Neither the Society nor the advisory group bears responsibility for the views expressed in this book. Mr. Wright has had the benefit of a diversity of views and has formed his own. The Society is very pleased to have contributed to the preparation of a work whose quality will, it is believed, attract much appreciation.

On the Society's behalf, I wish to thank Mr. Wright, the members of the planning and advisory groups, and The University of North Carolina Press. I wish also to record the Society's profound appreciation to the Ford Foundation, whose generosity has supported this and so many other Society endeavors.

Stephen M. Schwebel
Executive Director
American Society of International Law

Washington, D.C.
April, 1970

Preface

This book has been drawn from many sources. Much of the historical background has been compiled from numerous and often conflicting published studies; the details of many more recent developments have had to be pieced together from contemporary newspaper accounts, magazine articles, and discussions with Mexican and foreign participants and observers. My incursions into the realm of the economist have been made somewhat timidly and rely on published data and studies made by those far more qualified than I. The detailed descriptions and analyses of the laws and regulations that affect, directly or indirectly, foreign enterprise in Mexico, to which most of the book is devoted, have been taken directly from the statute books and reports of decided cases, but I have also had the benefit of opinions of Mexican lawyers and legal scholars, published legal studies, and my own experience in Mexico.

Most of what has been published on the regulation of foreign investment in Mexico—and there has been surprisingly little—has been limited to a description of existing legislation prohibiting or imposing quantitative restrictions on the entry of foreign capital into specific economic activities, with slight attention to the practical administration and application of the laws and even less to the policies that exist beyond the statutory scheme. In Mexico, perhaps to a higher degree than in most countries, much of the regulatory system governing the entry of foreign investment and the conduct of business generally is formulated within only the vaguest of statutory guidelines or completely outside the legislative process and often enforced under laws designed for entirely unrelated purposes. To the student of foreign investment regulation this poses substantial problems. Not only are the policies often difficult to uncover and define, but they are much more readily changed and exceptions more easily engrafted than when they are embodied in formal legislation. In many cases the adoption or change of an administrative policy is given little or no publicity and must be traced through its application to specific cases. As a result, substantial parts of the book have been drawn from long hours of discussions over extended periods of time with businessmen and government officials, but mainly with Mexican lawyers who are in touch day-to-day with the application of the laws and administrative policies to specific situations and transactions.

This ease with which practices are changed also means that a policy in existence today may not be entirely the same or may not be enforced with the same vigor tomorrow. New developments sometimes seem to occur almost overnight, without warning. Especially from one presidential administration to the next, there may be at least changes in attitude and shifts in emphasis. Nevertheless, while the present administration will have come to a close and a new president will have taken office shortly before the publication of this study, it seems likely that future developments will follow the trend evident in recent years and that the laws and major policies discussed in this book will continue in effect for some time to come. It is hoped that this study will be found a useful contribution to a deeper understanding of those laws and policies.

It is impossible to list here all those who have helped in the preparation of this book. I cannot fail, however, to acknowledge the contributions of some. This study was made possible and generously supported by the American Society of International Law. The members of the advisory group assembled by the Society, named by Stephen M. Schwebel in his Foreword, contributed their time and many valuable suggestions. Additional financial support was received for research in the spring and summer of 1967 from the United States Latin American Faculty Interchange of the Foreign Area Fellowship Program, a joint committee of the Social Science Research Council and the American Council of Learned Societies, through the Institute of Latin American Studies of The University of Texas at Austin. Of the numerous Mexican lawyers who helped guide me through the intricacies of the Mexican laws and regulatory process, I am especially indebted to Lic. Juan M. Steta, Lic. José I. Herrasti, and Lic. Mariano Soni. Lic. Ernesto Canales contributed helpful research assistance. In the preparation of Chapter X, I relied heavily upon Professor William C. Headrick, now visiting professor of law at the Universidad Católica de Puerto Rico. To all, I am deeply grateful. But it is my good friend Lic. Agustín Santamarina, of the firm of Miranda, Santamarina & Steta, to whom I am most profoundly indebted for his continuing interest and assistance. The views expressed in this book are, of course, my own.

For the typing of most of the manuscript in its numerous drafts, I wish to express my sincere gratitude to Anna Saldaña. María Cruz, María Eugenia Torres, and Gloria de Vega also assisted in the typing. Finally, to Lucía Santamarina, *un millón de gracias* for her readiness to assist in numerous tiresome chores that seemed constantly to appear.

Harry K. Wright

Bogotá, Colombia
June, 1970

Contents

Tables

FOREIGN ENTERPRISE IN MEXICO

Laws and Policies

I

The Environment: Economy, Government, and Law

To the foreign investor assessing the "investment climate" of the world's developing nations, Mexico surely ranks high. Many of the customary inducements to direct foreign investment seem to exist there to an unusually high degree. Its remarkable record of economic growth since about 1940 is a well-publicized fact and has led most observers to conclude that Mexico has successfully made the transition to self-sustained economic expansion. This performance is even more intriguing when one considers that Mexico has a large population, second only to that of Brazil in Latin America, and one of the highest rates of population growth in the world—a combination that translates into a lucrative and growing domestic market. The Mexican peso is freely convertible into United States dollars at a rate of exchange that has remained constant since 1954, and there are no restrictions on the transfer of profits or the repatriation of capital. These favorable conditions have been made possible to a large extent by the political stability that has existed in Mexico for nearly half a century and the firm commitment of the Mexican government to economic growth and industrial development. Furthermore, the attitude of the government to foreign investment, if not always unconditionally hospitable, at least has not often been openly hostile. Judging from the laws, in fact, there seems to be little distinction between indigenous and foreign enterprise. While no special incentives directed at foreign investment are found, a reading of the laws does not suggest either that public regulation of business is unduly burdensome or that the burdens of the regulatory process are any greater for foreign-owned enterprises than for the Mexican businessman. In a few areas, to be sure, foreign ownership of enterprises is prohibited or restricted, but on the whole the laws are notably non-discriminatory. And if corroboration of the evidence that Mexico offers outstanding opportunities for foreign investors is needed, one may readily point to the fact that large numbers of foreign-owned companies do, in fact, operate successfully in the country.

But there is always a danger that an outside observer, particularly one from the United States, may be misled by what he sees. Especially in interpreting and evaluating the laws and the regulatory process, he may assume similarities between the Mexican system and his own system that do not exist. He may make conclusions and judgments from the text of a law or regulation without sufficient regard for the background from which it arose, the goals sought to be achieved in its administration, and its implications for the economy in general and his business in particular. Too much reliance may be placed on principles of equality of treatment and nondiscriminatory application of the law and too little consideration given to the fact that the Mexican system allows much greater latitude for the exercise of administrative discretion in individual cases and provides much less rigid and explicit statutory standards than does his own system. He may fail to realize that the breadth of the regulatory system and the wide discretionary powers of the executive give the government at least potential control over most of the critical aspects of his activities and enable it to enforce policies that are not always static or consistent and that may not be reflected or, indeed, even suggested in the statute books. In particular, in his enthusiasm for the favorable "investment climate" of Mexico, the foreign investor may fail to consider that there are increasingly severe limits on the extent to which foreign participation in the Mexican economy is accepted or tolerated and that a reading of the laws alone will reveal only partially what those limits are.

Thus, the intent of this book is not only to describe the laws and regulations that affect, directly or indirectly, the entry and operation of foreign enterprise in Mexico, but also to examine the purposes and expectations behind them and the policy objectives sought in their application. If this study assists the foreign investor and his legal counsel in making a more realistic and sober appraisal of the extent to which his interests are consistent with the interests of Mexico and in finding his way through the Mexican laws and regulatory system, it will have served its main purpose. While the emphasis is on laws and policies affecting private direct foreign investment, that is, ownership of controlling or a substantial minority interest in business enterprises in Mexico, some attention is also given to matters of concern to foreign entities engaged in international trade with Mexico and to those that provide financing and technical assistance to Mexican enterprises.

To set the stage, we begin with an examination of the economic, governmental, and legal environment within which foreign enterprise operates in Mexico. Because this study deals primarily with Mexican law and its application, substantial attention is given in this chapter to a description of the legislative and judicial processes and the structure of the law. The somewhat detailed tour of the civil and commercial codes and the discussion of the Mexical legal profession, while they may seem tedious to some readers, will, it is hoped, be found a useful orientation to those not trained in, or familiar with, the civil-law systems.

Following this introduction the focus turns more specifically to foreign investment. Chapter II is an account of the role that foreign capital occupies and has occupied historically in the Mexican economy, which attempts not only to describe the relative importance of foreign investment in the development of Mexico but also to provide the background out of which the existing regulation of, and restrictions on, the entry of foreign capital have arisen. Restrictions against foreign investment are found both in the laws and, perhaps even more importantly, in policies established and administered by the executive branch of the federal government, and it is logically the first concern of a prospective foreign investor to know if and to what extent he will be permitted to establish and engage in his business in the country. These restrictions are described in Chapters III and IV. In the case of Mexico there are other regulatory policies and incentives that are extremely important to the operation of private enterprise, both foreign and domestic, and that may significantly influence a decision to establish operations in the country. These include import restrictions, price control, the so-called industrial integration policy, tax incentives, and others, and the most important of these policies are the subject of Chapter V.

Once the prospective investor has determined the conditions, if any, under which his investment will be received and that the regulations to which he will be subject are consistent with his interests, his attention turns to other questions. The problem of whether or not and under what conditions he will be able to secure the entry of alien managerial and technical personnel is discussed in Chapter VI. Also included in that chapter is a discussion of the qualification to do business in Mexico of foreign legal entities and the status of unqualified foreign companies—a matter of interest primarily to those who do not engage in business in the country on a continuing basis, since virtually every foreign enterprise that wishes to establish production facilities or other permanent operations in Mexico does so through a company incorporated under Mexican law, rather than through a branch of a foreign company. The Mexican law of business companies and the special problems it poses in the case of foreign-owned companies and associations between Mexican and foreign investors are the subject of Chapter VII. The fields of taxation and labor law are discussed in Chapters VIII and IX. The next two chapters, covering secured transactions and patents, trademarks, and licensing agreements, deal with subjects that are of concern both to Mexican-based enterprises and to foreign enterprises that provide financing or technical assistance or sell to enterprises in Mexico, whether foreign or Mexican controlled. Finally, some conclusions and observations on the outlook for foreign investment in Mexico are suggested in Chapter XII.

THE ECONOMIC STRUCTURE

The year 1940 marks the beginning of an era of impressive and sustained growth of the Mexican economy. Many of the conditions essential to economic development had, of course, previously been established, but before 1940 much of the country's attention was focused on consolidating the political gains of the Revolution of 1910-20 and making progress toward some of its social objectives. The coincidence of two factors beginning in 1940 brought about rapid changes—the first of a succession of presidents firmly committed to industrial development came to office, and the impact of World War II began to be felt, creating a major opportunity for the expansion of domestic production to supply traditionally imported goods.

In the decade of the 1940's, physical output of goods and services increased in real terms at an average annual rate of slightly over 6 percent.[1] While nearly half of this growth went to match the increase in population, which seems to have risen at an annual rate of about 2.8 percent, there was still a very healthy increase in per capita output of about 3 percent. The trend from 1950 to 1967 is shown in table 1. While there have been substantial fluctuations in growth from year to year, real annual increase in national product from 1950 to 1959 averaged about 6.3 percent, and the average increase per capita was something over 3 percent. Annual growth in the eight-year period 1960-67 picked up somewhat, averaging close to 6.5 percent, and even though the rate of population increase exceeded 3.5 percent annually, production on a per capita basis increased at a rate of about 2.8 percent. In terms of current prices, per capita annual income rose from $125 (U.S.) in 1950 to about $350 in 1960, and appears to have risen to slightly over $500 by 1967, a figure substantially in excess of the levels characteristically found in Africa, Asia, and much of Latin America.

Also striking have been the changes in the composition of Mexico's output. Whereas in 1930 agriculture and livestock accounted for some 22 percent of the value of national production and manufactures less than 13 percent, table 2 shows that by 1950 output of the manu-

Table 1

Annual Growth of Gross National Product of Mexico,
Total and Per Capital, 1950-1967
(based on 1950 prices)

Year	GNP (millions of pesos)	Percentage annual increase, total	Percentage annual increase, per capita
1950	40,600	9.4	6.6
1951	43,600	7.4	4.4
1952	45,400	4.1	1.3
1953	45,600	.4	*
1954	50,400	10.5	7.5
1955	54,800	8.7	5.7
1956	58,200	6.2	3.3
1957	62,700	7.7	4.7
1958	66,200	5.6	2.6
1959	68,100	2.9	*
1960	73,500	7.9	2.9
1961	76,000	3.4	*
1962	79,700	4.9	1.7
1963	84,700	6.3	3.0
1964	93,200	10.0	6.6
1965	98,200	5.4	1.9
1966	105,600	7.5	3.8
1967	112,400	6.4	2.7

SOURCES: For 1950-64, Nacional Financiera, *Statistics on the Mexican Economy* (1966), tables 5 and 10, based on Banco de México data; for 1965-67, Banco de México annual reports; some percentages derived by the author.
*No growth, by definition.

facturing industries made up one-fifth of the gross national product and
came close to equaling the contribution of agriculture and related primary activities—livestock, forestry, and fishing. The trend between
1950 and 1967 is also shown in table 2. In that period manufacturing
output increased at an annual rate of about 7.8 percent in real terms and
became the largest single contributor to national production. Dynamic
performances were also turned in by electrical power generation and
distribution, construction, and petroleum and coal output. Commercial
activities grew at about the same rate as total national product. Increase in output of the agricultural sector was not so rapid, and its
contribution to gross national product continued to decline, amounting
to only about 16 percent in 1967. Plagued by weak market conditions
and inhibiting domestic policies, mineral production, once Mexico's
major export, dropped to a mere 1.5 percent of total output despite important increases in iron ore, sulphur, and copper production.

Table 2

Gross National Product of Mexico by Activities, 1950-1967
(in millions of pesos at 1950 prices)

Activity	1950		1967		Percentage increase, 1950-67
	Value	Percentage of total	Value	Percentage of total	
Agriculture, live-stock, forestry and fishing	9,242	22.7	18,079	16.1	95.6
Mining	1,243	3.1	1,717	1.5	38.1
Oil and coke	1,129	2.8	3,694	3.3	227.2
Manufactures	8,437	20.8	30,283	26.9	258.9
Construction	1,287	3.2	4,489	4.0	248.8
Electricity	370	.9	1,756	1.6	384.6
Transport and communications	1,988	4.9	4,671	4.2	135.0
Commerce	10,750	26.5	29,655	26.4	175.9
Government	1,294	3.2	3,036	2.7	134.6
Other	4,837	11.9	15,008	13.4	210.3
TOTAL	40,577	100.0	112,400	100.0	177.0

SOURCE: Banco Nacional de Comercio Exterior, *Mexico 1968: Facts, Figures
and Trends* (1968), chart 5-1, p. 95, based on Banco de México data.
NOTE: Because of rounding, detail may not add to totals.

The changing structure of the Mexican economy and the rising living standards of a substantial proportion of the Mexican people are also indicated by a progressive increase in the number of jobs available in relation to the number of people and a shift in the distribution of the labor force. While the labor force has tended to remain about one-third of the total population, it increased from 55 percent of the adult population (fifteen to sixty-four years of age) in 1940 to 59 percent in 1950, rose to about 62 percent in 1960, and probably exceeded 63 percent in 1965.[2] At the same time, there has been a general shift from low-paying jobs into higher-paying ones. Between 1950 and 1968, for example, the number of persons employed in comparatively low-paying agricultural and related primary activities declined from 58 percent of the labor force to 47 percent. In the same period the number of workers employed in manufacturing grew from 11.7 percent to about 17 percent of the economically active population and more or less commensurate changes occurred in construction, commerce, transport, and the service industries.[3]

Despite these favorable trends, nearly half the population is still directly dependent on agriculture and other primary activities and accounts for only about 16 percent of total national product. The low productivity per worker in that sector suggests that much of the country's farming is still rather primitive and means that a considerable proportion of the agricultural workers are partially or wholly outside the money economy and insignificant as a market for the growing output of industrial commodities. Agricultural output has, nevertheless, increased substantially in recent years, outpacing population growth, with the result that the country is nearly self-sufficient in agricultural products and has a large export trade. But low productivity and inadequate living standards in many agricultural areas continue to represent one of the country's greatest problems.

Population pressure has been a major stimulus in the drive for economic growth. With an annual rate of increase that has averaged about 3.5 percent in recent years, the country's population in mid-1968 was estimated at 47.3 million inhabitants. At its present rate of growth, Mexico's population will exceed 51 million in 1970 and will double in twenty years. An obvious implication of this growth, and a matter of considerable importance to government planners, is the necessity of providing an increasing number of new jobs annually. The labor supply increased by more than 400,000 persons each year from 1960 to 1965, and the growth is expected to exceed 830,000 persons annually in the period from 1975 to 1980.[4]

Accompanying the acceleration in population growth is a trend toward greater urbanization of the Mexican people. In 1940 only 35 percent of the population was classified as urban, officially defined as persons living in communities of 2,500 or more inhabitants, increasing to 42.6 percent in 1950, 50.7 percent in 1960, and 57.8 percent in 1968. By 1970 it is estimated that the urban population will be 59.5 percent of the total, with only 40.5 percent in the rural areas. Indicative also of this trend and creating special problems for the government is the growth of the Federal District, which includes Mexico City proper, the capital of the country and by far its largest and most important city. The population of the Federal District jumped from 1.8 million in 1940 to 3.1 million in 1950 and 4.9 million in 1960, about 14 percent of the total population. For the metropolitan area as a whole, which takes in the Federal District and a number of contiguous municipalities and unincorporated centers in the State of Mexico, the estimated 1960 population was from 5 to 5.5 million and probably approached 7 million by 1968. On the basis of present trends, it has been estimated that some 15 million people will be concentrated around the capital by 1980.[5]

There is also an extremely high degree of concentration of industry in metropolitan Mexico City. In 1960, with 14 percent of the population, it accounted for over 50 percent of the total value added in all Mexican industry and had 48 percent of all persons employed in manufacturing, and these figures have probably increased since that date. This imbalance, besides creating strains on public services in Mexico City, tends to impede improvements in the economic conditions of the rest of the population and has led the government to discourage further industrial investment in the Federal District and surrounding communities and to take active measures to promote the development of other areas of the country.[6]

It is popular in Mexico to describe the country's economy as "mixed," which seems to suggest more or less equal participation by the public and private sectors and raises visions of a large public investment in the means of production. It is true that the public sector has played a vigorous role in the development of Mexico. Apart from the activities of governmental institutions proper, the government owns the petroleum industry, most of the electric power industry, the railroads, and a number of commercial and industrial banks. State-owned agencies are engaged in the distribution of basic foodstuffs and newsprint. Furthermore, the government has not seemed reluctant to invest in any industrial activity when the development of domestic production to replace imports has been considered important and private investment in adequate amounts has not been readily forthcoming, or to serve some other public or political purpose. As a result, the government owns total or a majority interest in companies producing such diverse things as fertilizers, steel, railroad cars, automobiles, trucks, buses, electrolytic copper, paper, sugar, and textiles and has investments in a variety of other industrial pursuits. Most of these investments are channeled through and managed by Nacional Financiera, a complex institution that serves as the government development agency.[7]

Nevertheless, in terms of its contribution to the country's gross national product, the public sector occupies a minor role in the economy. In 1959 the output of the public sector, including federal, state, and local governments as well as state enterprises, was less than 10 percent of gross national product and does not seem to have exceeded about 13 percent in the 1960's.[8] Measured by the relative importance of its contribution to investment, the public sector's position is somewhat larger. During the 1940's and 1950's, the public share of total new investment fluctuated moderately above and below 40 percent but increased to close to 50 percent in the early 1960's.[9] Most of the public investment goes into such overhead items as transportation and communications, electric power, and petroleum, but a substantial amount also goes into agriculture and manufacturing.

Government intervention in the economy cannot, however, be measured solely in terms of its output or its contribution to investment. Government regulation of the economy has been pervasive and takes many forms. In many ways public intervention has been aimed at fostering and protecting private enterprise or at least at creating conditions conducive to private investment. Careful fiscal management has brought monetary stability and has kept inflation within reasonable limits. Major efforts have been made to provide basic industrial infrastructure, including transport, communication, power, and water. Cheap governmental credits have been made available for important private investment projects. And the government's policy to encourage import replacement by providing protection against competitive imports has been extremely important in stimulating domestic investment.

Thus, it seems that the activities of the public sector have most often been directed at complementing those of the private sector rather than dominating or competing with them. At any rate, the relationship

between the two sectors is a complex one and both have made vital
contributions to Mexico's development. And it seems fair to conclude
that Mexico in the mid-1960's possessed a reasonably advanced and
well-balanced economy and a relatively diversified industrial sector
that enabled it to satisfy most of its domestic consumer goods requirements and a good part of its internal demand for processed raw materials
and intermediate goods.

MEXICAN GOVERNMENT

POLITICAL AND GOVERNMENTAL STRUCTURE

In form, Mexico is a federally organized republic composed of
twenty-nine states, two territories, and a Federal District.[10] However,
there is more form than substance to Mexican federalism; the dominance
of the federal government is overwhelming. While the Constitution provides that the states are "free and sovereign in all that concerns their
internal government,"[11] the constitutional division of powers is weighted
heavily in favor of the federal government, and the central government is
authorized under certain circumstances to intervene directly in state affairs.[12] The degree of subordination of the states is further indicated by
the fact that in practice no state governor could attain office if he were
unacceptable to the president of the republic and the circumstance that
the states are substantially dependent upon the federal government for
revenues.

Powers of the federal government are, according to the Constitution,
divided among three independent branches—the executive, the legislative, and the judicial.[13] Again, the theory is largely illusory. The executive arm is the real center of political power. The Congress, composed
of a Chamber of Deputies and a Senate, routinely approves proposals
submitted to it by the president and rarely takes independent action on
its own. Though more independent than the legislature, the federal
judiciary, discussed separately below, also plays a subordinate role. The
power of the courts to invalidate laws and administrative acts is cir-
cumscribed by the Constitution within narrow limits, and in matters of
national concern in which the president has taken a strong position the
courts are likely either to be swayed by executive pressure or to avoid a
direct confrontation by delaying a decision.

At the head of the complex executive branch and undisputed holder
of the reins of power for the term of his office is the president. He is

elected by popular vote for a six-year term, beginning December 1, and may never again hold that office. His powers include the initiation and veto of bills, the promulgation and execution of laws, appointment and removal of high officials of the federal government and the governments of the Federal District and territories, control of the military establishment, and conduct of the country's foreign relations. His broad powers of appointment and removal, one of the factors that assures his ultimate authority, are exercised fully, with the result that there is a large-scale change in administrative personnel every six years. Very significant also is his authority to appoint the heads or directors of the so-called decentralized institutions, such as the agencies charged with running the nation's petroleum, railroad, and electric power industries.

Depending from the presidency is what seems an endless array of ministries, departments, interministerial committees, independent administrative commissions, decentralized institutions, and corporations. The ministries are major centers of power and are the agencies of government with which the foreign investor customarily has greatest contact. Under the governing law,[14] there are fifteen ministries *(secretarías)*, each of which is headed by a minister *(secretario)*, one or more subsecretaries *(subsecretarios)*, and a chief clerk *(oficial mayor)*. The ministries are organized into various subdivisions, called bureaus *(direcciones generales)*, which are in turn divided into departments *(departamentos)*. In addition, there are three departments (not to be confused with departmental subdivisions of the ministries) of equal rank with the ministries.

While the operations of a particular foreign-owned enterprise may involve dealings with various ministries, direct authority in matters of general and immediate concern to foreign business is vested in only a few of them. The most important, both initially and on a continuing basis, is the Ministry of Industry and Commerce. Under its authority to administer quantitative import controls, it holds almost absolute power of life and death over industry, and by virtue of this authority it undertakes to regulate the entry of new direct foreign investments, control prices of domestic manufactures, and promote import substitution and industrial integration. The Ministry of Finance and Public Credit administers all fiscal and tax legislation, fixes import and export tariffs, and approves tax exemptions and subsidies. The finance minister also has a large measure of control over budgetary expenditures of government agencies, and by virtue of his control over the policies of the Banco de México, the country's central bank, and Nacional Financiera, its principal development bank, he exerts wide influence upon the economic development process. The Ministry of Foreign Relations, though concerned primarily with the conduct of Mexico's international relations, controls the formation of Mexican companies and the acquisition by foreigners of land, interests in Mexican companies, and certain other property rights. Finally, the Ministry of Internal Affairs (*gobernación*, often called the ministry of interior or government), under its authority in matters of foreign immigration, has absolute control over the entry of aliens into Mexico and may expel any foreigner whose presence in the country is deemed undesirable.

There is a surprising lack of co-ordination and even communication among the various ministers. While joint action by two or more ministries is required in some matters, for the most part they act independently of one another, jealously guarding their own spheres of power and resisting interference from others. They do not meet together as a cabinet, but each has direct communication with the president, who is the ultimate arbiter and whose authority may never be openly questioned.

The power and influence of the president derive not only from the fact that he heads the executive branch of government but also from his indirect but dominant influence over the official party. The Partido Revolucionario Institucional, or PRI, controls all branches of the federal government and all state governments. Much of the credit for the orderly transfer of power from one administration to the next and the highly effective operation of the government that have characterized Mexico for many years belongs to the effectiveness and broad-based support of the PRI. Its membership, divided into farm, labor, and popular sectors, encompasses groups of widely divergent interests and ideologies, and it provides the framework within which competing interests are adjusted and at the same time opposition and dissent held within tolerable limits.

Other political parties exist, but their combined strength is only a minute fraction of that of the PRI. The most vigorous of the opposition parties is the Partido de Acción Nacional, or PAN, representing mainly conservative, pro-enterprise interests. It is usually able to elect a handful of members of the Chamber of Deputies and occasionally it or another opposition party captures a local office, but in many contests none of the minority parties even offers an alternative to the PRI candidate. The existence of other parties serves mainly as evidence that the power of the PRI is not based on brute force and suppression, and the government fosters this role of the opposition.[15]

The PRI not only provides a power base of the president but also serves as a channel of communication to him from divergent interest groups and a subtle check on the exercise of his vast power. Important to an understanding of the operation of the Mexican government is the fact that, for all the president's power, there are practical limits on the exercise of his discretion. He must be constantly aware of and take into account the interest goals of the groups on whose support he and the system that has brought him to power depend. This does not mean, of course, that immediate gratification must be given to all their goals—the system allows great flexibility in the assignment of priorities and the selection of methods—but some assurance that at least a minimum of their objectives will ultimately be accomplished and some voice in basic policy decisions affecting their primary interests may not be denied if the system is to continue to function.

The PRI is not, however, the only channel of communication to the president, or probably even the most effective. There are many factions whose interests must be weighed in the delicate exercise of presidential power that do not operate within the machinery of the PRI. Many of these factions have their own organizations for dealing with the government that are not part of the formal political structure. Some are recognized by law and membership is compulsory for business enterprises. Manufacturing and commercial enterprises, for example, are required to belong to one of the various chambers of industry or commerce, which are grouped together into two major national confederations, the manufacturers' Confederación de Cámaras Industriales (CONCAMIN) and the merchants' Confederación de Cámaras Nacionales de Comercio (CONCANACO). The main organization channel of the banking community is the Asociación de Banqueros de México, and insurance enterprises are organized in the Asociación de Instituciones de Seguros. Also very important as a channel to the government from the business community is the Confederación Patronal de la República Mexicana (COPARMEX), a voluntary union of employer enterprises. These five organizations are informally grouped together in the Comité Coordinador de Actividades de la Iniciativa Privada, which in recent years has become considerably effective in handling important problems on behalf of the private sector. In addition, there are, inevitably, various small groups and individuals who have sufficient economic power or potential political strength to command direct communication with the president or important ministers.

THE LEGISLATIVE PROCESS

Ordinary federal legislation, that is, legislation other than the Constitution, is enacted by the Congress. Although bills may be introduced by members of Congress and legislatures of the states,[16] in practice virtually all legislation originates with the executive branch. Rarely does Congress do more than give formal approval to drafts of laws submitted to it by the president.

Article 70 of the Constitution states that every resolution of the Congress shall have the character of a law *(ley)* or a decree *(decreto),* and such terms as "ordinary law," "organic law," and "law regulating the Constitution" are also found in the Constitution, but as a practical matter there is little or no distinction among them. The passage of a law by the Congress is not sufficient to render it effective, however; it must be promulgated by the president and published before it becomes effective and binding. Promulgation is the act by which the president gives authenticity to and orders the entry into effect of a law. Publication is made in the federal daily official gazette, called the *Diario Oficial de la Federación.* The presidential act promulgating and ordering the publication of a law customarily specifies the date on which the law will take effect, which may be the date of publication or a subsequent date.

The *Diario Oficial* is the only official repository of federal legislation, but several private editions of laws exist and are considerably more useful than the official publications.[17] English translations of some of the laws are available, but many of them are not altogether reliable and must be used with caution.

Apart from his indirect practical control of the legislative process, the president has some authority to legislate directly on his own. Under his constitutional mandate to execute the laws and to provide "in the administrative sphere for their exact enforcement,"[18] the president has power to enact general rules in the form of regulations *(reglamentos).* Regulations have the purpose of explaining and supplying detailed rules for the application of specific laws, and most statutes are supplemented in this manner. They are, however, subordinate to ordinary legislation and may not contain provisions contrary to those of the statute they regulate. The enactment of regulations also takes the form of a decree *(decreto),* and promulgation and publication are made in the same manner as in the case of statutes.

What might be called other forms of executive enactment are the circular and the *oficio* (official communication). These are instructions issued by the heads of administrative services to their subordinates concerning the interpretation and application of laws. They are also sometimes used to notify private persons of administrative actions or decisions. While they are customarily of an internal nature only, they may be given the binding character of a regulation.

In a great many instances the president has exercised legislative authority directly by virtue of a statutory delegation from the Congress. Congressional delegations of "extraordinary legislative power" to the president were so frequent throughout the latter part of the nineteenth century and until the 1930's that there was often hardly even a pretense of an independent legislative branch. Much of the existing legislation was enacted directly by the president under such authority, including the Civil and Penal Codes for the Federal District, the Commercial Code, and many statutes, especially in the field of commercial law. After some initial vacillation on the part of the Supreme Court, beginning in 1879 it consistently upheld the constitutionality of these extraordinary powers.[19] In 1938, however, on the initiative of President Lázaro Cárdenas, article 49 of the Constitution, which was the theoretical basis for these delegations, was amended to make clear that authority to legislate could be granted only in connection with a suspension of individual guarantees in times of grave national emergency under article 29. Only once since the 1938 amendment have constitutional guarantees been suspended and legislative authority given to the president under article 29. That occurred following the entry of Mexico into World War II and lasted from June, 1942, to September, 1945. Decrees issued by the president were, for the most part, in effect only during the period of the emergency and were repealed by the congressional decree terminating the emergency. An important exception was a presidential decree issued in 1944 establishing the basis for quantitative restrictions on direct foreign investment, which is considered to be still in effect.[20]

In addition to delegations of legislative power under the conditions of article 29, since 1950 the Constitution has authorized Congress to empower the president to legislate directly in the field of foreign trade. Under article 131 he may be authorized to establish tariff rates on and to restrict or prohibit imports and exports. The only condition is that the president must report annually to Congress on the use that he has made of this power and obtain its approval. This authority has been delegated to the president, and import and export duties and restrictions on imports and exports are established by executive decree.[21]

ADMINISTRATION OF THE LAW

Not only does the president exercise a dominant role in the legislative process, but the executive branch is given wide latitude in the administration and application of the laws. This is particularly true in matters relating to the national economy and the conduct of business. In some cases regulatory authority is turned over to the president for him to exercise when and to what extent he sees fit. Under the federal law on price control, for example, the president has authority both to designate the specific products that are subject to price regulation and to establish maximum prices at which they may be sold. Under the monopolies law he may prohibit expansion of sectors of the economy through his power to declare an industry "saturated."

More importantly, regulation of business is frequently accomplished through the statutory requirement of a license or other authorization for a particular activity. Typically, laws that impose this requirement grant absolute discretion to the administrative agency concerned to issue or withhold a license in any individual case. Rarely are objective standards fixed by law for the granting of a license. At almost every turn, a private firm may find that the establishment and conduct of its business depend upon the favorable decision of some ministry or other agency of government. The formation of a new Mexican company or the acquisition of an interest in an existing company requires a permit from the Ministry of Foreign Relations; the importation of necessary machinery or raw materials depends upon licenses issued by the Ministry of Industry and Commerce; the entry of foreign managerial or technical personnel to work in the country requires authorization of the Ministry of Internal Affairs.

This latitude in the administration of the law is not only another example of the dominance of the executive arm of government but also reflects an underlying emphasis on the discretionary rights of the state, acting as guardian of the public interest, as opposed to the rights of the individual. As a consequence, there is a tendency to make decisions on an individual, *ad hoc* basis rather than by the automatic application of general rules. This means, of course, that persons in apparently similar circumstances may receive different treatment at the hands of the government and that it is often difficult to predict with certainty what an administrative decision will be in a particular case. It also means that, while most laws on their face make no distinction between foreign- and Mexican-owned enterprises, discrimination against foreign investors is entirely possible in the application of the law. One will search in vain for a statutory restriction on foreign equity ownership of companies engaged in any but a handful of industries, for example, but a prospective foreign investor is likely to discover that the existence of a substantial Mexican equity interest in the investment is essential if he is to obtain licenses for the importation of his machinery, equipment, and raw materials, or if he seeks protection against competing imports.

Despite the notable absence of statutory norms, there is nevertheless some degree of standardization in the administration of the law. For one thing, Mexican public officials are generally conscious of the desirability of achieving a measure of certainty and equality of treatment. For another, the volume of business of governmental agencies is often such that they are forced, as a practical matter, to adopt more or less standardized criteria and procedures, at least for the handling of routine matters. Thus, while the system allows great flexibility in the establishment and enforcement of policies, once specific policy goals are fixed and the methods and guidelines for achieving them decided, the administrative agencies generally operate within a framework of impersonal, nondiscriminatory standards that can be defined and usually relied upon. To be sure, the standards may be stretched and exceptions made, and policy goals and guidelines may be changed, but there is probably more certainty and predictability in the day-to-day dealings with government than many observers might think.

There is another facet to the administration of the law that should be mentioned. While the problem of favoritism and corruption exists in many countries and in varying degrees, it probably breeds more readily in a system in which the operations of business are substantially dependent upon the exercise of administrative discretion than in one in which rigid standards exist in the law. In the case of Mexico there is widespread belief that graft and malfeasance are pervasive in public life,[22] and one frequently hears the allegation that bribery and payoffs—the *mordida*—are essential features of doing business in Mexico and are necessary to favorable treatment by the government. The extent to which this is true is difficult to determine with any degree of certainty, but the assumption of pervasive corruption is undoubtedly more exaggerated than the reality.

In a few situations unlawful practices are flagrant and undoubtedly reflect unfavorably on the government as a whole. The fact that a policeman may readily accept an unlawful payment to overlook a traffic violation may lead to the belief that all law enforcement agencies, including the courts, are corrupt. From the fact that a customs inspector or a tax collector may accept a *mordida* to allow the entry of small quantities of smuggled merchandise or to overlook a discrepancy in a taxpayer's records, one may tend to assume that most officials in the finance ministry supplement their income in that manner. It is no secret that such practices exist, but they are probably confined to the lower echelons of civil servants, whose contact with the public and low salaries make them particularly susceptible to subornation. And in many cases the initiative comes from private persons who seek to obtain a privilege or avoid a penalty.

Also rather prevalent, but on quite a different level, is the practice of making payment to inferior government employees, such as clerical personnel, of what might best be called a tip in order to obtain the expeditious handling of a particular matter. In that case payment is not made to obtain something to which there is no right but rather to have something done more rapidly than it would normally be done.

At the higher echelons of government, however, it is extremely unlikely that any such collusion exists. To be sure, some officials may take advantage of their positions and the information to which they are party to increase their wealth. But there are ways of doing so that are legal and, though sometimes unethical, are generally regarded as acceptable practices. An official may, for example, exploit his knowledge that a new highway is to be built by buying land in the area. In other cases the rather modest salaries of government officials are augmented openly and legitimately by income from positions that are related and incidental to their public duties. Ministers and other key officials hold positions on the boards of directors of many industrial enterprises in which the government has equity interests, many of which follow the practice common in Mexican companies of paying substantial fees or distributing a percentage of profits to their directors.[23]

For the foreign investor, the critical point is that, while a particular important transaction with a government agency may be laced with subtle overtones arising out of a public official's interest in or liaison with the private sector, dealings between private business and the government do not in the vast majority of situations depend upon illegal payments or involve other forms of corruption or graft. Furthermore, the point is often made that there are influences at work that tend to reduce the instances of corruption. One is the trend toward increasing professionalization and higher salary scales of many civil servants. This is particularly noticeable among federal tax officials, who have greater professional training, higher technical standards, and perhaps more supervision than formerly. Also, the increasing volume of business handled by most government agencies tends to encourage the use of standardized methods, under which, so it is argued, there is less likelihood of corruption than where only occasional transactions are handled.

THE JUDICIAL SYSTEM

Because of the federated form of the Mexican government, there is a dual system of courts, federal and local. The federal courts have jurisdiction in all controversies of a civil or criminal nature arising out of the enforcement and application of federal laws or treaties; all cases involving admiralty law; suits to which the federal government is a party; suits between two or more states, between a state and the federal government, and between a state and citizens of another state; and cases involving diplomatic or consular officials.[24] In addition, federal jurisdiction extends to controversies involving constitutional issues—specifically, those arising out of laws or acts of public authorities that violate individual constitutional guarantees, those involving laws or acts of the federal government that infringe upon the sovereignty of the states, and those involving state laws or acts that encroach on the authority of the federal government.[25] Jurisdiction in these cases is invoked in *amparo* proceedings, discussed below. State courts have jurisdiction in suits arising out of state law and concurrent jurisdiction with the federal courts in cases involving federal laws or treaties when they affect only the interests of private parties.[26]

Federal Courts

The federal court system consists of a Supreme Court (Suprema Corte de Justicia de la Nación), circuit courts *(tribunales de circuito),* and district courts *(juzgados de distrito).*[27] There are fifty-six district courts in the country, eight of which are located in the Federal District. They are the usual courts of first instance. Each district court has one judge, appointed by the Supreme Court, who generally decides issues of both law and fact. Jurymen, more accurately a special jury court *(jurado popular),* are used to decide questions of fact submitted by the district judge only in criminal cases involving offenses committed through the press against public order or national security and cases of wrongdoing by federal officials.[28]

Circuit courts are of two types. The unitary circuit courts (tribunales unitarios de circuito), with one judge each, hear appeals from the district courts on questions of fact and law. The collegiate circuit courts (tribunales colegiados de circuito), composed of three judges each, were created in 1951 to alleviate the heavy case load of the Supreme Court and have original jurisdiction in amparo suits that are not reserved to the Supreme Court. There are eight courts of each type in the country, two of the collegiate courts sitting in Mexico City. Circuit judges, called magistrates (magistrados), are also appointed by the Supreme Court.

The federal Supreme Court consists of twenty-one judges or ministers (ministros), one of whom serves as presiding judge, called president, plus five auxiliary judges. They are appointed by the president of the republic, with the consent of the Senate, and serve during good behavior or until resignation or mandatory retirement at age seventy or because of permanent disability.[29] The Court has both original and appellate jurisdiction. The overwhelming majority of the cases it decides are brought by way of amparo on constitutional issues, and its work load is extremely heavy.[30] It sits en banc or in sections or chambers (salas). There are four chambers, each composed of five judges, which specialize in particular subject matters, and an auxiliary chamber to which the auxiliary judges are assigned. The first chamber hears primarily criminal cases; the second chamber has jurisdiction in administrative law cases; the third hears civil (including commercial) suits; and the fourth hears cases involving labor law. The auxiliary chamber takes the overload from the other four chambers and hears all types of cases.

Also classified as part of the judicial branch of the federal government is the office of the public attorney (ministerio público), headed by an attorney general (procurador general). It prosecutes all federal criminal cases, and its representative participates in other litigation, especially amparo proceedings, of concern to the government. The attorney general also has the role of legal advisor to the federal government.

Administrative courts, though not within the judiciary, are also important agencies for the administration of justice in two fields of law, tax and labor. The federal tax court (tribunal fiscal), which is divided into seven chambers, hears all litigation related to tax matters and cases involving the application to individuals of other financial legislation. Federal and local labor boards have jurisdiction over all types of labor conflicts, whether legal or economic and whether individual or collective. The decisions of administrative courts are subject to review for constitutionality by the federal courts in *amparo* proceedings.

The quality of federal judges at all levels has traditionally been quite high. Appointees to the Supreme Court are usually well qualified, experienced, and successful members of the practicing bar, many of whom are also academic lawyers of pre-eminence in their fields. Most have also served at one time or another as judges of lower courts. While political considerations do not seem to rank high among the criteria for selection, frequently judges have held political office. Appointment to the Supreme Court often requires financial sacrifices, but it is considered a great honor and the compensation is not inadequate.[31]

The fact that lower federal judges are appointed by the Supreme Court, a logical consequence of the principle of separation of powers, makes for a rather high degree of competence at the district and circuit court levels also. Most lower court judges have served an apprenticeship within the federal judiciary, and an approach is being made toward a career judiciary.[32] Almost all appointees to the circuit courts have served as district judges, and they are usually appointed directly from the district courts. In most cases district judges are selected from persons who have served as clerks, called secretaries, to the Supreme Court. The full Court and each chamber have a senior clerk *(secretario de acuerdos)*, and each member of the Court has two clerks *(secretario de estudio y cuenta)*, who study the files of cases, advise the judge, and prepare drafts of decisions. Because they do much of the judges' work, they are customarily selected for their ability and are usually experienced practitioners and often also professors of law.

Not only do federal judges generally rate high in ability, but the great majority are also above reproach in impartiality and integrity in the discharge of their trust, despite some belief to the contrary. They are prohibited by law to engage in the practice of law and to hold any public or private employment, except honorary positions in scientific, literary, or beneficent associations.[33] Conflicts of interest in specific cases are prohibited by a provision for disqualification for various reasons, including personal interest and acceptance of gifts or services from any of the litigants.[34] Outright corruption, such as the acceptance of a bribe or *mordida,* seems to be extremely rare in the federal judiciary and almost unknown in the Supreme Court. If its decisions can sometimes be faulted, this is probably because the large case load of the Court often prevents careful and unhurried deliberation and not because

of any improper influence. Also, the independence of the judiciary from
the other branches of government, notably the executive, is undoubtedly
more real in practice than may be commonly thought. It is doubtless
true that in some cases considered highly significant involving administrative law, political pressure is successfully exerted by the executive, either
to affect the outcome of the case or to delay indefinitely its decision, but
it is also probably true that in a substantial majority of cases the Court's
decisions are not influenced by the position of the president or the
administrative agencies under him.

Local Courts

Of the local court systems, that of the Federal District and federal
territories is the most important and is the model on which the state
court systems are patterned.[35] There are two levels of courts, the courts
of first instance and an appellate court, called the superior court of
justice (Tribunal Superior de Justicia del Distrito y Territorios
Federales), which has ultimate supervision of the lower courts and ap-
points all inferior judges, who serve for six-year terms.

The Federal District and territories are divided into seven judicial
districts (partidos judiciales); four of these are in the Federal District,
the most important being Mexico City proper; there are two in the
territory of Baja California Sur; and the territory of Quintana Roo is one
district. In the Mexico City district, the principal courts of first instance
in civil cases, as distinguished from criminal cases, are the civil courts
(juzgados de lo civil), the minor courts (juzgados menores), and the
peace courts (juzgados de paz). The competence of these courts depends
upon the amount in controversy and the subject of the litigation. At the
top of the hierarchy, the civil courts have jurisdiction in cases involving
claims exceeding 20,000 pesos, all cases of bankruptcy and composition
for the benefit of creditors regardless of the amount involved, all cases
involving questions of civil status or legal capacity, and certain other
cases. Parties may agree to have a civil court mediate any case, regardless of the amount in controversy, unless it is within the jurisdiction
of the special tribunals for minors and incompetents. The jurisdiction
of minor courts is limited generally to cases involving claims from 1,000
to 20,000 pesos. Peace courts are competent in civil cases involving
claims of 1,000 pesos or less.

Original criminal jurisdiction in the Mexico City judicial district is
exercised by the criminal courts (cortes penales) and, for less serious
cases, the peace courts, which are "mixed" courts in that they have both

civil and criminal jurisdiction. As in the federal courts, jurymen are used only in criminal cases involving offenses committed through the press against public order or national security and offenses of officials and employees of the Federal District and territories.

In judicial districts other than the Mexico City district, the organization of the courts of first instance is the same, except that the functions of the civil courts and the criminal courts are consolidated in mixed courts of first instance (*juzgados mixtos de primera instancia*).

Matters that affect the person or interests of minors and other incompetents under guardianship are decided by special judges, called pupillary judges (*jueces pupilares*).

Appeals on questions of law and fact from the courts of first instance are heard by the superior court of justice. The superior court is composed of thirty-one judges and three alternates and is divided into ten chambers (*salas*) of three judges each, eight sitting in the Federal District and one in each of the two territories. Five of the chambers in the Federal District have appellate jurisdiction in civil cases, and three hear appeals of criminal cases. Judges are appointed to six-year terms by the president of the republic, with the approval of the federal Chamber of Deputies, and must be lawyers with at least five years' experience in professional practice and meet other requirements. A presiding judge or president of the court is selected annually by the court itself and does not sit on a chamber.

Judicial ability and integrity are probably not so uniform at the level of the local courts as in the federal courts. Judges of the superior court of the Federal District and territories have in the past, for example, often been appointed on the basis of little other than political considerations or friendship, and this is probably still true to a substantial degree of the judges of many of the states. In the Federal District, however, considerable emphasis has been placed in recent years on improving the local judiciary, and Federal District judges at all levels now seem to be generally well regarded within the legal profession.

Authority of Decided Cases

Except under certain circumstances, judicial decisions are not considered a source of law and are not formally binding in future cases. This attitude, typical of civil-law countries, is a consequence of the traditional doctrine of strict separation of legislative and judicial power; only the legislature can make law, and the role of the judge is limited to finding, interpreting, and applying the proper legislative norm.

Despite this attitude, laws in Mexico, as elsewhere, are not always so clear, complete, and coherent as to reduce the judicial function to a mechanical application of the law to the facts of a particular case. The courts are in fact required to interpret laws, to fill the gaps in the legislative scheme, and to reconcile apparently conflicting statutes. And formally binding precedent, called jurisprudence *(jurisprudencia),* may be established by the highest federal courts in a series of uniform decisions. Under the law of *amparo* jurisprudence may be established by the Supreme Court sitting *en banc,* by individual chambers of the Court, and by collegiate circuit courts, on matters of interpretation of the federal Constitution, federal or local laws and regulations, and international treaties to which Mexico is a party.[36] Jurisprudence is formed when five consistent decisions on a point of law, uninterrupted by a contrary decision, have been reached by the court involved with the concurrence of a specified minimum number of members of the court. Decisions of the Supreme Court sitting *en banc* must have been approved by at least fourteen justices; decisions of the chambers require the concurrence of four justices; and those of the collegiate circuit courts must receive unanimous approval of the members of the court before they may be counted in the five decisions necessary to constitute jurisprudence. Once established, jurisprudence is binding on the court or chamber that established it and on all lower federal courts, all state and Federal District courts, and administrative tribunals. Jurisprudence is "interrupted" and ceases to be formally binding when the court or chamber that established it reaches a single contrary decision concurred in by the same minimum number of judges required for decisions that form jurisprudence and setting out the reasons for the reversal. Provision is also made in the law for resolution by the Supreme Court of conflicts in decisions of different chambers or collegiate circuit courts.

Judicial decisions that do not constitute jurisprudence, though not formally binding, are undoubtedly influencial in subsequent cases, at least when they are known. As a practical matter, it does not seem likely that lower court judges would often invite reversal on appeal by departing from known decisions of the appellate courts. Furthermore, the mere fact that the highest federal and local courts have the power of appointment of inferior judges within their judicial systems probably operates as some incentive to conform. At the level of the federal Supreme Court, while it is certainly true that inconsistencies and reversals are found among its decisions, citation and application of its prior decisions are sufficiently frequent to indicate that it, too, is affected to some extent by precedent.

Prior decisions, whether or not they constitute jurisprudence, are relied on almost entirely for their abstract statements of rules or principles, rather than for the similarity of the precise factual contexts in which they are rendered. Thus, the distinction between holding and dictum so carefully drawn in the common law tends to be obscured in the Mexican system, and an excerpt from a decision may sometimes be applied to cases substantially different from that for which it was rendered.

Reports of Decisions

This use of precedent, considered risky by the common lawyer, is encouraged by the form in which Mexican decisions are published. Decisions of the federal Supreme Court are officially published in the *Semanario Judicial de la Federación,* which was created in 1870 and has been published continuously, with few interruptions, since that time. It now comprises six series *(épocas)* and is published monthly (despite its title) in five separate parts, the first containing decisions of the full Court *(pleno)* and the other four containing decisions of the chambers.[37] Decisions that in the judgment of the Court lack all legal interest are not reported. Generally, only an extract of the case—the important rule or "thesis"—is published, with no statement of the facts of the case or only enough facts to make the rule intelligible. The full opinion is reported only when the Court so directs, when a dissenting or concurring opinion *(voto particular)* is written, or when the case involves legal questions of great importance or is so complex that it would be difficult to understand from an extract.[38] Extracts of important decisions of the Supreme Court and the collegiate circuit courts are also published monthly in the unofficial *Boletín de Información Judicial.*[39] Decisions of the federal district courts and unitary circuit courts are not customarily reported. Decisions of the federal tax court are published in its official organ, the *Revista del Tribunal Fiscal de México.*

Indices to the current sixth series of the *Semanario Judicial* are published semiannually, and the annual reports rendered by the president of the Court contain extracts of important cases decided by the Court during the year. Official digests or compilations of decisions that constitute jurisprudence and other important decisions have been published from time to time, most recently in 1955, covering the period 1917-54, and again in 1965, covering the years 1917-65.[40] There are also privately published compilations of Supreme Court decisions to 1963 that are more comprehensive than the official digests.[41]

At the local court level, reports of decisions are less reliable. Important decisions of the superior court of the Federal District and territories, and on rare occasions decisions of lower Federal District courts, are published in the official *Anales de Jurisprudencia,* which was initiated in 1933. Publications of state court decisions, however, are usually sporadic or nonexistent.

JUDICIAL PROTECTION AGAINST GOVERNMENTAL ACTS—THE AMPARO

The suit of *amparo* is considered by Mexican legal scholars to be the culmination and symbol of that country's struggle for the protection of individual rights and Mexico's unique and outstanding contribution to jurisprudence.[42] It is a type of action in the federal courts the purpose of which is to protect *(amparar)* private persons whose individual rights guaranteed by the Constitution have been violated through laws or acts of governmental authorities. Under it the federal courts have the ultimate role of construing and enforcing the Constitution, though their encroachment upon the legislative branch is minimized by the limitation of the judges' function to the protection of individual litigants; they may not make general declarations of invalidity of laws or acts. The *amparo* has also been developed into a method for appealing decisions of local courts and administrative tribunals to the highest federal courts, so as to constitute them courts of last resort on all questions of law.

The constitutional basis of the *amparo* is found in article 103, giving federal courts exclusive jurisdiction to decide controversies that arise out of laws or acts of authorities that violate individual guarantees, and article 107, which lays down basic requirements and rules of procedure for *amparo* litigation. The *amparo* is regulated in detail by the law of *amparo* of 1935, as amended,[43] and to some extent by the organic law of the federal judicial power.[44]

A suit for *amparo* may be brought in basically three types of situations. First, it is available in the case of direct violations by governmental authorities of individual guarantees contained in the first 28 articles of the Constitution. In a simple and very flexible procedure judicial protection may be obtained against official acts that result in or threaten, for example, deprivation of life, liberty, or property without essential procedural guarantees, excessive punishment for crimes, or denial of freedom of religion, occupation, speech, or assembly.

Secondly, an *amparo* suit may be brought to challenge the constitutionality of laws. There are two opportunities for bringing an action for this purpose. If the law in question is self-executing or has automatic application so that it is susceptible of affecting legal interests of the complainant by the mere fact of its enactment and promulgation, suit may be brought within thirty days of its effective date. Furthermore, all kinds of laws, whether self-executing or not, may be attacked judicially within fifteen days from the time the complainant learns of the first application of the law to his detriment. An action to test the validity of a law is brought directly against the governmental agencies responsible for its enactment—the federal Congress or state legislature that passed it, the president or state governor that promulgated it, and the officials who ordered its publication. Suit is brought in first instance in a federal district court and an appeal may be taken in some cases to the Supreme Court and in others to a collegiate circuit court. The relief granted is limited to protecting the individual requesting it, and no general statement of invalidity of the law in question may be made by the court. Thus, the effect of a favorable decision is merely to excuse the complaining party from compliance with the law. Other persons to whom the law is applied are not protected by the decision and must themselves seek protection against the law in similar proceedings. The legislature is not obligated to repeal the law, and it is not uncommon to find that laws that have been held invalid are still in effect and enforced by administrative agencies.[45] However, the legislature is considered to have a duty, though not a binding obligation, to repeal a law that has repeatedly and consistently been declared unconstitutional by the highest federal court.[46]

The most common use of the *amparo* is to obtain review by the highest federal courts of decisions of lower federal courts, local courts, and administrative tribunals that are not subject to appeal. It is primarily *amparo* suits of this nature that account for the staggering case load of the Supreme Court and that led to the creation in 1951 of the collegiate circuit courts to relieve some of the burden. The use of *amparo* for this purpose arises from article 14 of the Constitution, which establishes the principle that no person shall be deprived of life, liberty, property, or rights except "in accordance with laws issued prior to the act" and that in civil suits "the final judgment shall be according to the letter or the judicial interpretation of the law." This language has long been construed literally by the Supreme Court to establish a constitutional right to have all judicial decisions made according to law. Thus, the losing party in an ordinary civil suit decided by the highest appellate court of a state may, in effect, appeal the decision to the federal Supreme Court or a collegiate circuit court by alleging that the decision was not made according to law, in violation of his rights under article 14. Although the court may not re-examine the facts, the effect is that every question of law, whether strictly "federal" or not, is a constitutional question. This process is sometimes called *amparo*-cassation because of its relation to the power of cassation of the highest reviewing courts in France and some other civil-law countries. The form is still that of an original action, the nominal defendant or "responsible authority" being the court whose decision is attacked and the real opposing party, who may intervene in the *amparo* suit, being termed the "prejudiced third person."

THE STRUCTURE OF MEXICAN LAW

FEDERAL AND STATE LAW

An important aspect of Mexico's federated form of government is that there are two levels of legislative jurisdiction—federal and state. The federal government has only delegated powers, and article 124 of the Constitution provides that powers not expressly granted to the federal government are understood to be reserved to the states. There is, however, little concurrent authority; delegations to the federal government are generally exclusive and preclude state legislation in the same field. Furthermore, legislative authority delegated to the federal Congress is so broad as to leave relatively few areas to the states. Even in fields reserved to the states the federal Congress has exclusive authority to legislate for the Federal District and the federal territories, and the laws enacted for those jurisdictions have had a pervasive influence on the pattern of state law. As a result, the great majority of the laws affecting the foreign investor and the conduct of enterprises generally are either federal or are modeled after federally enacted legislation.

Under article 73 of the Constitution, the federal Congress is given the exclusive power to legislate on such important matters as commerce, hydrocarbons, mining, credit institutions, electric power, labor, maritime law, general means of communication, and immigration and legal status of foreigners. It is authorized to enact laws to prevent the establishment of restrictions on interstate commerce, and the power to regulate foreign commerce and to impose duties on imports and exports is reserved to the federal government by article 131. On the authority of section XXX of article 73, which empowers the federal Congress to enact all laws that may be necessary for giving effect to the powers enumerated in that article "and all others granted by this Constitution to the Powers of the Union," the federal government has at times pre-empted fields as to which its authority is not entirely clear.

In addition to the matters that are removed from the power of the states by the delegation of exclusive authority to the federal government, express limitations are imposed on the states by article 117 of the Constitution. They may not restrict or levy duties on goods entering, leaving, or passing through their territory; impose taxes or fees on the circulation or consumption of domestic or foreign merchandise; or en-act fiscal laws or other measures that discriminate against domestic or foreign goods on the basis of their origin. Under article 118, the states may not impose charges or fees on imports or exports in any form with-out the consent of the federal Congress.

The grant of exclusive authority to the federal government to legis-late in matters of commerce points up the division of Mexican private law into civil law and commercial law. While the civil law has its histor-ical origin in Roman law, commercial law developed in the middle ages with the revival of commerce in the Mediterranean area and grew out of the practices of Italian merchants and the statutes or ordinances of medi-eval guilds. From Italy it spread to other parts of Europe, including Spain, and eventually to the Spanish colonies in the New World. The dichotomy between commercial law and civil law has been preserved in Mexico, as in most of the countries of Europe and Latin America, and the two branches of law are the object of separate regulation. The Commercial Code and other commercial legislation is federal and applies throughout the country; whereas each state has its own civil code. By virtue of the exclusive jurisdiction vested in the federal Congress to legislate for the Federal District and federal territories, however, there is a federally en-acted civil code in effect in those entities which has significantly influenced the civil codes of most of the states.

Article 133 of the Mexican Constitution establishes the hierarchy of sources of federal law and the supremacy of that law over state law. The Constitution itself, federal legislation enacted pursuant to it, and treaties, in that order, are the supreme law of the land.

FEDERAL CONSTITUTION

The present Constitution of the United Mexican States became effective May 1, 1917, and has been amended numerous times and in significant respects since that time.[47] It contains 136 articles, plus 16 transitory articles, and is divided into 9 major divisions, called titles, some of which are further divided into chapters and sections. Title I, comprising the first 38 articles, establishes basic individual rights and civil liberties that are guaranteed to all persons in the country, defines and provides for rights and duties of Mexican nationals and citizens, and establishes certain limitations on the rights of foreigners. Title II, covering articles 39 through 48, provides for the political organization of the country as a "federal, democratic, representative Republic" and defines the territory of the country and its political subdivisions. Under Title III, comprising articles 49 through 107, provision is made for the division of federal powers among the legislative, executive, and judicial branches, and basic regulations for each of those branches are set out. Title IV, articles 108 through 114, deals with criminal and civil responsibility of public officials. Title V, articles 115 through 122, establishes basic requirements for the political organization of the states and imposes certain limitations on state powers and affirmative obligations on the states. Title VI consists of the lengthy article 123, establishing detailed rules for the protection of labor and directing the establishment of a social welfare system. Title VII, entitled "General Considerations" and covering articles 124 through 134, contains a variety of provisions that do not seem to fit elsewhere. The procedure for amending the Constitution is established in Title VIII, article 135, and Title IX, article 136, provides for its inviolability.

In many respects, particularly its political declarations and individual guarantees, the Constitution closely follows the pattern of its predecessor, the 1857 constitution, which borrowed heavily from the United States Constitution. However, it also reflects important social goals that arose out of the Mexican Revolution of 1910, relating principally to land ownership, authority of the church, and labor. The objective of achieving a more equitable distribution of wealth is reflected in article 27, which establishes the basis for the destruction of the large landed estates into which the country was divided in the pre-Revolution era and redistribution of the land among small owners and communal villages or *ejidos*. Restrictions on the acquisition by foreigners of land and concessions for the exploitation of natural resources, discussed in detail in

Chapter III of this study, are also established in article 27. Churches are prohibited to own real property and their powers are otherwise strictly limited in order to reduce their economic power and to prevent their influence in secular matters. The rights of labor in such matters as working conditions, minimum wages, compensation for injuries, collective bargaining, and strikes are established in unusual detail in article 123.

THE CODES AND STATUTE LAW

Mexico, like the great majority of countries within the orbit of the civil-law system, is a code jurisdiction. Each state has a civil code, a code of civil procedure, a penal code, and a code of criminal procedure. There are similar codes, enacted by the federal government, for the Federal District and federal territories. At the federal level there is a commercial code, a federal code of civil procedure, and a federal code of criminal procedure. The Civil Code and Penal Code for the Federal District are also applicable throughout the country to the extent they cover matters that are within the legislative jurisdiction of the federal government, and for that reason and because they are federally enacted they are sometimes referred to as federal codes. Certain other federal statutes are given the name code, such as the agrarian code, the sanitary code, the fiscal code, and the customs code, but they are not true codes.

While much of the law is found in the codes, there is a great volume of noncodified legislation, some of which supplements or amends provisions of the codes and some of which covers areas of the law entirely outside the codified topics. Except for criminal law and civil and criminal procedure, most public law, in particular, is contained in statutes rather than codes. Administrative law, financial law, labor law, and agrarian law are covered by legislation wholly independent of the codes. A number of these statutes directly implement provisions of the Constitution and are often called organic laws or regulatory laws. The statute implementing the constitutional provision restricting the right of foreigners to own land, for example, is the organic law of section I of article 27 of the general Constitution. The provision prohibiting monopolies is implemented by the organic law of article 28 of the Constitution in the matter of monopolies. There are also organic or regulatory laws covering such matters as petroleum, nationalization of private property, public education, and the organization of the federal judicial and executive branches. These titles do not, however, indicate a hierarchy among the various federal statutes; whether they are called organic laws or simply laws or decrees (not to be confused with presidential decrees), they are of equal rank. Most of these statutes are supplemented by presidential regulations, which are in effect integral parts of the laws under which they are issued but are subordinate to them.

In the field of private law, noncodified legislation is the source of most of the commercial law. While there is a commercial code, the enormous changes in the economy and needs of business since its enactment in 1889 have made new legislation necessary, most of which is contained in separate statutes. The law on business corporations, negotiable instruments, banking, insurance, and bankruptcy, for example, is now found in special statutes rather than in the Commercial Code.

The Civil Codes

In Mexico, as in other civil-law countries, the civil code is the repository of the fundamental private law. It is, in theory at least, a systematically organized and complete statement of the general principles and specific rules that regulate legal relations among private persons. As the "general law," it also provides the background for and fills the lacunae in other legislation, in much the same way as the common law is the bedrock upon which statutory law is based in the Anglo-American system. Although it is traditionally regarded as private law, many of its rules are also applicable to relations between individuals and the government, a fact that tends to make the distinction between public law and private law of less practical significance in Mexico than in some other civil-law countries.[48] An agreement between a public body and an individual or private company, for example, is governed by the civil law just as is one between two individuals. In other areas classified in Mexico as public law, reference to the civil law is often essential. The labor law regulates labor contracts, but to determine whether a contract exists, one must look to the rules of the civil code on formation of contracts. The agrarian law governs agricultural land and its use, but its point of departure is the basic property law contained in the civil code. Thus, despite the increasing importance of governmental activity and public law, the civil law is still the fundamental law.

Although each of the Mexican states has its own civil code applicable within its territorial limits, there is substantial uniformity among them resulting from the dominant influence of the federal government. Most states have been content to adopt virtually intact the provisions of the code enacted by the federal Congress for the Federal District and territories. Of the twenty-nine states, all but eight have civil codes patterned after the Civil Code for the Federal District and Territories of 1928. The codes of two of these, Puebla (1901) and Zacatecas (1890), follow the earlier Federal District code of 1884. The states of Tlaxcala (1928) and Yucatan (1941) have drawn from both the 1884 and the 1928 codes for the Federal District. Three states, Morelos (1945), Sonora (1949), and Tamaulipas (1961), have codes based on the 1928 federal code but with many original features. Finally, the 1967 Guanajuato code, though patterned after the Federal District code, is somewhat more complete and advanced.

The present Civil Code for the Federal District and Territories was enacted in 1928 and took effect October 1, 1932.[49] Its predecessors, the codes of 1870 and 1884, had drawn heavily upon the French Civil Code and reflected its emphasis on individual autonomy in such matters as private property and freedom of contract, a philosophy consistent with the dominant individualism of the nineteenth century. The drafters of the 1928 codification, however, were confronted with vastly different social and economic conditions, most importantly a new social philosophy that arose out of the revolutionary movements of the 1910-20 period demanding greater social justice, more equitable distribution of wealth, and limitation of individualism for the protection of the weak and ignorant and in the interest of society as a whole. Some of these ideals had been incorporated into the 1917 Constitution and necessarily influenced the recodification of the private law, whose drafters set out to transform the code into a "Private Social Code."[50] These attitudes were not, of course, limited to Mexico, but were aspects of the evolution of thought in the twentieth century throughout most of the western world.

Despite the stated goals of its drafters, the 1928 code is not a revolutionary document or even very socialistic; to present-day observers it seems at most mildly progressive. The general structure and style of the code closely follow those of the 1884 code, and many of its basic concepts are very similar to those of its predecessor. Private property and freedom of contract are still fundamental tenets, though certain limitations on property and contract are found that tend to modify in some respects the extreme individualism reflected in the earlier codes. For example, the general obligation is imposed on property owners "to use and dispose of their property in such a manner as not to harm the community,"[51] and the specific limitations on the exercise of property rights are broadened somewhat, though not radically.[52] The government is authorized to occupy, use, and even destroy private property "if that is indispensable to prevent or remedy a public calamity, to save a town from imminent peril, or to execute works of evident collective benefit,"[53] and the basis for expropriation by the state is expanded to authorize taking of land for resale for family homesteads or for the construction of low-rent housing for the poor.[54] Parties have contractual autonomy, but the inequality in the positions of the parties in some bargaining situations is recognized and protection afforded to the weaker party, especially lessees and the extremely ignorant, inexperienced, and poor.[55] Consistent with this tendency toward liberalization of the law are provisions for the recognition and protection of certain social groups and interests: the family is given added protection under new provisions for family homesteads; illegitimate children are afforded more liberal treatment; concubinage is recognized as a method of family formation and certain protections are given to the concubine; employees are entitled to compensation from their employers for injuries and diseases incurred in their work without regard to fault or negligence; and labor, professional, and similar associations are recognized as legal entities. Another tendency of the code is found in new provisions designed to simplify and facilitate the circulation of property and the formation of contracts, among which are those giving greater protection to persons in possession of property, reducing the formal requirements for contracts, and recognizing the promise of sale or option contract and the installment sale contract.

The code is divided into four main divisions, called books, which are subdivided into titles and chapters, and contains 3,044 articles plus 9 transitory articles. The first 21 articles are classified separately as Preliminary Provisions and contain rules on the application of the code and laws in general, the sources of law, and certain fundamental legal principles, some of which relate to the subject matter of specific books of the code and seem out of place in the Preliminary Provisions. Under article 2, for example, women are given equal legal capacity with men, a rule of the law of persons; article 16, imposing the obligation on property owners to use or dispose of their property in such a manner as not to harm the community, is a part of property law; article 17 contains a rule of contract law, giving a party from whom an "excessive profit" has been obtained a right of rescission as against one who has taken advantage of his "gross ignorance, notorious inexperience, or extreme poverty."

Book One.—The first book (articles 22-746) contains the law of persons, including family law. The classification of persons as natural persons or legal or artificial persons, and rules on their legal capacity are the subject of the first two titles of the book. The third title covers domicile. The fourth title provides for the civil register and the recording of matters of civil status, such as birth, adoption, guardianship, marriage, divorce, and death. The remaining eight titles deal principally with family law—marriage and divorce, relationship and maintenance, paternity and filiation, parental authority, guardianship, emancipation and majority, absent and missing persons, and family homestead. The title on marriage also covers marital property rights, and it is interesting to note that the marital property regime may take the form of either the community property system *(sociedad conyugal)* or the separate property system *(separación de bienes),* as the spouses agree. The law does not impose either system but rather requires that an election be made by agreement between the spouses, which must be filed in the civil register with the marriage record.

Book Two.—The subject of the second book (articles 747-1280) is property. Following a brief introductory section, the second title provides for the classification of property as immovable or movable (generally equivalent to the common-law classifications of real and personal property) and public or private, and establishes rules for property whose ownership is unknown. The third title deals with possession, principally rights and obligations of persons in possession of property. The fourth title covers the broad subject of ownership. Private property rights are defined and limitations on the use of property are imposed, mainly for the protection of adjacent property owners. The basis for expropriation by the state, "by reason of public utility and through indemnification,"[56] is established. Certain methods of acquiring ownership, the so-called original titles, are established—appropriation of animals, discovery of treasure trove, and accession. Finally, this title establishes rules on co-ownership, including a general provision on condominiums, which are regulated in detail by a special law enacted in 1954.[57] The two succeeding titles deal with the so-called real rights— usufruct, use, habitation, and the various servitudes. The subject of the seventh title is prescription, including both acquisition of ownership by adverse possession, called positive prescription, and the extinction of obligations by the passage of time, called negative prescription. The rules on limitation of actions or negative prescription in this title are not limited to property actions but cover actions to enforce obligations generally, including those arising from contract and tort. This title does not, however, contain all the law on limitation of actions; it deals only with actions to enforce obligations, as distinguished from actions to annul or rescind obligations, which are covered elsewhere in the code.[58] The final title of this book, covering copyright, has been repealed and replaced by a special federal copyright law.[59]

The coverage of Mexican property law may seem somewhat preplexing to the lawyer trained in Anglo-American common law. Not only does the code speak of *ownership* rather than title to or estates in property, but much of the law of property as it is conceived in the common law is missing. There are no provisions for transfer of ownership, and a whole range of what common lawyers consider estates or interests in land are omitted—notably leaseholds, future interests, and security interests. These phenomena are explained by basic conceptual differences between the civil law and the common law. The fundamental principles of Mexican property law are derived from the Roman law concept of ownership, the principal characteristic of which was its absoluteness. The owner of property had absolute title, an absolute right to dispose of his property, and a right of use limited only by a few restrictions of a public-law character. The kinds of incumbrances with which property could be burdened were few and were carefully distinguished from and did not affect the ownership of the property. Thus, there was no fragmentation of property rights into separate interests or estates. This absoluteness and resistance to fragmentation differ markedly from the relative nature of the common-law concept of better title and the common-law propensity for dividing the beneficial property interest into estates.[60] This treatment of ownership is the basis of Mexican property law and largely explains the content and arrangement of the second book of the Civil Code.

Of the broad range of interests that common lawyers regard as estates, only certain limited interests known as real rights, as distinguished from personal rights, fall within the coverage of Mexican property law. Other interests recognized in common law either do not have the status of real rights or simply do not exist in Mexican law. The lease, for example, is not a conveyance of an interest in land but is a contract, creating personal rights, and is covered in the fourth book, on obligations. Likewise, security interests—the pledge and the mortgage— are contracts and are included in the fourth book. Because of the absence in Mexican law of any distinction between rights in equity and rights in law, there is no division between equitable and legal title. It is true that a limited form of the trust has been adopted in Mexican law, but it is a matter of commercial law and no reference to it is found in the Civil Code.[61] Future interests—reversions, remainders, and the like —do not exist in Mexican law. Transfer of ownership or of real rights is omitted from the provisions governing property, again because of a fundamental conceptual difference. The concept of a conveyance, such as a deed, does not exist in Mexican law; a transfer is effected by contract, whether it is for value or is gratuitous. Consequently, the provisions governing transfers of property are found in the fourth book, on obligations.

Book Three.—The third book of the code (articles 1281-1791) covers the law of succession or decedents' estates. The first title contains preliminary provisions defining inheritance, distinguishing between testate and intestate succession and between heirs and legatees and providing for the alienation of inheritances. The distinction between heirs and legatees reflects a fundamental difference between civil law and common law. Under the civilian institution of universal succession, an heir succeeds to the obligations, as well as to the property, of the deceased, while a legatee receives his devise or bequest unconditionally.[62] The second and third titles deal with succession by will and the formal requirements for wills. The fourth title covers intestate or "legal" succession. The last title contains certain provisions common to both types of succession: protection of pregnant widows and posthumous children, vesting and acceptance or rejection of an inheritance, executors and administrators and their duties, and rules on partition.

Book Four.—The largest book of the code is the fourth and last (articles 1792-3044), covering the broad subject of obligations. In it are found provisions on what are classified in common law into contracts, torts, unjust enrichment, sales, conveyances, landlord and tenant, bailments, agency, creditors' rights, and even company law. The notion underlying these provisions and unifying them is the concept of obligation. Contracts, torts, unjust enrichment, and certain other acts all give rise to obligations that are considered legally similar in nature, and they are thus classified and treated together in one field of law.

The fourth book is divided into three parts. The first contains provisions on obligations in general and begins with general provisions on the various sources of obligations: contracts; unilateral declarations of will, which are public offers;[63] unjust enrichment; *negotiorum gestio,* which is a type of voluntary or unauthorized agency; torts, which are called obligations arising from illicit acts; and employers' obligations for workmen's injuries and diseases. Next come provisions that are presumably applicable to all obligations regardless of their source, though most of them seem appropriate only to obligations arising from contracts. These cover various kinds of obligations, such as conditional obligations, term obligations, and joint obligations; transmission of obligations; effects of obligations, that is, performance and nonperformance and effects of obligations with respect to third persons; methods of extinguishing obligations; and nonexistence and nullity of obligations.

The second part of book four contains specific provisions dealing with the various types of contract: the preparatory contract or promise to contract, similar to the option; the sale contract, called *compraventa* or purchase-sale; barter; donation or gift; *mutuo,* a type of loan of money or fungible goods against a promise to redeliver goods of the same kind and quality; lease; *commodatum* or gratuitous bailment; deposit and sequestration; agency, or more precisely mandate, which is one kind of agency contract; service contracts, including contracts for professional services, independent contractors, transportation, and lodging; associations and companies; aleatory contracts, which include gambling and wagering, life annuity, and what is called "purchase of hope" *(compra de esperanza),* a contract for the purchase of future products of a thing or event under which the purchaser assumes the risk that such products may not come into being; suretyship; pledge; mortgage; and compromise.

The third part of book four contains two titles, the first covering composition for the benefit of creditors and priorities among creditors, and the second containing provisions for the public register and the recording of civil documents.[64] The section of the code dealing with the public register is supplemented by regulations on the public register of property issued in 1940.[65]

It is difficult to avoid the conclusion that the law of obligations contained in the fourth book of the code is primarily contract law and that the other sources of obligations receive rather summary treatment. Tort law, for example, is reduced to a relatively few general principles, contained in only 25 articles, articles 1910 through 1934. Article 1910, for instance, states the basic concept of liability based upon fault: "Anyone who, acting illicitly or against good customs, causes damage to another is obligated to repair it . . ." and article 1913 provides for strict liability for damage resulting from the use of dangerous mechanisms or substances, the so-called created risk or objective liability principle.

However, since tort liability arises from unlawful acts, some provisions of what might be considered tort law are found elsewhere in the code, such as the provisions in book two limiting the rights of use of property.[66] Many penal offenses also give rise to private remedies in damages, and certain provisions of the Penal Code and the Code of Criminal Procedure in effect amplify the general provisions of the Civil Code.

It is important to bear in mind that the provisions of the Civil Code are applicable to "civil" acts, as distinguished from "commercial" acts. The dichotomy between civil and commercial law is especially significant in the field of contract law. Both the Civil Code and the Commercial Code contain provisions on many of the same types of contracts—sale, exchange, deposit, loan, pledge, and transportation, for example—the applicability of which depends upon whether the transaction is classified as civil or commercial. Another important example is the dual sets of provisions on companies, which are traditionally regarded as created by contract and therefore one of the types of contract. The Civil Code governs only civil companies and associations, which are limited to those whose purpose is not primarily to engage in profit-making activities.[67] On the other hand, companies whose purpose is commercial and companies organized in the *form* of commercial companies, whatever their purpose, are governed by the commercial law, specifically the general law of commercial companies. Also, the Civil Code provisions on composition for the benefit of creditors relate to civil insolvency, as distinguished from bankruptcy of merchants and commercial companies, which is governed by the rules of the commercial law on bankruptcy. The method of distinguishing between civil and commercial transactions is provided for in the Commercial Code and is discussed below. Despite this dichotomy, however, as pointed out below the Civil Code is very important as a supplemental source of law in commercial matters, and its provisions are frequently applicable to commercial transactions.

The Commercial Code

The present Mexican Commercial Code was issued in 1889 and became effective January 1, 1890.[68] The commercial development and changing economic conditions of Mexico over the many years since its enactment have rendered the code obsolete in many respects and inadequate in others. Rather than undertake a complete reform of the code, however, as was done in the case of the Civil Code, the government has from time to time, especially since about 1930, enacted special legislation to replace specific sections of the code or to supplement it. As a result, only about one-third of the original 1,500 articles of the code are now in effect, and most of the commercial law is found in statutes rather than in the code itself. Although drafts of a new code covering the entire field of commercial law now divided among the 1889 code and these various statutes have been prepared, no serious effort has been made by the government to adopt a recodification.

The code is divided into five main divisions or books. The first book (articles 1-74), which is still in effect, provides for the applicability of the code and contains provisions on merchants, commercial brokers, and their obligations. Merchants, a classification that includes commercial companies as well as individuals, are defined, and rules on capacity to engage in commerce are set out. The duties of merchants relate to the publication of notice of a new business establishment and subsequent changes in its operation, recording certain acts and contracts in the public commercial register, and maintaining accounting records, minute books, and correspondence.

The second book (articles 75-640) covers the broad subject of commerce on land. Its general provisions on commercial contracts and provisions dealing specifically with various types of such contracts— commissions, deposits, loans, sales, and transport contracts—are still in effect. Various portions of the book have, however, been repealed and replaced by special statutes. Commercial companies are now governed by the general law of commercial companies of 1934; negotiable instruments and other credit documents are covered by the general law of credit instruments and operations of 1932; and insurance contracts are covered by the law on the contract of insurance of 1935.

The subject of the third book (articles 641-944) is maritime commerce, and it is in effect as originally adopted except for amendments made in 1946 to certain provisions dealing with maritime insurance contracts.

Of the two titles of the fourth book, the first, covering bankruptcy (articles 945-1037), has been replaced by the law of bankruptcy and suspension of payments of 1943. The second title (articles 1038-1048), still substantially in effect, provides for the prescription of suits arising from commercial acts.

Although separate commercial courts were abolished in Mexico and jurisdiction of commercial suits was transferred to the ordinary courts soon after its independence from Spain, separate rules of procedure for commercial suits have been maintained. These rules are contained in the fifth book of the code (articles 1049-1500), which has not been amended except for the repeal of title four on special rules of procedure for bankruptcy proceedings, now contained in the bankruptcy law.

In addition to the statutes that have replaced parts of the code, a number of important statutes have been enacted that supplement it, that is, that regulate matters not originally covered by the code. These include the general law of insurance institutions of 1935, the federal law of bonding institutions of 1950, the general law of credit institutions of 1941, and the law of mutual funds of 1955.

With respect to the method of distinguishing commercial law from civil law, the Commercial Code adopts an objective criterion, the act of commerce. That is, the commercial law applies to commercial acts considered objectively, regardless of whether or not the persons who perform them are merchants. Article 1 of the code states: "The provisions of this Code are applicable only to commercial acts," and article 4 provides that persons who occasionally engage in commercial transactions are subject to the commercial law with respect to such transactions, even though they are not merchants. There is no general definition of commercial acts, but article 75 lists various types of acts that are classified as commercial, ending with an omnibus category "any other acts which are of a nature analogous to those specified in this Code."

Unlike the Civil Code, the Commercial Code does not purport to be a complete statement of the law on all subjects that it embraces. The general provisions on commercial contracts, for example, contained in only twelve articles (articles 77-88), are quite sketchy, especially in comparison with the detailed provisions of the Civil Code. To fill these gaps article 2 provides that as to matters on which the code is silent the provisions of the civil law shall be applied to commercial acts.[69] The Civil Code is thus an important supplemental source of commercial law, especially in matters of contract. Since commercial law is within the exclusive legislative jurisdiction of the federal government, it is the civil code enacted by the federal Congress—that is, the Civil Code for the Federal District and Territories—that is the supplemental source of law in commercial matters, rather than the civil codes of the various states.[70]

THE LEGAL PROFESSIONALS

Division of the legal profession is much less pronounced in Mexico than in many civil-law countries, and there is substantial overlapping and interchange of personnel among the various divisions. Judges are custom-

arily selected from the practicing bar and often return to private practice, although, as mentioned above, a move is being made toward a
career judiciary in the federal courts. Most law professors are also
successful practicing attorneys or, in some cases, judges. Even government lawyers sometimes engage in private practice in addition to their
employment by the state. Law school instruction is the same for all
lawyers and significantly influences the manner in which they approach
law, and some understanding of it is helpful to the foreign investor and
his counsel who deal with Mexican lawyers.

LEGAL EDUCATION

Legal education is widely available in Mexico, and many persons
who pursue the study of law do not enter the active practice or engage in
law-related work.[71] There are over thirty law schools in the country,
representing nearly every state. The great majority are state supported
and are attached to a university or to an institute of science or of
science and arts. By far the most important and influential is the
Faculty of Law of the national university, the Universidad Nacional
Autónoma de México, located in Mexico City and the major source
of the Mexican legal profession. Of the privately supported schools,
the Free School of Law (Escuela Libre de Derecho), also located in
Mexico City, is especially well regarded for the caliber of its faculty and
its high standards of education.

A student typically enters law school following six years of primary
school and six years of intermediate education, which is divided into
secondary (three years) and preparatory (three years). Since prelegal
education totals twelve years, it is not uncommon for a student to begin
his law study as young as eighteen. The standard law course lasts five
years, and upon successful completion the student is awarded the degree
of *licenciado en derecho*.

The curriculum of the national university law school, which is typical of the leading law schools in the country, includes five to seven
subjects each year.[72] All subjects are required, with the exception of
two elective courses in the last year. The basic courses reflect the structure of Mexican law: civil law (three years), civil procedure (two
years), constitutional law and individual guarantees (two years), criminal law and procedure (three years), administrative law (two years),
commercial law (two years), and labor law (two years). There are one-
year courses in contracts, public international law, private international

law (conflict of laws), agrarian law, and philosophy of law. The list of elective courses includes such subjects as mining law, commercial companies, admiralty, taxation, banking law, and legal accounting. In the first and second years, substantial emphasis is given to courses of a nonlegal or background nature, such as political economy, sociology, general theory of the state, and Roman law, not only because they are considered important, but because, in the absence of university-level prelaw education, the student has no other opportunity to study them. Upon completion of the required number of courses, the student must submit a professional thesis approved by the director of one of the seminars and must pass an oral examination, mainly on the subject of his thesis, by a board of five professors.

The orientation of law study is largely theoretical and the learning process is passive, with emphasis on memorization. The lecture method is followed almost entirely, and both the lectures and the assigned textbooks are concerned mainly with the explanation and classification of definitions and concepts and abstract analysis of the provisions of the codes and statutes. Despite the fact that the overwhelming majority of law professors are successful practitioners with ample practical experience, there is little concern in the classroom for analysis of factual situations or techniques of problem-solving. Apart from the thesis requirement, there is also a notable lack of training in legal research and writing. Even the examinations are oral, and at best they tend to develop proficiency in the verbal discussion of abstract concepts and principles.

This theoretical study of law is balanced to some extent by practical experience gained outside law school. A large percentage of law students, especially those in the last two or three years of school, work as clerks or *pasantes* in private law offices, in the courts, or in government agencies, and class schedules are tailored to accommodate working students. Fourth- and fifth-year students may, under the law of professions of the Federal District, even be authorized to engage in practice under the direction of a licensed attorney.[73]

THE PRACTICING BAR

Article 4 of the federal Constitution guarantees everyone the right to engage in the lawful profession or occupation of his choice, but empowers the states to require a degree for the practice of a profession and to determine the requirements for obtaining it. Most, but not all, of the states have adopted regulatory laws, under which a law degree is required for the practice of law. The exercise of professions, including law, in the Federal District, federal territories, and before federal courts and other federal authorities throughout the country is governed by the law regulating articles 4 and 5 of the Constitution, the so-called law of professions, and its implementing regulations.[74]

Under the law of professions, admission to the practice of law requires a law degree issued by an institution recognized and authorized by the Ministry of Public Education, registration of the degree with the general bureau of professions of the ministry, a license issued by the bureau, and Mexican citizenship.[75] There is no bar examination or other similar qualification for a license; once a law degree is obtained from a recognized Mexican law school, it is merely registered and a license is issued as a matter of routine.

The requirement of Mexican citizenship seems inconsistent with the obvious fact that there are foreign lawyers, mostly from the United States, engaged in practice in Mexico. While some exceptions to the requirement are allowed for foreign political refugees and law professors or consultants in educational institutions,[76] very few of the foreign lawyers in Mexico come within those exceptions. Some are technically classified as consultants in foreign law and are not licensed to practice. Others, probably a majority, after fulfilling the degree requirement, have successfully challenged the validity of the citizenship requirement in *amparo* litigation. The Mexican Supreme Court has consistently and repeatedly held that the requirement of Mexican citizenship in the law violates article 4 of the Constitution, which is applicable to aliens as well as Mexicans and makes no reference to citizenship as a requirement for the practice of a profession.[77] However, since a decision in an *amparo* suit applies only to the person who brought the suit and not to others in the same situation, each alien who seeks admission to the practice of law must file suit and prosecute it to final judgment in his favor. There has been no move to amend the law, and the general bureau of professions of the Ministry of Public Education continues to deny licenses to aliens and actively defends *amparo* suits brought against it.

There is no integrated bar in Mexico; that is, membership in a professional association is not required for the practice of law. A movement to adopt an integrated bar in the early 1960's met with bitter controversy, and opposition to it seems widespread within the profession. Although the administration has taken no official position on the issue, the main objection seems to be based on fear that it might be used as an instrument for increased government intervention and control of the legal profession.[78]   There are, however, several voluntary associations of lawyers, the most important of which are the Barra Mexicana—Colegio de Abogados and the Ilustre y Nacional Colegio de Abogados. While only a small minority of licensed lawyers are members of those associations, their membership includes many of the most highly reputed and successful practitioners, and their influence is consequently much greater than might be guessed from their size.   They sometimes conduct legal education programs for their members and are occasionally consulted by the government on proposed legislation.

Traditionally, the legal profession in Mexico has been characterized by the independent practitioner, conducting his business on a personal basis and from his own office. Within about the past twenty-five years, however, there has been a trend toward greater specialization within the profession and the formation and expansion of law firms. One reason for this is that, with the growth and diversification of the country's economy, the law, especially public law, and administrative and corporate practice have become increasingly complex. Another influence has been the entry into Mexico of growing numbers of foreign companies, some of which have adopted Mexico as the base for their Latin-American or Western Hemisphere operations. There are now several firms in Mexico City that are quite large by Latin-American standards, the largest having from thirty-five to forty-five lawyers.[79] Many of these firms have substantial representation of international business enterprises. Some have foreign, as well as Mexican, members and associates, and a few are associated in some form with foreign law firms.

NOTARIES

The notary in Mexico, as in most civil-law countries, bears little resemblance to the notary public in the United States. He is a lawyer specially licensed and controlled by the state and vested with public authority and faith.[80] He authenticates important legal instruments, including articles of incorporation, contracts, conveyances, powers of attorney, and wills. His functions also include attesting the existence or occurrence of important facts, such as legal notifications, demands, protests of commercial instruments, the accuracy of copies of documents, and the entry and existence of documents in his notarial records. He often also drafts instruments that are executed under his supervision, but in some cases the parties retain other lawyers, especially in non-standardized transactions, to prepare the instruments, which are then signed in the presence of and authenticated by a notary.

Notaries are also responsible for seeing that taxes incurred on numerous transactions in which they intervene are paid. In many cases they withhold federal income and stamp taxes and local taxes on transfers of title to property, and they are also required to give notice to the tax authorities of transactions that are subject to tax.

Certain types of instruments are required by law to be executed before a notary, and even where that requirement does not exist notarial authentication is sometimes obtained because of the evidentiary value of a notarial instrument. An instrument attested by a notary is known as a "public instrument" or "public document" and is conclusive evidence that the persons who executed it manifested their intention to make the agreements and recitals expressed in the instrument, that the statements and acts attested by the notary were made and did occur, and that the notary complied with the formalities stated in the instrument.[81] The conclusive nature of a public instrument can be upset only by judicial declaration.

As a public official, a notary is obligated to serve anyone who requests his services, but he may not perform any official function outside the district to which he is appointed. He is prohibited to hold any public or private employment and to engage in business, and he may not represent clients in court or engage in the practice of law in contentious matters. He may, however, serve as guardian or executor; be a member of the board of directors, *comisario,* or secretary of a company; render legal opinions; serve as arbitrator or secretary in arbitrations; and represent clients in judicial and administrative proceedings necessary for the recordation of public instruments.

The keeping of notarial records, called protocol books *(protocolo),* is governed in detail by law. Ordinarily, the original of any instrument executed before and attested by a notary must be kept permanently in his records. Authenticated copies, called *testimonios,* are delivered to the parties to the transaction and have the same evidentiary value as the original.

A notary receives no salary, despite the fact that he is a public official, but is remunerated by his clients. The fees he may charge are rigidly fixed by law and are generally a percentage of the amount involved in the transaction.[82] For example, execution of the articles of incorporation of a company having a capital stock of $100,000 or a transfer of title to land for that amount involves a notarial fee of about $125.

In view of the public authority vested in notaries, they are subject to strict control. The number of notarial positions is fixed by law, and a notarial license is issued only to fill a vacancy in an authorized position, usually upon the death or resignation of an incumbent notary. Admission to the notariat is made on the basis of a difficult competitive examination administered each time a vacancy occurs. In order to take the examination, the candidate must hold an aspirant's license, which is issued upon the successful completion of an examination following an eight-month apprenticeship in the office of a notary and for which he must be a native-born Mexican citizen and a licensed lawyer. Before assuming his position the notary must post security in the amount of 20,000 pesos to guarantee discharge of any civil liability and payment of any fines levied against him. Notaries are personally liable in the event of malpractice and are subject to administrative sanctions ranging from official warning to removal from office for violations of the law.

This, in part, is the institutional framework within which foreign enterprise operates in Mexico today. The names of the ministries and other executive agencies that have been mentioned will appear time and again throughout this study, and the fundamental importance of their role in shaping and applying policies that affect foreign enterprises will become evident. The availability of the suit of *amparo,* as important to foreigners as it is to Mexicans as a device for obtaining judicial review of administrative decisions and other governmental acts, will be referred to on numerous occasions. While many of the areas of law that will be discussed are governed by special statutes, it is the civil and commercial codes that provide the background against which these statutes are devised, and in many cases the codes themselves furnish the rules governing the foreign investor's legal relations with others. And in all of his legal relations, whether with the government or with private companies and individuals, it is the Mexican lawyer with whom the foreign businessman and his foreign legal counsel are likely to have the most immediate contact and upon whom they rely most heavily for an understanding of the laws and policies and for assistance in surmounting the obstacles that may seem to appear at every turn to the successful operation of his business.

Another aspect of the environment for foreign enterprise in Mexico, perhaps too little known or appreciated by many foreign investors, but one that is essential to an understanding of current attitudes and policies toward foreign capital, is the role that foreign investment has played through Mexican history. Let us now turn to that.

II

The Role of Foreign Investment

If available estimates are accurate, foreign investment in Mexico in the late 1960's probably accounted for little more than one-tenth of the total fixed investment in the country's economy. Mexico's economic growth during the past thirty years, impressive by any standard, has been financed largely from domestic resources.

This has not always been the situation. Foreign enterprise in Mexico has had a long and often turbulent history. Much of the country's basic industrial facilities—transport, communications, and power—were originally developed by foreign capital and initiative, but the dominant position in the economy that foreign enterprise acquired in the process ultimately brought on a half century of almost unyielding reaction and struggle for economic independence.

Phenomena that are obvious to even the casual observer of today—economic nationalism and antiforeign sentiment, concern over the effects on the economy of foreign investment, the steady restriction of economic activities in which foreign capital is welcome, and growing insistence that new direct foreign investment should be limited to a minority position in association with Mexican capital—can be understood only against the background of the role that foreign investment has played in Mexican history.

THE PORFIRIAN ERA: 1876-1911

The history of foreign investment in Mexico had its real beginning following the assumption of the presidency by General Porfirio Díaz in 1876. Before that time, during nearly half a century after its independence from Spain in 1821, civil and international strife and chronic political instability made Mexico less than attractive to most potential foreign investors.[1] True, an illusion, nourished by numerous promotion schemes, that the newly independent countries of Latin America contained inexhaustible untapped riches and offered brilliant investment possibilities enabled the Mexican government to sell two issues of bonds in the London market in 1824 and 1825. However, only the brokers profited; of the total $32 million (U.S.) of debt incurred, Mexico received less than half, or about $15.6 million, and the country's inability to pay interest on the debt was a source of friction for many years to come. Following a series of adjustments under which unpaid interest was capitalized and interest rates reduced, the original English debt had grown to more than $100 million by 1885.[2]

English investors were also enticed to invest substantial sums of money in the rehabilitation of Mexican silver and gold mines, which had been devastated during the country's war of independence. After the mining laws were amended in 1823 to allow foreign participation in the industry,[3] a large number of mines were acquired by British companies. Substantial quantities of silver were extracted, but poor administration and the high cost of unrealistic production methods brought financial disaster to most investors.

By 1867, when the French intervention ended with the defeat of the forces of Maximilian by Benito Juárez, Mexico's reputation abroad was at a low ebb. Though some new foreign investment began to enter the country in the decade of the 1860's, principally in the Mexican Railroad linking Mexico City and Veracruz and to some extent in banking and commerce, it was not until after Porfirio Díaz brought order and political stability that Mexico's international reputation was re-established and foreign investment began to enter the country, with official encouragement, on a large scale—such a scale, in fact, that it would ultimately dominate the country's economy. To a great extent the emotionalism that the debate over foreign investment evokes in Mexico today is a reflection of the reaction to the position that foreign capital and foreigners attained during the thirty-four years of the Díaz dictatorship, one of the longest in modern history.

Díaz and the *científicos* under the leadership of Finance Minister José Limantour[4] embraced an interpretation of economic liberalism and laissez-faire that was given credit for the phenomenal industrial development of Western Europe and the United States in the nineteenth century. The insufficiency of Mexican capital and the unwillingness of the moneyed class in Mexico to invest in industry led the government to open the door wide to foreign capital on the supposition that large investments in mining, communications, electric power, and basic consumer goods industries would automatically carry the country into a spiral of industrialization not unlike that experienced in the more advanced nations. The welfare of the *campesinos* and laborers received little consideration, and if they were exploited in the process, they would have to wait for the benefits of the expected economic growth to trickle down to their level.

The deliberate policy to attract large amounts of foreign capital paid off. Beginning in the 1880's and reaching tidal-wave proportions in the years before the fall of Díaz in 1911, foreign investments poured into railroad construction and mining and to a lesser extent into public utilities, real estate, banking, manufacturing, and commerce. Although available estimates are not consistent and are subject to question, data from a careful recent study, shown in table 3, place total foreign investments in 1911, direct and indirect, at $1,700 million (U.S.), of which almost $650 million was from the United States, $500 million from Great Britain, and $450 million from France. One contemporary estimate placed United States investments alone in 1911 as high as $1,045 million.[5] Whatever the actual figures, it appears that by the end of the Díaz era foreigners probably owned over half the total wealth of the country and that foreign capital dominated every area of productive enterprise except agriculture and the handicraft industries.[6]

Mexico's external credit also was re-established under the Díaz regime. Before 1888, virtually the entire external debt, with the exception of $112 million of government obligations issued by Maximilian and subsequently repudiated by the republican government, arose out of the original bond issues of 1824 and 1825. Through a series of conversions between 1886 and 1888, the external debt was reduced to about one-third of its prior amount, and service on the debt was resumed, paving the way for substantial foreign borrowings on increasingly favorable terms throughout the last two decades of the Díaz administration. Though foreign loans to the country never reached the magnitude of direct foreign investment, table 3 indicates that the external debt had risen to about $250 million by 1911 and accounted for 15 percent of the total amount of foreign capital in the country.[7]

Direct foreign investment, especially North American and British, was oriented principally toward the production and transportation of primary commodities for the export market. Government subsidies, tax and import duty exemptions, and the right to take property under condemnation proceedings attracted foreign capital into railway construction, which claimed almost 40 percent of all foreign investment in

Table 3
Foreign Investment in Mexico in 1911

	Millions of U.S. dollars					Percentage of total investment	Percentage of direct investment
	Total	U.S.A.	Gt. Britain	France	Other		
TOTAL	1,700.4	646.2	494.7	454.3	105.1	100	
Indirect (public debt)	249.0	29.7	41.4	164.1	13.9	15	
Direct	1,451.4	616.5	453.4	290.3	91.2	85	100
Railroads	565.3	267.3	200.7	58.1	39.1		38.9
Mining	408.6	249.5	58.4	89.8	10.9		28.2
Public services	118.9	6.7	105.8	5.0	1.3		8.2
Real estate	97.2	40.7	45.5	8.0	3.0		6.7
Banks	82.9	17.2	8.8	50.0	7.0		5.7
Manufacturing	65.5	10.6	5.4	36.0	13.5		4.5
Commerce	61.1	4.5	.1	40.0	16.4		4.2
Petroleum	52.0	20.0	28.6	3.4	—		3.6

SOURCE: Luis Nicolau D'Olwer, "Las inversiones extranjeras," in *Historia moderna de México*, ed. Daniel Cosío Villegas, vol. 7, *El Porfiriato: La vida económica* (Mexico, D.F.: Editorial Hermes, 1965), tables 65 and 66, pp. 1154-55. Amounts were converted from pesos to U.S. dollars by the author at the prevailing exchange rate of 1 peso = .50 dollar.

NOTE: Because of rounding, detail may not add to totals.

the country in 1911.[8] From the modest 335 miles of railroad that Díaz inherited, the Mexican railroad system was virtually completed in the last years of his administration, growing to over 15,000 miles by 1911. Despite this achievement and the fact that the railroads helped to stimulate industrial development and agricultural production and to increase trade and the mobility of the population, there was a notable absence of government planning and co-ordination. Lines were laid for the main purpose of providing outlets from the mining areas to United States markets and the principal ports, and competing lines operated on the most profitable routes, while large areas of the country were left isolated.

In the production of raw materials for export, mining was by far the most attractive area to foreign investors. Under the liberal mining laws of 1884 and 1892,[9] and with the encouragement of the Díaz administration, foreigners acquired vast mining properties from private Mexican owners and from the government, opened up important new mining districts, and established the smelting industry. Early investments were directed mainly toward the extraction of silver and gold, but the production of industrial minerals—notably copper, lead, and zinc—increased tremendously after 1897. Although there were large French and British investments in mining, United States capital was dominant; by 1911 North American interests accounted for at least 60 percent of the total investment in Mexican mining. Many of the companies that dominate the industry today, though no longer entirely foreign owned, achieved prominence during this period: American Smelting and Refining Company, controlled by the Guggenheim interests; Cananea Consolidated Copper Company, organized and later lost by "Colonel" William C. Greene; The Fresnillo Company, founded by Robert Safford Towne; and Compañía Minera de Peñoles, controlled by German-American interests.[10]

Development of the Mexican oil industry was begun in the last decade of the Díaz administration through the efforts of two foreigners. Edward L. Doheny, an American, acquired large areas of promising oil-producing land in the Tamaulipas–Veracruz–San Luis Potosí area, consolidating his holdings in the Huasteca Petroleum Company. Weetman D. Pearson, an Englishman, later given the title of Lord Cowdray, concentrated on the Tehuantepec region, operating through Compañía Mexicana de Petróleo "El Aguila," S.A. Although the most rapid growth was to come in the decade of the Revolution, significant investments had been made in the industry by 1911.

Investment in oil exploration and production was facilitated to an even greater extent than in mining operations, for which at least a concession from the government was required. The traditional principle of Spanish property law that title to land does not include any rights in the minerals of the subsoil, which are retained by the sovereign, was surprisingly abandoned when the first federal Mexican mining code was adopted in 1884, providing that surface title carried with it ownership of subsurface deposits of bituminous and other mineral fuels and nonmetallic minerals. This provision, allowing the surface owner freely to produce oil and coal from his property without governmental authorization, was reaffirmed in the first petroleum law, enacted in 1901,[11] which also authorized the government to grant oil concessions on federally owned lands and in federal zones. Oil operations were further stimulated by an exemption from all taxes and duties except a negligible stamp tax.

Public utilities also developed rapidly under foreign control during the Porfirian era. Telegraph lines paralleled the railroads; an electric power industry was established to provide service to the mines, industries, and major cities; street railways were built; and a telephone system was installed.

French and British interests led the way in establishing a commercial banking system in the country, primarily to provide banking services to foreign investors in export-oriented activities and merchants engaged in foreign commerce. As in the case of most other activities, the insufficiency or unwillingness of Mexican capital to enter this field and the lack of knowledge and experience of Mexicans in the banking function left the field to foreigners by default.

Of much less importance in amount than other sources of foreign capital, but very significant to the development of industries serving the domestic market, were investments by European immigrants. Mostly French and Spanish, but also German, British, and North American enterprise and capital went into manufacturing and commerce. French capital dominated the cotton textile industry, Mexico's major manufacturing industry, and was found in paper and flour mills, breweries, distilleries, steel mills, and a number of other small manufacturing plants. The French were also the most important investors in retail trade, and a large number of commercial firms dealing in such things as dry goods, clothing, and novelties were established.

The most misguided of all of Díaz' policies, and the one that proved least successful, was his agricultural policy. Not only were substantial amounts of Mexican territory permitted to fall into foreign hands, but the grossly inequitable distribution of land that resulted from it was to be one of the basic causes of the bloody Revolution that followed his downfall and brought nationalism and antiforeignism to the surface of Mexican political philosophy.

Concentration of the productive land in the hands of a few owners and protection of the huge haciendas against disturbance seemed to be regarded by the Díaz administration as the only necessary measures, in a laissez-faire economy, to bring new agricultural techniques that would increase production and the income of the rural population. Although large haciendas had been established under Spanish rule, the *latifundios* grew to an unprecedented extreme under Díaz, at the expense of the holdings of the Catholic Church, small agricultural properties, and the communal lands of the Indian villages. By the end of the Díaz rule, it is reported that over 90 percent of the rural families were without land and that a few thousand haciendas controlled more than half of all privately owned land and contained within their boundaries 50 percent of the rural population and 82 percent of the rural communities in the country.[12]

The legal basis for this massive land-grab had been unwittingly laid by the liberal group that had succeeded in finally overthrowing the Santa Anna dictatorship in 1855. They saw the existing land tenure system, under which half the country's land, much of it unproductive, was held by the Church, as the basis of the country's social and economic problems. Substitution of thousands of small landowners for the relatively few large landowners, principally the Church, and free circulation of real property would remove a great obstacle to the prosperity and growth of the country and would provide a stimulus to the economy. To this end President Ignacio Comonfort issued the famous *Ley de desamortización* (mortmain law) of June 25, 1856,[13] which provided that all property held by civil and ecclesiastical corporations—that is, all institutions that had a perpetual or indefinite duration—was to be sold to the lessee or person who worked the land at a price calculated on the basis of the amount of rent paid. If the lessee failed to purchase the land within three months after publication of the law, anyone could request a sale of the land, receiving as a prize one-eighth of the price at which the land was sold.

The law did not have the desired effect.[14] Most of the Indians who worked the land either could not pay the price or were too innocent to buy the land they occupied or would not risk doing so because of the threat of excommunication, and the purpose of the law to break up the

Church's holdings was largely evaded. Benito Juárez, the great liberal leader, responded to Church resistance to the law and the Church's financial support of the reactionary faction in the Reform War of 1857-60 by nationalizing all Church property in 1859.[15] As a further effort to promote land redistribution and development, in 1863 Juárez issued the law on occupation and alienation of vacant lands,[16] giving anyone resident in the country the right to make claim to as much as 2,500 hectares (about 6,200 acres) of public land.

What began, under Comonfort and Juárez, as an attempt to stimulate the economy through the encouragement of a large class of small farmers who owned and worked their own land had exactly the opposite result. The well-intentioned law of 1856 had the devastating effect of opening the way for the destruction of the Indian communal and village lands, which had traditionally been respected by the Spanish. Since the village governments were considered corporate groups, their lands were also covered by the law, but instead of going to the individual villagers, as was intended, they were absorbed, along with large amounts of public land, into huge estates. The Díaz government encouraged the process of separation of the Indians from their land and the extension of the hacienda system, and the country came to be divided into semifeudal principalities. A large percentage of the rural Indians were forced to leave their homes and work on the haciendas, often in a virtual state of bondage. The landed families, who usually preferred to live in comfort in the capitals of Europe or the large cities of the republic, were not concerned with increasing the productivity of their estates and left the management of the land to often inept and brutal administrators.[17] The consequences for the country were serious. Agricultural production declined to the point that by the latter part of the Porfirian era it was necessary to import large amounts of corn and other products of primary necessity.

Although most of the large estates were held by a small number of Mexican families who formed the social elite and privileged class during the Díaz regime, foreigners also participated in the gigantic land-grab. In addition to extensive cattle ranches and plantations producing agricultural products for the export market and land acquired for oil exploration and mining operations, foreign-owned companies acquired huge tracts of land for the purported purpose of colonizing the country with foreign settlers.

Viewing the agricultural problem as one of insufficient production and sparse population to develop the large areas of uncultivated land,

Díaz' advisors believed that the solution was to promote colonization by foreigners, especially Europeans. The United States and Argentina provided ample evidence that foreign colonizers would bring prosperity. The law of 1863 had proved ineffective to stimulate the interest of foreign settlers, and new laws were issued in 1875 and 1883, authorizing colonization operations through government concessions or by means of contracts with private companies.[18] Numerous companies, mostly foreign owned, were authorized to survey vacant public lands, receiving as compensation for their services one-third of the land surveyed and the right to purchase the remaining two-thirds at ridiculously low prices. Lands acquired by such companies were required to be sold to colonists in tracts not exceeding 2,500 hectares.

The government's attempts to attract foreign settlers were a dismal failure, but the land companies and foreign contractors benefited enormously. Landholders who did not have clear title to their land were at the mercy of the companies. Extensive areas occupied by persons who had no concept of private titles and other properties to which title was beclouded were surveyed and added to the growing holdings of the companies and their occupants ejected with the blessing of the Díaz administration. Unable to fulfill their obligations, the contractors pressed the government for relief, and a new law was issued in 1894,[19] relieving them of all colonization commitments, securing their land titles against forfeiture, and removing the prohibition of the 1883 law against conveyance of title to tracts exceeding 2,500 hectares. Long-standing prohibitions against the acquisition by foreigners of land along the borders and coasts were openly evaded, and large parts of the territory of the northern states bordering on the United States were acquired by North Americans. By the end of Díaz' rule, nearly one-third of the country had been surveyed, and foreigners probably owned one-fourth of the country's total land area.[20]

Unlimited admiration for the foreigner and everything foreign came to be a hallmark of the government of Díaz and the society that surrounded it. The Mexican Indian was regarded as inherently inferior, suited only to till the soil and perform menial tasks in the mines and factories. Foreign companies shared this view and preferred foreign skilled workers. Mexicans were denied training and opportunity to advance to positions of responsibility, and the few skilled Mexican workers were the victims of widespread wage discrimination.[21]

Even before the Díaz government was toppled, there was evidence, especially after 1905, of discontent both within and outside the government over the growing foreign influence in the economy and life of the country, and fear of a pacific conquest by the United States. A preponderance of foreign personnel and use of the English language on the railroads intensified the appearance of United States domination. Foreign immigrants, especially North American and British, were increasingly subject to criticism for maintaining their own language, customs, and schools and making no attempt to integrate into Mexican life.[22] Growing antiforeign and nationalist sentiment was reflected in the slogan "Mexico for the Mexicans." Under the inspiration of Finance Minister José Limantour, who came to favor European capital to offset the dominant position of United States investors, the government in 1906-8 nationalized the major railroads by acquiring 51 percent of the voting stock in the three largest lines and integrating them into the government-controlled National Railways of Mexico system, reportedly to prevent the large trunklines from passing under the control of a continental system in the United States.[23] Attempts were made to impose some restrictions on foreign investment in mining and to extend coverage of the mining legislation to petroleum in the new mining law of 1910, but they failed; the only innovation in this respect was the prohibition of foreign ownership of mining claims within 80 kilometers of the border.[24] Popular resentment was stirred by a series of strikes against foreign-owned companies arising out of protests against the favored position of foreign employees. The 1906 miners' strike at the North American–owned Cananea Consolidated Copper Company properties in Sonora and the 1907 strike of the textile workers at the French-controlled mills at Río Blanco, Veracruz, were brutally suppressed by the government with no redress of grievances.

It cannot be disputed that foreign capital and enterprise made vital contributions to the economic development of Mexico during the Díaz administration. The massive injections of foreign capital were undoubtedly necessary, in the absence of domestic resources, to help build the base required for further development. The investments of European immigrants in the nascent manufacturing industries provided the beginnings of an entrepreneurial class and a consumer goods industry oriented toward the domestic market. A beginning was made in the development of a labor force outside of agriculture.

Despite these contributions, it is difficult to find in present-day Mexico much recognition of the benefits left to the country by either the foreign investor of that period or the government of Porfirio Díaz. What is most remembered and emphasized is that the natural resources of the country were taken for the benefit of the industrial apparatuses of the more advanced countries, with little permanent wealth left in Mexico; Mexican labor was exploited; and the economic penetration of the country by foreign enterprises resulted in almost complete loss of control of the country's destiny to foreigners and foreign interests.

Furthermore, the industrial and fiscal policies of Díaz, superimposed as they were upon the feudal hacienda system, failed substantially. The small domestic market was insufficient to support large-scale industrialization, and nothing was done to improve agricultural production and the income and social conditions of the rural masses—80 percent of the total population—which would have stimulated demand for manufactured products. At the end of the Díaz administration the average annual income per capita of the population was $80.00 (U.S.),[25] and worst of all, there seemed to be no hope for improvement in the situation of most of the people.

Díaz was insensitive to the fact that the country's material progress was limited to a privileged few and that the masses would not accept indefinitely the proverty and denial of human dignity that was their lot. The reaction to the political and economic system of the Porfirian era erupted in the civil war that was to change the course of Mexican history.

THE REVOLUTION AND INTER-WAR PERIOD: 1911-1940

The epic Revolution of 1910-20 marks the beginning of modern Mexican history. What started as a political revolt, under Francisco I. Madero's banner of "effective suffrage and no re-election," against an administration that had been too long in power evolved into a broad agrarian and social movement that is regarded as continuing to this day.[26] The ideals and aims that emerged during ten years of civil struggle—emancipation of the rural and laboring classes and recovery of the country's economic destiny—have been basic to the philosophy of every administration since that time.

In view of the dominant position that the foreigner and foreign enterprise had attained under Díaz and the growing antiforeign sentiment in the country, it is surprising that the initial reaction to foreign investment was as mild as it was. In his revolutionary proclamation, the "Plan of San Luis Potosí," Madero promised that obligations undertaken by the Porfirian administration with foreign governments and corporations would be honored and called on the Mexican people to respect the persons and interests of foreigners.

Latent antiforeignism, however, fed by the rediscovery of Mexican culture and nationalism, charges that foreign business interests were giving aid to one faction or another during the ten-year struggle for power, and United States meddling, inevitably became open hostility after the Madero revolt. The machinations of United States Ambassador Henry Lane Wilson brought him a place of honor in the ranks of the villains of Mexican history. The ill-conceived policies of President Woodrow Wilson, culminating in the occupation of Veracruz in April, 1914, at a cost of at least two hundred Mexican and nineteen North American lives, and his continuing efforts to influence Mexican domestic affairs brought the two countries to the brink of war and flamed the anti-Yankee sentiment in Mexico to a fever pitch.[27] By late 1914 Venustiano Carranza, bidding for popular support in his struggle for power against Pancho Villa and Emiliano Zapata, was promising nullification of foreign contracts and monopolies along with social, economic, and political reforms.

Although no reliable figures are available for this period, it is highly unlikely that, outside of the petroleum industry, any significant amounts of new foreign capital were invested in Mexico during the Revolution. Because of their location along the coastal periphery of the country and by paying for protection, the foreign-owned oil companies largely escaped property damage and, stimulated by wartime demand, expanded their production very substantially throughout the Revolution. By 1921 Mexico had become the second largest oil-producing country in the world, with a production of 193 million barrels—a quarter of the world's output. Other foreign-owned enterprises were not so fortunate. Railroad equipment and rolling stock and mining properties were destroyed wholesale during the renewed armed conflict that followed Madero's assassination in 1913. The mining companies were particularly hard hit, and most of the major mining areas in the country were shut down.[28]

Not long after Venustiano Carranza succeeded in consolidating his control over the major parts of the country, he set about to incorporate the social and economic aspirations and political reforms of the Revolution in a new fundamental law. The Constitution promulgated February 5, 1917, has been in effect, with significant amendments, ever since. Based largely on the liberal 1857 constitution of Juárez, it contained important innovations designed to replace the old order with a new. The legal basis was laid in article 27 for the destruction of the large haciendas and redistribution of the land to communal villages and small private holders. Article 123 incorporated the most advanced program of labor legislation to that time in the world.[29] Important restraints on foreigners and foreign economic activities in the country were also adopted, reflecting a policy to limit the role that foreign capital should play in the new society. Article 27 established the nation's direct ownership of all subsurface mineral deposits, abolished private property rights in petroleum deposits, and reincorporated petroleum into the legal system that governed other mining. Foreigners would be permitted to acquire title to land or waters or concessions on mines, waters, or combustible minerals only on the condition that they agreed to renounce the diplomatic protection of their home governments. By no means could foreigners acquire title to land within 100 kilometers from the land borders or 50 kilometers from the seacoasts. Antiforeign sentiment was also reflected in article 33, which gave the president full power to deport, without trial, any foreigner whose presence in the country he deemed inconvenient.

The struggle that thus began to reassert Mexican control over the natural resources and economy of the country has run through the fabric of Mexican history since that time—its course often irregular and slow, even seeming to disappear at times, but always reappearing to move a step forward.

The first object of attack was the foreign-owned oil industry, which was to occupy the center stage of Mexico's international relations for the next twenty-five years. There was no attempt, or even desire, at that time to oust the oil companies—to do so would have been suicidal—but Carranza considered it important that the industry be subjected to government control and that the government's share in the country's natural wealth be increased. Furthermore, since there was virtually no Mexican investment in the oil industry, it furnished a convenient whipping boy to rally popular support which Carranza needed to stay in power, especially in view of his feeble efforts to carry forward the agrarian and labor reforms promised in the new Constitution. To these ends, beginning in 1917 Carranza issued a series of decrees imposing new taxes on the industry, effectively ending the tax exemptions granted by the Díaz administration, and requiring oil producers to obtain governmental drilling concessions.

The oil companies bitterly fought Carranza's attempts to apply the Constitution and to increase taxes in the press, the Mexican courts, and especially through vigorous protests by the United States Department of

State. In the face of this pressure Carranza backed down, and in January, 1920, a stalemate was reached. His decrees had little effect except to increase taxes, which the companies paid under protest. They successfully ignored his attempts to require concessions, and he abandoned further efforts to regulate the industry. At this point it seemed that the constitutional aspirations of 1917 were empty promises.[30]

Following the ouster of Carranza by Alvaro Obregón in May, 1920—the last successful military *coup* in Mexican history—the United States resorted to the device, as it had before, of withholding recognition to force the Mexican government's hand on the status of the oil companies and other foreign holdings. The State Department refused to accept Obregón's private assurances that article 27 would not be applied retroactively and that no action would be taken against North American–owned properties; Carranza had given similar assurances and had reneged. Obregón's promises were strengthened by a series of decisions handed down by the Mexican Supreme Court between August, 1921, and May, 1922, in favor of foreign oil companies, enunciating the doctrine of "positive acts"—if the landowner had erected drilling equipment or had otherwise performed some "positive act" before the effective date of the new Constitution, May 1, 1917, he was exempt from the requirement of obtaining drilling permits.[31] This was not enough for the State Department, and in view of Obregón's continued refusal to settle the controversy by treaty, the two countries agreed to discuss the entire matter of foreign holdings.

Out of the ensuing discussions from May to August, 1923, known as the Bucareli conferences in honor of their meeting place on Bucareli street in Mexico City, came an extraofficial pact, by which the Mexican representatives agreed to adhere to the doctrine of positive acts and to recognize the perpetual rights of owners who had legitimately acquired oil properties before the 1917 Constitution became effective.[32]

But the controversy was not yet settled. For a time after Obregón's successor, Plutarco Elías Calles, assumed the presidency in December, 1924, it appeared that he would not regard the extraofficial pact as binding on him. In December, 1925, a new petroleum law was adopted, recognizing existing rights in oil properties for a period of only fifty years.[33] However, negotiations on the part of highly effective and popular United States Ambassador Dwight Morrow resulted in a change in Calles' position, and in January, 1928, the petroleum law was amended to provide for the confirmation in perpetuity, through a system of "confirmatory concessions," of rights in oil lands acquired before May

1, 1917.[34] With this, the controversy with the oil companies was put to rest for ten years. The companies, with the active support of the United States government, had won the first round. Even though Mexico continued to assert its ownership of subsurface mineral deposits and succeeded in imposing a sort of concession system in place of the fee simple titles the companies formerly held, the change was more one of form than substance.

The Mexican government also showed a willingness during this period to settle the numerous claims that had accumulated against it on behalf of United States citizens and other foreigners for damage to property and loss of life, principally during the Revolution. Another achievement of the Bucareli conferences was an agreement to establish United States–Mexican special and general claims commissions, and most of the European countries were invited to settle mutual claims with Mexico through similar mixed commissions. None of these commissions was entirely successful despite the fact that their work extended over a number of years, but foreign claims against Mexico would eventually be settled for a fraction of their total face value.[35] Most of the foreign mining concerns, which had probably suffered the greatest losses during the Revolution, agreed to drop their claims in 1926 for political and strategic reasons, in the hope of receiving a more conciliatory attitude from the Mexican government.[36]

Following the military phase of the Revolution and during the controversy over the status of the oil companies, foreign investors were understandably hesitant to risk much new capital in the country. The major mining companies survived the civil war and began to increase their production and exports, and some new foreign capital went into manufacturing and assembly operations, which began to grow rather rapidly during the decade of the 1920's. But the oil industry was the only sector in which the value of foreign investment during that period substantially exceeded the pre-Revolution figure. According to one estimate, direct foreign investment in 1926 was about $1,700 million (U.S.),[37] an amount not to be reached again until the mid-1960's. The increase over the estimated $1,450 million in 1911 undoubtedly resulted from the increased value of the foreign-owned oil industry. Looking ahead at table 7, we see that direct United States investment in Mexico was about $683 million in 1929, only slightly more than the $616 million estimated for 1911, but reflecting a ten-fold increase in petroleum investment and a decline in most other activities.

From the late 1920's through the 1930's, foreign investment was on the decline. In part this was the result of the financial collapse of 1929 and the Great Depression that followed. But there were other factors. The international oil companies, fearful that their property rights would be restricted or abolished, were unwilling to commit the large amounts of capital necessary for new exploration and began to concentrate their efforts in Venezuela. Oil production steadily declined after 1921, reaching a low of 33 million barrels in 1932 before the trend was reversed by the discovery of the rich Poza Rica field. Table 7 indicates that North American investments in petroleum declined from $206 million (U.S.) in 1929 to $69 million in 1936.[38] The railroad system had been severely damaged during the Revolution, and, while some investment went into railroad facilities after 1925, there was little incentive for the investment of substantial new foreign capital to rehabilitate it. The foreign-controlled electric power industry increased installed capacity very considerably from 1920 to 1930, but new investment and further expansion were sharply reduced after the establishment of government rate regulation in 1933 and the resulting decline in profits.

Table 4
Presidential Administrations in Mexico, 1915-1970

President	Dates of office
Venustiano Carranza	February 5, 1915 — May 21, 1920
Adolfo de la Huerta	May 22, 1920 — November 30, 1920
Alvaro Obregón	December 1, 1920 — November 30, 1924
Plutarco Elías Calles	December 1, 1924 — November 30, 1928
Emilio Portes Gil	December 1, 1928 — February 4, 1930
Pascual Ortiz Rubio	February 5, 1930 — September 1, 1932
Abelardo L. Rodríguez	September 2, 1932 — November 30, 1934
Lázaro Cárdenas	December 1, 1934 — November 30, 1940
Manuel Avila Camacho	December 1, 1940 — November 30, 1946
Miguel Alemán	December 1, 1946 — November 30, 1952
Adolfo Ruiz Cortines	December 1, 1952 — November 30, 1958
Adolfo López Mateos	December 1, 1958 — November 30, 1964
Gustavo Díaz Ordaz	December 1, 1964 — November 30, 1970
Luis Echeverría	December 1, 1970 —

The most important factor accounting for the decline of foreign investment in the 1930's was the nationalistic policies of President Lázaro Cárdenas. With Cárdenas came a renaissance of the Revolution, and the slogan "Mexico for the Mexicans" acquired real meaning for the first time. Taking office in December, 1934, he set about to push forward two important revolutionary aims that had been largely side-tracked during the period of political consolidation that followed the Revolution—redistribution of land and loosening the hold of foreigners on the country's economy. Although he disclaimed any intention of closing Mexico to foreign investors and invited foreign capital to assist in financing the country's economic development, Cárdenas was suspicious of the foreign "monopolies," especially in the extractive industries, and blamed the country's economic ills on a conspiracy among foreign capitalists. If foreign investors came, they should be prepared to take a minority interest and establish their homes and reinvest their profits there. These terms and Cárdenas' actions made Mexico less than attractive to most potential investors.

Under the agrarian reform program, the Cárdenas government distributed over 44 million acres of land to collectivized *ejidos,* more than twice the amount distributed by all previous revolutionary governments, most of it expropriated from private owners, many of them foreign. Much of the best agricultural land in the country was taken in the sweep. The 1936 expropriation of the large landholdings in the cotton-rich Laguna district of Durango, mostly foreign owned, has been described as one of the spectacular events of the Cárdenas administration.[39]

The attack on foreign holdings in other areas took different forms. An effective instrument was the expropriation law issued on November 23, 1936, authorizing the federal executive to declare the expropriation of private property for a broad range of purposes, including the "preservation of an enterprise for the collective benefit."[40] Radical labor unions were organized and were supported by the government in their demands for greatly increased benefits under the recently enacted labor law of 1931. If a company refused or was unable to abide by the award of the arbitration tribunals made in response to the union's demands, the government often expropriated the enterprise and turned it over to the workers to operate as a co-operative. Foreign concerns were the primary target of the unions, and a number of small and medium-sized companies, including mining companies, could not withstand the pressure and either withdrew or were turned over to co-operatives.[41]

In order to strengthen the government's control of the major railroads and to remove the threat of interference in their management by the railroad bondholders, mostly British and North American, in June, 1937, Cárdenas expropriated the government-controlled National Railways of

Mexico system, absorbing the railroad obligations into the national debt.[42]

But the most dramatic and far-reaching event of this period was, of course, the expropriation of the foreign-owned oil companies.[43] Despite Cárdenas' antipathy toward the companies, which he regarded as exploiters of Mexican labor and resources, the decision to expropriate was not premeditated or part of an over-all plan. It was virtually forced upon him by the intransigence and miscalculation of the companies and was required, in his view, to preserve the country's honor and integrity. Nevertheless, the event resulted in the elimination of one of the largest blocks of foreign capital in the country and was a giant step in the process of reducing foreign participation in the economy. It is hailed by Mexicans as the beginning of their "economic independence."

Whereas the earlier dispute with the oil industry had concerned the status of their landholdings, the controversy leading up to the expropriation revolved around labor relations. Early in 1936 the small independent unions in which the workers in the various companies were organized were merged into a single national union, the Petroleum Workers Union of the Mexican Republic. Representing all the workers in the industry, the national union in November of that year demanded an industry-wide collective contract from the companies, in accordance with the 1931 labor law, including increased wages and other benefits, a closed shop, and forced unionization of office employees. The companies were willing, in principle, to execute a collective contract, but they rejected the demands for wage increases and inclusion of office staff within the union. In the face of a threatened general strike, Cárdenas intervened and called for a 120-day cooling-off period for negotiation (termed a labor-management convention in Mexican labor law jargon). In spite of government efforts to bring the parties together, the period ended without agreement in May, 1937, and a general strike was called. The union's demands, which by the companies' estimates amounted to an increase in wages and other benefits of about 70 million pesos, were claimed by the companies to be exorbitant and beyond their capacity to pay. They offered 15 million pesos.

Faced with little public support for the strike and no hope of an agreement on its terms, the union changed its tactics. On June 9, 1937, it filed a petition with the federal board of conciliation and arbitration claiming that the controversy was what the labor law terms a "conflict of economic order," required to be resolved by the board. A three-man commission was appointed to investigate company profits and other matters, and after several months' exhaustive study the commission rendered its report. The companies were accused of contributing little to the national interest and social progress of Mexico and were charged with making huge profits, especially in comparison with industry earnings in the United States, selling their products at substantially higher prices in Mexico than abroad, and paying low wages. The commission concluded that the companies were capable of increasing wages by 26.3 million pesos annually. Accepting virtually all of the commission's recommendations, the board issued its award on December 18, 1937, ordering the companies to sign the collective contract, increase wages by 27 percent, estimated at about 26 million pesos, and provide additional benefits. The companies refused to comply and took the controversy to the Mexican Supreme Court, attacking the constitutionality of the board's award and complaining that compliance would mean an increase in wages of 64.5 million pesos and a total increase in benefits of over 100 million pesos, which they were incapable of paying. On March 1, 1938, the Supreme Court affirmed the award, and the federal board of conciliation and arbitration ordered compliance by March 7. The companies were defiant—they repeated that they were unable to comply and reportedly announced that the next step was up to the government. Cárdenas personally intervened to assure the companies that the wage increase would not exceed the 26.3 million pesos estimated by the board. The companies offered 24.5 million and made the serious tactical blunder of indicating that they were not satisfied with the personal pledge of Cárdenas.

At this point it seemed that the controversy might be settled. Although the reports of the discussions between representatives of the government and the companies are in dispute, it appears that the companies were holding out mainly for a modification of the award to remove office employees from union control. Cárdenas seemed conciliatory on this point but refused to commit himself in writing. Neither side conceded. On March 15, the final deadline for compliance with the award, the last straw was added to the scale when the companies flatly announced their refusal to comply.

The companies misjudged the situation and overestimated their power. Perhaps concerned that a dangerous precedent might be established, not only in Mexico but in other Latin-American countries where they operated, if they knuckled under to the government's demands and interventions in their finances, they apparently felt that if they were firm nothing much would happen—the government would be forced to accede or risk economic bankruptcy of the country and perhaps even the fall of Cárdenas himself. But Cárdenas had been pushed to the wall. Although it is doubtful that he had ever intended to resort to expropriation, he decided that there was no alternative.[44] On March 18, 1938, he announced in a nationwide radio broadcast his intention to nationalize the industry, and the decree expropriating the assets of all the major companies was issued the same day.[45] Realizing their miscalculation, the companies immediately offered to pay the 26 million peso wage increase, but it was too late.

Cárdenas' heated charges against the companies, including failure to contribute to the economic and social improvement of the country, discrimination against Mexican workers, and even persistent intervention in Mexican politics, and the companies' bitter counterattacks through the press and economic sanctions against the country served to deepen the widespread antiforeign feelings and touched off an increased flight of private capital, both foreign and domestic.

By the end of the Cárdenas era the role of foreign capital in Mexico had been drastically altered. In contrast to the dominant position it once occupied, in 1939 foreign capital financed only 15 per cent of the total investment in the country.[46] As table 6 shows, total direct foreign investment in 1940 was under $500 million (U.S.), slightly more than one-quarter of the estimate for the mid-1920's. Of the four areas traditionally dominated by foreign capital—railroads, oil, mining, and electric power—foreign control had been eliminated from the first two. Foreign enterprise still controlled the mining and electric power industries, which together accounted for close to 90 percent of total foreign investment in the country in 1940, but even in those fields the amount of foreign capital had been reduced. The course of direct investment from the United States, summarized in table 7, probably reflects the trend of foreign investment generally. By 1943 investment in mining had fallen to less than half the amount invested in 1929. United States private investment in utilities and transportation declined from $164 million in 1929 to $106 million in 1943. The agrarian reform program took its toll of foreign-owned land. North American investment in agriculture dropped from $59 million in 1929 to $10 million in 1940. Manufacturing seems to have been the only area in which foreign investment increased during this period, but the investment was still small, and even though manufacturing expanded swiftly during the Cárdenas era, foreign capital did not play a significant role.[47]

RAPID GROWTH: 1940-1968

The year 1940 marks the beginning of important changes in Mexico's economic policies and attitudes toward foreign enterprise. The basic institutional changes accomplished by the previous revolutionary governments, especially that of Cárdenas, in redistribution of land, strengthening of organized labor, and reduction of foreign participation in and control over the economy set the stage for a shift in emphasis to industrialization as the primary goal of economic policy.

MANUEL AVILA CAMACHO AND MIGUEL ALEMAN

After Manuel Avila Camacho took office in December, 1940, the agrarian reform program was substantially slowed, the relative power of labor was weakened,[48] expropriations of going concerns came to a stop, and the country's attention turned to industrial development. World War II was a powerful stimulus to the process of rapid industrialization. The virtual halt of imports of manufactured goods that had traditionally been purchased abroad and the increased external demand for Mexican products such as textiles, foodstuffs, fibers, tobacco, and chemicals created excellent opportunities for investment in production facilities to supply Mexico's domestic market and to take advantage of the export possibilities.[49]

This shift in economic emphasis was accompanied by a change in attitude toward foreign capital. Steps were taken by Avila Camacho to settle the country's international obligations that he had inherited from prior administrations and thus to improve the climate for foreign participation in the growth of the economy.[50] The most important step in this direction was the signing, on November 19, 1941, of the Mexican-American General Agreement, under which many of the problems between Mexico and the United States were resolved. The agrarian and general claims of United States citizens against Mexico, principally arising from land expropriations under the agrarian reform program, were settled in full for $40 million (U.S.), including accrued interest. Mexico had already paid $3 million toward this debt, another $3 million was paid upon the exchange of ratifications, and the balance of $34 million was to be paid in annual installments of $2.5 million.

Probably the most important feature of this agreement was the establishment of a procedure to settle the outstanding debt to the United States oil companies arising from the 1938 expropriation of their Mexican properties. Cárdenas had broken the united front of the companies by making a separate settlement with the Sinclair oil interests on May 1, 1940, for $8.5 million, but the other companies had resisted his invitations to negotiate a settlement and had placed what the government considered exorbitant values on their holdings. The general agreement provided for a joint commission of one Mexican and one United States expert to evaluate the expropriated properties and recommend terms of payment. The commission's report, issued on April 17, 1942, was accepted, and Mexico agreed to pay almost $24 million for the North American–owned properties, plus 3 percent interest from March 18, 1938, to September 30, 1947, the date of payment of the final installment, amounting to $5 million.[51]

Settlement of the debt to Compañía Mexicana de Petróleo "El Aguila," S.A., a Dutch Shell subsidiary and the largest foreign-owned oil company in Mexico, was delayed by the rupture in diplomatic relations between Mexico and Great Britain resulting from the expropriation. Before the end of Avila Camacho's term of office in 1946, however, direct negotiations were initiated with the company, and on August 29, 1947, an agreement was reached under which Mexico agreed to pay $81.25 million (U.S.) for its expropriated holdings, plus interest amounting to a total of about $49 million from March 18, 1938, to September 17, 1962, the final payment date. All told, the government was to pay over $170 million for the expropriated oil properties.

Another problem facing Avila Camacho was that of the old bonded external debt and the debt to foreign bondholders of the National Railways of Mexico, which had been assumed by the federal government upon the expropriation of the lines in 1937. By the early 1940's the Mexican government's general external debt, including principal and interest, amounted to nearly $510 million (U.S.) and the railroad debt was over $550 million. Although debt service on the defaulted bonds had been resumed under a 1922 agreement between the Mexican government and the International Committee of Bankers on Mexico (known as the De la Huerta–Lamont agreement), Mexico had been unable to continue payments under that agreement, and service on the public debt had been suspended for over fifteen years. In 1942 an adjustment of the direct external debt was negotiated, the bondholders accepting a reduction of the government's obligation to about 20 percent of the nominal principal amount of the bonds and a large reduction in interest payments. A somewhat similar arrangement was made with the railroad bondholders in 1946 for adjustment of the defaulted debt of the National Railways.

These settlements cleared the slate, for all practical purposes, of Mexico's pending external obligations. To her credit, Mexico has faithfully complied with the obligations established in the various agreements. The oil expropriation debt was totally liquidated with the final payment to El Aguila on August 31, 1962; the outstanding bonded debt and a substantial part of the railroad debt were prepaid in 1960, and the remaining outstanding railroad bonds have been redeemed on schedule.

With its external credit thus re-established, the Mexican government began to look increasingly to foreign loans to help finance the expansion of the country's economy. From 1941 to the end of 1950 Mexico negotiated loans totaling almost $400 million (U.S.), mostly from the United States Export–Import Bank but also from the International Bank for Reconstruction and Development and private North American banks. These loans were invested primarily in such overhead facilities as highways, railroads, electric power, and irrigation, and a variety of industrial projects.

The industrialization policy emphasized by Avila Camacho was given even greater impetus during the administration of Miguel Alemán, who took office in December, 1946. Because of his desire to accelerate the rate of industrialization, Alemán openly invited foreign capital to participate in Mexico's economic development. No Mexican government since Porfirio Díaz has welcomed foreign investment so warmly. Indicative of his attitude was the administration of a decree issued in 1944 by Avila Camacho establishing for the first time the basis for limiting new direct foreign investment to a minority position in association with Mexican capital. Intended as an emergency wartime decree for the stated purpose of controlling the disruptive effect that temporary investments of flight capital might have on the Mexican economy, the decree authorized the Ministry of Foreign Relations to require Mexican control of companies organized after its enactment. Although the decree was retained as permanent law after the war emergency ended, its effect was limited under Alemán to a small list of insignificant activities.[52]

Although by far the greatest percentage of private investment during the decade of the 1940's was Mexican, foreign enterprise began to be attracted by the rapidly expanding economy and the receptive attitude of the Mexican government. As table 5 shows, direct foreign investment increased slowly during the war years—the average annual rate of new foreign investment in the period from 1941 through 1946, including reinvested earnings, was only about $26 million (U.S.), and total direct foreign investment increased moderately from about $450 million in

Table 5
Annual Direct Foreign Investment in Mexico, 1939-1968
(in millions of U.S. dollars)

Year	Total	Net new investment	Reinvested earnings & intercompany items
1939	22.3	13.6	8.6
1940	9.3	9.5	− .2
1941	16.3	13.5	2.7
1942	34.4	16.0	18.4
1943	8.9	7.8	1.1
1944	39.9	21.1	18.8
1945	46.0	22.4	23.6
1946	11.5	8.4	3.1
1947	37.3	16.3	21.0
1948	33.3	39.7	− 6.4
1949	30.4	15.2	15.2
1950	72.4	38.0	34.4
1951	120.6	49.6	71.0
1952	68.2	36.5	31.7
1953	41.8	37.2	4.6
1954	93.2	77.8	15.4
1955	105.4	84.9	20.4
1956	126.4	83.3	43.1
1957	131.6	101.0	30.6
1958	100.3	62.8	37.4
1959	81.2	65.6	15.6
1960	78.4[a]	62.5[a]	16.0
1961	119.3	81.8	37.4
1962	126.5	74.9	51.6
1963	117.5	76.9	40.5
1964	161.9	95.1	66.9
1965	213.9	120.1	93.8
1966	109.1[b]	109.1	c
1967[d]	88.6[b]	88.6[e]	c
1968[d]	115.1[b]	115.1	c

SOURCE: Banco de México, S.A.

NOTE: Because of rounding, detail may not add to totals.

a. Does not reflect disinvestment of $116.5 million (U.S.) resulting from government's purchase of equity interests in foreign-owned electric power companies.

b. Does not include reinvested earnings (see note c).

c. In 1967 Banco de México discontinued the practice of publishing reinvested earnings as not representing international movements of funds. The preliminary estimate of reinvested earnings and intercompany items in 1966 was $88.7 million (U.S.).

d. Preliminary estimates.

e. Does not reflect disinvestment of $64.4 million (U.S.) for purchase of foreign-owned sulphur companies.

1940 to $575 million in 1946. The declining trend of the 1930's in direct investment from the United States continued to 1943, when a low of $287 million was reached, but there was a steady increase in the inflow of private North American capital after that year.

The rate of direct foreign investment in the country accelerated rather sharply under Alemán, particularly during the latter half of his administration, to an annual average of slightly over $60 million (U.S.). By the end of 1952, despite devaluations of the peso in 1948 and 1949, total foreign investment was estimated at close to $730 million, a net increase of more than $150 million over the 1946 figure. The stake of

Table 6
Total Direct Foreign Investment in Mexico, 1940-1965
(in millions of U.S. dollars at year end)

Year	Amount
1940	449.1
1941	452.9
1942	477.4
1943	491.2
1944	531.8
1945	568.7
1946	575.4
1947	618.6
1948	608.8
1949	518.6
1950	566.0
1951	675.2
1952	728.6
1953	789.5
1954	834.3
1955	952.8
1956	1,091.4
1957	1,165.1
1958	1,169.5
1959	1,244.7
1960	1,081.3
1961	1,130.4
1962	1,285.9
1963	1,417.3
1964	1,552.4
1965	1,744.7

SOURCE: Banco de México, S.A.

United States private capital in the Mexican economy rose to over $400 million by 1950 and to about $550 million in 1952, accounting for some 75 percent of all direct foreign investment in that year.

More significant than the amount of capital invested by foreign enterprise, however, was the dramatic change in the direction of that investment. The foreign investor of this period was basically different from his predecessor. No longer was he attracted mainly into production of primary commodities for export, public services, and government bonds. Rather, he was lured by the growing domestic market and the tariff protection offered to Mexican-based industry into establishing production facilities, at least assembly and processing operations, to supply local demand. Whereas in 1940 direct foreign investment in the traditional fields of mining, public utilities, and transportation accounted for 90 percent of the total, new investment after that year increasingly went into industry. In the period 1941-44 an average of 36 percent of new direct foreign investment was in manufacturing, and from 1945 through 1949 it rose to 59 percent of the total.[53] By 1950 foreign investment in manufacturing had surpassed that in any other single activity, and at the end of 1952 it accounted for over 30 percent of the total foreign private capital in the country.

Despite this increased influx of foreign funds, both private and public, investment during the decade of the 1940's was financed largely from domestic savings, and there was even a decline in the relative importance of the foreign contribution to investment. Whereas foreign capital financed 16 percent of total investment during the period 1939-45, from 1946 through 1950 its share of the total was only 9 percent. This trend was also reflected in foreign participation in industrial investment—in the years 1941 through 1945 foreign investment in industry averaged 10 percent of total investment in that field but declined to about 7 percent of the total in the postwar years 1946 through 1949.[54]

ADOLFO RUIZ CORTINES

By the time Adolfo Ruiz Cortines took office in 1952, the economic boom of the prior decade had begun to cool. Highly profitable investment opportunities in the production of consumer goods for the domestic market were becoming less plentiful, and, after a brief spurt during the Korean war, external demand for Mexican exports had begun to decline. These factors, together with initial hostility toward direct foreign investment on the part of the Ruiz Cortines administration, undoubtedly con-

Table 7
Total United States Direct Investment in Mexico, Selected Years, 1929-1967
(in millions of U.S. dollars at year end)

Activity	1929	1936	1940	1943	1950	1954	1956	1958
Mining and smelting	230	213	168	108	121	142	165	139
Petroleum	206	69	42	5	13	12	18	32
Utilities and transportation	164	148	116	106	107	90	94	120
Manufacturing	6	8	10	22	133	217	309	336
Trade and finance	9	11	7	23	32	45	71	84
Agriculture	59	17	10	14	3	a	a	a
Other groups	8	13	5	9	6	17	18	34
TOTAL	683	479	358	287	415	523	675	745

Activity	1960	1961	1962	1963	1964	1965	1966	1967[b]
Mining and smelting	130	129	121	116	128	104	108	100
Petroleum	32	54	73	66	56	48	42	43
Utilities and transportation	119	29	26	25	27	27	29	27
Manufacturing	391	418	442	503	607	756	802	890
Trade and finance	85	97	97	93	111	138	152	166
Agriculture	a	a	a	a	a	a	a	a
Other groups	39	104	107	104	106	110	114	115
TOTAL	795	830	867	907	1,035	1,182	1,248	1,342

SOURCE: United States Department of Commerce, Office of Business Economics.
NOTE: Because of rounding, detail may not add to totals.
a. Not separately reported.
b. Preliminary estimates.

tributed to the marked decline in the rate of inflow of foreign capital in 1953 shown in table 5.

However, balance of payments pressures that began to appear early in 1954, leading to the devaluation of the peso from 8.65 pesos to the dollar to 12.50 pesos to the dollar on April 18, 1954, brought about a change in the government's attitude toward foreign investment. With this change and the rapid recovery of the economy following the devaluation, foreigners again began to pour funds into the country. As table 5 shows, over $100 million (U.S.) in new direct foreign investments and reinvested earnings went into the country in every year from 1955 through 1958. By the end of 1958 total direct foreign investment was estimated at close to $1,200 million, an increase of more than 50 percent over the 1952 total. Although foreign capital increased in every sector of the economy, the great bulk of new investment continued to go into manufacturing, which accounted for over 34 percent of the total in 1957. There was also a notable increase in the relative position of investment in trade, from just under 16 percent in 1952 to over 18 percent in 1957. Together the two fields accounted for well over half the total foreign investment in the country, a startling jump from the 6 percent registered in 1940.[55]

During this period the Mexican government also increased its reliance on foreign credits to finance the country's public investment. Table 8 indicates that from 1955 through 1958 net public foreign loans rose at an average annual rate of over $60 million (U.S.), exceeding $75 million in 1957 and $100 million in 1958. In the period 1950-59 capital from this source represented 14 percent of total public investment and 30 percent of the investment of decentralized organisms and state enterprises.[56]

The rapid growth in the inflow of foreign capital and a decline in the rate of increase of domestic investment, both public and private, during the decade of the 1950's resulted in a rise in the relative role of foreign investment. Whereas foreign investment averaged only 8 percent of total annual investment in the country's economy in the period 1939-50, foreign capital financed about 12 percent of total investment during the 1950's.[57]

This increase in investment from abroad brought new pressures to limit the role of foreign enterprise in the country. The group of young and nationalistic Mexican industrialists who had come onto the scene during the boom years of the 1940's, with the Cámara Nacional de la Industria de Transformación (CANACINTRA or CNIT) as their principal spokesman, stepped up their propaganda offensive against direct foreign investment, seizing on the argument that the effect of such investment is to "decapitalize" the country and thus to add to the balance of payments problems because more capital is taken out of the country annually by foreign firms in the form of profits than is brought in as new investment. Government economists too were becoming concerned over the long-term effect on the payments balance of foreign investments and

Table 8
Public Foreign Loans to Mexico, 1952-1968
(in millions of U.S. dollars)

Year	Received	Repaid	Net
1952	55.3	33.8	+ 21.5
1953	31.6	31.2	+ 0.4
1954	63.5	49.9	+ 13.6
1955	102.7	64.5	+ 38.2
1956	114.7	79.3	+ 35.4
1957	158.2	82.3	+ 75.9
1958	238.9	137.9	+101.0
1959	221.0	158.4	+ 62.6
1960	332.8[a]	167.3	+165.5[a]
1961	357.3	183.7	+173.6
1962	400.9	267.9	+133.0
1963	420.9	230.6	+190.3
1964	695.3	335.0[b]	+360.4[b]
1965	366.5	365.7	+ 0.8
1966	548.5[b]	451.9	+ 96.6[b]
1967[c]	714.8[b]	446.4	+268.4[b]
1968[c]	777.3[b]	550.1	+227.1[b]

SOURCE: Banco de México, S.A. Receipts and repayments of loans to Nacional Financiera and other government agencies and net changes in government debt, reported separately in source, have been combined.
NOTE: Because of rounding, detail may not add to totals.
a. Includes $60 million (U.S.) debt incurred on acquisition of foreign-owned electric power company.
b. Reflects foreign credits granted by Mexico to stimulate Mexican exports.
c. Preliminary.

public loans and also were fearful of a slowdown in the rate of industrial development unless the pattern of investment in assembly and processing operations, characteristic of the 1940's, could be broken and greater use of domestically produced intermediate materials encouraged to stimulate import substitution.

Although Ruiz Cortines did not give in fully to these pressures, the reality of Mexican politics did not permit him to ignore them altogether. Foreign investors were encouraged to accept Mexican capital in their ventures, and even though there was little if any real pressure in this respect and the legal restrictions on direct foreign investment continued to be insignificant, an increasing number did so.[58] As a stimulus to the process of "integration" of Mexican industry—that is, the domestic manufacture of intermediate products and components to replace imports—the law on new and necessary industries, which had been enacted in 1939 to attract investment in industry through the authorization of certain tax concessions, was amended in 1955 to apply only to manufactured products that had a minimum of 60 percent of domestic content. It does not appear, though, that these measures discouraged potential investments, and foreign firms continued to be attracted by Mexico's political and economic stability, tariff protection, and profit potential.

ADOLFO LOPEZ MATEOS

If Ruiz Cortines' attitude toward direct foreign investment was somewhat ambiguous, his successor, Adolfo López Mateos, soon made his nationalistic inclination unmistakably clear. Despite sluggishness in the economy and a declining rate of private investment in the late 1950's, the new president set about to reduce sharply the participation of private foreign investment in the country, at least in some activities. The announcement in his first annual report to the Congress on September 1, 1959, that the administration had adopted the policy that all firms producing raw materials or basic products should have a majority of Mexican capital was a warning of what was to come.

Even before he took office, in 1958 López Mateos, as president-elect, had given his blessing to the elimination of foreign ownership of the country's prinicipal telephone system through the purchase by a group of private Mexican investors of controlling interest in foreign-owned Télefonos de Mexico, S.A. This policy was also applied to the emerging petrochemical industry. During the new administration's first year in office regulations were issued limiting foreign participation in enterprises in that industry to a minority role.[59]

But his most important step in this direction was one that rivaled Cárdenas' expropriation of the oil industry and represented another spectacular advance in the revolutionary goal of elimination of foreign control from the country's basic economy—this time the electric power industry. However, both the circumstances and the technique of the nationalization of the foreign-owned electric companies were vastly different from those involved in the 1938 oil expropriation.[60]

In 1960 the electric power industry in Mexico was divided among the state-owned Comisión Federal de Electricidad (CFE), two major foreign-owned companies, and numerous small local public and private plants. Up to about 1945 the two foreign companies had virtually monopolized the industry—Mexican Light & Power Company, controlled by the Belgian holding company Sofina, supplied power to the Federal District and surrounding states, and American & Foreign Power Company, the Latin American subsidiary of the United States–owned Electric Bond & Share system, owned all the major generating and transmission facilities elsewhere in the country. After the war the CFE, which had gotten off to a slow start following its creation by Cárdenas in 1937, expanded its capacity much more rapidly than the private utilities, increasing its share of the total installed capacity from 5 percent in 1945 to 40 percent in 1960. In the same period the share of the two large private companies was reduced from 60 percent to about 33 percent. The small service plants accounted for approximately 27 percent of the installed capacity. Despite the great expansion of the CFE's facilities, the private companies continued to control the distribution systems and were the major purchasers of the commission's energy output.

The private companies also began to expand their generating capacity after 1945, following a period of almost complete stagnation beginning in the mid-1930's, but the rate of growth of the industry did not keep pace with the needs of the country for its industrial development. Substantial indirect governmental assistance to the companies, mainly in the form of sales of CFE-generated power to the companies at low prices and guarantees of loans to the companies from foreign credit institutions, upon which the companies largely depended to finance their expansion programs, was insufficient to stimulate the necessary growth, and the government consistently refused to revise the rate structure in the industry to permit what the private utilities and international lending agencies considered adequate profits to warrant substantial additional investments. By the late 1950's it appeared that additional loans to the industry from international and United States agencies would not be forthcoming in the absence of a complete revision of the rate structure. But the political implications involved in a rate increase, so long as the industry was dominated by foreign companies, were too great. The government, facing continuing increases in the country's requirements for electric power, and the companies, unwilling or unable to make the heavy new investments necessary to meet those requirements, thus came to an impasse.[61]

It is not entirely clear which side made the first move, but the companies had been giving serious consideration to selling out to the government, and it appears that American & Foreign Power took the initiative in offering to negotiate a sale to the government.[62] At any rate, nationalization seemed the logical solution.[63] In two separate transactions in 1960 the government acquired the two major foreign utilities. On April 26 the properties of American & Foreign Power Company were purchased for $65 million (U.S.), of which $5 million was paid in cash, and the balance, represented by dollar obligations of Nacional Financiera guaranteed by the government, was to be paid over a period of fifteen years with tax-free annual interest of 6.5 percent. Nacional Financiera also assumed the $34 million outstanding debts of the company's subsidiaries. As part of the deal, the company agreed to reinvest the payments it received from Nacional Financiera in nonutility enterprises in Mexico. A few months later the government purchased directly from Belgian Sofina and individual shareholders in various countries 95 percent of the outstanding common shares and 73 percent of the preferred shares of Mexican Light & Power Company and assumed control of the company on September 27. The total purchase price of $52 million paid was somewhat higher than the stock exchange quotations for the shares before negotiations began. The Mexican Light & Power debt assumed by the government amounted to $78 million. To complete the nationalization, the following year the government purchased the remaining privately owned generating systems.

The administration was careful to avoid offending foreign entrepreneurs; there were no cries of "foreign imperialism" or attacks on foreign investment generally. In his second annual report to the Congress on September 1, 1960, President López Mateos stated, perhaps for the benefit of the international business community, that the acquisitions had been made "without harming any legitimate rights or interests, and in a manner in keeping with our general development." The companies also publicly announced their satisfaction with the fairness of the transactions. Because of the manner in which the Mexican government accomplished the nationalization of the industry, paying what seemed a fair price when it undoubtedly could have achieved its goal at a much smaller cost in view of the weak position of the companies, the country maintained the good will of the utilities themselves and international financial circles. It was even reported that the initial payments for the properties were financed by an unconditional loan made to the Mexican government in March, 1960, by a large United States insurance company.

Even if nationalization of the electric power industry was accomplished with fairness to the foreign investors and was the only practicable solution to the impasse between the government and the companies, it nevertheless represented another giant step toward the elimination of foreign control of Mexico's basic economy and was the source of great jubilation and pride on the part of the Mexican people. Of the four traditional areas of foreign dominance—railroads, mining, petroleum, and public utilities—only the mining industry, about 90 percent of which was in the hands of foreign-owned companies, was still controlled from abroad.

López Mateos did not delay in moving to Mexicanize that industry. On February 5, 1961, a new mining law was issued, providing that no new concessions for mining or metallurgical operations could be issued to foreigners or to Mexican companies the majority of whose capital stock was not owned by Mexicans. The law further established that existing concessions, which had an unlimited duration under prior law, would expire within twenty-five years and were not renewable unless they were held by Mexicans or Mexican-controlled companies. Although no requirement was imposed on existing concession holders to give up control to Mexicans, very substantial tax concessions were incorporated into the mining tax law for companies that did so, and most foreign-owned companies lost no time in negotiating sales to Mexican investors of controlling interests in their mining operations.[64]

Though not so important or spectacular as the electric power and mining industries, the government under López Mateos also moved to displace foreign investment in other selected fields. An example was the purchase by government-controlled Altos Hornos de México, S.A. from North American investors of the majority interest in a major Mexican steel company, La Consolidada, S.A.[65]

Pressures were also stepped up during this period on foreign entrepreneurs wishing to make new investments in manufacturing activities to accept a minority position in association with Mexican investors. Outside of a few areas, such as mining, petroleum, petrochemicals, transportation, public utilities, and the rather insignificant list of activities that had been closed to majority foreign ownership under the emergency decree of 1944, there was no legal restriction on the amount of foreign participation in Mexican industrial enterprises. But the administration had other weapons to enforce its wishes and seemed to prefer the flexibility in shaping its policies to individual investment projects that was allowed by the absence of a general law on foreign investments. The greatest potential threat, especially to enterprises that depended on imports from abroad of raw or intermediate products, machinery, or equipment, was that vital import licenses, which the Ministry of Industry and Commerce could grant or deny at its discretion, would be withheld. In order to assure themselves that their investments in new facilities would be favorably received, foreign businessmen and their legal representatives increasingly felt it necessary or advisable to sound out the government on its attitude toward their projects, and an informal clearing process for new investments developed. Often prospective foreign investors were informed that import licenses and other permits would more likely be forthcoming if they were associated with a majority of Mexican capital.[66] Another means of encouraging joint ventures was the withholding of tax concessions under the law on new and necessary industries from foreign-controlled enterprises.

The vigorous efforts of the Mexican government under López Mateos to accelerate the process of import replacement also affected the position of the foreign entrepreneur. No longer was the government receptive to the establishment of plants for the mere assembly or final processing of imported parts or intermediate products, and prospective investors in such facilities were informed that import licenses for their activities would not easily be obtained. The administration also moved to force existing plants that depended heavily on imports to develop domestic production of their intermediate products. The most important area in which the government applied this policy was the automobile assembly industry, which imported about 80 percent of the value of assembled vehicles, but it was also applied to such industries as the manufacture of mechanical typewriters, agricultural machinery and implements, and heavy construction equipment.[67]

Other events early in the López Mateos administration further gave prospective foreign investors second thoughts about committing new capital in Mexico. The Communist take over of Cuba and fear that Communism might spread to other Latin-American countries made the whole area less than attractive to many foreign businessmen, and Mexico's independent stand in refusing to apply the sanctions against the Castro government decreed by the Organization of American States further caused concern about the direction of the Mexican government. This fear was intensified by the leftist, pro-Castro stand taken by former president Lázaro Cárdenas and his followers, who were threatening the unity within the PRI, and the need apparently felt by López Mateos to make concessions to the left and prove himself a standard-bearer of their cause. These undoubtedly were important factors behind the reluctant attitude toward direct foreign investment and other measures taken by the administration that were unsettling to domestic as well as foreign private investors. One example was López Mateos' statement that his administration's policy was to follow a path "on the extreme left within the Constitution." In the area of agrarian reform also, López Mateos seemed determined to prove that he was a true revolutionary leader; the rate of distributions of land for *ejidos* was accelerated to such a degree that by the end of his term of office almost 40 million acres had been converted to *ejidos,* more than one-third of the amount distributed by all his predecessors since the Revolution.

These measures, which were taken by many businessmen as an attack on business generally, coincided with a period of sluggishness in the economy. Whatever the contributing causes, there was a sudden drop in the rate of private investment from both domestic and foreign sources.[68] Tables 5 and 6 reveal that new direct foreign investment fell substantially in both 1959 and 1960, and by the end of the latter year total direct investment in the country had declined to a level below the 1956 amount. However, the administration responded in 1961 and 1962 by reassuring the domestic business sector in a series of major speeches of the government's esteem for and support of private enterprise, and by offering such inducements as tax and other concessions for manufacturing enterprises in the border zones and other areas outside of Mexico City and for the export of Mexican manufactured products. The publication of a list of some six hundred industrial products the domestic manufacture of which the government was anxious to stimulate was a further attempt to encourage new investments by the private sector.

The administration's efforts brought renewed confidence to the business community, and with an increase in private domestic investment came a significant rise in the inflow of foreign capital, as shown in table 5. In the four years from 1961 through 1964 new direct foreign investment, including reinvested earnings, averaged over $130 million (U.S.) annually, reaching the impressive amount of almost $162 million in 1964, the last year of the López Mateos administration. The recovery of the economic growth rate was probably also an important stimulus; the average annual rate of growth of 5.4 percent projected in the government's Plan de Acción Inmediata[69] for the three-year period 1962-64 was exceeded, and in 1964 there was a startling increase in gross national product of 10 percent over the prior year, resulting largely from heavy investments of the public sector.

To help finance the sizable investments made by the public sector during this period, the government increased substantially its reliance on foreign public funds, with the results shown in table 8.[70] The largest amount of foreign public credit, over a quarter of the total, went into expansion of electric power, but substantial amounts were also directed to state-controlled manufacturing industries, petroleum, hydraulic works, railroads, agriculture, petrochemicals, and highways.

Highly significant in the field of public borrowing was the successful international marketing on three occasions in 1963 and 1964 of Mexican government bonds in the total amount of $100 million (U.S.). This was the first time in fifty years that Mexican government securities had entered the international market and, not only demonstrated the confidence of the foreign investing public in Mexico, but produced other favorable consequences for the country by lengthening the average maturity of its foreign indebtedness, thus easing its debt service burden, and by opening a new source of public financing and paving the way for further reliance on this practice in the future.

GUSTAVO DIAZ ORDAZ

The change of administrations on December 1, 1964, was one of the smoothest in Mexican history. Although the new president, Gustavo Díaz Ordaz, felt it necessary to severely restrict public investment during his first year in office to counterbalance and correct the excessively heavy rate of investment of the last year of the López Mateos administration, the confidence of private businessmen remained strong, and the country did not experience the decline in economic activity that had been customary during the first years of preceding administrations.

The government's attitude toward private foreign capital continued to be one of cautious acceptance. Reflecting the position of almost all recent Mexican governments, Díaz Ordaz early announced on several occasions that foreign investment was welcome to complement domestic investment but that it should preferably be associated in a minority position with Mexican capital.[71] Foreign investors apparently felt reassured that there would be no drastic change in official policy under the new administration and shared in the general confidence in the Mexican economy. As table 5 shows, direct foreign investments in the country jumped to over $200 million (U.S.) in 1965, of which $120 million was net new capital inflow from abroad. By the end of that year total foreign investment had reached an all-time high of almost $1.75 billion.

If the pronouncements of Díaz Ordaz seemed to reflect no departure from the position of prior recent administrations, there were other developments in the mid-1960's that caused a degree of concern among foreign businessmen. The process that had begun under López Mateos of clearing proposed new foreign investments and important expansions of existing facilities with the Ministry of Industry and Commerce, though still not required by law, was virtually institutionalized, and in almost all cases the ministry insisted that the project be shared with Mexican investors, usually in a majority position. For example, of the industrial investment projects approved by the Ministry of Industry and Commerce between January 1, 1965 and April 15, 1967, only about one-fifth were for enterprises with majority foreign capital.[72] Although government spokesmen stated that the policy of Mexicanization of industry was directed primarily at investments in new facilities and important expansions of existing facilities, most foreign-owned enterprises felt at least a psychological pressure to accept Mexican investors in their operations. Furthermore, President Díaz Ordaz seemed to downgrade the importance to the country of direct foreign investments when, in his second annual report to the Congress on September 1, 1966, he assigned to them third place—following intergovernmental loans and indirect or portfolio investments—among the sources of foreign capital considered suitable to help finance Mexico's economic growth.

On top of this, increasing governmental insistence on industrial integration to replace imports and the government's refusal to allow price increases on basic consumer goods despite rising production costs also affected foreign enterprises and undoubtedly gave pause to some foreign businessmen who were considering making new investments in the country.[73]

Unquestionably the most significant single step taken in the early years of the Díaz Ordaz administration was the Mexicanization of the sulphur industry—more accurately, the largest sulphur-producing company—the only important mining activity that remained under foreign control. Although sulphur was covered by the new mining law of 1961 and sulphur-producing companies were thus required to be Mexicanized within twenty-five years in order to retain their rights, the royalties and taxes payable to the government were established in the companies' concessions, and the tax relief provided for in the 1961 amendments to the mining tax law offered no incentive to the companies to surrender control of their operations to Mexican investors before they were obligated to do so. But the Mexican government had made known its policy with respect to the extractive industries and apparently was not willing to wait.

Pan American Sulphur Company (Pasco), the giant of the Mexican sulphur producers, had been organized by a group of private United States investors in 1947 to explore and drill concessions in the Isthmus of Tehuantepec, after failure to interest the Mexican government and Mexican banks and businessmen in investing in the venture had forced the concession holders to look abroad for the necessary financing.[74] Under aggressive management and favorable conditions the company, operating through its Mexican subsidiary Azufrera Panamericana, S.A. de C.V., developed the huge Jáltipan dome and by 1960 had grown to be the world's third largest sulphur producer, with expectations of a long and profitable life. Its success was also profitable for Mexico; on the most important concession the government received a 20 percent royalty on production in addition to the standard production and income taxes, and according to a 1960 company estimate, 69 percent of its gross income remained in the country in the form of labor and material costs, royalties, and taxes. Other companies sought to share in the Tehuantepec sulphur boom, but only one survived—North American–owned Gulf Sulphur Corporation, operating through Compañía de Azufre de Veracruz, S.A.

Especially after 1963, with increased world demand, Mexican sulphur production and sales grew substantially, reaching over 1.8 million tons in 1964, the great bulk of production, about 95 percent, being exported. By 1964 Mexico was second only to the United States in sulphur production, and sulphur occupied sixth place among Mexican exports. Riding the boom in the world market, Pasco, which accounted for about 80 percent of production and exports, planned to increase its exports in 1965 to 2.5 million tons from about 1.5 million tons in 1964, and Gulf Sulphur planned a similar increase.

In April, 1965, however, the companies received a rude shock when the Mexican government suddenly halted exports and announced, through the minister of national properties, that export permits would no longer be freely issued and that future exports would be limited to 10 percent of new reserves discovered annually. Pasco, it was later clarified by the minister of industry and commerce, would be limited to a maximum of 1.5 million tons of exports per year until the company had proven reserves of 25 million tons, about double the company's existing reserves estimated by the government, and thereafter would be permitted an increase based on reserves in excess of 25 million tons. Similar limitations on exports of Gulf Sulphur were imposed. The stated reason for the move was conservation for domestic needs—to assure that sufficient reserves of the vital mineral would be available for domestic requirements for the next fifty years. According to government estimates, national reserves amounted to under 24 million tons (the United States companies estimated reserves at between 50 and 100 million tons), and at the increased rate of exports planned by the companies, Pasco's reserves would be exhausted in five years and those of Gulf Sulphur within nine years. It was further estimated that only one-fifth of the prospective sulphur-producing areas had been explored, and the companies were criticized for failing to make adequate new explorations and develop new reserves. Although the announcement made no mention of Mexicanization or nationalization of the companies and expressly stated that their concessions would be respected, a leading Mexico City daily stated in an editorial that the government seemingly planned to force the sale of controlling interest in the industry to Mexican investors.[75]

In response to this move the companies embarked on vigorous new exploration programs to increase proven reserves. Government spokesmen, including the president himself, further made it clear that the administration was bent on stimulating the development of industries utilizing the country's sulphur resources. Within a few months it was announced that Pan American Sulphur would invest in a major new fertilizer complex designed to produce primarily for the export market, in which it would own a 35 percent interest, 51 percent to be underwritten and later sold to the Mexican public by Banco Nacional de México, the country's largest commercial bank. In view of the government's great interest in promoting domestic manufacture of fertilizers and the report that the company was required to borrow a substantial sum on not entirely favorable terms to finance its investment in the project, it is not unlikely that the company's decision was the result of some degree of government pressure.

Under the new export control system, Pasco was allowed to export 1.5 million tons of sulphur in 1965, substantially less than it had planned for that year, but about the amount of its exports in 1964. Early in 1966, however, it appeared that the squeeze was being tightened; Pasco was advised by the Mexican authorities that its initial export quota for the year would be only 830,000 tons. Although a special export permit for an additional 400,000 tons was issued in August, the total export quota for 1966 was less than that for the prior year.

Whether or not these moves were designed to pave the way for the eventual Mexicanization of the company may never be known. At any rate, it was announced by the Ministry of National Properties in early

October, 1966, that a Mexican group had offered to buy 66 percent of Pasco's Mexican operations, 43 percent to be acquired by the federal government and 23 percent by a group of private Mexican investors headed by the Banco Nacional de México. It was reported that a representative of the Mexican group "expressed the conviction of his associates that the acquisition of a substantial interest in Azufrera Panamericana by the Mexican group would greatly enhance the company's future prospects in Mexico and throughout the world."[76] Other inducements were reported: export allowances would be considerably raised, and the government would set minimum export prices in line with current spot prices and substantially above the current average contract price; the company would probably be exempted from the Mexican distributable profits tax on dividends to its shareholders, a saving of over $2 million (U.S.) a year; and the 20 percent government royalty would be reduced to 12 percent, resulting in an estimated annual saving of $3 million. These factors, together with the rapidly rising world demand and prices, might mean that Pasco would earn as much from a 34 percent interest in a Mexicanized operation as it had with full ownership.[77] Pasco had little choice. Although company officials emphasized that the Mexican government had not exerted any pressure on the company to Mexicanize, the control over the company's exports and the mere fact that the principal member of the offering group was the Mexican government were, in themselves, sufficient inducements to insure that the offer would be accepted.[78]

The sale of controlling interest in Azufrera Panamericana, S.A. de C.V., was approved by Pasco in June, 1967, and the transaction was effected on June 30. For 66 percent of the outstanding shares, the Mexican group agreed to pay $49.5 million (U.S.), approximately half within one year and the balance within two years, with annual interest of 7.75 percent. Pasco also received about $20 million in cash, the amount of the net current assets of Azufrera, and was guaranteed an additional amount of close to $12 million, equivalent to 50 cents per share of Pasco stock annually for five years, as dividends from Azufrera or additional purchase price. Under a five-year management assistance contract, Pasco would act as Azufrera's exclusive management consultant and operator of its sulphur mines.[79]

The Mexicanization of Pasco's operations and the growing pressure on foreign enterprises in other activities to achieve a majority participation of domestic capital brought warning notes in the foreign press that the investment climate in Mexico might be less attractive than formerly[80] and perhaps contributed to the decline of new investments from abroad in 1966 to an estimated $109 million (U.S.), still a healthy amount and well above the average in recent years. However, the enthusiasm of many foreign companies to participate in the growing Mexican economy and perhaps the long-term export opportunities offered by Mexico's membership in the Latin American Free Trade Association did not seem to be dampened, and many were willing to accept a minority position in new enterprises.[81] Even in the sulphur industry, where foreign capital was strictly limited to a minority interest, there was a frenzy of activity as foreign companies rushed to gain a share of Mexico's rich deposits and the booming world market. By early 1967, with government encouragement, a number of companies, mostly North American, but also Canadian and French, had taken minority interests in newly formed Mexican companies with two-thirds Mexican ownership, some with government participation, to apply for new sulphur concessions. Though new foreign investments continued their declining trend in 1967, preliminary estimates for 1968, shown in table 5, indicated a substantial increase in that year to $115 million.

Another development that was increasingly evident in the mid-1960's was the sale to foreign concerns of operating Mexican companies by their local owners. Some foreign businesses had entered Mexico in this way in the past, but the number of Mexican companies being sold to foreigners, especially in the fields of food products and drugs, increased to such an extent that by 1966 the government felt compelled to restrict the trend by refusing in many cases to grant permits necessary for such transactions.

In one branch of the economy—banking and insurance—the government moved swiftly to prevent this possibility. Although the Mexican banking system had been initiated by foreign interests in the nineteenth century, Mexican bankers had gradually acquired control of the country's private banks, and foreign capital invested in banking had been reduced to a relatively minor level. However, there existed the threat that this trend would be reversed and that sizable interests in certain Mexican financial institutions would be sold to foreign concerns. Noting that foreign capital should not be allowed to enter economic activities in which domestic investment is sufficient, Díaz Ordaz late in 1965 pushed through amendments to the laws governing banking and insurance companies to forbid ownership of their stock by foreign governments or official agencies, "financial entities from abroad, or groups of foreign persons or legal entities."[82] Government spokesmen and

Mexican bankers were quick to point out that the move did not signify a change in general policy toward foreign investment and that foreign capital was welcome within the limitations of Mexican law and economic policy.

In the field of public finance, the government reduced its reliance on foreign public loans during the first two years of the Díaz Ordaz administration, as shown in table 8, though there was a sharp reversal of this trend in 1967 and 1968. The policy to replace short- and medium-term credits with long-term obligations and to diversify Mexico's sources of credit was also strengthened. From November, 1965, to May, 1967, four additional issues of government bonds in the total amount of $77.5 million (U.S.) were placed in the international market. European sources of public financing were increasingly sought, and the May, 1967, bond issue, in the amount of $25 million, was sold entirely in the European market. The confidence in Mexico of the international financial community was further demonstrated by the successful placement in Europe in 1966 of $20 million bond issues by the Comisión Federal de Electricidad and Nacional Financiera.

FOREIGN INVESTMENT TODAY

Mexico has had a long and varied history as a capital-importing country. During the latter part of the nineteenth century and early years of this century, foreign capital poured into the country to develop its mines, build railroads, and install electricity and communications. The contributions to Mexico's long-term development made by foreigners is unquestionable, but in the process the country's economy came to be dominated from abroad to an extent perhaps unparalleled in any other modern nation.

The Revolution of 1910 marked the beginning of the reversal of that trend. In the traditional areas of foreign dominance, foreign capital has been eliminated or sharply reduced, and the economic activities open to majority foreign investment have been steadily restricted. This process has at times resulted in extreme hostility on the part of foreign businessmen and severe declines in the inflow of capital from abroad, but Mexico has long since regained its reputation as a highly attractive country for international investments.

Beginning in the early 1940's, foreign capital again began to enter the country in increasing amounts. In the twenty-five year period from 1940 through 1965 direct foreign investment almost quadrupled in amount, and from 1961 through 1968 net new foreign investments entered the country at an average annual rate of over $95 million (U.S.), not counting reinvested earnings. By the end of 1968 the total stake of foreign enterprise in the country undoubtedly exceeded $2 billion. There has, however, been a drastic change in the structure of that investment. Whereas in 1940 the traditional fields of mining, public utilities, and transportation and communications still accounted for about 90 percent of the total direct foreign investment, with a meager 6 percent in manufacturing and commercial activities, by the end of 1967 the share of foreign investment in manufacturing had jumped to over 65 percent of the total, and investment in the traditional activities had been reduced to about 12 percent.[83] Judging from United States investments in Mexico, it appears that of the total new foreign capital entering the country in recent years over 90 percent has gone into manufacturing, largely to supply consumer and capital goods for the growing domestic market, but to some extent to produce manufactured products for export.

Inevitably, the most important supplier of foreign capital has been the United States, which in 1940 furnished about 80 percent of the value of direct foreign investment in Mexico. The interest of entrepreneurs in the developed countries of Western Europe and Japan has grown substantially, however, and Mexico has attempted with considerable success to diversify its sources of foreign capital in recent years, with the result that by the end of 1965 the stake of United States investors had been reduced to something under 70 percent of the total.

Despite this influx of foreign capital, the impressive growth of the Mexican economy since 1940 has been financed largely from domestic resources. In the period 1942-65 new direct foreign investment accounted for only 5.7 percent of the gross fixed private investment in the country, while public foreign loans financed 11.4 percent of the gross fixed investment of the public sector. The total contribution of foreign capital from all sources in that period is estimated at about 10.7 percent of the total gross investment in the economy.[84]

It is unlikely that there will be any drastic change in the role of foreign investment in Mexico's economy within the next few years. Mexico has clearly demonstrated that it is capable of financing the great bulk of its economic development from domestic sources and will continue to do so, but the government also realizes that the country derives substantial benefits from foreign investment. An important consideration, and one that is often mentioned by government spokesmen as a condition to favorable reception of new investment projects, is that the foreign investor brings with him technological skills and advances. At its present stage of growth Mexico lacks the technically trained personnel and capital necessary for the research and development that are essential if its manufactured products are to compete in the world market. And increasing emphasis is being placed on exports as a means of stimulating economic growth.

Also important is the realization that a satisfactory growth rate cannot be maintained without financial assistance from external resources. The government is firmly committed to continuing the process of industrialization as the best means of raising the living standards of its booming population and to provide employment for the more than 400,000 new job seekers who enter the labor market annually. In his second annual report to the Congress on September 1, 1966, President Díaz Ordaz predicted an annual increase in population of 3.6 percent during the period 1966-70 and stated that an annual increase in gross national product of 6.5 percent would be required to achieve an acceptable rise in the standard of living in the country. This goal, he said, would require an investment of 275 billion pesos, the equivalent of $22 billion (U.S.), over the five-year period—95 billion pesos from the public sector and 180 billion pesos from private investors, of which he estimated about 90 percent would be financed from domestic sources. On the basis of these figures, it appears that the administration is counting on an average annual inflow of foreign capital of close to $450 million (U.S.), considerably more than the average net inflow of direct foreign investment and foreign public loans combined of about $240 million in the years 1960 through 1965. Even greater amounts of foreign capital than the president estimated may be needed; many observers believe that the investment goal assigned to the private sector cannot be reached without a substantially higher contribution from external sources than 10 percent.

III

Restrictions on Foreign Investment—The Laws

It is impossible to study the history of foreign investment in the Mexican economy without reaching some understanding of the process by which certain economic activities have been closed to foreign control and the types of conditions that have been placed on the entry of foreign capital. The process has been a gradual one, however. The initial groundwork was laid with the adoption of the Constitution of 1917, which established restrictions and conditions on foreign acquisitions of land and concessions. Except for the closing of the petroleum industry to private investment following the 1938 expropriation, those were the only important limitations until the emergency decree of June 29, 1944 was issued, establishing the basis for the imposition of restrictions on foreign investment on a broad front. That decree did not, however, fulfill the promise it seemed to hold out to some, and the government resorted instead to the practice of adopting specific statutory restrictions in selected industries as it felt the need or desirability arose.

All administrations have resisted the temptation to enact a general law on foreign investment. Attempts to press for a general law have failed, and even less ambitious efforts to codify the existing restrictions into a single law have been abandoned. Each successive administration has preferred to shape its policy toward foreign investment unfettered by a statute of general application and has perhaps been apprehensive that such a statute might have the effect of frightening away desirable foreign capital. Consequently, the statutory restrictions are found scattered among a number of laws and decrees, each of which must be examined to determine its effect.

The activities in which foreign investment is prohibited or restricted by law are relatively few. It is important to realize, however, that the fact that there is no statutory restriction on foreign investment in a particular industry does not necessarily mean that the industry is wide open to the entry of foreign capital. The policy of the government, though not codified in a law, that most private foreign capital should take a minority interest in association with Mexican capital is becoming increasingly firm and is enforced by other but equally effective means. This policy and its implementation are discussed in the next chapter. Because of the flexibility thus afforded and the effectiveness of enforcement of government policy in the absence of a general statute, it seems highly unlikely that any serious attempt will be made to enact a law on the subject within the foreseeable future. If a need was ever felt for such a law, that need is passing as its objectives are being achieved without it. It is entirely possible, however, that additional statutory restrictions will be imposed on the entry of foreign capital into certain sectors of the economy if the government feels that the importance of the activity or the adequacy of domestic investment in the field makes it advisable.

The existing statutory restrictions and conditions take various forms. A few basic sectors of the economy, such as the petroleum industry, electric power generation, and railroads, have been reserved to the state, and all private investment, domestic as well as foreign, is excluded. Some activities are closed to foreign individuals or foreign companies, though not necessarily to foreign-owned Mexican companies. The most important restrictions, however, take the form of limitations on foreign equity ownership of Mexican companies operating in certain designated industries. In most cases in which this limitation is imposed, foreign ownership is restricted to a simple minority interest. In some instances foreign participation is more severely limited. Foreign investment in companies producing regulated petrochemicals, for example, may not exceed 40 percent of the total capital, and the maximum allowed in the case of companies seeking special mining concessions on national mineral reserves is 34 percent. The requirement of majority Mexican ownership of enterprises, whether imposed by statute or by administrative policy, is widely known as "Mexicanization."

While the activities and industries in which foreign participation is limited by statute are not always susceptible of easy classification, most of them, nevertheless, relate to the exploitation of natural resources or are activities for which a license, concession, or other administrative authorization is required. A condition imposed on all direct foreign investment is the requirement that the investor expressly renounce the diplomatic protection of his government, which is the subject of the first section of this chapter.

THE CALVO CLAUSE

Mexico has long adhered to the principle that foreigners who wish to own property or engage in business in the country must enter into an express agreement with the federal government, through the Ministry of Foreign Relations, under which the foreigner agrees that he will be considered a Mexican national and waives the right of diplomatic protection of his home government. This type of agreement, common in the Latin-American countries and usually referred to as the Calvo clause, is often a source of confusion and mystery to foreign investors in Mexico.

The requirement of this agreement is found in several provisions of Mexican law. Under article 27 of the Constitution the agreement is a prerequisite to the acquisition by foreigners of land, waters, or concessions for the exploitation of mines or waters. The law and regulations implementing that article extend the requirement to foreigners who acquire stock or other equity interests in Mexican companies that have the right to acquire such properties or concessions.[1] In practice, the agreement is contained in every permit issued by the Ministry of Foreign Relations for the formation of a Mexican company, except where foreigners are expressly excluded from owning any interest in the company, and by law it must be inserted in the company's articles of incorporation and stock certificates. By the mere acquisition of stock or other equity interest in the company the foreigner is considered to have agreed to the terms of the clause. Since virtually all direct foreign investment in Mexico is effected through the medium of a Mexican corporation or other form of business association, it is difficult for a foreign investor to avoid the agreement.

The agreement is also required in all contracts entered into between federal or local governmental agencies and foreign individuals or companies or Mexican companies in which foreigners are permitted to own equity interests, and in all governmental concessions and permits to such persons or entities.[2] This requirement seems obviously to apply to all contracts between the government and foreign enterprises, whether they operate in Mexico or abroad, but for many years it has been overlooked or for other reasons not enforced in cases of sales or services to governmental agencies made or rendered abroad by foreign companies not operating in Mexico. Nor is the agreement required of foreign entities that enter loan or financing contracts with the Mexican government or its agencies. Recently, however, the requirement has been applied in connection with government contracts under which foreign companies have been engaged to perform services in Mexico, particularly construction work, and it has been necessary for those companies to obtain a permit from the Ministry of Foreign Relations containing the Calvo agreement.

Although the language of the Calvo clause as it appears in Mexican legislation is not entirely the same in all situations, the stipulation most commonly employed is that the foreigner agrees "to be considered a Mexican" with respect to his properties in Mexico or his contract with or concession from the government and further "not to invoke the protection of his government" in connection therewith. The exact meaning of this rather vague and imprecise language does not appear to have been satisfactorily established by judicial interpretation, but the intent seems evident.[3] The agreement that the foreigner shall be considered a Mexican national implies that his rights with respect to the contract or property involved and the means available to him of enforcing those rights are the same as are accorded by Mexican law for the protection of its own citizens, but no more. He must, therefore, pursue any claim that he has, including claims against the Mexican government, in accordance with the procedures established by Mexican law. Other recourses, including his right to seek the diplomatic intervention of his own government and, presumably, the submission of his claim to international claims tribunals, are waived. This agreement is a private undertaking between the foreigner and the Mexican government and is regarded as consideration for the granting of the permit or concession or execution of the contract by the government. The penalty for breach of the agreement not to seek diplomatic intervention is severe— forfeiture to the nation of the property in connection with which the agreement was undertaken or rescission of the contract or concession and loss of the investments the foreigner has made under it.

This unusual agreement and its apparent importance to the Mexican government can be appreciated only against its historical background. The nineteenth century was a period of large investments of capital from Europe and later North America in the underdeveloped areas of the world, including the newly independent countries of Latin America. These investments were of tremendous importance to the major powers of that time to develop sources of raw materials and markets for their manufactured products, and they considered it their duty to provide protection for their citizens investing in those areas, where law and justice were often regarded as below "civilized" standards. Under the international law principle that a state has the right to protect its citizens residing in a foreign country if the treatment accorded them does not meet with what are considered to be internationally recognized standards, the major investor countries developed procedures for the protection of their citizens residing in the underdeveloped countries. In Latin America these procedures took the form of what is known as the institution of diplomatic protection, whereby a citizen abroad could appeal to his home government for protection if an injury to his person or property was not redressed through the remedial processes available in the foreign country.[4] The doctrinal justification for a state's intervention on behalf of its citizens was the theory devised by Emmeric de Vattel that an injury to an alien was actually an injury to his home state, which was thus entitled to compensation under international law.[5] However, the institution of diplomatic protection was too often abused by the world powers through the sponsoring of dubious claims on behalf of their citizens and served as an excuse for armed intervention and occupation of the weaker countries of Latin America.

Reacting to these abuses and the use of armed force on behalf of foreign creditors, and out of fear that they might lead to outright occupation and colonization, many of the Latin-American countries embraced the writings of Carlos Calvo, an Argentine diplomat and publicist of the nineteenth century, as a defense against diplomatic protection. The doctrine enunciated by Calvo consists essentially of two fundamental principles: sovereign states have the right to freedom from any kind of interference by other states, and foreigners are not entitled to any rights and privileges that are not accorded to nationals and consequently may not seek redress of grievances except before the local authorities. This doctrine, though never recognized as a principle of international law, has been a cardinal policy of most Latin-American countries for close to a century, and the so-called Calvo clause has been the most successful attempt to implement it.[6]

The validity of the clause as a bar to diplomatic intervention has been the subject of substantial controversy, principally between the Latin-American countries and the United States. Its effect seems to have been directly decided only in a series of international arbitrations before various Mexican claims commissions in the 1920's and early 1930's. Beginning with the landmark decision rendered in 1926 by the United States–Mexican General Claims Commission in the case of

United States (North American Dredging Company of Texas) v. The United Mexican States,[7] a line of precedents was established that may have resolved some of the issues. In those decisions the clause was held binding on the individual alien contracting party to preclude him from presenting to his government any claim relating to the validity or performance of his contract, and it was further held that the clause operated as a bar to a claim before an international tribunal despite a general waiver in the arbitration agreement of the requirement that local remedies be exhausted. However, under the language of the *Dredging* decision and those that followed it, the agreement is binding only on the foreigner himself and not on his home state, whose rights under international law to protect its citizens are not affected.

In practice this distinction may be of little effect; if the foreigner is prohibited from seeking the protection of his government, this will usually preclude intervention since his government will likely not otherwise have knowledge of his claim. Furthermore, he does not waive the protection of his government against breaches of international law by the local government, such as a denial or delay of justice as that term is used in international law. In that case his complaint is not based on the violation of his contract or property rights but rather on a violation of the international law rule guaranteeing him certain minimum standards of justice. Therefore, if he has exhausted the local remedies available to him and these standards of justice have been denied, then, presumably, an appeal to his government for protection would not be considered a breach of his agreement nor would an international tribunal refuse to take jurisdiction of the claim under an international arbitration agreement.

Mexico, the principal spokesman in favor of the complete validity of the clause as a bar to diplomatic intervention, and the United States, the leader of the opposition to the validity of the clause, seem to have approached acceptance of this view.[6] It must be recognized, however, that the exact meaning and effect of the clause have not yet been satisfactorily established by international agreement or tribunals and that the interpretation of a particular clause will depend to a large extent on its precise wording.

Despite the international uncertainty surrounding the Calvo clause as it is used in Mexico and the severe penalties imposed for its breach, it does not seem to have been the source of any serious concern on the part of foreign investors in Mexico in recent years or to have deterred foreign enterprises from contracting with the Mexican government or engaging in other activities in the country. Among the reasons for this undoubtedly is the fact that capital-exporting countries have virtually abandoned the use of diplomatic intervention. Also, private foreign investors themselves are more hesitant than they once were to incur the hostility of their host countries and to endanger their foreign operations through the invocation of their government's protection, and, especially in the case of Mexico, are largely willing to rely on the stability of the local government and to accept the remedies and standards of justice afforded by local law and practice. The very existence of the clause, in itself, has probably also served as a deterrent to requests for diplomatic protection. In most circumstances, the severity of the penalty for breach of the agreement and the possibility that it might be invoked would give pause to any foreigner considering resort to his government for diplomatic intervention on his behalf.[9]

THE EMERGENCY DECREE OF JUNE 29, 1944

The most important single law relating to foreign investment in Mexico and the one that has caused the greatest confusion and misunderstanding is an executive decree issued by President Avila Camacho on June 29, 1944, often called the emergency decree of 1944.[10] This decree is the basic statutory instrument for the regulation of private foreign participation in the Mexican economy. This control is vested, oddly, in the Ministry of Foreign Relations by virtue of the requirement that the authorization of that ministry be obtained for the incorporation of any Mexican company and for the acquisition by foreigners of certain property rights in Mexico. If an alien seeks to invest in a sector of the economy in which foreign participation is restricted by law, the ministry simply denies the necessary authorization. Not only are the various statutory restrictions enforced in this manner, but the ministry has broad powers under the decree, on its own initiative, to limit foreign investment. These powers are a source of concern and misunderstanding to foreigners and Mexicans alike, and many Mexicans, including even some lawyers and many government officials, believe that the decree lays down an absolute requirement that Mexicans control all companies organized after its enactment.

PURPOSE AND REQUIREMENTS OF THE DECREE

The decree was motivated by governmental and private concern over the growing influx of foreign capital into Mexico during World War II,

presumably flight capital from nations in which investments were restricted or were considered unsafe, attracted by the booming wartime
Mexican economy. As stated in the preamble to the decree, it was
feared that this capital would be used to displace existing Mexican investments and to monopolize sectors of the economy and that a large-
scale inflow of capital having no permanent ties to the economic and
social interests of the country and its subsequent withdrawal to the
country of origin after the war would result in severe damage to the
Mexican economy.[11] The decree was designed to prevent such an occurrence and to channel excess capital in the country into new and stable
enterprises that would aid in the war effort and be of permanent benefit
to the economy.

The decree was clearly intended to be only a temporary measure. It
was issued by the president under extraordinary legislative powers
granted him by a 1942 law approving the suspension of certain constitutional guarantees for the duration of the war.[12] The decree itself stated
that it was an emergency measure to be applied "during the time the
suspension of guarantees decreed June 1, 1942, remains in effect."[13]
Presumably, then, the operation of the decree should have ended when
the Congress enacted a decree terminating as of October 1, 1945, the
1942 suspension of guarantees and re-establishing "constitutional order
in all its plenitude."[14] The Ministry of Foreign Relations, however, has
continued to enforce the decree, basing its action on article 6 of
the 1945 decree, which provided that executive orders issued during the
emergency and relating to state intervention in the economic life of the
country were ratified with the force of law.[15] Thus the emergency decree
has, in effect, become permanent legislation though its validity is at least
questionable.

The decree provides that a permit must be obtained from the
Ministry of Foreign Relations for the acquisition of any of the following
interests by a foreigner or a Mexican company that has or is permitted
to have foreign owners: control of existing enterprises or companies
engaged in any industrial, agricultural, livestock, or forestry activity or
dealing in or developing real estate; any type of real property for any
purpose; and concessions on mines, waters, or combustible minerals.[16]
A permit is also required for the formation and all amendments to the
articles of incorporation of a Mexican company that has or may have
foreign owners and whose purpose is to engage in any of the named
activities or to acquire real property or concessions on natural resources.
Since there is no general restriction on foreign ownership of Mexican

companies, the effect of this provision is to require a permit for the organization of any such company whose articles of incorporation do not expressly prohibit foreign participation. But the application of the decree is not limited to those companies. Even companies whose articles expressly exclude foreigners may not be incorporated nor may they acquire the interests covered by the decree without the ministry's authorization.

The ministry is given broad discretionary powers to deny, grant, or condition permits as it considers appropriate to fulfill the purposes of the decree, and specific conditions are expressly imposed or authorized. For example, foreigners must be permanent residents of the country with *inmigrado* or immigrant status in order to obtain a permit for the direct acquisition of an interest covered by the decree.[17] But most important is the ministry's authority to impose the requirement that majority ownership in Mexican companies be held by Mexican nationals and that a majority of their directors be Mexicans. It is this provision that has been the source of confusion and has led many to believe that Mexican control is required in the case of all Mexican companies.

Property interests acquired in violation of the decree—that is, without the authorization of the Ministry of Foreign Relations—are subject to forfeiture to the government, and penal sanctions are imposed in the case of false statements or concealment of the fact that the party in interest is a foreigner. Notaries, judges, and other officials who authorize or record written instruments for which the required permits have not been issued may be suspended or fined.

ADMINISTRATION OF THE DECREE: RESTRICTED ACTIVITIES

For almost a year after the decree was issued apparently little was done to regulate foreign participation in Mexican companies. On April 17, 1945, the minister of foreign relations instructed the legal department of the ministry to formulate a table "specifying the percentage of Mexican capital that should be required for the constitution of various enterprises" and ordered that, in the meantime, permits not be issued for the incorporation of companies to engage in a few named activities unless a majority of their capital was held by Mexicans. Until administrative regulations were issued, it was directed, the minister or his representative should be consulted in cases of permit applications for companies that, because of the nature of the activities in which they were to engage or the amount of their capital, might have repercussions on the country's economy.

This situation continued virtually unchanged for two years. Neither the table called for nor regulations for the administration of the decree were issued. Because of the confusion that existed with respect to the various laws and rules governing foreign investment and in order to co-ordinate their administration and application by the governmental agencies involved, in May, 1947, President Miguel Alemán created a "mixed interministerial commission" to make a systematic and continuing study of problems under the laws relating to foreign investment and to maintain a proper balance between investments of domestic and foreign capital.[18] The commission was made up of representatives of the president and each of the Ministries of Internal Affairs, Foreign Relations, Finance, Economy (now Industry and Commerce), Agriculture, and Communications and Public Works, and it was to formulate and communicate to the ministries concerned, at least every three months, general rules for the application of the laws involved.

Despite its broad mandate, the commission contributed little to the formulation of a unified governmental policy toward foreign investment. It functioned irregularly from September, 1947, to October, 1953, and produced a total of twelve general rulings or "norms" to be followed in the application of the various laws. The commission's meetings were held in secret, apparently no hearing being given to private interests, and its rulings were distributed in mimeograph form within the government and without publicity.[19] Although it enlarged somewhat the list of activities in which Mexican control was required and ruled on a few rather technical questions that had arisen under the laws, it largely ratified the practices already adopted by the Ministry of Foreign Relations under its discretionary powers. The decree by which the commission was created has never been repealed, but there seems to be no evidence that it has functioned since 1953.

The failure of the commission to bring any substantial order into the foreign investment picture has not deterred the vigorous enforcement of the decree, and the Ministry of Foreign Relations has even expanded its application beyond the literal wording of its provisions. In 1949 it issued instructions to notaries and officials of the public registers that permits were to be required for the incorporation or amendment of the articles of any company, whatever its nature or purpose, even though by its terms the decree applies only to companies engaged in certain named activities.[20] The ministry has steadfastly maintained this position, and no company may be constituted nor may the articles of incorporation of any company be modified without its authorization.

The original list of activities issued by the minister of foreign relations in 1945 in which majority Mexican ownership is required includes radio broadcasting, the motion picture industry, domestic air transport, urban and interurban transportation, fishing and fisheries, the production of carbonated beverages, and publishing and advertising.[21] With the exception of a May 27, 1947, ruling of the minister expanding the restriction on the carbonated beverage industry to include distribution and sale in addition to production, this list was unchanged until the creation of the interministerial commission.[22]

From 1948 to 1953 the commission enlarged the list to include companies engaged in either domestic or international air transport; the production, sale, and distribution of carbonated or noncarbonated beverages and essences, concentrates, and syrups used for their manufacture; shipping; and the rubber industry. Companies engaged in coastal shipping were required in all cases to be Mexican controlled, but those in international shipping might be foreign controlled if there was not sufficient available Mexican capital. Applications relating to companies whose purposes included any activity connected with the oil industry were required to be submitted to the Ministry of Economy and to Petróleos Mexicanos for a determination of the conditions that should be imposed.

The only other additions that seem to have been made before 1960 were the preparation and bottling of fruit juices, which first appeared in 1952, apparently as an extension of the soft drink restriction, and agriculture and forestry, in which there are specific statutory limitations on foreign investment.

It is difficult to conclude that this rather strange assortment of industries, some of which have no fundamental economic importance, reflects any over-all planning or general policy with respect to foreign participation in the Mexican economy. Though some of the restrictions obviously relate to national security and public welfare, there are indications that others resulted from pressures brought for the protection of private Mexican interests against foreign competition.

Between 1960 and 1963 several new industries were added to the restricted list.[23] In some cases, such as mining, television, and petrochemicals, the additions were made as a result of the adoption of special laws expressly limiting foreign investment in those fields. Other additions were made solely on the basis of policy decisions by the Ministry of Foreign Relations acting either on its own initiative or, more likely, on the initiative of, or at least with the concurrence of, other governmental agencies. These activities were the packing of marine products, the preservation and packaging of food products, and the manufacture and distribution of fertilizers, insecticides, and basic chemical products. The restriction of the food packing industry resulted from the rather sudden rush of several United States companies to enter Mexico either by establishing new operations or by acquiring existing ones and the government's concern over the rapid occupation of the field by foreign companies. The addition of fertilizers, insecticides, and chemicals may have been an outgrowth of the 1959 statutory restriction on foreign investment in the petrochemical industry.

The ministry's practice has generally been limited to a routine examination of applications for permits to incorporate or amend the articles of Mexican companies or for the acquisition of interests covered by the decree. If the corporate purposes of the company concerned do not fall within the list of activities for which Mexican control is required or foreign participation excluded, the necessary permit has been issued without any limitation on foreign ownership of the company. However, for the constitution of companies to operate in certain industries that are regulated by special laws, such as oil and gas, mining, and petrochemicals, specific authorization or concurrence of other governmental agencies must be obtained before the ministry may grant a permit. Otherwise, no attempt seems to have been made to consider on its own merits each application, despite the broad discretionary powers given the ministry by the decree. Until about mid-1967 each permit issued for a company whose articles did not limit foreign ownership contained a provision that the company could not engage in any of the restricted activities, which were listed at length, unless its articles were amended to restrict foreign ownership.

If the purposes of the company for which a permit is sought include any of the restricted activities, the permit is automatically refused unless the articles also contain an appropriate limitation on foreign ownership of the company. Since no public hearings are held by the ministry in connection with its policy decisions and no publicity or notice is given to additions to the restricted list, in some cases a foreign businessman has learned that the industry in which he is operating or which he contemplates entering has been added to the list only when his permit application is denied.

To prevent evasion of the law through the use of bearer shares, at least 51 percent of the shares of companies engaged in restricted activities must be registered or nominative. This requirement also applies to the dividend coupons attached to those shares, but it has not been strictly enforced in practice, and bearer coupons are often used. The possibility of acquisition of effective control of such a company by a minority group through the limitation of voting rights of the majority is prevented by the requirement that the Mexican-held majority shares have full voting rights on all matters.[24]

The addition of a previously unrestricted activity to the list of industries in which Mexican control is required does not have retroactive effect. Nevertheless, the fact that the permit requirement of the decree extends to amendments to the articles of exising companies may pose a substantial problem in the case of a foreign-controlled company engaged in an activity that has been added to the list of restricted industries after its incorporation. Even though its original permit to incorporate does not contain the restriction, under the practice of the ministry the permit to amend its articles will be subject to the condition of Mexican control. This practice has been successfully challenged at the administrative level in a limited number of instances and by judicial action at least once, but in most cases the effect of the practice is to prevent amendments to the articles of such companies or to require that a majority interest be surrendered to Mexicans. Probably the most common amendment is to effect a modification of capital, and some protection from this risk may be achieved through the use of a company organized in the form of a variable capital company.[25] No permit is required for the increase or decrease of the variable portion of the capital of such a company since no amendment to its articles is necessary for that purpose.

The ministry has also on occasions in the past attempted to impose the condition of Mexican control in permits to acquire real property, where the activity in which the company is engaged is limited to minority foreign ownership at the time the application for a permit is made. This clearly contravenes a 1949 ruling of the interministerial commission that Mexican companies constituted with the ministry's authorization and without the requirement of Mexican control may acquire real property necessary to carry out their corporate purposes without changing the ownership of their capital stock,[26] and attempts by the ministry to impose that condition have been abandoned.

The foreign investor may be faced with special problems when he seeks to incorporate a Mexican company even though it is to operate in an industry in which no legal restrictions on foreign ownership have been imposed. Since nonresident foreigners and foreign companies not qualified to do business in Mexico may not execute directly in Mexico contracts and other instruments such as articles of incorporation, it was at one time common practice for Mexican nationals, often members or employees of the law firm representing the foreign investor, to act as incorporators of foreign-owned Mexican companies, assigning their rights to the real owners upon incorporation. However, the requirements of the decree extend to the acquisition by foreigners of existing "businesses or enterprises, or control of them" and to the assignment of ownership interests "by virtue of which control of any of the enterprises [covered by the decree] passes to foreign shareholders or members."[27] Consequently, a permit is required for the assignment of majority shares from a Mexican incorporator to a foreigner because the company is then an existing one, and, as pointed out below, the ministry has since 1966 denied permits for the acquisition by foreigners of control of existing Mexican companies. Many Mexican attorneys overlook this requirement and allow the assignment of majority interests to foreigners without the necessary authorization. The risk that the forfeiture penalty will be imposed makes this inadvisable. More cautious attorneys have adopted the procedure of having the foreigner himself appear as an incorporator, through a Mexican agent acting under a power of attorney executed abroad, and the practice of furnishing incorporators is declining. No special permit has traditionally been required by the ministry for the original subscription of shares in a company by a foreigner apart from the usual permit to incorporate. In some instances resident foreigners or qualified foreign companies, where they are available, have acted as incorporators since a permit has not been required for the transfer of shares from one foreigner to another.

Some confusion seems to exist in the case of acquisitions by foreigners of minority interests in existing companies. The wording of the decree seems limited to acquisitions of controlling interests, but the Ministry of Foreign Relations is of the opinion that authorization is necessary for a foreigner to acquire any number of shares, even though not a majority. This opinion is based on article 2, paragraph II of the decree, which requires a permit for the "modification or transformation of Mexican companies . . . especially when, thereby: (a) foreign owners are substituted for Mexican owners. . . ." In Mexican corporation law terminology the term "transformation" refers to a change from one form of business association to another, such as a change from a partnership (*sociedad en nombre colectivo*) to a corporation (*sociedad anónima*).

Nevertheless, the ministry has interpreted the provision more broadly to mean any transaction by which a foreigner acquires an ownership interest from a Mexican.[28] Many Mexican attorneys, however, have not in practice requested permits for transfers of minority shares, and no cases are known in which sanctions have been imposed.

RECENT DEVELOPMENTS

Following the assumption of the presidency by Gustavo Díaz Ordaz in 1964, highly regarded lawyers were appointed to the offices of subsecretary and director of legal affairs of the ministry, and under their leadership certain questionable practices have been changed. Industries that were added to the restricted list under the prior administration without specific statutory authority—food packing and the production and distribution of fertilizers, insecticides, and basic chemical products— were removed in 1965 and 1966. (The requirement of Mexican control of companies in the fertilizer industry was, however, imposed by a 1970 presidential degree, discussed in the last section of this chapter.) Furthermore, certain permit forms were corrected to eliminate disputable provisions. At times in the past the ministry had seemed to exceed its authority in the case of companies in which foreign ownership is absolutely prohibited by law by imposing the condition that such companies not admit as members or shareholders other Mexican companies unless their articles also contained a clause excluding foreign ownership. Recognizing the lack of statutory authority for this practice, the ministry in 1966 discontinued the use of permits that contained that condition and redrafted the permit form to follow the statutory language limiting ownership of such companies merely to "Mexicans," which includes Mexican companies regardless of the nationality of their shareholders or members. Finally, the unnecessary practice of inserting the complete list of restricted activities in every permit for the formation or modification of a company was abandoned.

If these changes seemed to indicate a softening of the government's policy toward foreign investment, at least to the extent that it is administered by the Ministry of Foreign Relations, there were other changes in the application of the 1944 decree that were much more significant and considerably less heartening to the foreign investor.

The first of these changes came in 1966. A source of concern to the Mexican government in recent years had been the increasing tendency of foreign investors wishing to engage in business in Mexico to do so through the acquisition of existing Mexican companies. Logically, the Ministry of Foreign Relations had never authorized the acquisition by foreigners of a majority interest in an existing company engaged in an activity in which Mexican control is required, but permits for the acquisition of majority interests in other companies had been routinely issued. The displacement of existing domestic investments by foreign capital, unlike the establishment of new enterprises, is considered of little economic benefit to the country, and at least in some industries the tendency had reached what were considered alarming proportions. In order to halt this trend, in August, 1966, the ministry quietly adopted the policy, undoubtedly on instructions from or at least with the approval of the president, to deny permits for the acquisition of majority interests in any existing Mexican companies, regardless of the activities in which they are engaged, by foreigners from Mexican owners. This policy has not been extended to the acquisition of such interests by foreign-controlled Mexican companies, so that its purpose may be circumvented through the use of a Mexican holding company. There is no assurance, however, that this loophole will not be closed in the future, especially if there are substantial violations of the spirit of the policy.

Potentially more far-reaching was a policy adopted in November, 1967, apparently on direct instructions from the president, which seemed to promise tighter control of new direct foreign investment than had existed in the past. Under this policy every application for a permit to incorporate a Mexican company in which the applying incorporator is a foreigner or whose name contains a foreign word or indicates that it is a subsidiary or affiliate of a foreign company is to be referred to the Ministry of Industry and Commerce for a resolution on the amount of foreign ownership that will be authorized in the company under the permit of the Ministry of Foreign Relations.

It is too soon, at this writing, to estimate the full effect of this policy. The Ministry of Industry and Commerce is obviously a more appropriate agency to formulate foreign investment policy than the Ministry of Foreign Relations. It has, in fact, assumed the function of controlling the entry of private foreign capital on a broad front where no statutory restrictions exist, as will be discussed in the next chapter. In some cases, however, it has been possible for foreign investors to circumvent the policy restrictions of the Ministry of Industry and Commerce. The requirement that permit applications for new companies be cleared with that ministry where foreign ownership is indicated may significantly extend its control over new foreign investments. Judging from the policy now being followed by the Ministry of Industry and Commerce, it seems likely that applications for new Mexican companies will be closely examined on a case-by-case basis and that restrictions on the proportion of foreign ownership in such companies may well be extended to most industries. If so, the list of restricted activities heretofore followed almost unquestioningly by the Ministry of Foreign Relations will become less significant. But by maintaining formal control within the Ministry of Foreign Relations under the discretionary authority that already exists by virtue of the 1944 decree, the government retains complete flexibility to adjust its policies to each individual case.

The new policy does not seem to be airtight, however. Since permit applications are to be referred to the Ministry of Industry and Commerce only when foreign ownership is indicated by the nationality of the applicant or the name of the proposed company, it is possible that not all applications for companies in which there is a foreign interest will be covered. And the Ministry of Foreign Relations has indicated that there will be no change in the treatment of other applications.

DISPUTES OVER VALIDITY OF THE DECREE

Most Mexican lawyers and legal scholars seem to be of the opinion that the emergency decree of 1944 is invalid and that the policies adopted by the Ministry of Foreign Relations under its authority have no legal basis. Protests against its legality and the manner of its administration have, however, been largely ineffective.[29] The argument against the validity of the decree is based on two points. In the first place, the decree was issued by the president under extraordinary legislative powers, which may be given him under article 49 of the Constitution only in the case of a suspension of guarantees pursuant to article 29. Upon the termination of the emergency for which legislative authority was given to the executive, his power to legislate ends and all emergency legislation enacted thereunder ceases to have effect. Congress has the power, within constitutional limits, to ratify and re-enact into law emergency legislation of the president, and it did so in certain cases. However, by the terms of article 5 of the 1945 law lifting the suspension of guarantees and re-establishing constitutional order, laws issued by the president for a term limited to the emergency and those which were expressly stated to be based on the suspension of individual guarantees were not ratified. The 1944 decree came within both of those conditions and therefore was not ratified by the Congress. Secondly, it is argued that, even if the

Congress intended to re-enact the decree into law, it had no power to do so under the Constitution. The freedom of commerce and industry guaranteed by article 4 of the Constitution to both Mexicans and foreigners may not be restricted except as otherwise authorized by the Constitution. The only limitations on this freedom are those permitted under article 27 relating to acquisitions of property and certain corporate activities. Since the emergency decree imposes greater restrictions on economic activities than are authorized under that article, so the argument goes, it is unconstitutional.

Those who support the government's position that the decree is valid and effective argue that the applicable provision of the 1945 law is article 6, which provides for the ratification of laws issued by the president during the emergency relating to state intervention in the economic life of the nation. Since the emergency decree clearly relates to state intervention in the economy, Congress intended to re-enact it. Furthermore, they maintain, the decree does not restrict the freedom of industry or commerce guaranteed by the Constitution but merely establishes conditions on the ownership of commercial companies. Article 4 does not guarantee the right of any person to constitute or to be a shareholder or member of a commercial company, nor does it guarantee recognition of separate legal personality to such companies or the benefits of limited liability to their owners.[30]

On at least one occasion the validity of the decree has been challenged by judicial action. In the case of *Química Industrial de Monterrey, S.A.*,[31] petitioner was a Mexican corporation organized in 1955, with the necessary permit of the Ministry of Foreign Relations, for the principal purpose of producing chemical products. There was no limitation on foreign ownership of shares in the company, and its shares were issued to bearer. In 1961 the company petitioned the ministry for a permit to amend its articles to increase capital. By that time the manufacture and sale of basic chemical products had been added by the ministry to the list of industries in which foreign investment is restricted. Consequently, although the company apparently was Mexican controlled, the ministry refused to grant authorization for the capital increase unless the corporation changed its shares from bearer to nominative and unless assurances were given the ministry that a majority of the members of its board of directors were and would continue to be Mexican citizens. The company would not submit to these conditions and brought suit for *amparo*,[32] which was granted by the trial court. On appeal, the federal Supreme Court affirmed the grant of *amparo*, reasoning that the emergency decree was repealed by virtue of the provisions of article 5 of the 1945 decree lifting the wartime suspension of guarantees and rejecting the ministry's argument that the emergency decree came within the terms of article 6 of that decree. By basing its decision on this reasoning, the Court avoided ruling on the issue of the constitutionality of the emergency decree.

Since a grant of *amparo* runs against the government only in favor of the individual who obtained it and a court may not make a general declaration of invalidity of a law, the decision in the *Química Industrial* case is not binding on the Ministry of Foreign Relations except in that case, and it has had no effect on the ministry's continued enforcement of the decree. Presidential and congressional inaction seems to indicate that those branches of the government are in accord with the ministry's position. Furthermore, it is not likely that a sufficient number of companies will be willing to bring suit challenging the ministry's action under the decree in order for the five consecutive decisions necessary to constitute binding judicial precedent to be reached. And if binding precedent were established, the executive and legislative branches might choose to ignore it or the government might be forced to the alternative of enacting new legislation on foreign investment and perhaps even an amendment to the Constitution if that should be necessary. Nevertheless, it seems clear that the ministry is anxious to avoid further litigation of the question of the decree's validity and in a few instances has retreated from positions based solely on the authority of the decree where *amparo* suits have been filed or threatened.

In practice, therefore, the decree seems to be well established as a permanent instrument for the control of foreign investments in the Mexican economy. Although the authority of the Ministry of Foreign Relations to limit foreign investment has until recently been exercised only in the case of a limited number of specified industries, many of them relatively unimportant, the decree may acquire new and broader significance with the participation of the Ministry of Industry and Commerce in its administration.

REAL PROPERTY

The acquisition of real property for the installation of plants, offices, and other facilities generally poses no particular problem for foreign-owned Mexican enterprises, outside of certain restricted areas. However, there are important limtitations on the ownership of land by foreign individuals and foreign companies and certain requirements and geographic limitations that are applicable to Mexican companies that have foreign shareholders or members.

The basic principle concerning the acquisition by foreigners of real property is established in the sixth paragraph of article 27 of the Constitution:

> Only Mexicans by birth or by naturalization and Mexican companies have the right to acquire ownership of lands, waters and their accessions or to obtain concessions of exploitation of mines or waters. The State may grant the same right to foreigners, provided they agree before the Ministry of Foreign Relations to be considered nationals with respect to such properties and not to invoke, therefore, the protection of their Governments for anything referring thereto; under penalty, in case of breach of the agreement, of forfeiting in favor of the Nation the properties they have acquired by virtue of the same. Within a zone of one hundred kilometers from the borders and fifty from the seacoasts foreigners may not acquire for any reason direct ownership of lands and waters.

The precise meaning of the provision that "the State may grant the same right to foreigners" has apparently not been settled by judicial decision and has been the subject of some debate among Mexican legal scholars. The principal associations of lawyers have taken the position that, outside the so-called prohibited zone, foreigners have the same right to acquire real property as Mexicans, the only condition being that they enter into the required agreement with the Ministry of Foreign Relations, and that this right may not constitutionally be denied them nor may further conditions or requirements be imposed. The position of the Mexican government, perhaps more widely accepted, is that article 27 does not create an absolute right in favor of foreigners but merely gives the state discretionary power to grant that right to them, and that, therefore, the authority of foreigners to acquire real property may be subjected to any conditions the government deems appropriate and may even be completely denied. This interpretation is based not only on the term "may grant" in article 27 but also on the power of the federal Congress under article 73, section XVI, of the Constitution to enact laws on the legal status of foreigners and on its power to restrict private property rights as required in the public interest pursuant to the third paragraph of article 27.[33] Apparently on the basis of this interpretation, conditions on the acquisition of real property interests by foreigners in addition to that contained in article 27 have been imposed by several laws.

PROHIBITED ZONE

The constitutional prohibition against the acquisition by foreigners, including foreign companies, of title to land or bodies of water within the so-called prohibited zone—that is, within 100 kilometers (about 62 miles) of the land borders or 50 kilometers (about 31 miles) of the sea-coasts—is virtually absolute.[34] While the Constitution merely prohibits foreign ownership in those areas, it early became evident that the result sought to be proscribed could easily be accomplished through a foreign-owned Mexican company, and the prohibition was enlarged by the law and regulations implementing that provision of the Constitution to forbid foreigners to have any type of ownership interest in Mexican companies that own land in the prohibited zone. Mexican companies wishing to acquire such land must first obtain a permit for that purpose from the Ministry of Foreign Relations and must expressly agree that no foreign individual or legal entity may be a shareholder or member of the company.[35]

This type of restriction, perhaps strange to foreign entrepreneurs of this day, obviously arose out of considerations of self-defense and was not new in Mexican law when the drafters of the 1917 Constitution adopted it. Almost since Mexico gained its independence from Spain and first opened its territory to foreigners, similar limitations have been found in the country's laws,[36] even though they were notoriously evaded during the Porfirian era. Perhaps because of lingering fear of foreign designs on Mexican territory, they were carried forward into post-revolutionary legislation and are firmly established in Mexican law.

The sanctions for violation of the prohibition are stringent. Under the implementing law and its regulations, acts and contracts executed in violation of the prohibitions of the law are void, and in the case of the acquisition by a foreigner of an interest in a Mexican company that owns land in the prohibited zone, that interest and the certificates representing it are "without any value" and the company capital is considered to be reduced in the amount of the foreign participation.[37] These provisions seem to indicate merely that the act or contract of acquisition of title to land in the prohibited zone or an interest in a Mexican company owning such land has no effect in law and that the parties to such an act or contract will be returned to their original positions, the foreign purchaser recovering the consideration he has given and the seller recovering the land title or reducing its capital in the case of a company in which the foreigner has acquired an equity interest.

However, an additional and more drastic sanction seems to be imposed by the emergency decree of 1944, which provides that acts in violation of the decree will have no effect in favor of the parties to the act and that the properties that are the object of such acts will become the property of the nation. Furthermore, if the provisions of the decree are violated by means of false declarations, concealment of the fact that the person involved is a foreigner, or through the use of an intermediary, the responsible persons will be subject to imprisonment for six months to three years and a fine of up to 10,000 pesos.[38] Since the decree contains the requirement that foreigners and Mexican companies that have or are permitted by their articles of incorporation to have foreign members or shareholders must obtain a permit from the Ministry of Foreign Relations in order to acquire certain property rights, including "ownership of lands, waters and their accessions to which section I of article 27 of the Constitution refers,"[39] and since that ministry will obviously not issue such permits where prohibited-zone land is concerned, it is not unlikely that the penalty provisions would be interpreted to mean that any property in the prohibited zone acquired by a foreigner or a Mexican company having foreign owners without the required permit or through false representations is subject to forfeiture to the government. Furthermore, the Ministry of Foreign Relations seems to interpret the decree to provide for forfeiture of any shares or other ownership interests acquired by a foreigner in a Mexican company that owns or is permitted to own property in the prohibited zone, since that is the penalty provided for in the permits currently being issued by that ministry for the incorporation of such companies.

As a further safeguard against violations of the law, notaries, Mexican consuls, and other such officials are forbidden to authorize instruments that purport to convey or transfer to foreigners land titles or company interests in violation of the prohibited-zone restrictions, under penalty of losing their office or employment, and a similar prohibition is imposed against the recording of such instruments by officials of the public registers.[40] Additional penalties of suspension or fine are imposed by the emergency decree of 1944 on notaries, judges, and other officials who authorize or record instruments that violate the provisions of that decree.[41]

Despite these prohibitions, it is well known that many foreigners own residences and other properties in the prohibited zone, especially in the coastal resort areas. Evasion of the law is undoubtedly facilitated by the fact that there is no legal prohibition against the issuance of bearer shares, the holders of which may remain anonymous for most purposes, by Mexican corporations that are authorized by the Ministry of Foreign Relations to acquire such property, provided their articles of incorporation contain a provision excluding foreign ownership of shares in the company. No cases are known in which the penalties of the law have been applied, and there is no indication of any desire on the part of the government to confiscate illegally owned property in the prohibited zone, at least in the case of private residences, where there is no threat to the country's security and there are evident advantages to the economy of the area. Nevertheless, most Mexican lawyers consider the risks of incurring the penalties of the law sufficient to avoid practices that may evade the law.

There are, however, methods by which foreign enterprises may acquire the use of real property within the prohibited zone without violating the law. Under the applicable regulation, Mexican companies authorized to acquire land in that area must agree that no foreigner or foreign entity may own any interest in the company. Since a company organized under Mexican law is considered a Mexican national regardless of the nationality of its members or shareholders, the ownership of shares in a landholding company by another Mexican company in which there are foreign shareholders would not violate the prohibition. The Ministry of Foreign Relations has not always followed the literal wording of the law in its permits for the incorporation of those companies and has at times also prohibited the ownership of such interests by Mexican companies unless their articles also forbid foreign members.[42] The practice of the ministry since 1966, however, has been to permit the acquisition of prohibited-zone land by Mexican companies all of whose shares are owned by Mexicans or Mexican companies, regardless of the nationality of their members or shareholders, so that a foreign-controlled Mexican company may be the principal shareholder in a company holding title to such land.

A lease for a term of ten years or less may also be validly executed by a foreigner or foreign-owned Mexican company on prohibited-zone land. The emergency decree of 1944 provides that for purposes of the decree a lease of real property for a term longer than ten years is considered an acquisition, for which a permit is required. No permit is necessary, however, for a lease of ten years or less.[43] A device that has sometimes been employed for the acquisition of land use for a longer term is the simultaneous execution of a series of ten-year leases. This seems clearly to violate at least the intent of the law, and its validity is doubtful.

It has on occasion been found useful by foreign-owned companies to acquire title to buildings within the prohibited zone, even though their interest in the land on which the buildings are located may not exceed a ten-year leasehold. The prohibition against foreign ownership contained in article 27 of the Constitution and its implementing law applies only to "lands" *(tierras),* rather than to the broader classification, real property. The regulations to the implementing law extended the prohibition to cover "lands and their accessions" *(tierras y sus accesiones),* which arguably might include buildings and fixtures attached to the land. However, the term "accessions" has no clearly defined meaning in Mexican law and, furthermore, the addition of this term is presumably invalid since the Constitution may not be changed by a mere statute. The Ministry of Foreign Relations has accepted this reasoning and has permitted foreign-owned companies to acquire buildings in the prohibited zone, though not, of course, title to the land on which they sit.

An important additional method by which foreigners may acquire the use of prohibited-zone land was authorized by the minister of foreign relations in March 1967 by a resolution that permits would be granted to authorized institutions to enter into trust agreements covering such property.[44] The effect of this resolution is to authorize the acquisition by appropriate trust banks of title to land in trust for foreign beneficiaries, who have the beneficial interest in and use of the land for the term of the trust agreement.[45] This very significant change in the ministry's policy probably resulted from a realization that foreign investments in the border and coastal areas are desirable, and it may well open the way for substantial new foreign investments in the prohibited zone.

REAL PROPERTY OUTSIDE THE PROHIBITED ZONE

Acquisition by Foreign-Controlled Mexican Companies

Under current practice foreign entrepreneurs who effect investments in Mexico through the medium of a company incorporated under Mexican law usually encounter few impediments to the acquisition of real property outside the prohibited zone necessary for their operations. Mexican companies with foreign owners may acquire such land under two conditions: first, a permit must be obtained from the Ministry of Foreign Relations for each conveyance to the company, in addition to the permit required for its incorporation, under which any foreigner who holds an interest in the company agrees to the terms of the Calvo clause, discussed earlier in this chapter; and second, the company may not acquire more land than is necessary to fulfill its purposes as stated in its articles of incorporation. While these conditions are easily fulfilled in most cases, special problems are presented in connection with foreign investments in agricultural activities, and even companies engaged in industrial or commercial operations may be confronted with serious complications if the land they wish to acquire for their facilities has been affected by the agrarian reform program.

The requirement of a permit from the Ministry of Foreign Relations is imposed on Mexican companies that have or are permitted to have foreign shareholders or members—that is, companies whose articles of incorporation do not expressly prohibit the ownership of shares or other interests in the company by foreigners. In addition to the acquisition of title to real property, the requirement applies to the execution of leases for a term exceeding ten years and trust agreements under which such a company is the beneficiary and to the acquisition of controlling interests in existing enterprises that deal in real property.[46] Broad discretionary power is given to the ministry to deny such permits or to limit them to Mexican-controlled and managed companies.[47] The practice of the ministry, sanctioned by a rule adopted by the interministerial commission on investment of foreign capital, is, however, to issue such permits to Mexican companies regardless of the percentage of foreign ownership in the company.

The ruling of the interministerial commission calls on the ministry to require "proof that the real properties concerned are really indispensable to the corporate purpose" of the company.[48] A similar provision, but applicable only to commercial stock companies, is found in the Constitution, under which such companies are denied the right to acquire, possess, or administer rural agricultural property (fincas rústicas), but companies incorporated to engage in activities other than agriculture may own the amount of land "strictly necessary for the establishments or services" to carry out their corporate purposes and "which the Executive of the Union or those of the States shall establish in each case."[49] The Ministry of Foreign Relations interprets this provision to apply only to rural land—that is, land located outside the limits of a city, town, or village—so that a Mexican company wishing to acquire urban property is not required to prove that the property is "strictly necessary" for its activities. Furthermore, in practice the ministry does not normally

require the evidence of necessity called for by the ruling of the interministerial commission where urban land is involved. In the case of rural
property, the company must present evidence with its permit application
that the land is essential to its corporate purpose. This requirement must
be satisfied by a statement of consent from the governor of the state or
federal territory in which the land is located or from the Federal District
Department if the land is located in the Federal District. Since local
authorities in most cases are anxious to promote the establishment of
new businesses, these statements are usually obtained without difficulty.

Acquisition of Ejido Land

In many instances the most suitable land for new industrial and commercial facilities is found in suburban areas outside the limits of cities
and towns. The acquisition of such property may present important
problems to the investor, for it is precisely the land surrounding cities
and towns that is most likely to be communal or *ejido* land protected by
the agrarian code. Land that has been dedicated to communal or *ejido*
use may not be conveyed, leased, or mortgaged. Any act or contract
violating that prohibition is void, and a private person or company that
attempts to acquire such land has no recourse against an order to
vacate.[50] Nor may a prospective purchaser of rural land rely on an apparently valid deed of record in the appropriate public register of property; its status can be accurately determined only through a search of
the records of the local agrarian delegation and the federal agrarian
register.

If it is found that the land concerned is *ejido* or communal land, the
law provides for two methods by which it may be acquired for private
use—expropriation and exchange *(permuta).* The exchange of such
land for privately owned land, which in turn becomes *ejido* land, is
permitted with presidential authorization, on the request and with the
consent of the members of the *ejido,* and with the approval of the agrarian department and other federal agencies.[51] The practice of the agrarian department for several years, however, has been not to authorize
exchange transactions, and that method of acquiring *ejido* land for
private use seems no longer available. A further impediment to the
acquisition of such land for industrial or commercial purposes is imposed by a 1959 regulation requiring a private person who acquires *ejido*
land in an exchange to devote the land exclusively to agricultural purposes.[52]

In practice, therefore, the only available means of a[cquiring] land is through expropriation. The purposes for which the [law] authorizes the expropriation of communal land are quit[e broad and] include the "creation, promotion and preservation of an e[nterprise in] the interests of the community.[53] If the agrarian departme[nt and other] agencies concerned find that the proposed use of the land satisfies this condition, it may be expropriated by presidential resolution and conveyed to the private person upon payment of the compensation established. In many cases the required compensation takes the form of another tract of land for the *ejido* from which the expropriation is made. The procedure is complicated and normally requires at least two years to complete. Nevertheless, if the business for which the land is to be used is considered sufficiently important, the state government will not likely hesitate to sponsor the expropriation request and assist in obtaining its approval.

Acquisition by Foreign Individuals and Companies

The acquisition directly by foreigners of real property outside the prohibited zone is substantially more restricted than in the case of a foreign-controlled Mexican company. There are differences of opinion on the proper interpretation of the constitutional provision that "the State may grant the same right [to acquire title to land] to foreigners," but the most widely accepted view seems to be that this provision applies only to foreign individuals and not to foreign legal entities and that foreign companies may not acquire title to real property in Mexico.[54] There is no restriction, however, on the execution by a foreign company of a lease for a term not exceedng ten years. Also, there is no objection to the execution of a mortgage on Mexican land to a foreign company or the subsequent acquisition of title to the land on a foreclosure. The law implementing article 27, section I, of the Constitution authorizes the Ministry of Foreign Relations to permit "any foreign person" to acquire a right prohibited by the law by adjudication "by virtue of a pre-existing right acquired in good faith." A land title so acquired must be conveyed to a qualified person within a specified period of time, customarily two years.[55]

Foreign individuals, on the other hand, may directly acquire land outside the prohibited zone under certain conditions. By law the authorization of both the Ministry of Foreign Relations and the Ministry of Internal Affairs must be obtained, and permits are generally available

only to residents of Mexico. The applicable laws do not entirely over-
lap, however, and the requirement of a permit from the Ministry of
Internal Affairs is often overlooked.

As in the case of Mexican companies with foreign owners, a permit
from the Ministry of Foreign Relations containing the Calvo clause
agreement is required for each conveyance to a foreigner of title to real
property, including leases for a term exceeding ten years and trust
agreements under which a foreigner is the beneficiary, and for the acquisition of control of existing real estate companies. Again, the
ministry has discretionary power to grant, deny, or impose conditions on
such permits.[56]

The requirement of a permit from the Ministry of Internal Affairs,
imposed by a 1960 amendment to the population law and the subject of
considerable controversy,[57] is substantially broader in scope. The law
requires such a permit for the acquisition not only of real property
but also "shares or real rights therein." The term "shares" is defined in
the regulations as shares of stock issued by companies whose purpose
is to deal in real property. The requirement is not limited to the acquisition of a majority or any other specified minimum interest in such a
company, and the law is literally applicable to the acquisition of any
number of shares in a real estate company. Real rights are stated to
include "those which affect or limit in any way the right of ownership,
including those derived from a trust on immovables, but excluding those
derived from judicial attachments and authorized certificates or obligations secured by mortgage."[58] The legislative intent is apparently to
require a permit for the execution of any contract, such as a lease, by
which a foreigner acquires the right to use or occupy real property in any
way, regardless of the period of the use or occupation, or by which he
acquires a mortgage. The exception of obligations secured by mortgage
would seem to be limited to securities, called *cédulas hipotecarias,* issued by licensed mortgage loan companies and guaranteed by mortgages
held by those companies.

In practice the authorizations of both ministries are usually routinely
issued to foreigners who fulfill certain conditions. These conditions relate
to the status of the foreigner under Mexican immigration law[59]—the type
of visa or permit under which he is authorized to enter and remain in the
country—and are obviously intended to restrict the ownership of land in
Mexico to persons who reside more or less permanently in the country
and to prevent ownership by nonresident aliens.

The permits of both ministries are generally limited to persons with the status of *inmigrado* or immigrant. The emergency decree of 1944 requires that, in order to qualify for the authorization of the Ministry of Foreign Relations, the foreigner must have his principal source of business or investments in Mexico and "a residence sufficient to evidence his settlement" in the country.[60] Under a 1947 ruling of the interministerial commission the residence requirement is stated to be satisfied if the alien has either immigrant or *inmigrado* status,[61] and that fact is, in practice, also taken as evidence that his principal source of business or investments is in the country. The criteria of the Ministry of Internal Affairs are somewhat different. Its permits are freely issued to *inmigrados*,[62] but immigrants are permitted to acquire only dwellings for themselves and their dependents, despite a regulation that they may be authorized to acquire certain other properties.[63] In the case of rural land the ministry does not allow an immigrant to acquire a larger area than it considers necessary for a dwelling place.

Persons having a status that does not require residence in Mexico generally do not qualify for the necessary permits from either ministry. In no case, for example, may a foreigner with tourist or transmigrant status be authorized to acquire real property.[64] Some discrepancy exists in the law with respect to foreigners in Mexico as visitors *(visitantes)*. The Ministry of Foreign Relations has authority to permit a visitor to acquire the amount of land necessary for a dwelling or for the business for which he has been authorized to enter the country by the Ministry of Internal Affairs.[65] However, permits of the Ministry of Internal Affairs are expressly prohibited to visitors under the regulations to the population law,[66] and in practice the Ministry of Foreign Relations no longer issues permits to foreigners with visitor status. An exception to this rule is made in the case of acquisition by inheritance. A foreigner who acquires an interest in land by devise or succession is normally authorized to enter the country as a visitor and is issued the necessary permits to receive title to the land on the condition that he convey it to a qualified person within a designated period of time, usually two years.[67]

The enforcement of these laws is not always consistent. The requirement of a permit from the Ministry of Foreign Relations is one of long standing and is strictly enforced. Violations are sanctioned by forfeiture of the property concerned, and notaries and other officials who authorize or record contracts or other instruments by which a foreigner acquires a property interest covered by the law without the necessary permit are subject to suspension or fine.[68] The more recent requirement of a permit from the Ministry of Internal Affairs, however, is often ignored, and in many cases notaries and officials of the public registers of property authorize and record deeds to foreigners with only the permit of the Ministry of Foreign Relations. In fact, no case is known in which recordation of a deed to a foreigner has been denied because of lack of a permit from the Ministry of Internal Affairs. In the case of acquisitions of leasehold interests and shares in real estate companies, enforcement of the permit requirement is especially difficult since lease contracts are not necessarily notarized or recorded and since shareholders in real estate companies are often anonymous because of the use of bearer shares.

This does not mean, however, that a foreigner may always violate the law with impunity. Public officials and notaries are required to notify the Ministry of Internal Affairs of all acts and contracts which they authorize and to which foreigners are parties,[69] and if an infraction of the law comes to the attention of the ministry, it may impose a fine on the foreigner concerned of 200 to 10,000 pesos.[70]

What seems a rather illogical interpretation is given the population law and its regulations by the Ministry of Internal Affairs in the case of the execution of a mortgage or conveyance in trust in favor of a foreigner not physically present in Mexico or a foreign company that does not operate in the country. As pointed out above, the law requires a permit for a foreigner to acquire either of those types of interest in real property. The ministry has taken the position that, since the law applies only to foreigners who are in Mexico, the permit requirement is not applicable to the execution of contracts by foreigners not located in Mexico.[71] The effect of this interpretation is that a foreigner outside Mexico or a foreign company not doing business in the country may acquire a mortgage or a beneficial interest in real property held in trust; whereas, a foreigner temporarily in Mexico, as a tourist for example, is denied that authority.

Acquisition of Agricultural Land

Foreign investors wishing to engage in agriculture in Mexico face special problems. The acquisition of rural land for agricultural purposes is subject to special regulations relating both to foreign ownership and to the surface area of land that may be held privately under the agrarian laws.

Foreigners and Mexican companies having foreign owners are subject to the same requirements of permits from the Ministries of Foreign Relations and Internal Affairs and other conditions as are applicable generally for the acquisition of real property. In the case of foreign individuals, the practice of the Ministry of Internal Affairs not to allow immigrants to acquire more land than is necessary for a dwelling effectively limits the acquisition of agricultural land to *inmigrados*.

Investments in agriculture may be made by other foreigners and by foreign companies through the medium of a company incorporated under Mexican law. For historical reasons and to prevent the concealment of the true ownership of rural land, commercial stock companies are prohibited to "acquire, possess or administer" rural agricultural properties.[72] This prohibition applies to the two forms of business association whose capital is represented by shares of stock, the stock corporation *(sociedad anónima)* and the limited partnership with shares *(sociedad en comandita por acciones),* but it does not exclude ownership of such land by the other types of entities recognized by Mexican law.[73] The most commonly used form of company for agricultural activities is the limited liability company *(sociedad de responsabilidad limitada).*

A further limitation provides that the Ministry of Foreign Relations may not issue permits for the acquisition of agricultural property to Mexican companies in which foreigners hold a majority interest.[74] Under this restriction the ministry has at times in the past imposed in its permits the condition that a majority interest in such companies must be held by Mexican nationals or Mexican companies controlled by Mexican nationals, but the current practice of the ministry is to allow majority ownership by another Mexican company regardless of the nationality of its shareholders or members. It is possible, therefore, for a foreign-controlled Mexican company, such as a stock corporation, to be the majority owner of an agricultural landholding company. Also, since no permit is required for the execution by a foreign-controlled Mexican company of a lease for a term not exceeding ten years, such a company may obtain the use of agricultural land for a limited period of time by that method.

One of the principal causes of the Mexican Revolution of 1910 was grossly inequitable distribution of land, and an important objective of the Constitution of 1917 was the destruction of the great land estates that characterized the Porfirian era and the limitation of the amount of land that could be privately held. Any investor in agriculture must take these limitations into account or risk expropriation for *ejido* or communal use. The maximum area of land that may be privately owned depends upon either the quality of the land or the use to which it is put.[75] The limitations range, for example, from 100 hectares (247 acres) of irrigated or humid land to 800 hectares (1,976 acres) of arid mountain or grazing land. In the case of irrigated land devoted to the cultivation of certain crops, larger areas may be held—150 hectares (370.5 acres) for cotton raising and 300 hectares (741 acres) for other designated crops. Agricultural landholdings that do not exceed these limitations, called "small agricultural properties," are protected against expropriation provided they are under cultivation, and a procedure is established by which the owners may obtain "certificates of agricultural inaffectability" *(certificados de inafectabilidad agrícola)* evidencing their protection under the agrarian laws.[76] Land used for livestock raising is classified as small property and thus protected against expropriation if it does not exceed the area necessary to maintain a maximum of 500 head of major livestock or its equivalent in minor stock, and "certificates of livestock inaffectability" *(certificados de inafectabilidad ganadera)* are available to the owners of such land.[77] For the additional protection of the livestock industry, which has been adversely affected by the agrarian reform program, the law also authorizes the issuance of "concessions of livestock inaffectability" for a period of twenty-five years on larger areas of land than those classified as small properties.[78] The requirements for these concessions are numerous, and in practice they are no longer being issued.

OIL AND GAS

The oil and gas industry has been largely closed to private enterprise since Cárdenas' spectacular expropriation of the properties of the principal oil companies in 1938. Following that event, a wholly owned state enterprise, Petróleos Mexicanos, was created to take over the Mexican oil industry,[79] and in 1940 article 27 of the Constitution, which had embodied since its promulgation in 1917 the principle of state ownership of subsoil resources, was amended to prohibit the grant of concessions on petroleum and other hydrocarbons.[80]

Private operations were not, however, entirely excluded from the industry at that time. Several small independent companies, mostly foreign owned, were not affected by the expropriation decree and continued to operate. Confirmatory concessions created by the 1925 petroleum law and its amendment of 1928[81] were respected by the new law enacted in 1941.[82] This law also permitted the state to contract with private persons or companies for the exploration and production of oil, and especially during the administration of President Miguel Alemán a decline in the discovery of new reserves necessary to meet the requirements of the country's expanding economy and the need for outside technical skills led the government to reopen the industry to some degree to private enterprise. In the late 1940's and early 1950's Pemex, as it is often called, entered into numerous drilling contracts with private companies. A small number of contracts were executed with foreign-owned companies for exploration and production, providing for reimbursement of the contractors' expenses out of production and payment of a 15 percent royalty in the event production was obtained.

These doors have now been largely closed. Beginning in about 1948 Pemex bought up most of the remaining private holdings, and the new petroleum law enacted in 1958[83] and a 1960 amendment to article 27 of the Constitution[84] terminated existing concessions and provided that only the nation, through Petróleos Mexicanos, may operate in the industry. Though contracts with private persons are still permitted, compensation in the form of royalty payments out of production is no longer allowed.

Under the existing law and its regulations only the state, through Pemex or other public agency that may be created in the future, may engage in the petroleum industry. The law defines the petroleum industry broadly as the exploration, production, refining, transportation, storage, distribution, and firsthand sales of petroleum, gas, and products that are obtained from the refining thereof, and the manufacture, storage, transportation, distribution, and firsthand sales of artificial gas and petroleum derivatives that are susceptible of serving as basic industrial raw materials.[85]

The role of private enterprise is limited to the performance of certain services under contract with Pemex. Construction, drilling, and technical services, such as geological and geophysical services, may be and often are contracted for by Pemex with private companies. Contracts for these services must provide for payment in cash, and in no case may royalties or participations in production be established.[86] While domestic pipeline transportation is limited to Pemex, other forms of transportation and gas distribution by pipeline within cities and towns may be effected by contractors. Storage facilities, outside of oil fields and refineries, may be operated and distribution up to the time and place of the first sale may be made also by private persons under contract.[87] Specialties may be produced by private persons from products of the refining process with the authorization of the Ministries of National Properties and Industry and Commerce, which are required to consult Pemex before issuing a permit.[88]

Neither the law nor its regulations impose any limitation on foreign investment in companies that contract with Pemex. However, the Ministry of Foreign Relations routinely notifies Pemex and the Ministries of Industry and Commerce and National Properties of all applications for permits under the emergency decree of 1944 for the incorporation of companies whose stated purpose is to engage in any branch of the oil industry, and no permit will be issued without the approval of those agencies. It is said that the general practice of Pemex is to require that companies with which it contracts be controlled by Mexicans, but numerous exceptions are made.

The distribution of liquid petroleum gas is governed by a special regulation, under which foreigners are totally excluded from that activity. Private enterprises may engage in the storage, transportation, and distribution of liquid petroleum gas only with authorization of the Ministry of Industry and Commerce, and permits are expressly limited to Mexicans and Mexican companies owned entirely by nationals.[89]

PETROCHEMICALS

The petrochemical industry, largely influenced by foreign technology, has in recent years become one of the fastest growing and most attractive fields of investment in Mexico. Government regulation of the industry, however, has been fraught with difficult problems and indecision, and only in early 1967 did some order emerge from the confusion.

Regulation of the production of petrochemicals was first introduced into the law in the new petroleum law of 1958, which provides that the petroleum industry, reserved to the nation, includes the "preparation, storage, transportation, distribution, and firsthand sales of those derivatives of petroleum that are susceptible of serving as basic industrial raw materials."[90] The 1959 regulations[91] to that law laid down more detailed guidelines concerning the areas of the petrochemical industry from which private investment was excluded and the conditions under which private enterprise would be allowed to participate. Under the regulations certain categories of petrochemical products may be produced only by the state, through Petróleos Mexicanos or its subsidiaries or affiliates created by the state, in which private participation is prohibited. Other products may be produced either by the government or by private industry, alone or jointly with the state. The manufacture of those products requires governmental authorization, which is issued only to companies having a specified minimum percentage of Mexican ownership. Not all products that may be technically classified as petrochemicals are necessarily covered by the regulations, and no permit is required nor is there any restriction on foreign investment in the manufacture of products that are not covered. It is in the determination of what products are regulated and thus subject to the permit requirement that the main difficulty has arisen.

Under article 27 of the regulations the production of two categories of products is reserved to the state: first, those that result from "petrochemical processes based on the first important chemical transformation or the first important physical processing" of products or by-products of the refining process or natural petroleum hydrocarbons, and second, those that "have a fundamental social economic interest for the State." Since there is no definition of what is of fundamental economic interest, virtually any petrochemical product may be declared to be reserved to the state, and the regulations provide in article 29 that cases of doubt as to whether a particular product is so reserved shall be determined by ruling of the president, with the participation of the Ministries of National Properties and Industry and Commerce, and after consulting Petróleos Mexicanos.

An initial step was taken in April, 1960, to define more specifically the area reserved to the nation when a presidential ruling was issued listing sixteen basic petrochemical products that could be produced only by Petróleos Mexicanos or its affiliates.[92] It was provided in the ruling that the list could be enlarged or changed by the executive on the basis of considerations of a technical character or of fundamental economic interest for the state.

Products that may be produced by private industry under governmental permit are defined in article 28 of the regulations as those that "result from petrochemical processes subsequent to" the first important chemical transformation or the first important physical processing of petroleum or products of the refining process. By implication, products that do not come within that definition are not subject to the requirements of the law and may be produced freely by the private sector, including foreign-owned enterprises. The meaning of that definition has been the subject of considerable dispute, however.

Two interpretations of article 28 have been put forth. On one hand, it has been argued that it refers only to the first processing of products whose production is reserved to the nation—that is, the manufacture of products in which there is used as a raw material a product acquired directly from the state. The broader interpretation is that the article covers all products for the production of which there is used either a product acquired from the state or any product derived, however remotely, from such a product.

For several years after the 1959 regulations were issued, a number of private interests, who saw the possibility of eliminating competition on a broad front, applied for and obtained government permits for the manufacture of a wide range of products in which a raw material derived from petroleum is used. Some government officials took this as an interpretation by the private sector generally that article 28 applied to all products of that nature and adopted a similar position.

A crisis in the industry was precipitated in 1966 when, on the basis of this broad interpretation of article 28, the petrochemical department of the Ministry of Industry and Commerce began issuing communications to companies manufacturing products for which raw materials derived from hydrocarbons are used, stating that they were violating the requirement of a permit for their operations and calling on them to appear before the ministry to correct their situation. These communications went to numerous Mexican- and foreign-controlled companies, many of which had been in operation long before 1959 regulations were adopted and manufactured products as far removed from the petrochemical industry as aspirin and paint. The resulting uncertainty over what was included in the petrochemical industry and governed by the regulations brought new investments to a virtual halt.

A committee representing private enterprise was quickly formed to discuss the problem personally with the minister of industry and commerce and the general director of Pemex. As a result a commission made up of representatives of the Ministry of Industry and Commerce, the Ministry of National Properties, and Petróleos Mexicanos and representatives of the private sector was appointed to study the problem. The private representatives made a strong argument. First, since article 26 of the regulations defines the petrochemical industry as the manufacture of products totally or partially from natural petroleum hydrocarbons or hydrocarbons that are products or by-products of refining operations, then the chapter of the regulations dealing with petrochemicals, including article 28, must have been intended to apply only to the manufacture of products from hydrocarbons. Therefore, the production of a product from a raw material that is not a hydrocarbon is not governed by the regulations, even though the raw material is a product or by-product of the petroleum refining process and is produced by and bought from the state. According to the accepted definition, hydrocarbons are composed exclusively of hydrogen and carbon, and once either element is removed or a third element added, the product is not a hydrocarbon. Secondly, it was argued, the language in article 28, "petrochemical processes subsequent to those specified," and the spirit of article 26 indicate that only the first processing of hydrocarbons produced by and acquired from the state is included, and any further processing of products privately produced, even though they are hydrocarbons, is excluded from the coverage of the regulations and is not subject to the permit requirement.

While the governmental agencies involved recognized the logic of the argument of the private sector, they were reluctant to adopt it as official policy because permits had previously been issued authorizing the production by private enterprises of products that would not be covered by the regulations under the interpretation put forth, and official acceptance of that interpretation would mean recognition that the government's earlier position had been erroneous and that subsequent producers of those products would not be subject to the permit requirement. The only way out of the dilemma seemed to be to designate specific products whose production was subject to the requirement of governmental authorization. As a result of the commission's work, in March, 1967, four lists of products were released, the first two covering basic products whose production is reserved to the nation, the third covering secondary products that may be produced either by the state or by private enterprise under presidential authorization, and the fourth covering products for the manufacture of which no permit is required. Many of the products contained in the third group are not produced directly from hydrocarbons but had been the subject of presidential authorization before a solution to the problem was found.

There is no limitation on foreign investment in companies that manufacture products for which no permit is required—that is, products contained in the fourth group. The proportion of foreign ownership is, however, restricted in the case of enterprises manufacturing products for which a permit is required. Article 30 of the regulations provides that the granting of such permits will be subject to the provisions of the emergency decree of 1944 "and other legal provisions applicable with respect to foreign investments." Normally, in companies in which Mexican control is required under the 1944 decree, ownership by Mexicans of 51 percent of the shares is considered sufficient. In the case of companies producing regulated petrochemicals, however, the policy has been established that at least 60 percent must be Mexican owned, and no permit will be issued to a company more than 40 percent of whose shares are held by foreigners.

Another result of the work of the commission was the establishment, on the insistence of the private sector representatives, of internal guidelines to clarify the procedures and requirements for obtaining petrochemical permits. Under these regulations, permit applications are submitted to the petrochemical commission, composed of the ministers of industry and commerce and national properties and the general director of Petróleos Mexicanos. An application must be accompanied by a copy of the articles of incorporation or proposed articles of the producing company and detailed studies of the product to be produced and its manufacture; the market for the product and its proposed distribution; plant location, capacity, and investment; production costs; and financing. After a technical subcommission studies the application and makes its recommendation, the petrochemical commission issues an opinion on whether or not a permit should be granted, taking into account such considerations as whether or not the future market, including planned exports, for the product supports the proposed investment. While the commission's internal regulations call on the technical subcommission to issue its opinion within fifteen days after an application has been presented and on the commission to reach a resolution within ten days thereafter, delays are often encountered. A favorable opinion of the commission is transmitted to the president for final action.

In addition to the limitations on foreign investment, the government has also adopted the policy of imposing other requirements and restrictions in petrochemical permits, which vary according to the circumstances of each particular case. The maximum price is specified at which the product covered by the permit may be sold, stated as a percentage above the domestic price in the country of origin of the product, in most cases the United States. The price allowed is customarily 15 percent above the United States price, but it is usually provided that this may be increased if the cost of raw materials is substantially higher than in the United States. Plant capacity and maximum periods for the commencement of plant construction and initiation of operations are also established, and a bond must be posted, normally in an amount equal to 5 percent of the total investment, to guarantee commencement and termination of the plant.

MINING

Of the traditionally foreign-dominated sectors of the Mexican economy, mining is the most recent to be subjected to statutory restrictions on foreign investment. Unlike railroads, oil, and electric power, which have been nationalized by expropriation or government purchase, mining has been left largely in the hands of the private sector, but the mining law of 1961 for the first time in over a hundred years drastically restricted new foreign investment in the industry and, together with important amendments to the mining tax law, paved the way for the Mexicanization of existing companies.

Basic to Mexican legislation in this field is the theory, inherited from Spanish legal tradition, that title to subsurface minerals is in the state rather than in the private landowner and that private persons may extract them only with the authorization of the government.[93] This principle is embodied in article 27 of the Constitution of 1917, which provides that the nation has "direct dominion" of deposits of all minerals and other substances "whose nature is different from the components of the lands" and that the state's title is "inalienable and imprescriptible." Minerals may be worked only under concessions granted by the federal executive, pursuant to the rules and conditions established by law.[94]

The field of mining has been governed exclusively by federal law since the first Mexican mining code was enacted in 1884, following the amendment of the 1857 constitution to confer power on the federal Congress to legislate for the entire country on this subject.[95] The first law implementing article 27 of the existing Constitution was adopted in 1926[96] but was soon replaced by the mining law of 1930,[97] which was in effect with amendments for over thirty years. On February 5, 1961, a new mining law was issued and, together with its 1966 regulations, governs the field at this time.[98] Some knowledge of the general regulatory scheme of the law is helpful to an understanding of the restrictions imposed on foreign investment in mining.

MINING EXPLOITATION RIGHTS

The law applies to the exploitation and use of all mineral deposits with the exception of petroleum and other hydrocarbons and substances found in suspension or dissolution in subterranean waters which are not from a mine. Exploitation includes exploration, extraction, and treatment.[99]

Mining operations may be carried out by the state, acting through public mining entities, by so-called state participation companies, or by private persons or companies.[100] Public mining entities, the most important of which are the Comisión de Fomento Minero (mining development commission) and the Comisión Nacional de Energía Nuclear (national nuclear energy commission), exploit minerals in specifically designated zones that are assigned to them by the Ministry of National Properties or by resolution of the president.[101]

State participation companies are constituted "when the federal executive deems it advisable for the development of the industry."[102] These companies must be in the form of variable capital stock corporations, and a majority of their shares are subscribed by the federal government. Private investors, whether Mexican or foreign, may not own more than 49 percent of their shares. Their exploitation rights are derived from concessions issued by the president. The law does not preclude the government from acquiring less than majority interests in mining companies, and the government has demonstrated its willingness to occupy a minority position in the 1967 acquisitions jointly by the government and private Mexican groups of control of the foreign-owned sulphur companies and its association with private Mexican and foreign investors in new companies organized to explore for and develop additional sulphur deposits.[103] These companies are not, however, state participation companies as defined in the law since the government does not own a majority of their shares.

Private persons and companies may engage in mining exploitation only under concessions granted by the federal executive. With certain exceptions, mining concessions may be issued only on "free lands," which are defined as any lands in the country except those assigned to a public mining entity or covered by an existing concession, those on which an application for assignment or concession has been filed, and those included in the national mining reserves. The continental shelf, submarine portions of islands, keys and reefs, and the federal maritime land zone are also excluded from "free lands," but special concessions may be issued on them.[104]

Maximum land area and minerals covered and term of concessions are set out in detail in the law and regulations, as well as the rights and obligations of concession holders.[105] Each concession covers one mining lot of a maximum surface area of 500 hectares, and no person or company may hold exploitation rights on a total surface area exceeding specified maximum amounts that vary according to the mineral covered from 1,000 hectares for mercury, tungsten, and molybdenum to 8,000 hectares for mineral coal. However, the area covered by a concession is calculated at one-third of its actual surface area until the end of the five-year exploration period of the concession. Concessions are issued for a term of twenty-five years but may be renewed for an indefinite period on the application of the holder if the requirements for workings have been met. The obligations of concession holders include payment of taxes, execution and proof of specified minimum workings, and fulfillment of requirements relating to such matters as the furnishing of data, information, and inspection facilities to the Ministry of National Properties.

Mining concession holders have the right to install and operate, for their private use, treatment plants or mills with a capacity of less than 100 tons of mineral in twenty-four hours. Separate concessions, issued jointly by the Ministries of National Properties and Industry and Commerce, are required for larger private mills and mills operated for public service. These concessions also have a twenty-five year term and may be renewed, and the rights and obligations of their holders are specified.[106]

EXPLOITATION OF NATIONAL MINING RESERVES

National mining reserves are subject to special regulation. The establishment of these reserves was first authorized in 1934 by amendments to the 1930 mining law, and the system was retained, with some changes, in the 1961 law.[107] Either specifically designated minerals or mining zones, provided they are not covered by an existing concession or application, may be incorporated into the national reserves by presidential decree issued to the Ministry of National Properties. Minerals that are so incorporated are classified in one of three categories: first, those that may be exploited only by the state, under assignments to public mining entities; second, those considered essential for the industrial development of the country, which may be exploited by public mining entities under assignment or by state participation companies or private persons under special concessions; and third, minerals or zones set aside to cover future needs of the country that may not be worked at all. The president is authorized to disincorporate minerals or zones from the national reserves and to change their classification from one category to another.

Over the years a number of important mineral deposits and mining zones have been incorporated into the national reserves, including the rich sulphur deposits in the Isthmus of Tehuantepec, uranium and other radioactive minerals, coal, manganese, all minerals in the iron-bearing Las Truchas and Plutón areas of Michoacán and Guerrero and the Peña Colorada zone of Colima and Jalisco, phosphorites in parts of Zacatecas, copper in areas of Jalisco and Colima, and other minerals. Many of these have been assigned to the mining development commission. Substantial additions to the national reserves were made by President Adolfo López Mateos in the late 1950's and first half of the 1960's, but the pace of new incorporations has declined under the administration of President Gustavo Díaz Ordaz.[108]

Minerals classed in the first category that have been assigned to a public mining entity may be exploited only by that entity. Before the adoption of the 1961 law the mining development commission was authorized to enter into contracts with private persons for the exploitation of national reserves, and the sulphur production rights acquired in the 1940's by such companies as the Mexican subsidiaries of Pan American Sulphur Company and Gulf Sulphur Corporation were obtained under government contracts. Such contracts are not authorized in the 1961 law, however, and reserve minerals in the first category must now be released by the public mining entity to which they have been assigned and reclassified by presidential order into the second category in order for private persons to acquire rights in them. The government has not been unduly reluctant to do this. A number of sulphur mining concessions were issued to newly formed companies in 1966 in areas formerly assigned to the mining development commission.

Special mining concessions may be granted to private persons on national reserve minerals classified in the second category.[109] Upon receipt of an application for a special concession, the Ministry of National Properties is required to issue a call for public bids and to grant the concession to the person submitting the most advantageous bid. Since the original applicant is preferred in the case of equal bids and is given the right to match the bid selected as the most advantageous, there is little incentive for others to submit bids, and no case is known in which a special concession has been granted to a person other than the original applicant. In addition to the obligations that accompany ordinary mining concessions, certain requirements are imposed by the terms of special concessions relating to minimum investment, obligation to supply domestic industry, and payment of royalties, usually a total of 6 percent of the official value established for purposes of the tax on production, to the mining development commission and the Consejo de

Recursos Naturales no Renovables (nonrenewable natural resources board).

LIMITATIONS ON FOREIGN INVESTMENT IN MINING

Among the most fundamental innovations of the 1961 law are the Mexicanization provisions—the limitations on direct foreign investments in the industry. No law in Mexico contains such clear and complete restrictions on foreign participation as do the mining law and its regulations.

Under article 14 of the law only Mexican citizens and Mexican companies a majority of whose capital is subscribed by Mexicans may obtain ordinary mining or mill concessions. Foreign governments and sovereigns are absolutely prohibited to acquire concessions or other mining rights or to hold ownership interests in mining companies. In the case of special concessions on national mining reserves, the limitation on foreign ownership is even greater. Pursuant to article 76 of the law, those concessions may be granted only to Mexican citizens or to Mexican companies in which at least 66 percent of the capital is owned by Mexicans. Articles 8 and 15 prohibit the assignment of rights under concessions or any mining exploitation rights to persons or companies that do not qualify to obtain concessions directly. An assignment or exploitation contract made in violation of these prohibitions is void. An exception is made, however, for acquisitions of concessions by inheritance or adjudication in payment of debts.

Article 26 of the regulations fills in the details of these restrictions. In the case of stock companies, their shares must be divided into series A and series B, and a minimum of either 51 percent or 66 percent designated series A, depending upon whether they wish to acquire ordinary mining or plant concessions or special concessions on national mining reserves. If redeemable or limited vote shares are issued in addition to common shares, each class must likewise be divided into series A and series B (designated subseries in the law) in the same proportion, so that it is not possible to confer voting control on the minority shareholders by limiting the voting rights of the majority. All shares of the same series must be of equal value, and the series A or Mexican shares may not confer less rights than or be subordinate in participation in earnings to the series B shares.

Series A shares must be registered and may be subscribed or acquired only by Mexican citizens or the following Mexican companies:

those whose articles prohibit foreign ownership and in which interests may be held only by Mexican citizens, companies in which foreign ownership is also prohibited, or other companies in this list; those which fulfill the requirements of articles 14 or 76 of the law and applicable provisions of the regulations and which are registered in the book of Mexican members and shareholders of mining companies in the public mining register; Mexican credit institutions or investment companies that meet certain conditions; or Mexican companies that establish that a majority of their capital is owned by Mexicans, Mexican companies with majority Mexican capital, or Mexican credit institutions or investment companies, provided the companies and the evidence of their ownership are registered in the book of Mexican members and shareholders of mining companies. It seems obvious that most of these conditions are designed to prevent foreign control of mining companies through the use of holding companies, a loophole that exists in other laws. Ownership of series B shares is unrestricted, except that they may not be held by foreign sovereigns or governments.

Stock certificates representing different series of shares must be clearly distinguishable by color and form, and series A certificates must contain a provision that assignment may be made only to qualified persons and that acquisition of the shares by others will be void. Series B certificates are subject to the usual requirement that they contain the so-called Calvo clause.

In the case of an assignment of series A shares, the company must require proof that the assignee is qualified to hold them before the transfer may be made on the company's books, and if such proof is not made or is unsatisfactory, it must notify the Ministry of National Properties. Failure of compliance with these requirements subjects both the company and the assignee to criminal sanctions.

Foreign management of Mexican mining companies is also restricted. If the company is managed by a sole administrator, he must be a Mexican citizen, and if there is a board of directors, a majority must be Mexicans and the series A or Mexican shareholders must have the right to elect at least half plus one of the directors.

Mining companies organized in the form of a business association other than a stock company[110] are subject to similar restrictions on foreign ownership and management.

In the event that more than the authorized percentage of shares in a Mexican mining company is acquired by foreigners or unqualified Mexican companies, the company must notify the Ministry of National

Properties, which then establishes a period of one to two years for correction of the irregularity.[111] The acquisition by unqualified persons of shares by inheritance or adjudication in payment of debts is authorized, but shares so acquired must be assigned to a qualified holder within one year.[112] If at the end of those periods the shares involved have not been acquired by qualified persons, they are sold at public auction under judicial order.

If the shareholders of a company authorize foreigners or unqualified Mexican companies to acquire more than the permitted interests in the company, the concessions held by the company are subject to forfeiture.[113] Criminal sanctions of imprisonment and fine are imposed where the ownership of interests in mining companies by unqualified persons is concealed or falsified.[114]

The 1961 law did not require the Mexicanization of existing mining companies. Concessions issued under prior laws were continued in effect but were limited to a term of twenty-five years counted from the anniversary date of their issue immediately following the date of issue of the law. Renewal at the end of that period, however, may be obtained only if the holder fulfills the minimum Mexican ownership requirements established in the law.[115] Foreign-owned companies could, therefore, continue to work their pre-existing concessions for the twenty-five year term without surrendering control to Mexicans, though they could not obtain new concessions or renew their concessions upon the expiration of their term.

Nevertheless, a highly effective stimulus to transfer controlling interests to Mexicans before that time was incorporated into the mining tax law simultaneously with the adoption of the 1961 mining law. Effective January 1, 1962, Mexican-controlled mining companies—holders of existing concessions that fulfill the Mexicanization provisions of the 1961 law and holders of concessions issued under that law—were granted an automatic reduction of 50 percent of the net federal portion of the production and export taxes on minerals from their concessions, which amounts to 84 percent of the total of those taxes, and the right to request further reductions under special tax agreements. Foreign-controlled concession holders were denied the tax reduction.[116] The amount of the tax concession was so substantial that many foreign-owned companies estimated that the return from a 49 percent interest in a Mexicanized operation would be more than their return if full ownership was retained. Understandably, most companies did not delay long in negotiating sales of majority interests to Mexican investors. Though some smaller companies are still owned by foreigners, by mid-1965 control of all major companies, except the existing sulphur companies, had been acquired by Mexicans.

In the light of the history of foreign investment in Mexico, it is not difficult to recognize the country's legitimate desire that its citizens participate more fully in the development and use of its natural resources. The long-existing foreign domination of this basic area of the economy was regarded by many as inconsistent with the national interest. It does not seem likely, however, that, as the then minister of national properties indicated,[117] the Mexicanization of the industry will alone free it from reliance on the international market for its principal minerals or that domestic consumption could not be stimulated without limiting foreign investment. Furthermore, if the intent was to attract many small Mexican investors into the industry, this has not been realized. Finding Mexican buyers for their shares has been extremely difficult for foreign companies trying to comply with the Mexicanization requirement, and with very few exceptions, control of the important mining companies has passed from a large number of foreign investors into the hands of a small group of Mexican owners. Unless more Mexicans are willing to invest in the industry, this concentration of ownership may operate to restrain needed new investments. In the absence of other potential Mexican investors, foreigners seeking Mexican associates in new mining ventures may find that they are limited to the existing small group of Mexican owners, who are able to and sometimes do impose conditions that are impossible for their prospective foreign partners to accept.

FORESTRY

The exploitation of timber and other forest vegetation is governed by the federal forestry law of 1960 and its regulations.[118] Efforts to revise the law have been made, and in July, 1967, a draft of new law was published, but no action has been taken on it.[119] The law is applicable to all forest land, whether privately or publicly owned, and owners of such land are obligated to register their titles and all acts and contracts relating to the exploitation of their forest resources in the national public register of forest property kept by the Ministry of Agriculture and Livestock.[120]

With minor exceptions, all exploitations of forest resources require the authorization of the Ministry of Agriculture.[121] Under article 87 of the law permits for commercial exploitation may be granted only to persons of Mexican nationality or to "associations of persons, also Mexican" that actually organize or undertake the operations. These permits may not be transferred except with the written consent of the ministry and unless the transferee fulfills the requirements for direct acquisition. The term "associations of persons" apparently is intended to distinguish the so-called associations of capital—the corporation and the limited partnership with shares—and the adjective "Mexican" seems to refer to the association rather than its members. Under this construction of the law, therefore, while a Mexican corporation could not obtain a permit, a limited liability company or one of the forms of partnership organized under Mexican law would qualify, irrespective of the nationality of its members.[122] The policy of the Ministry of Agriculture, however, is to require majority Mexican ownership of companies to which it issues permits, and the Ministry of Foreign Relations does not authorize the incorporation of companies to engage in such operations unless a majority of their capital is owned by Mexicans. Furthermore, it was announced in August, 1966, that the policy of the Díaz Ordaz administration is to give preference in the issuance of exploitation concessions to enterprises owned entirely by Mexicans.[123]

The constitutionality of the law, insofar as it applies to all forest land in the country, and the implied prohibition against acquisition of permits for commercial operations by foreigners has been questioned.[124] The Constitution does not expressly delegate to the federal Congress power to legislate with respect to forests. However, constitutional authority for the law is said to be found in section III of article 27, which grants to the nation the right to impose restrictions on private property required in the public interest. Article 2 of the law declares that the conservation and use of forest resources are of public interest. With respect to the prohibition against acquisition of permits by foreigners, it is argued that since foreigners may be permitted to acquire title to real property, including, logically, timber lands, and since title to land includes the trees on it, Congress has no authority to prohibit foreign landowners from using what legally belongs to them. A possible answer is that the purpose of the law is conservation and protection of forest resources and that, consequently, it is a valid restriction in the public interest under article 27. Despite these arguments, the validity of the law has not been challenged by legal action.

FISHING

The fishing industry is regulated by the federal fishing law of 1950, which applies not only to the act of capturing biological marine life but also to all other prior and subsequent acts that have a direct and immediate relation thereto.[125] This includes hatchery operations, but not processing and packaging.

The right to engage in any type of activity related to fishing, with the exception of fishing for the domestic consumption of the fisherman, is subject to government concession or permit,[126] issued by the general bureau of fishing of the Ministry of Industry and Commerce. Article 6 of the law provides that this right is recognized only in favor of Mexicans by birth[127] and Mexican companies. That article further provides, however, that aliens may obtain permission to engage in fishing for domestic consumption, exploitation, scientific purposes, or sport. There is no restriction in the law on foreign ownership of Mexican companies that receive permits for fishing operations, and further evidence that no general restriction is intended is found in the provision in article 6 that holders of concessions and permits may not admit foreign governments or sovereigns as members or shareholders. Article 19 of the regulations to the law specifically recognizes the possibility of private foreign owners by requiring that the Calvo clause be inserted in every concession granted to a Mexican company. Nevertheless, a long-standing policy of the Ministry of Foreign Relations under the emergency decree of 1944 is to require majority Mexican ownership of companies formed for the purpose of engaging in the fishing industry. Furthermore, the Ministry of Industry and Commerce does not, as a matter of policy, currently issue concessions for commercial fishing activities to anyone other than fishermen's co-operatives.

COMMUNICATIONS, TRANSPORT, AND SHIPPING

A concession or permit of the federal executive, issued through the Ministry of Communications and Transport, is required by the law of general means of communication for the construction, establishment, or commercial use of "general means of communication."[128] These are defined broadly to include territorial waters and navigable interstate and international rivers and canals; most railways, roads, and bridges; national airspace; and telephone and electric power lines.[129]

Under article 12 of the law these concessions may be granted only to

Mexican citizens or to companies incorporated under Mexican law. The law contains no general restriction on foreign ownership of such companies, the only requirement being that foreign shareholders or members must adhere to the terms of the Calvo clause. However, the Ministry of Foreign Relations has for many years followed the policy, under the emergency decree of 1944, of requiring majority Mexican capital in its permits for the incorporation of such companies, and it is the policy of the communications ministry to issue concessions only to Mexican-controlled companies. Furthermore, concessions for the use of federal roads and bridges for public transportation of persons or freight are, under the law, available only to native-born Mexican citizens and companies constituted by them.[130] It is implied that there may be no foreign participation in those companies, and such concessions are expressly prohibited to companies having shares in bearer form.

Mexican registry of aircraft for public transport service or for private air photography, air topography, and other similar services is limited to Mexican citizens and companies, but there is no prohibition in the law against foreign investment in such companies.[131] Again, however, majority Mexican ownership is required in practice and the policy is enforced both by the Ministry of Foreign Relations in its permits for incorporation and by the Ministry of Communications and Transport.

Shipping and navigation are regulated by the law of maritime navigation and commerce of 1963.[132] Coastal shipping is restricted by article 53 of the law to vessels of Mexican registry. Under article 92 a company may not possess Mexican-flag vessels unless it is incorporated under Mexican law and domiciled in the country and a majority of its capital is owned by Mexicans. The members of its board of directors and its manager must also be Mexican. Since the law uses the term "possess" rather than "own," this requirement seems to extend to possession and use of a vessel under any title, such as a bare-boat charter.

There is no specific prohibition against Mexican registration of vessels by alien individuals, but this seems implicit in artcle 95, section I, which provides that Mexican registry is lost by sale, adjudication, or transfer to foreign persons or countries.

RADIO AND TELEVISION

Radio and television broadcasting is considered an activity of public interest and consequently is regulated by federal law.[133] A concession is required for the operation of a commercial station, and a permit must be obtained for cultural or experimental stations and for radio schools. Both concessions and permits are issued by the Ministry of Communications and Transport and may be granted only to Mexican citizens or to companies whose shareholders or members are Mexican. The shares of stock companies must be registered, and those companies are required to furnish annually to the communications ministry a list of their shareholders.[134] Any shares or other ownership interests in those companies acquired by a foreign government or person are automatically forfeited without compensation to the Mexican government, and the concession of a company that admits foreign members is subject to cancellation.[135]

Concessions and permits may be assigned only with the authorization of the communications ministry and only to persons or companies that qualify to receive them directly. This restriction applies to encumbrances and transfers of concessions by any means, including inheritance, adjudication, or assignment in trust. Nor may a concession holder encumber or transfer his transmission equipment, installations, or other properties used in connection with his broadcasting activities to a foreigner. Violation of these prohibitions subjects the concession holder to forfeiture of both his concession and the property involved.[136]

ELECTRIC POWER

At the same time the Mexican government nationalized the major electric utility companies in 1960, a prohibition against private operations in this field was incorporated into the Constitution:[137] "The generation, transmission, transformation, distribution, and supply of electric power for the purpose of rendering public service corresponds exclusively to the Nation. In this field concessions shall not be granted to private persons and the Nation shall exploit the properties and natural resources that are required for those purposes."

Since the constitutional prohibition applies only to public service utilities, it is possible for private persons and companies to generate electric power for their own use. The 1939 electric industry law provides that, if natural resources belonging to the nation are used for this purpose, a government permit must be obtained,[138] but in practice a permit is always required for the generation of electric power. Also as a matter of policy, a permit is not issued for generation for private use when a public service company can supply the electric power needs of the applicant. Under article 15 of the law these permits may be issued only to Mexicans and Mexican companies, though there is no restriction on foreign ownership of such companies.

BANKING, FINANCE, AND INSURANCE

Private financial institutions—banks, investment companies, bonding companies, and insurance companies—are governed by special federal legislation. Under each of the applicable laws specific authorization of the federal government is required to engage in the activities covered by the law. These authorizations are issued by, and in the discretion of, the Ministry of Finance and Public Credit, which consults the Comisión Nacional Bancaria (national banking commission) and the Banco de México in the case of banking institutions, and the Comisión Nacional de Seguros (national insurance commission) in the case of insurance companies. Authorizations may not be transferred. The laws on banking and insurance institutions permit the authorization of branches of foreign companies to operate in Mexico, but investment and bonding companies must be Mexican corporations. Each of the laws was amended in 1965 to restrict new foreign investments in this sector of the economy.

Institutions of the private banking system are governed by the general law of credit institutions and auxiliary organizations of 1941.[139] Most credit-granting institutions are called "banks," and the law applies not only to deposit and savings banks but also to financial companies *(financieras)* that issue financial bonds *(bonos financieros)* and other debt instruments, mortgage loan companies that issue bonds and *cédulas hipotecarias* (mortgage-participation certificates), capitalization banks, trust institutions, and savings and loan associations. Government authorization is required for each of these institutions, and requirements relating to form of organization, minimum invested capital, management, and other matters must be met.[140] A company that is not authorized under the law may not use in its name such terms as *banco, financiera, crédito,* or other words indicating that it is a bank or other credit-granting institution.[141] So-called auxiliary credit organizations (general deposit warehouses, clearing house associations, securities exchanges, and credit unions) are also regulated by the law. Authorization of the finance ministry must be obtained for the establishment of general deposit warehouses and securities exchanges, and credit unions must be authorized by the national banking commission. All of the auxiliary institutions must be registered with and are subject to the control of that commission.[142]

The law provides that foreign banking institutions may establish branches or agencies in Mexico only for the purpose of acting as deposit banks and only under concessions issued by the finance ministry. They must qualify as foreign companies under the commercial companies law, fulfill the minimum capital requirements of the law, and agree to respond for their Mexican operations to the full extent of their assets whether located in Mexico or abroad. These requirements are also applicable to agents and representatives that engage in banking and credit operations for the account of foreign banks unless their activities are limited to correspondent relations with authorized Mexican banks.[143] While the law authorizes the grant of concessions for the establishment of branches by foreign banks, only one such concession exists, that held by First National City Bank of New York, and it is highly unlikely that the Mexican government will be persuaded to authorize the entry of other foreign banks. A number of foreign banks, however, maintain representatives in Mexico, with the authorization of the Ministry of Finance, for purposes of liaison with correspondent banks and others.

Investment companies are regulated by the investment companies law of 1955.[144] A concession from the finance ministry, with the approval of the national securities commission, is required for the incorporation of an investment company, which must be in the form of a corporation (*sociedad anónima*).[145] Although it is not specifically provided that such a company must be constituted under Mexican law, there is no express authorization of concessions to foreign companies, and it is undoubtedly the intent that only Mexican corporations qualify.

Bonding institutions, defined as corporations authorized by the federal government to issue bonds for consideration, are governed by the federal law of bonding institutions of 1950. The necessary authorization may be issued only to Mexican corporations that fulfill certain requirements.[146]

The general law of insurance institutions of 1935 applies to insurance companies, which include private Mexican companies authorized to engage in insurance operations and branches of foreign insurance companies authorized to operate in Mexico pursuant to the law.[147] Companies other than insurance institutions may not use the words *seguro, reaseguro, aseguramiento,* or other similar terms in any language in their names, and the public commercial register is prohibited to record public instruments of companies whose names include any of these words without authorization of the Ministry of Finance.[148]

Under the law foreign insurance companies may be authorized by the finance ministry to establish branches in Mexico if they qualify to do business under the commercial companies law, prove that they have been in operation for at least five years and that they are authorized to operate under the laws of their country of incorporation, and fulfill other requirements.[149] In practice, however, no authorization of a foreign insurance company is known.

The law prohibits the contracting of insurance against most types of Mexican risks with foreign companies. This prohibition applies to insurance of persons when the insured is in Mexico at the time of execution of the contract, insurance of property that is transported from or to Mexican territory when the risks are on persons domiciled in Mexico, insurance of hulls of ships or aircraft or any type of vehicle of Mexican registry or owned by persons domiciled in Mexico, insurance of debt when the insured is subject to Mexican law, insurance against civil liability resulting from events that may occur in Mexico, and other insurance against risks that may occur in Mexico. When no authorized insurance company can or considers it advisable to write a specific insurance contract, the finance ministry may permit the contract to be executed with a foreign company through an authorized insurance institution.[150]

Foreign investment in Mexican companies covered by these laws was sharply restricted in 1965. By decrees of December 27, 1965, each of the laws was amended to prohibit any type of participation in the capital of such companies, either directly or through an intermediary, by "foreign governments or official agencies, financial entities from abroad, or groups of foreign persons, whether individuals or legal entities, whatever their form."[151] Existing Mexican institutions were required, within one year from the effective date of the amendments to the laws, to amend their articles of incorporation to include the prohibition and a provision that violation would result in forfeiture to the nation of the share or shares concerned. The amendments further provided for revocation of the concession or authorization of a company that violates the prohibition or "establishes evident relations of dependency with" any of the designated foreign entities or groups.[152] The provisions of the banking and insurance laws permitting the authorization of foreign companies to operate in Mexico, discussed above, were not changed, and the only limitation on ownership of those companies is that a majority of their shares may not be acquired by a foreign government.

The language of the prohibition of ownership by "financial entities from abroad, or groups of foreign persons," which was used in the amendments to all four laws, is not altogether clear. Presumably, the prohibition covers any kind of foreign bank, investment company, surety company, or insurance company, and it would probably not be unreasonable to construe "groups of foreign persons" to include any foreign-owned company or association, whatever its nature or purpose. But it seems obvious that the drafters did not intend to prohibit stock acquisitions by individual foreign investors, perhaps because shares of a number of Mexican banks and other financial institutions are publicly held and traded and because there is little risk that an individual alien would acquire a large or controlling interest in such a company. The meaning of the prohibition against establishing "evident relations of dependency" seems even more ambiguous. The only clarification is found in the amendments to the banking law, which provide that relations of dependency shall not be deemed to exist "where the Mexican institution acts as a trustee for a foreign institution." The imprecise wording of the amendments may well have been deliberately chosen in order to allow substantial flexibility in the interpretation of the laws.

Existing foreign shareholders of Mexican financial institutions were not specifically required by the 1965 amendments to transfer their interests to Mexicans, even though they come within the prohibition against ownership by foreign entities and groups. However, authorization of the finance ministry of their investments was required, at least by implication, by a provision in transitory article first of each of the amending decrees giving the ministry the power to authorize such investments that were held on the date of the decrees. The ministry has been very liberal in the administration of this provision; no case is known in which a foreign investor has been required to transfer his interest in a company to which the prohibition applies.

Considering that the banking and financial sector of the Mexican economy has not in recent times been dominated by foreign capital and that, on the contrary, foreign investment has declined to a relatively small position, it perhaps seems strange that the government should have felt it necessary to adopt formal restrictions of this type. In his statement of reasons for the amendments, President Díaz Ordaz noted that these institutions should be reserved to Mexican investors, "given their decisive importance in the process of our development," and that precautions were required "to avoid that this sector might lose its autonomy or weaken its close relations with the national interests."

More specifically, he stated that the move resulted from "the insistence of foreign interests to obtain an important participation in our financial apparatus."[153] This seemed to corroborate open rumors in Mexican financial circles that several important foreign banks were actively negotiating for the purchase of large interests in Mexican banks and that the prohibition was adopted to forestall the possibility that existing Mexican ownership would be displaced. Also, the president's reference to the possible weakening of the close relations between the banking sector and domestic interests indicates that there was some fear that if Mexican banks were allowed to fall under foreign control, the country's limited credit resources might be channeled to foreign-controlled companies in Mexico rather than preferentially to Mexican-owned operations, contrary to governmental policy.[154]

OTHER BASIC INDUSTRIES

The most recent restrictions on foreign investment are contained in a decree issued by President Díaz Ordaz on June 30, 1970,[155] as his administration was coming to an end. Under that decree foreign ownership in new companies formed to engage in the steel, cement, glass, fertilizer, cellulose, or aluminum industry may not exceed 49 percent of the capital stock. Existing companies in operation on the date of the decree are not affected by it, but companies that wish to acquire or install new facilities in any of those industries must comply with the ownership requirements of the decree.

The decree provides that at least 51 percent of the capital stock of companies engaged in the industries named must be subscribed by Mexicans or Mexican companies whose articles of incorporation contain a clause prohibiting foreign ownership. If, however, the vote of more than 51 percent is required by the articles of a company for the adoption of resolutions relating to the operation of the company, that percentage of the capital stock must be Mexican owned. Shares or other ownership interests required to be owned by Mexicans must have full voting rights. If the company concerned is a corporation (sociedad anónima), its capital stock must be represented by two series of shares, one restricted to Mexicans and the other freely transferable. The certificates representing the Mexican shares must state that they may not be assigned to foreigners or to Mexican companies in which foreign ownership is permitted.

Furthermore, the articles of incorporation of affected companies must provide that a majority of the directors shall be elected by the Mexican members or shareholders and that those directors must have Mexican nationality.

Enforcement of the decree is effected through the control of the Ministry of Foreign Relations over the formation of new companies and amendments to the articles of existing companies. The ministry is directed to ensure that the requirements of the decree are met before it issues permits for new incorporations, for amendments to the articles of existing companies, and for acquisitions of businesses or installations in the industries named.

It appears that the initiative for this new measure may have come, at least in part, from the Mexican industrial sector with the concurrence of the Ministries of Industry and Commerce and Finance. Almost certainly, the decree and the policy behind it had the support of President-elect Luis Echeverría, who takes office December 1, 1970, as well as President Díaz Ordaz.

It seems entirely possible, also, that this decree foreshadows the restriction of foreign investment in additional selected industries. The decree recites the necessity of Mexican control of certain basic industries of great importance to the national economy, and it may well be that other industries considered basic to the economy will be subjected to similar restrictions by presidential decree in the future.

IV

Restrictions on Foreign
Investment—The Policies

The fact that the Mexican government has seen fit to enact legislation restricting direct foreign investment in only a relatively small number of industries does not mean that the government has been willing to admit foreign investment without limit in other fields. The absence of a general law on foreign investment has, however, permitted each administration to shape its policies according to its view of the needs and limitations of the economy and, probably to some degree also, the emotional impact of the argument that foreign investment threatens the independence of the country. There has been little consistency in these policies and even less in their enforcement, both from one administration to another and among government agencies within the same administration. Furthermore, where a more or less permanent policy has emerged, its implementation has often been marked by numerous exceptions. In this situation it is, of course, quite difficult to predict with any degree of certainty what the official attitude toward foreign investment generally will be in the future or how that attitude might affect an individual foreign-owned enterprise. There is, nevertheless, a readily discernible and unmistakable trend toward the imposition of increasingly strict conditions upon the entry of foreign investment, and it would be reckless to suppose that there will be any reversal of this trend in the foreseeable future.

Every president since the Revolution has emphasized economic independence as a fundamental principle, and most have gone on record as viewing direct foreign investment with some degree of caution. From the end of the Cárdenas administration in 1940 until near the close of the decade of the 1950's, however, it is difficult to find any clear attempt or even a very strong desire on the part of those in power to take any positive action to limit on a broad front the amount of foreign capital entering the country or otherwise to restrict direct foreign invest-ments in the Mexican economy. The emergency decree of 1944, as we saw in Chapter III, was issued by Avila Camacho as a temporary war-time measure and was not intended as a permanent basis for such limita-tions, and even though it was kept on the statute books by subsequent administrations, its effect was held to a small number of rather insignif-icant industries. The drive that gathered steam in the 1940's toward im-port replacement as a method of stimulating domestic industrialization had the effect of accelerating the already evident trend away from invest-ment in purely assembly operations and toward the establishment of local manufacturing operations by foreign firms, but it did not otherwise restrict foreign investments. Most administrations, firmly committed to industrialization as the key to economic progress and improvement of the lot of the Mexican people, seemed to feel that the continued and largely uncontrolled inflow of foreign capital was necessary even though for political reasons they did not consider it prudent to appear, to the Mexican public at any rate, overly hospitable toward foreign enterprise.

This position seems understandable. After all, the relative amount of foreign investment in the country had been drastically reduced, foreign companies did not pose the threat to economic and political independence that was once feared, and new foreign investments ac-counted for a small portion, about 10 percent, of total investment and were being directed primarily to the production of consumer goods for the domestic market rather than to the sensitive areas of exploitation of natural resources and public services. The emphasis of governments of that period often reflected concerns of the past and took the form of mere verbal insistence that foreign investors should not expect any preferential treatment or meddle in the country's political affairs and should scrupulously adhere to Mexican law and legal institutions and adjust to the "Mexican way of life." They were further told that they should make an affirmative contribution to the country's economic growth by increasing the national product, stimulating diversification of foreign trade, especially to reduce exports of raw materials and imports of manufactured products, and introducing and employing advanced technology. It was sometimes also stated that foreign companies should take a "complementary" role and not compete "unfavorably" or "dis-loyally" with Mexican firms or draw financing from domestic capital sources, which should be reserved for Mexican-owned enterprises. But these conditions may have seemed little more than platitudes and were not the source of any serious reservations on the part of foreign businessmen, especially since there were few real obstacles in the path of new investment projects.

If government spokesmen were often cautious in their public statements, the most important segment of the Mexican business community, adhering to a lingering nineteenth-century liberal philosophy favoring free enterprise generally and opposing state intervention in the economy, openly welcomed private foreign investment. This faction was composed of the representatives of the leading banks and the older established manufacturing and commercial firms, who controlled and made their views known through the confederations of chambers of commerce and industry—CONCANACO and CONCAMIN.[1]

One clear voice had, however, emerged in the mid-1940's in opposition to virtually all foreign enterprise. The difficulty of obtaining traditionally imported goods during World War II had stimulated the establishment of numerous small manufacturing operations, mostly Mexican owned and financed, to supply the domestic market. A common fear of threatened competition from abroad, especially the United States, as wartime conditions and shortages began to subside, drew these small new industrialists together into a cohesive group under aggressive and effective leadership and with well-defined economic policies designed to further their own interests. With the Cámara Nacional de la Industria de la Transformación (national chamber of manufacturing industries— CNIT or CANACINTRA) as their spokesman, they launched a masterful propaganda campaign through the late 1940's and early 1950's, demanding increased government intervention in the economy and maximum protection for domestic industry and attacking direct foreign investment in all forms. Highly nationalistic, they placed the blame for Mexico's main problem, lack of capital, on the "decapitalizing" effect of "colonial" investments and "unplanned" new foreign investments. Even companies with joint Mexican and foreign capital were regarded as harmful to the extent that profits were taken out of the country or reinvested in profit-making operations that would ultimately only compound the balance-of-payments problem. They urged strict government controls to prevent foreign acquisitions of existing Mexican-owned firms and to prohibit all foreign investments in competition with established domestic industries, in the production of articles of direct or intermediate consumption and basic products, and in commercial activities. By references to the United States "policy of economic imperialism" and the use of such terms as "trusts," "monopolies," and "international capital," they appealed to latent Mexican resentment against foreigners, particularly North Americans, and what most Mexicans view as the ruthless exploitation of the country's natural and human resources by giant foreign mining and petroleum companies of the pre-World War II era.[2]

As the rate of inflow of private foreign capital accelerated in the decade of the 1950's, most government economists, though firmly committed to rapid industrialization, came to view foreign investment with increasing concern and tended to regard what they considered its negative effects on the economy as outweighing its contributions to the industrialization process. Many of their arguments seemed to give credence to the emotional appeals of the CNIT: foreign investments are ultimately a drain on the country's foreign-exchange reserves because more capital is exported in the form of profit remittances than enters the country as new investment; foreign-owned companies prefer to import their machinery and intermediate products rather than buy or produce them locally, thus restricting the industrialization process; foreign investments in the production of raw materials for export increase the country's reliance on world market conditions and subject the economy to decisions of foreign firms that have numerous sources of supply and that would have no concern for the effects on the Mexican economy of a decision to close down their operations in Mexico; and foreign-owned companies have the financial resources and technology to destroy incipient Mexican competitors and thus constitute "unfair" or "disloyal" competition.[3] While the merits of many of these arguments are undoubtedly subject to question,[4] they raised issues of genuine concern and were debated with considerable passion.

It was probably impossible for the propaganda offensive from an important segment of the private sector and the arguments of the economic technicians to be entirely disregarded by those responsible for formulating official policies. Whatever the extent of these influences, government attitude toward foreign capital began to shift notably in the late 1950's and early 1960's under the administration of President Adolfo López Mateos. It became increasingly clear that the unrestricted entry of foreign capital into Mexican industrial and commercial activities controlled from abroad would no longer be viewed with a wholly benign eye. Of course, the government still felt that foreign industrial investment was an essential source of capital and technology and government spokesmen were careful not to offend or unduly frighten prospective foreign investors. But the main emphasis came to be "Mexicanization" —that new foreign investors should associate with Mexican capitalists and should ideally take a minority position in new undertakings.

This shift in official policy was accompanied and to some extent preceded by a similar change in the attitudes of the private sector. The commercial interests, feeling the effects of such formidable foreign competition as Sears, Roebuck & Company and F. W. Woolworth & Company, were the first to cool their earlier welcome of foreign investment, and by the mid-1950's spokesmen for CONCANACO were voicing open opposition to further direct foreign investment in commercial activities.[5] The larger industrialists, represented by CONCAMIN, also became more reserved in their advocation of an open-door policy as the growth of their financial and technical resources made them more confident of their own ability to carry the burden of private investment requirements in manufacturing and more eager to share in new projects sponsored by foreign companies anxious to enter the Mexican market. At about the same time, CNIT was becoming less vocal in its opposition to foreign enterprise as many of its members matured into larger and better established concerns and were presented with favorable opportunities to associate with foreign companies. As a result of these shifts in attitude, the divergencies between the two industrial groups tended to disappear and a substantial consensus emerged that foreign investment was a beneficial aid to Mexican economic development if it took a "complementary" role to domestic investment and if foreign firms accepted a minority position in association with Mexican investors so that control would not remain abroad.[6]

The policy of the López Mateos administration to expand the restrictions on foreign investments was most obvious in the field of production and processing of natural resources, where it took the form of statutory limitations, discussed in Chapter III, on investments in mining, petrochemicals, and forestry. In addition, as we have seen, foreign investment was removed from the electric power industry, the only public service remaining under foreign control, through the nationalization of the principal companies in 1960. The tightening of government policy was also reflected in a change in attitude within the two government depart· ments that most directly regulated the entry of foreign enterprise, the Ministries of Foreign Relations and Internal Affairs. The foreign relations ministry began to scrutinize more carefully applications of foreign firms for permits for the formation of new companies and the acquisition of existing companies and, either on its own initiative or on the initiative of other policy-making agencies, expanded the list of activities in which majority Mexican capital was required to include the important industries of food packing and the manufacture of fertilizers, insecticides, and basic chemical products.[7] The Ministry of Internal Affairs, which controls the entry of aliens, became increasingly tightfisted with visa authorizations for foreign management and technical personnel.

Outside of the fields specifically regulated by law or practice of the Ministry of Foreign Relations, implementation of the Mexicanization policy began to take form almost by accident and seemingly with the unwitting assistance of foreign businessmen themselves and their cautious Mexican attorneys. This development took place in the Ministry of Industry and Commerce. The discretionary authority of that ministry is such that the success or failure of an industrial undertaking often rests squarely in its hands. Through its control over import permits, it may prevent the importation of essential machinery, equipment, and raw materials, and may deny import protection to manufacturing firms and allow the entry of competing foreign products that usually sell at lower prices than Mexican-made products.[8] Through persuasion and influence, it may indirectly hamper the import of raw materials for which import permits are not required by bringing about an increase in import duties or at least a denial of a request for a tariff reduction. It may also exercise its influence to prevent the granting of tax exemptions and export subsidies to firms that otherwise qualify for such assistance. In view of this life-or-death power over industry, it is understandable that many foreign companies contemplating the establishment of new industrial facilities in Mexico, often involving large sums of money, wanted some advance assurance that they would be well received and would not be prevented from obtaining necessary imports and in some cases that they would receive tax benefits authorized by the law. Out of this need there began to develop an informal practice of submitting investment projects or manufacturing programs, as they are often called, to the Ministry of Industry and Commerce.

This practice of presenting manufacturing programs had its beginnings in a few industries, including the automobile, automotive parts, office equipment, and tractor industries, in which the government had decided to force domestic production of more intermediate products and component parts. Companies in the automobile industry were required by decree to present programs under which their products would be produced in Mexico with a minimum of 60 percent of domestic cost. In other industries in which the government wished to compel "integration," existing producers were called in by the Ministry of Industry and Commerce and requested to present acceptable programs.[9] Enforcement was effected through the ministry's control over imports; producers were simply told that if they did not come up with satisfactory integration programs, they would not be allowed to import and would be out of the market. While this requirement was not imposed in more than a handful of industries, it at least served as a precedent for the practice that developed among many prospective investors from abroad to clear their projects with the ministry in advance.

In the initial stages of the development of this practice the ministry refused to issue any sort of formal or binding assurance to the prospective investor, but it was usually willing to give an informal indication that the undertaking would be well received but often only after a long period of delay marked with requests for additional information and informal negotiations. Increasingly, the ministry used this clearance process to press prospective foreign investors to associate with Mexican investors, indicating that necessary import permits and other government favors might not be readily available if the project was wholly foreign owned.

There was no requirement in most cases, however, that investment projects be cleared in this way, and many foreign companies continued to establish facilities in the country without any government approval except a permit to incorporate from the Ministry of Foreign Relations. This was especially true in the case of companies that were not dependent to any great extent on imports or other government permits and thus were less vulnerable to such pressures. In a few instances, cautious foreign firms that submitted their projects to the ministry sat helplessly by, waiting out the slow processing and apparent indecision within the ministry, while rival firms that were willing to risk by-passing the clearance process beat them into production. Furthermore, the practice extended only to manufacturing enterprises, and there was little or no effort to control the unrestricted entry of foreign capital into domestic commercial operations.

Whether by accident or design, this practice was the beginning of what became, early in the administration of President Díaz Ordaz, a rather formal, institutionalized procedure for the approval of new investments in manufacturing facilities and substantial expansions of existing operations. This procedure has provided the means for implementing and enforcing government policy to limit foreign-controlled operations and foster associations of capital without the limitations of binding rules and without resort to the enactment of a general law on foreign investments or other broad statutory measures that might unduly alarm foreign businessmen and have the unwanted effect of discouraging the entry of needed foreign capital and technology.[10] Additionally, the government has taken advantage of this clearance procedure to further and enforce policies to achieve other economic goals of high priority—continued import substitution through the stimulation of domestic production of intermediate products and control of prices of finished products to protect the Mexican consumer and restrict inflation and to encourage exports of Mexican manufactures.

Under this procedure as it became formalized in the mid-1960's, the prospective investor presents a written request for approval of his manufacturing program to the Ministry of Industry and Commerce. A detailed description of the program must be filed containing such information as the amount of the projected investment in land, plant, machinery, equipment, and working capital; a time schedule for commencing and completing the project; cost studies showing the distribution of production costs between items of Mexican origin and imported items; and price studies. Although an applicant may save considerable time by filing detailed information on his program with his original application, in most cases the ministry requests additional information or clarification, and final approval of a program usually takes from three to six months.

The ministry's approval of a manufacturing program is conditioned on the fulfillment of certain specified conditions relating not only to percentage of foreign ownership but also, as will be explained in Chapter V, to percentage of production cost of Mexican origin and prices. While these conditions are somewhat flexible and are sometimes negotiable, the terms of the conditions have become rather standardized and at least set a basis for negotiation if the applicant feels that they are not reasonable in his individual case.

The percentage of foreign ownership permitted depends to a substantial extent upon the ownership of existing companies in the same industry. If the applicant seeks to enter an activity in which one or more companies having majority Mexican capital are already engaged, the new company must likewise have majority Mexican ownership. The ministry does not always insist that the percentage of Mexican ownership be the same as in the existing company, and it will usually permit the establishment of a company with Mexican ownership of a simple majority of the shares even though a greater proportion of the shares in the existing company or companies is Mexican owned. If the prospective investor seeks to enter a field in which a wholly foreign-owned company is already engaged or if he seeks to establish a completely new industry, the Ministry of Industry and Commerce tends to be more lenient in permitting foreign control. Even though the ministry attempts to achieve as high a percentage of Mexican participation as it considers possible, often asking for 35 or 40 percent Mexican ownership, the amount is usually subject to negotiation and is often reduced if the applicant is able to convince the ministry that it is not feasible to obtain Mexican investment in the proportion requested. It is not uncommon also for the ministry to allow a period of time, usually two years, for the sale of the specified percentage of shares to Mexican investors. In many cases, especially where a new industry is to be established, the ministry has authorized a wholly foreign-owned company to commence operations on the condition that a portion of its shares will be sold to Mexicans within a designed period of time. During that period the shares to be sold are normally required to be placed in trust with a Mexican bank.

Two important exceptions have been made to the general requirement that new foreign investments be made only in association with Mexican capital. In order to foster employment in the northern border area, the ministry authorizes the establishment of wholly foreign-owned manufacturing and processing operations in the border cities provided Mexican labor is used and the finished products are exported.[11] The low cost of Mexican labor makes this particularly appealing in the case of operations in which labor is an important factor, such as the needle trades and the electronics industry, and a growing number of foreign companies are establishing operations of that type along the border. Also, the ministry has demonstrated a willingness to permit the establishment of a new industry in Mexico with exclusively foreign capital where at least half of its production will be exported.

Despite the fact that there is no legal requirement that a prospective foreign investor submit his program to the Ministry of Industry and Commerce, it is doubtful that many operations of any significance have been established in Mexico by foreign firms since the mid-1960's without the advance approval of that ministry. Not only does this afford some assurance of government co-operation in connection with imports and tariff protection and facilitates obtaining tax concessions by companies that qualify, but it offers other advantages as well. An important consideration has been that firms with an approved manufacturing program have often been given preference over other companies to import the product they will manufacture in Mexico during the period of installation of their plant and other preparations for domestic production. The prospective producer may be the only authorized importer, and he is in effect protected against competing products and is able to develop the market for his product even before he commences production in Mexico. This preferential treatment has been limited primarily to firms that are entering production of a product not being manufactured in the country. If a producer is already established and the new investor will enter competition with it, the Ministry of Industry and Commerce has in most cases heeded the demands of the existing firm for protection against imports of competing finished products and has allowed only limited imports. Nevertheless, in a few instances, apparently in cases in which the government considers that the interests of consumers or established dealers require protection, substantial imports of foreign products have been permitted despite the fact that domestic producers are hard pressed to compete with them.

Not all enterprises have felt it necessary to submit their programs to the Ministry of Industry and Commerce and thus subject themselves to the conditions imposed by the ministry. Some foreign companies effectively avoided this and achieved other advantages by buying controlling interests in existing Mexican companies. Others, particularly firms entering smaller operations and those that do not rely substantially on government authorizations, have proceeded to establish wholly foreign-owned or at least foreign-controlled Mexican companies with only an incorporation permit from the Ministry of Foreign Relations. As pointed out earlier, the purchase by foreigners of existing Mexican companies was halted by the Ministry of Foreign Relations in 1966 under its authority under the emergency decree of 1944, but otherwise there was apparently little co-ordination of policy between the various agencies dealing with foreign investment before late 1967. A prospective investor in a manufacturing facility usually had little difficulty in obtaining a permit from the Ministry of Foreign Relations to form a wholly owned Mexican company, but if he presented his manufacturing program to the Ministry of Industry and Commerce he was normally required to find and associate with Mexican investors and was sometimes told that his Mexican associates must be majority owners.

Toward the end of 1967 there was evidence of a move to unify and co-ordinate government policy in this regard and to broaden the control of the Ministry of Industry and Commerce over the entry of new foreign direct investment and the enforcement of the policy to discourage wholly foreign-owned operations and to promote associations of capital. The first sign of this came in October or November, when it was quietly revealed by the Ministry of Foreign Relations that applications submitted to it for permits to incorporate Mexican companies under the emergency decree of 1944 from which it appeared that the companies concerned would be owned by or affiliated with foreigners or foreign firms would be referred to the Ministry of Industry and Commerce for its consideration as to whether limitations on the percentage of foreign ownership should be imposed. It was implied that the foreign relations ministry would be guided by the opinion of the Ministry of Industry and Commerce and would condition its permits to the terms suggested by that ministry. It thus appeared that the role of the Ministry of Industry and Commerce as the principal foreign investment policy-making agency of the government was to be considerably strengthened and that all new foreign investments would be subjected to its examination. Enforcement of its policy would not be dependent upon pressures based on its control over imports but would be effected directly by the foreign relations ministry. Since it already had power under the 1944 decree to impose limitations on the percentage of foreign ownership of a Mexican company as a condition of its incorporation, no additional statutory authority was required.

The extent to which this policy has been carried out is not entirely clear, nor does it appear certain that it will be fully implemented. The Ministry of Foreign Relations has referred some permit applications to the Ministry of Industry and Commerce, but perhaps because of its heavy workload or because of lack of adequate co-ordination between the two ministries, the Ministry of Industry and Commerce has often failed to reply or has delayed a decision for an unreasonable length of time.

Another potentially significant development came in March, 1968, when plans were disclosed for the establishment of an interministerial committee for the specific purpose of reviewing foreign investment projects. The composition and operating procedures of this committee have not been revealed at the time of this writing, but it is understood that it is intended to be a working group of representatives of various ministries and that all applications for foreign investment projects will be submitted to it for consideration. Presumably, it will have authority to impose restrictions on foreign ownership of new enterprises in all activities and its decisions will undoubtedly be enforced through the control of the Ministry of Foreign Relations over new incorporations. However, whether or not this committee will actually come into being and, if it does, whether or not it will prove more effective than its predecessor of the late 1940's and early 1950's[12] are still matters of conjecture.

The pressures on foreign enterprises to admit Mexican investors have not been limited to new undertakings. Although the policy can more readily be enforced in the case of new investments, most foreign-owned or -controlled companies in operation before the establishment of the present policies have felt some degree of pressure to admit Mexican investors. These pressures have been most direct in the case of larger and more important companies that depend significantly on import permits and other government authorizations, but all foreign enterprises have felt at least a psychological pressure to associate with Mexican capital. In many cases existing companies have been pressed to submit programs to achieve greater integration and have been informed that one of the requirements under the integration programs will be the sale to Mexican investors of a majority or substantial ownership interest. These pressures to Mexicanize existing foreign-controlled companies reached a peak in about mid-1966, but in the face of strong resistance the government retreated somewhat and the Ministry of Industry and Commerce let it be known that companies that were already in operation would not be required to Mexicanize merely because of an integration program. Nevertheless, companies that wished to engage in a new line of production, it was revealed, would be treated the same as entirely new producers and would be subject to the Mexicanization requirement with respect to their new activity. This meant that if an existing company wanted to go into a new line of producton, it was faced with the alternative of either selling to Mexican investors an interest in the company itself or forming a new company in association with Mexican capital to engage in the new undertaking. As a result of these pressures and in some cases because companies have decided that it will be to their advantage, especially in the long run, a number of foreign-controlled companies that have been in operation for years have sold share interests publicly or to private Mexican investor groups.

These pressures have also encouraged foreign-controlled enterprises to increase the role of Mexicans in their management. There is no general statutory requirement relating to the nationality of management personnel of Mexican companies, but it is obvious to most observers that companies in which Mexican directors and managers predominate receive more favorable treatment in their dealings with the government at all levels than do companies that have substantial numbers of foreign personnel. That is not to say that there is flagrant discrimination, but some differences in attitude and willingness to assist are noticeable.

There seems to be little doubt that Mexicanization of industry is a long-range policy, and no reversal of that policy is foreseen. Highly significant also is the Mexican government's attitude that this policy should be extended to the other members of the Latin American Free Trade Association. The president and other officials have stated that industry in LAFTA should be controlled preferably by domestic capital, next by Latin-American capital, and with lowest priority, foreign capital. In his annual report to the Congress on September 1, 1967, President Díaz Ordaz stated: "We see Latin-American integration as a great effort of all our people to constitute an economic community capable of dealing equitably with the rich and powerful country to the north. We do not attempt to create, opposite a great agricultural and industrial power, another that comes to quarrel with it, but to understand one another on the highest planes of respect and dignity."

Thus far, the policy to encourage foreign investors to associate with Mexican capital must, on the whole, be judged a success. Most foreign enterprises have accepted it as a necessary price for admission to the lucrative Mexican market and have been pleased with their associations with Mexican investors.[13] From Mexico's standpoint, it does not seem likely that the Mexicanization policy has deterred the entry of new foreign capital essential to its continued economic progress.[14]

V

Other Policies Affecting the
Conduct of Enterprises

Enterprises in Mexico, whether foreign owned or indigenous, operate within a complex framework of laws, institutions, and policies for the control and development of the economy. The Mexican government has for many years been firmly committed to industrialization as the most effective means of increasing the real income and living standards of its population and has made substantial efforts to promote industrial development. Many of the policies formulated for this purpose have encouraged the entry of foreign enterprises and have operated to their benefit, though no special incentives have been offered to foreign investment as such. As development policy has been adapted to meet changing circumstances and as the government's attention has been directed toward objectives other than mere industrialization, however, controls have been imposed that have increasingly restricted the freedom of operation of private industry. One important objective of economic policy, promotion of Mexican participation in enterprises and discouragement of wholly foreign-owned companies—Mexicanization, as it is often called—has been discussed in Chapter IV. This chapter focuses on some of the other important economic policies that affect the conduct of enterprises in Mexico.

IMPORT CONTROLS

Most developing countries bent on industrialization to provide jobs for a fast-growing population and to achieve adequate rates of growth find it necessary at one time or another to protect domestic industry against the competition of imports. Mexico is no exception. Protectionism has always been a feature of Mexican import policy, but it has been only since World War II that the policy has been applied broadly as an instrument for import replacement and industrial development.[1] Issues of protection and industrialization have not always been the only, or even the primary, consideration in the formulation of Mexico's import policy—other and more complex objectives have been sought from time to time relating to such matters as balance-of-payments difficulties, government revenue requirements, and issues of internal price levels and inflation. However, protectionism has always been at least a by-product of import policy, and restrictions and tariffs adopted to handle other problems have operated to encourage the development of domestic production to replace imports.

This policy has had a dramatic impact on the role of foreign enterprises in the country's economy. Companies that once supplied the Mexican consumer goods market by export sales from their plants in foreign countries were forced to establish production facilities in Mexico or forfeit the market as prohibitive tariffs or import restrictions were imposed on their products. At the same time, companies that entered production in Mexico were assured a protected market, amounting in many cases to a virtual monopoly. As a result, investment in manufacturing increased substantially and imports of consumer goods fell sharply. In the 1940's and into the 1950's these facilities were often merely assembly operations—a manufacturer could usually circumvent the import restrictions and obtain protection for his product by installing a plant for the assembly or final processing of raw materials and semifinished goods that he imported, perhaps from his factory across the border in the United States or elsewhere. Beginning in the early 1960's, however, the Mexican government began to move decisively against the indiscriminate establishment of assembly plants and to extend the protectionist policy to secondary and auxiliary industries. As a result of this policy of industrial integration, discussed in the next section of this chapter, new investments are being channeled into the production of intermediate goods and integrated manufacturing operations, and a foreign enterprise that seeks to establish an assembly plant dependent primarily upon imported raw materials and parts will no longer likely find a receptive ear.[2]

Until recently, the Mexican government has largely avoided international commitments that would restrict its freedom to shape import policy to meet its needs and circumstances. The only exception to this before 1960 was a reciprocal trade agreement entered into with the United States in 1942, which bound the parties not to increase tariff rates or impose quantitative controls on certain products. Opposition that developed in Mexico, however, led to termination of the agreement by mutual consent in 1950. Furthermore, Mexico has consistently declined to participate in the General Agreement on Tariffs and Trade (GATT). The only significant departure from this no-agreement policy was made in 1960 when Mexico became a party to the Treaty of Montevideo, creating the Latin American Free Trade Association. Its participation in LAFTA has resulted in a substantial increase in trade with other Latin American countries.

Import policy is effectuated through two types of control—tariffs and quantitative restrictions—formulated and administered by the executive branch of the federal government. Article 131 of the Constitution gives to the federal government the exclusive power to levy duties on imports and exports and provides that the Congress may authorize the executive to establish, modify, or abolish tariff rates and to restrict or prohibit imports and exports "to regulate foreign trade, the economy of the country, the stability of domestic production, or to accomplish any other purpose to the benefit of the country."[3] This authority was customarily granted to the executive each year in the annual revenue laws until 1961, when a permanent law was enacted for this purpose.[4] Under this law the executive has complete authority to fix tariff rates, the only requirement being that the Congress be informed annually of the exercise of this authority and its approval requested. The executive is also authorized to establish quantitative controls by determining the maximum amount of financial resources applicable to specific imports. Authority to impose restrictions on imports and exports is also found in the 1950 law on powers of the federal executive in economic matters.[5]

Within the executive branch the administration of import controls is divided between the Ministry of Finance and the Ministry of Industry and Commerce. The 1961 act provides that authority over tariff rates shall be exercised by both ministries, "pursuant to provisions in effect." This seems to be a reference to the law of state ministries and departments of 1958, which makes the Ministry of Industry and Commerce responsible for fixing tariffs "in consultation with the Ministry of Finance."[6] With respect to quantitative controls, the 1961 act provides that the finance ministry shall determine the total financial resources that may be applied to imports and assigns responsibility to the Ministry of Industry and Commerce for fixing import restrictions and determining what products will be restricted. A decree issued in 1948 also authorizes the Ministry of Industry and Commerce to amend the list of products subject to import control, directing that the finance ministry be consulted in cases in which national revenue might be affected.[7] The coordination between the two ministries contemplated in the laws of 1958 and 1961 has been put into practice only to a limited extent. In fact, the Ministry of Industry and Commerce administers quantitative controls and the Ministry of Finance continues to be primarily responsible for tariff policy, though the Ministry of Industry and Commerce has had an increasingly larger voice in the formulation of that policy in recent years.

The existing tariff system was originally adopted in 1947 and has been revised from time to time since then, mainly to establish new specific classifications to reflect changes in the composition of imports. The current import tariff became effective in 1964,[8] restructuring the classification system to conform to the Brussels nomenclature.

Duties are levied by a system of compound rates—specific and ad valorem. Specific duties are based on weight or, in some cases, units of merchandise. The ad valorem duty is levied on either the invoice price or an official valuation, whichever is higher. Official prices are established by the Ministry of Finance on the basis of market price studies to prevent underinvoicing and exist on most products. Individual tariff rates are subject to frequent change and basically reflect a policy to protect the market for domestic goods and to discourage imports of luxury items. The rates are generally high—50 to 100 percent or even higher—on consumer goods and other items produced in Mexico and articles considered luxury goods but moderate on raw materials and capital goods not domestically produced or produced in insufficient quantity. An additional ad valorem duty of 10 percent has been provided for on a large number of products in the annual federal revenue laws since 1963.[9] In addition to the import duties, a customs surtax of 10 percent of the duty is levied on imports by mail and 3 percent on other imports.

Total or partial exemption from import duties and customs surtaxes may be granted to companies that qualify for tax benefits under the law for the promotion of new and necessary industries[10] and to certain enterprises operating under a government concession. Temporary exemptions from duties or subsidies amounting in effect to reductions of duties are occasionally granted to private enterprises, especially those that are in the process of establishing a plant for the manufacture of a new product. Under the border industrialization program discussed below and in certain other instances, the Ministry of Finance may authorize the temporary importation of goods free of duty, for which a bond must be posted to guarantee that the goods will be subsequently exported or will not be used for purposes other than those for which their entry was permitted.

Even more effective than tariff policy as an instrument of import control are quantitative restrictions imposed under an import-licensing system. Since the license requirement was initially applied in 1947,[11] the number of items subject to import license has steadily increased in response primarily to balance-of-payments crises and requests of private producers for protection. Regardless of the reason for subjecting an item to the license requirement, however, once it is added to the list it is rarely removed. Import licenses are now required for some 80 percent of the products imported into Mexico.

The Ministry of Industry and Commerce has virtually unlimited authority over the granting of import licenses. Annual quotas are assigned for some products, mostly luxury goods such as cigarettes, wines, whiskey, quality fabrics, and wrist watches, and are allocated to individual importers in proportion to the amounts they previously imported. For most products, however, the ministry decides whether to approve or deny applications on a case-by-case basis according to the circumstances, and its decisions are not a matter of public record. It may thus reduce or restrict imports of certain products without prior notice or grant licenses to some importers and deny them to others.

Representatives of the private sector play an active and important role in the decision-making process. License applications are customarily submitted to advisory committees that function within the ministry, which recommend granting or denying a license. Each committee is responsible for a specific group of products or industry and is made up of an official of the Ministry of Industry and Commerce, who acts as chairman, and representatives of the organizations of private industry and commerce, according to the product group covered by the committee. In mid-1967 there were 55 committees meeting twice a week and handling some 20,000 import license requests a month. The growing importance of these committees is indicated by the fact that their number more than doubled in the six-year period 1961-67.

The criteria for the committees' recommendations on license applications are based on regulations issued by the ministry in 1956.[12] These regulations establish a presumption against granting a license. Licenses may be issued "when the domestic product is obtainable only under conditions that compare unfavorably with the foreign product, with respect to quality and time of delivery." Also, licenses may be issued when no domestic substitute is available, local production is insufficient to supply the internal market, temporary scarcity occurs, or a reserve of raw materials or manufactured goods is needed. In practice, the most important consideration has been whether the product or a substitute for it is or can be produced in Mexico. If a private sector representative on the committee demonstrates that a domestic manufacturer can produce the product in sufficient quantity and of satisfactory quality, it is usually recommended that the import license be denied.

Until rather recently, prices of domestic products were not generally taken into consideration in individual decisions. The government was committed to the view that industrialization and the creation of employment justified the higher cost of domestic products. Beginning in 1966, however, attention has increasingly been directed toward the price element, and in many cases the ministry has granted licenses for competing imports where the price of the domestic product greatly exceeds that of the foreign product.

Despite the importance of the committees on import licensing, their role is still purely advisory and the ministry may accept or reject their recommendations. Since the ministry does not notify the committees of the ultimate disposition of the applications they have considered and is not even bound to submit all applications to them, it is difficult to verify to what extent their recommendations are followed. At times in the past it has appeared that little heed has been paid to the advisory committees, but during the mid-1960's the ministry seemed to place substantial reliance on them and apparently adopted their recommendations in the great majority of cases.[13]

If an application for an import license is denied, the applicant may request reconsideration by the ministry. Importers do not usually resort to formal appeals, however, since refusal of a license does not necessarily mean that a subsequent application will be denied and because importers consider it important, given the lack of consistent and objective criteria for granting licenses, to maintain the good will of the government officials responsible for making import-licensing decisions.

Beginning in 1965, the ministry has in recent years taken several steps to simplify and expedite the administrative handling of applications for import licenses. A procedure for issuing open-end licenses for products not manufactured in Mexico has been initiated, under which an importer may be permitted to import merchandise required for a period of six months to a year without obtaining separate licenses for each transaction. Also, while decisions on license applications normally take at least one to two weeks, a procedure has been established by which importers who are in urgent need of parts and accessories may obtain licenses within seventy-two hours if the quantities to be imported do not adversely affect domestic producers. There has also been established a special office to expedite the handling of license requests from importers located outside Mexico City.

INDUSTRIAL INTEGRATION

The term industrial integration is applied in Mexico to the domestic production of a commodity from domestic raw materials and intermediate products and other Mexican-source supplies. It does not necessarily imply that a manufacturer itself controls sources of supply and carries through production from the raw material stage to the finished product but merely that its supplies are domestically produced rather than imported. The degree of integration of a particular manufacturer or industry thus indicates the percentage of its end product that is of Mexican origin or the proportion of its direct cost of production that is expended in Mexico. The promotion of integration has become a cornerstone of Mexican economic policy of the 1960's, and most new investments in industry and many established enterprises are affected by it. Though import replacement has long been a primary objective of government policy, active promotion of the domestic manufacture of production goods is of rather recent origin. It is, nevertheless, an understandable consequence of changes in the Mexican economy that began some years earlier.

For several years after World War II the government's protectionist policy was successful in encouraging heavy investments in domestic production to supply the expanding internal market and a rapid rate of import replacement. It was probably inevitable, however, that the policy of simply eliminating competitive imports, directed mainly at consumer goods, did not produce the sustained and accelerated economic growth that was expected of it. For one thing, while imports of consumer goods were sharply reduced, demand for imports shifted to raw materials, intermediate products, and capital goods, upon which domestic producers were largely dependent. Even though the industrial sector gradually increased somewhat its use of domestic production goods, the policy of granting protection more or less indiscriminately to domestically produced consumer goods encouraged the establishment of numerous plants for the mere assembly of imported components. Furthermore, the possibilities for expanding domestic production of consumer goods began to disappear. By the mid-1950's it seemed apparent that the existing import replacement policy was nearing the end of the line and that the country's reliance on imports of production goods was a restraint on further industrialization.[14]

An effort to discourage the establishment of assembly operations and to stimulate industrial integration was first made through the restriction of tax benefits available under the law for the promotion of new and necessary industries of 1955 to businesses in which at least 60 percent of direct cost of production is incurred in Mexico. This seems to have had little success, however, in accelerating the rate of integration. Investors in production facilities were apparently willing to forego the tax exemptions offered by the law, particularly as long as their imports of intermediate products and machinery were not cut off, and the problems involved in shifting from imports to domestic goods—higher costs and difficulties with quality control and delivery schedules—discouraged voluntary integration to any significant degree.

The need to stimulate the import replacement process through industrial integration became increasingly acute between 1955 and 1960, when a decline in the growth of exports and an increase in quantity and cost of imports resulted in heavy deficits in the current account of Mexico's balance of payments. The government, however, was slow to concentrate on industrial integration to meet the problem of this drain and resorted instead to the easier alternative of increasing its reliance on foreign capital, both public and private, to cover the deficit in current account. The reasons for this refusal to extend the protectionist policy to production goods are not entirely clear, but it has been suggested that the government may have been motivated by a desire to avoid price increases that would inevitably result from the use of higher cost domestic products and the desire to attract foreign investment, especially in industry.[15]

After 1959, however, the government's attention turned increasingly to integration as a means of accelerating industrialization, and import replacement of production goods has become an objective of high priority. In some cases the government has persuaded producers to increase their use of domestic raw materials and intermediate products by threatening to allow competitive imports unless an acceptable degree of integration is achieved. At times particular industries have been singled out because of their importance to the domestic economy or the relative amounts of their imports, either of finished goods or of intermediate products, and the policy has been enforced by the imposition of more or less formal requirements on all producers or importers in an industry. More recently, the policy has been extended to most new producers that seek government co-operation in connection with imports. The automobile industry was the first to be subjected to a formal requirement of integration and is a good example of how the policy has been applied.

Automobile assembly plants were established in Mexico by the principal United States producers as early as the 1920's and 1930's to supply the domestic market, but they continued to rely heavily on foreign parts and supplies. While some domestically produced parts were being used by the early 1960's, components representing an estimated 75 to 80 percent of the cost of the vehicles were still being imported. The fact that vehicles and automotive parts and supplies made up the largest single category of imports was undoubtedly an important consideration in the government's selection of that industry as the first major target of its integration policy. Furthermore, the industry's reliance on many auxiliary suppliers offered the opportunity to achieve import replacement of a large number of products.

A necessary step for the development of a national automobile industry was the reduction of the number of models on the market. The advantages of large-scale production could not possibly be achieved if an attempt was made to produce component parts locally for the large number of motor vehicle types that were then being assembled in Mexico. As what was later officially, though illogically, explained as the first step in the reduction process, the government in 1959 authorized a substantial increase in the number of models on the market and permitted the importation of small finished cars, which had been prohibited since 1947. Of the forty-four makes and some one hundred models that were available as a consequence, the government gradually reduced the number of makes and models allowed, apparently on the basis of consumer preference, eliminating most of the highest priced cars.

This reduction in the number of models paved the way for the establishment of a national automobile industry, but government compulsion was necessary. On August 23, 1962, a decree was issued[16] requiring assembly plants to present to the Ministry of Industry and Commerce integration programs that would lead to the production, by September 1, 1964, of vehicles at least 60 percent of whose direct cost of production was incurred in Mexico. These programs were required to set out plans for the domestic manufacture of parts, the amount of new plant investment proposed, parts whose continued import was considered necessary, and other details. The automobile companies themselves were required to establish facilities for engine machining, but all other domestic parts to be used were required by the ministry to be obtained from independent suppliers. The decree provided that after September 1, 1964, the importation of complete motors and assembled mechanical components for cars and trucks would be prohibited. Enforcement of the integration requirement was thus simple and direct—a company either complied or was out of the Mexican market. An incentive to reach a higher degree of integration than the required minimum was established by a provision in the decree allowing the ministry to grant exemptions from the requirement of import permits for components to companies at least 70 percent of whose direct cost of production is incurred in Mexico. To stimulate exports, the decree also permits the ministry to authorize approved companies to import special parts and vehicles not produced in Mexico of a value equal to their exports of Mexican-made vehicles, parts, and tools.

The period allowed for the submission of these programs—less than two months—was too short for such a large undertaking and was extended twice. By the end of 1963 integration plans had been presented by eighteen companies, of which only ten were found to comply with the requirements of the decree. Two of the companies whose plans were accepted failed to proceed with their projects, but by 1964 eight companies had begun to carry into effect their programs under government authorization for the manufacture of a total of approximately 100,000 vehicles.[17] The government was sympathetic to the problems of the companies in meeting the original deadline of September 1, 1964, and new periods for compliance were established administratively for each company according to the difficulties encountered. By the end of 1965, however, most of the producers had met the requirements of the integration program and were turning out basically Mexican-made cars and trucks.

The biggest problem that the companies had to overcome was the location of domestic suppliers of parts that the companies were not themselves allowed to make, approximately 45 percent of the 60 percent Mexican content required.[18] Heavy investments were made in the auxiliary industries, but the automobile companies were often required to seek out and furnish financial and technical assistance to their suppliers to enable them to meet their needs, and difficulties with quality control, high costs, and unreliable delivery schedules were substantial. Although a majority of the capital stock of new auxiliary companies was required by government policy to be Mexican owned, a number of foreign companies associated with Mexican investors to establish plants to manufacture parts and supplies for the industry.

While application of the integration policy has been most spectacular in the automobile industry, other important industries have been subjected to similar requirements, including the diesel engine, electronics, construction machinery, tractor, and office equipment industries. In industries that have not been singled out for this purpose, the policy is applied to prospective producers that seek assurance from the Ministry of Industry and Commerce that they will be protected against competing imports or will be granted permits for parts and machinery required to be imported. The development of the extra-legal procedure for the clearance of new manufacturing projects and substantial expansions of existing operations with the ministry, described in Chapter IV, has facilitated implementation of the policy. As a sort of *quid pro quo* for the ministry's approval of a manufacturing program, the manufacturer is required to agree that a specified percentage of his direct cost of production will be incurred in Mexico. The government's control of import licenses gives it a highly effective means of enforcing a company's commitment in this respect.

The ministry's objective in most cases is to require 60 percent integration, and it is customary to allow a period of time to achieve this goal, usually two years from the commencement of production. However, neither the amount of Mexican cost nor the time for reaching it is entirely inflexible, and different requirements may be established by negotiation in individual cases. Primary considerations are the price at which the finished products will be sold, the possibility of developing export sales, and the importance of the industry to the Mexican economy. If the use of a high percentage of domestic parts and supplies would result in domestic prices that are excessively above international levels, if a substantial part of a firm's production will be exported, or if the industry in question will make an important contribution to economic growth, there is greater likelihood that the firm will be permitted to import a larger proportion of its supplies or that it will be allowed a longer period of time to reach the level of integration required. Once these requirements are established for the initial producer in an industry, they are applied to all subsequent producers in the same industry.

The integration requirement is stated in terms of "direct cost of production," the meaning of which is taken from the law for the promotion of new and necessary industries.[19] As defined in that law, direct cost of production comprises the cost of raw materials and intermediate components, fuel and power, wages and fringe benefits paid to workers participating directly in production, and a factor for depreciation of machinery, equipment, and buildings that may not exceed 10 percent of the aggregate of the other direct-cost components. The portion of direct cost that is considered to be of Mexican origin is the total cost of direct labor even if the company employs some foreign workers, raw materials and components either produced in Mexico by the company itself or bought from other domestic manufacturers, fuel and power bought in Mexico, and depreciation. A component produced locally, either by the manufacturer of the finished product or another domestic producer, is considered to be of Mexican origin even though it may contain imported parts. Thus, the true domestic content of the final product may be less than 60 percent, but as the integration policy is extended to the secondary and auxiliary industries, this will undoubtedly increase. Furthermore, where the cost of components acquired from other producers represents a substantial part of the cost of the finished product, or where components are produced by a company affiliated with the manufacturer, the present policy of the Ministry of Industry and Commerce is to consider only the content of the component that is of Mexican origin for purposes of determining the percentage of the finished product that is of Mexican origin.

The government seems to have had considerable success in stimulating import replacement of intermediate products by compelling industrial integration. This is not to say that there have been no difficulties. Although many new auxiliary industries have been established, producers who formerly depended heavily on imports have often been plagued with problems of costs, quality, and delivery schedules. In many cases suppliers with no past experience in the production processes involved have had to go into production with undue speed, and resulting inefficiencies, together with market limitations on volume, have often resulted in high costs, defects in quality, and unreliable deliveries. These probems should tend to decrease in importance as suppliers learn how to produce more efficiently and as the size of the market increases. The government has also directed considerable attention to the problem of holding prices within reasonable limits, which is the subject of the next section.

PRICE CONTROL

Two basic concerns have given rise to government regulation of prices of domestic goods—protection of Mexican consumers, especially those in lower- and middle-income brackets, against excessive increases in the cost of essential goods, and more recently the realization that the country must increase its exports of manufactures if it is to maintain a satisfactory rate of industrial growth. The high cost of production of most Mexican manufactured goods is the principal obstacle to export sales, and much of the blame is placed on high prices of many domestic raw materials and semifinished products that have resulted from the indiscriminate protection of local industry against foreign imports and the difficulty of achieving economies of scale because of the limited size of the domestic market. The government has attacked these problems both through specific price-control legislation, aimed primarily at basic consumer goods and raw materials, and by administrative action to control prices of manufactured goods.

The statute under which prices are regulated, the law on powers of the federal executive in economic matters,[20] has been described as the country's most important legislation on state intervention in the economy with the sole exception of certain provisions of the 1917 Constitution.[21] Although certain price control authority, primarily in connection with basic consumer necessities, had existed for a number of years under the monopolies law of 1934, discussed below, this law went substantially beyond any prior legislation in its grant of regulatory authority over prices and other aspects of the country's economy as well. Enacted at the end of 1950 for the stated purpose of protecting domestic industry and consumers against shortages and excessive price increases that were being felt and were feared would be intensified as a result of the Korean war and the restriction of exports from the United States,[22] the law has been retained as an instrument of permanent economic policy.

The law on economic powers of the executive grants authority to the federal executive branch to establish maximum wholesale and retail prices and to freeze existing market prices on products included in any of six broad categories—basic foodstuffs, articles of clothing, raw materials essential to domestic industry, products of basic industries, goods produced by important domestic industries, and generally "products that represent considerable items of Mexican economic activity."[23] By a 1959 amendment, services that affect the production and distribution of those goods, except services for which rates are established by the government, were included within the law, and an exception originally made for luxury goods was deleted. The president is given the authority to designate the goods and services to be included under those general categories and thus is empowered to determine precisely what will be subject to control.

In addition to control over prices, broad authority is given to the executive to regulate the distribution and production of goods covered by the law and to control imports and exports. Under the authority over distribution, priorities may be established and rationing imposed when supplies are insufficient to satisfy demand, preferences in the use of goods may be fixed, channels of distribution may be regulated to prevent price increases by reason of unnecessary or excessive intermediaries, and stores of merchandise may be required to be sold to prevent hoarding. Producers of raw materials and manufacturers are required to satisfy the domestic market before they may export their products, and their domestic prices may not be higher than those at which they sell in foreign markets. Production of covered products may be regulated through the authority to specify what goods factories must produce and the authority to effect temporary occupations of industrial enterprises when that is necessary to maintain or increase production or to enforce government action under the law.[24]

The powers granted by the law are exercisable by either the president or the minister of industry and commerce, who is also entrusted with the administration of the law, except that designations of goods and services to be covered and requirements as to production and temporary occupations of production facilities may be made only by presidential decree.[25] Penalties for violation of the law may be imposed by administrative action and include fines of up to 50,000 pesos, temporary or permanent closing in the case of retail establishments, and detention.[26]

Shortly after enactment of the law, President Miguel Alemán issued a decree specifying the products to be included in each of the first five categories covered by the law, and some additions have been made to the list by subsequent decrees.[27] No designation of services has been made, and consequently price regulation has not been extended to them. The more important of the goods included in each category are as follows:

Basic foodstuffs: most food grains; flour; bread; beans; potatoes; salt; lard; vegetable oils; fresh, condensed, powdered, and evaporated milk; coffee; sugar; ice; meat; eggs; fish; bottled waters and soft drinks; and all packaged food products.

Articles of clothing: commonly used cotton fabrics; shoes; and hides and leather for the manufacture of shoes.

Industrial raw materials: most metallic minerals, such as copper, lead, zinc, tin, and iron; coal and coke; sulphur; scrap iron, steel, and copper; certain industrial chemicals, such as caustic soda, soda ash, sulphuric acid, and copper sulphate; crude rubber; latex; nylon; alcohol; lumber for construction; animal feed; and cotton, sesame, and flax seeds.

Industrial products: products of the iron and steel industry; petroleum fuels and lubricants; cement; paper products; and certain construction materials.

Products of important domestic industries: medicines; rubber tires and tubes; cotton and wool; soap and detergents; cellulose; artificial vegetable fibers; kraft paper; automobiles; trucks and buses; agricultural tractors, implements, and tools; automotive parts and accessories; containers for articles of primary necessity; cigarettes; and matches.

Prices may be controlled either by the freezing of existing market prices or by the establishment of official maximum prices. In almost all cases, the presidential decrees designating products to be covered by the law have also frozen the wholesale and retail prices of those products existing on the dates of publication of the decrees. Official prices on many products have subsequently been established by the Ministry of Industry and Commerce upon requests for price increases. Under either type of control, prices may not be increased without authorization of the ministry pursuant to criteria and procedures set out in the regulations to the law.[28] In determining whether to authorize price increases, for example, the ministry may not take into consideration increases in costs that can be absorbed by the producer or distributor, so long as there remains a reasonable profit.

To assist the minister of industry and commerce in the exercise of his functions under the law, the regulations provide for a national price commission, an advisory body composed of representatives of various government ministries and financial institutions and representatives of the commercial and industrial chambers and labor and farm worker organizations. Provision is also made for special committees for various branches of producton and distribution to make studies of costs, prices, problems of production and distribution, and other matters on the ministry's request, and for local price and distribution committees throughout the country to perform similar investigatory functions and to assist in the enforcement within their geographical areas of resolutions issued under the law.[29] It does not appear, however, that these organizations have ever been very active, if they have in fact functioned at all, and investigatory and other administrative functions are performed primarily by the ministry's general bureau of prices.

Enactment of the law caused considerable consternation in the business community, and it was severely criticized by almost all the commercial and industrial chambers and other organizations, one responsible critic even warning that it might lead to "collectivism and totalitarian tyranny."[30] It has also been argued that the law is unconstitutional, in that the Constitution contains no delegation of power to the federal government to regulate prices, and that it violates certain fundamental rights guaranteed by the Constitution, such as the right to engage in the occupation of one's choice under article 4, the right of property under article 14, and the guarantee of free competition under article 28.[31] It was perhaps in anticipation of those objections that the constitutional basis for the law was set out in some detail in its statement of purposes: article 4, under which exercise of the freedom of industry, commerce, and occupation may be limited "when the rights of society are offended"; article 27, by which private property rights may be limited in the public interest; and article 73, section X, granting legislative jurisdiction to the federal government in matters of commerce. While its validity does not seem to have been decided directly by the courts, the Supreme Court has on several occasions rendered decisions interpreting the law and has upheld price control resolutions issued under it, an apparent indication that the Court considers it valid.[32]

In the eighteen years since its enactment, exercise of the authority granted by the law has been limited to the regulation of prices, principally of important consumer goods and industrial raw materials. While the importance of these controls cannot be denied, the large-scale state intervention in the economy permitted by the law and originally feared by many has not materialized and does not seem likely. Nevertheless, legislative sanction exists not only for the establishment of price controls on virtually any product that the president may consider of sufficient importance and related services, but also, under some circumstances, for government regulation of distribution and even direct intervention in the country's production facilities.

More recent concern on the part of manufacturers and merchants has centered on the extreme reluctance of the Ministry of Industry and Commerce to approve price increases on many goods covered by the law, especially basic foodstuffs and other consumer products of general use, despite rising costs of production. However, with respect to other products there has been little or no pressure for price increases, and in some cases present market prices are lower than the authorized ceilings. In part this is a result of the fact that ceiling prices for many articles were established or frozen shortly after World War II, when existing prices were artificially high.

Apart from this statutory authority to regulate prices, the Ministry of Industry and Commerce has for several years exerted effective administrative control over prices of many manufactured products not covered by the law on powers of the federal executive in economic matters. Under what has become, especially since about 1965, a formalized procedure, discussed in Chapter IV, many new industrial investments are submitted to the ministry's scrutiny before they are made. While this is not required by law, the ministry's control over imports is such that most prospective investors in manufacturing facilities, especially if imports of machinery, raw materials, or components are required or if protection against competing imports is to be sought, consider it essential to obtain advance approval of the ministry. Because this procedure enables the ministry to enforce important economic policies, including control of prices, the ministry understandably encourages the practice and since late 1966 has even attempted with some success to force a number of established manufacturing enterprises to submit similar programs for approval.

One of the conditions invariably imposed for the approval of a manufacturing program is the maximum price at which the product to be manufactured may be sold. This price is usually calculated as a percentage of the price in the country of the product's origin, and in some cases the specific price is established in the ministry's authorization. Customarily, the Mexican price may not exceed 125 percent of the price in the country of origin, which is considered to be the country in which the product was first manufactured, provided it is still manufactured there. In a few instances, a notable example being the automobile industry, higher prices have been permitted where domestic manufacture of the product is considered important to the country's economic development and where the cost of domestic production has been shown to require higher prices. The proportion of the direct cost of production that is incurred in Mexico has in some instances also been taken into account in fixing prices. If, for example, Mexican cost is only a small percentage of total production cost, the maximum price may be lower than is normally permitted. Any increase in prices authorized under a manufacturing program must be approved by the ministry on the basis of cost studies, and many manufacturers have found the ministry less than receptive to requests for price increases, even where a significant increase in production cost is shown. In view of the government's determination to increase exports of manufactures, it seems unlikely that the ministry will loosen its hold on prices within the foreseeable future.

TAX EXEMPTIONS

FEDERAL TAX EXEMPTIONS

A program of tax concessions has been an important part of the Mexican government's policy to stimulate industrial development at least since 1941. During the decade of the 1940's tax exemptions were granted rather indiscriminately to almost any new industry, but by the early 1950's the government had adopted important administrative restrictions to control more carefully the amount of tax relief granted. These restrictions were incorporated in a new law, the law for the promotion of new and necessary industries of December 31, 1954,[33] which became effective in 1955 and is still in force. Application of the tax exemption program under this law has been more selective and has tended to favor larger and more important enterprises. At the same time, tax concessions have come to be used to promote policies and objectives other than mere industrialization, for example, the encouragement of Mexican control of domestic industry, the promotion of employment and training of Mexicans in technical and other positions, and the limitation of remittances abroad for foreign licenses and technical assistance. In fact, the implementation of these policies through the imposition of conditions on exempted firms has seemingly become, from the standpoint of the government, the most important aspect of the tax exemption program, and tax concessions are used primarily as a device for encouraging new enterprises to submit voluntarily to government regulation. While these conditions have undoubtedly discouraged some firms from seeking benefits under the law, it seems to be generally admitted that the tax concessions available may have the effect of significantly increasing a company's profits. Furthermore, import duties on capital goods and raw materials have tended to increase over the past few years, with the result that exemptions have acquired greater economic importance.

Under the law for the promotion of new and necessary industries and its regulations, exemptions from or reductions of various federal taxes may be granted to Mexican companies engaged in industrial production or services that are considered important for the economic development of the country. Although the law provides for the division of the more important administrative responsibilities between the Ministry of Industry and Commerce and the Ministry of Finance, in practice the law is administered jointly by those ministries and to some extent by the Banco de México.

Qualification of a manufacturing enterprise for tax benefits under the law depends upon its classification as either new or necessary.[34] New industries are defined as those which are engaged in the manufacture or fabrication of goods not previously produced in Mexico, provided that they are not mere substitutes for goods already being produced and provided that they are an important contribution to the country's economic development.[35] Necessary industries are those that are engaged in the manufacture of goods that are produced in the country but in quantities insufficient for domestic consumption, provided that the shortage is substantial and not merely temporary.[36] The regulations provide that a substantial shortage exists if domestic production falls short of apparent domestic consumption by at least 20 percent and if existing industrial capacity is insufficient to satisfy the demand, and a company must be able to meet at least 20 percent of the existing deficit in order to qualify as necessary,[37] but these requirements are rarely applied in practice.

In no case may an enterprise be considered new or necessary unless it performs a significant amount of manufacturing, that is, adds substantial value to the raw materials or semifinished products used. Value added is considered substantial if it is at least 10 percent of the total direct cost of production.[38] A further requirement for qualification is that at least 60 percent of direct cost of manufacturing be incurred in Mexico.[39] For purposes of both of these requirements, direct cost is defined as the aggregate cost of raw materials and finished and semifinished articles used in the end product, fuel and other materials required in the manufacturing process, electric power used directly in production, direct labor, and depreciation of buildings, installations, machinery, and equipment in an amount not exceeding 10 percent of the total of the other components of direct cost.[40]

In addition to manufacturing enterprises, the law provides that certain extractive, assembly, service, and export industries may qualify for tax concessions.[41] Qualifying extractive industries are those engaged in the mining of nonmetallic minerals which they refine or process for use as raw materials in domestic industry. Industries engaged in the mining or improvement of metallic minerals are not eligible for exemptions under the law, but they may be entitled to tax benefits under the mining tax law. Enterprises engaged in assembly operations may qualify if all of the parts they use are manufactured in Mexico or if they produce themselves at least 35 percent of the parts used and do not use foreign parts of a value exceeding 40 percent of direct cost of production. The law provides that service industries in economically important activities may qualify, but the regulations limit the application of this provision to firms that can supply complete services for the repair of ships of a certain size, locomotives, railroad cars, or airplanes, and enterprises rendering services to combat diseases affecting domestic agriculture and livestock.[42] Manufacturing enterprises that export finished or semi-finished products may qualify if at least 60 percent of their direct cost of production is incurred in Mexico and if one or more of the tax exemptions authorized, except the exemption from import duties, are required to enable them to compete in the export market.

Apart from the requirements for qualification established in the law, applicants for exemptions must meet certain conditions that are imposed as a matter of policy. It is a usual condition, for example, that a company will not be granted tax benefits unless a majority of its capital stock is owned by Mexican nationals. This requirement is not entirely inflexible, however, and in a very limited number of instances companies with minority Mexican capital have been given exemptions because of the amount of their investment and the importance of the industry for the country. It is also present policy to limit payments made abroad by tax-exempt companies for technical services, patent and trademark licenses, and interest. Customarily, technical service and licensing fees may not exceed 3 percent of the amount of the company's sales, and interest on loans from foreign sources is limited to 9 percent. Exempt companies must also meet certain conditions relating to foreign employees and the training of Mexican personnel. Salaries and other compensation to foreign employees are normally limited to 10 percent of the total amount of remuneration paid to all employees engaged in the manufacture of products covered by the exemption. It is also a usual condition that a company may employ only one foreign technician, who may remain in the country for a maximum of one year from the date the exemption is granted and must train Mexicans in his specialty, and that other foreign personnel may remain in Mexico for only two years from that date. These limitations on foreign personnel and the length of their stay have been modified in some instances to meet the requirements of specific companies.

Qualifying companies may be granted total or partial exemptions from one or more of the following federal taxes:[43]

1. Import duties. Manufacturers may be totally or partially exempted from the import duty and customs surtaxes on machinery, equipment, raw materials, and other items required for the manufacture of the products covered.[44] The exemption is granted only for goods that are not produced in Mexico, that are not produced in sufficient quantity or with the required specifications, or that cannot be adequately replaced by domestic products. An enterprise that has filed an application for exemption may import or export dutiable goods free of duty for two years following its filing if it furnishes a bond or makes a deposit in the amount of the duties payable if its application is denied.

2. Export duties. Enterprises that manufacture for export, if at least 60 percent of their direct cost of production is incurred in Mexico and if tax exemptions are essential for them to be able to export, may be granted an exemption from the general export duty and the additions thereto.

3. Stamp tax. Qualifying enterprises may receive a total exemption from the federal stamp tax.

4. Commercial receipts tax. An exemption may be granted from the federal portion (1.8 percent) of the commercial receipts tax.

5. Income tax. Partial exemption from the income tax may be granted to qualifying enterprises. Under the law the exemption may not exceed 40 percent of the tax payable, but government policy in recent years has been to grant the maximum exemption only to industries classified as basic. In the case of semibasic industries, the exemption is currently limited to 30 percent, and secondary industries normally receive an exemption of not more than 20 percent.

The law provides that the determination of the extent of the exemption granted in each individual case shall be made on the basis of the importance of the enterprise for national or regional economic integration and the following specific factors: the size and quality of its labor force; its technical efficiency and research facilities; the extent to which it uses Mexican materials, machinery, and equipment; the portion of the domestic market that it supplies or will supply; the amount of its investment; the use to which its products are put; and the social benefits granted to its workers in excess of those required by law.[45]

For purposes of determining the length of time for which an

exemption is granted, and to some extent its amount, qualifying industries, except service industries, are classified as basic, semibasic, or secondary, depending upon their importance for the country's industrial development.[46] Basic industries are those that produce raw materials, machinery, equipment, or vehicles that are essential for one or more activities of fundamental importance for the development of domestic industry or agriculture.[47] The regulations impose the additional requirement that an enterprise must have sufficient productive capacity to satisfy at least 20 percent of the apparent needs of the domestic market,[48] but it does not appear that this requirement is applied in all cases. Enterprises that qualify in this category receive tax exemptions for a term of ten years. The exemption may be extended for an additional term not exceeding five years if the activities of the enterprise are of paramount importance for the economic development of the country, for which it must be shown that its activities have been beneficial to various sectors of national production and to consumers in general and that it has failed to recover in profits at least 20 percent of its total initial investment at the time of its application for an extension.[49] Again, these requirements are seldom applied in practice.

Semibasic industries are those that produce goods to satisfy directly the vital necessities of the population, or tools, scientific apparatus, or articles for use in later industrial processes that are considered important. The enterprise is required to have capacity to satisfy at least 15 percent of the apparent needs of the domestic market,[50] but this is not often enforced. The exemption granted to enterprises in this group is for seven years and may be extended for an additional period not exceeding five years under the conditions applicable to basic industries.[51]

Secondary industries are those that cannot be classified as basic or semibasic. Exemptions granted to enterprises in this category are for five years, and there is no provision for extension of this term.[52]

Tax exemptions to service industries are for a term of not less than five nor more than ten years. Enterprises that manufacture for export may receive exemptions for a maximum term of ten years, subject to annual confirmation.[53]

Once an exemption is granted to an enterprise in a particular industry, it must be extended to all others that produce the same goods or render the same services, provided they otherwise qualify under the law. These exemptions are granted only for the unexpired term of the original exemption.[54]

Enterprises to which exemptions have been granted are subject to rather elaborate inspections of books and plants to ensure compliance with the conditions of the exemption and must furnish periodic reports and financial information on their operations. To cover the cost of this service, exempt enterprises pay a fee equal to 2 percent of the amount of the taxes to which the exemption applies.[55]

STATE TAX EXEMPTIONS

Virtually all states offer exemptions from various state and municipal taxes to new or necessary enterprises and to established companies that expand their plant capacity.[56] While the state laws for the promotion of industry are not uniform, they generally follow the pattern of the federal law but usually provide relief for a longer period, often as much as twenty years, during which the amount of the exemption gradually declines. For example, the State of Mexico, which adjoins the Federal District and is the most highly industrialized area outside the Federal District, offers to industries that locate within designated industrial zones partial exemptions from the commercial receipts tax, special taxes on commerce and industry, and registration fees of the public register. Exemptions are authorized for a term of fifteen years and in the amount of 75 percent of the taxes covered for the first five years, 50 percent for the next five years, and 25 percent for the last five years. However, pursuant to the government policy to encourage decentralization of industry, exemptions are no longer being given for plants in the areas of concentrated industry immediately adjacent to the Federal District.

It is highly doubtful that the state tax exemption laws have had any real influence on the location of industry in Mexico.[57] State taxes are a relatively insignificant burden on industry by comparison with federal taxes and are not likely to outweigh such factors as the availability of raw materials, power, water, transportation, and labor in the determination of a plant location. Furthermore, since similar laws have been enacted in almost all states, they offer little incentive to a company to locate in one state rather than another.

MONOPOLY POLICY

The Mexican scheme for the regulation of monopolies and restrictive trade practices is relatively unsophisticated and of very limited application. While the Constitution lays down broad principles for the protection of free and unrestricted competition, those principles have been largely sacrificed in favor of what are considered more compelling economic policies and the requirements of Mexican economic development. Some government policies have, in fact, deliberately limited competition and fostered monopolies by protecting domestic producers against competing imports and even, in some cases, against the establishment of additional local producers. Lack of competition is also an unavoidable consequence of the realities of the Mexican economy; in many cases the market is simply too small to support more than one or a few producers. As a result, the existing legislation is directed more at maintaining order and stability in the economy than at safeguarding competition in a free market economy.

The constitutional basis for the restriction of monopolistic practices is found in article 28, which categorically states that "there shall be no monopolies or *estancos* of any kind; nor exemption from taxes; nor prohibitions under pretext of protection to industry," with the exception of such activities as the coinage of money and issuance of currency and operation of the mails and telegraph, and copyright and patent protection. That article further directs that there shall be proscribed every concentration in the hands of one or a few persons of necessary consumer goods for the purpose of obtaining an increase in prices; every act that prevents or tends to prevent free competition in production, industry, or commerce, or services to the public; every agreement or combination of producers, manufacturers, merchants, common carriers, or those engaged in any other service to prevent competition among themselves and to require consumers to pay exaggerated prices; and in general whatever constitutes an exclusive and undue advantage in favor of one or more specified persons and to the prejudice of the public in general or of any social class.

The implementing legislation is the so-called law of monopolies, enacted in 1934 and in force, with minor amendments to certain penalty provisions, since that time.[58] While there are regulations to specific provisions of the law, no general regulations have been issued under it and the regulations to the prior law of 1931 are still in effect.[59] Despite the language of article 28 of the Constitution, the law of monopolies makes clear that government concern for restrictive trade practices is centered on prices and that the constitutional prohibitions against protection of industry and tax exemptions are not to be taken too literally. It is a fundamental premise of the law not only that the public should be protected against excessive prices but also that unlimited competition may be equally harmful in that it may result in price reductions that jeopardize employment and wage levels and impede industrial development.[60]

Article 1 of the law repeats the constitutional prohibition of monopolies and *estancos*. An *estanco* is defined in article 2 as a monopoly of the state established for the purpose of obtaining some advantage for the treasury. Monopoly is defined in article 3 as "every industrial or commercial concentration or cornering and every situation deliberately created which permit one or more specific persons to impose prices of goods or rates of services, to the prejudice of the public in general or of some social class." Thus, it appears that the principal criteria by which the existence of a monopoly is determined are the ability to set prices and detriment to the public.

Under article 4 the existence of a monopoly shall be presumed, unless the contrary is proved, from any of the following circumstances: (1) any concentration or cornering of necessary consumer goods; (2) any agreement or combination of producers, manufacturers, or owners of service establishments, made without authorization and regulation of the government, which allows the imposition of prices of goods or services;[61] and (3) any situation of a commercial, industrial, or service-rendering nature, deliberately created, which allows the imposition of prices of goods or services. This presumption does not apply to public service enterprises operating under government concession with officially approved rates or to enterprises in which the state is a shareholder or associate.[62]

The presumption under article 4 against agreements among and combinations of competitors does not apply if they are authorized and regulated by the government, and provision for the granting of such authorization is set out in a 1935 presidential decree.[63] Under that decree authority may be granted to organizations of competitors upon application to the Ministry of Industry and Commerce (formerly National Economy) if they have one or more of the purposes listed in the decree, such as the integration of an industry that permits a price reduction, the elimination of intermediaries, the elimination of ruinous or unfair competition without an unjustified price increase, the establishment of a new industry or commerce, the preservation of useful or necessary activities, or "other activities which by their nature demonstrate that the possibility of imposing prices will not be exercised to the prejudice of the public." Furthermore, any organization, whatever its purpose, may be authorized if it agrees that the ministry may establish maximum prices on the goods or services involved. If authorization is granted, the ministry may retain regulatory powers over the organization, including the power to establish maximum prices, and may also grant exemptions and subsidies if the organization is beneficial to the national economy and is in need of financial assistance.

In addition to the presumption of the existence of a monopoly, the law provides in article 5 that certain activities shall be presumed to tend to a monopoly: (1) sales of goods or services at less than cost except under certain limited circumstances; (2) importations of goods which, because of the circumstances under which they are produced, can be sold in Mexico under conditions of unfair competition; (3) wilful destruction of goods by producers or merchants without government authorization which may cause scarcity or price increase; (4) sales by lottery or raffles without government authorization; and (5) allowances or bonuses to consumers in the form of vouchers, coupons, certificates, or similar objects giving the right to receive money or goods, except as permitted by the regulations.

Lotteries and similar contests as a means of promoting sales and the use of cash or merchandise coupons are subject to special regulations designed to protect consumers against deceptive practices and to prevent the use of those devices by merchants to compete unfairly by selling at less than cost.[64] Those practices must be specifically authorized by the Ministry of Industry and Commerce upon the application of the interested party and must conform to the requirements established in the regulations. Since about 1966 the ministry has followed a very restrictive policy with respect to such sales promotions, and very few authorizations have been granted.

While the definition of monopoly is limited to situations "deliberately created," the law of monopolies authorizes the president to take certain action when in fact there exists a concentration or cornering of goods or any other situation not deliberately created that allows price fixing to the detriment of the public. In those circumstances the president may establish maximum prices of the goods or services concerned, require that the goods be placed on sale and that necessary services be rendered to the public, and promote the establishment of similar businesses or industries by granting subsidies or exemptions. These measures may be taken with respect to necessary consumer goods whenever market conditions so require.[65] Necessary consumer goods are listed and price control authority over them is implemented in regulations issued in 1941,[66] but the power to control prices was substantially enlarged and is now exercised almost entirely under the law on powers of the federal executive in economic matters of 1950, discussed above under Price Control.

Apart from the regulation of monopolies, the law repeats the constitutional proscription of "prohibitions under pretext of protection to industry" but so limits its application by authorizing the president to restrict competition and to take other regulatory action as to render it virtually meaningless. Specifically, he may (1) regulate the initiation of new industrial activities in specific branches of production when there is danger that excessive competition may cause reductions in workers' salaries or prejudice to the public in general or to some social class; (2) restrict the production of specific articles when their supply is excessive in relation to domestic and foreign demand and a crisis may result from overproduction to the prejudice of the public; (3) prohibit the use of necessary consumer goods for purposes different from those for which they are normally used when that may cause scarcity in the market and price increases; (4) prohibit industrial integrations that create the danger of a monopoly or threaten serious economic disturbances; and (5) restrict imports and exports under certain circumstances.[67]

The power to limit the expansion of an industry has in practice been exercised through presidential declarations that a specified industry is "saturated," which has the effect of preventing both the entry of new enterprises and additions to the equipment of existing plants without prior authorization. While this is a potentially powerful instrument for the control of industrial development and the channeling of investments into areas that the government wishes to see developed, in fact only five industries have been declared saturated: silk and rayon (1937), matches (1941), flour milling (1943, 1963), rubber (1943), and cigarettes (1944). Control of the rubber industry was imposed because of shortages of supply and was removed in 1946 when the supply situation eased. In most of the other cases, however, the imposition of controls seems to have resulted merely from pressures from interested producer groups.[68]

Finally, the law of monopolies limits the constitutional prohibition of tax exemptions by providing only that it shall apply when a specified person is relieved of payment of taxes applicable to other taxpayers in the same circumstances or when taxes already due are forgiven or remitted in favor of some taxpayers but not others and by expressly excluding certain subsidies and grants from the prohibition.[69]

Penalties for violations of the law consist of fines and temporary closings of establishments and may be imposed by administrative action.[70]

Despite the rather broad authority under the monopolies law, the government has made very little use of it as an instrument for the control of restrictive trade practices. In many cases prices are controlled by other means—under the law on powers of the federal executive in economic matters of 1950 in the case of basic consumer goods, and by the Ministry of Industry and Commerce as a condition to its approval of new manufacturing programs, discussed in Chapter IV, in the case of many manufactured products—so that there has been no need to use the monopolies law for that purpose. Furthermore, during some periods the desire to promote industrialization, even where a monopoly resulted, has outweighed other considerations. Until recently government policy, enforced primarily by the Ministry of Industry and Commerce by virtue of its control of imports, has been to permit the entry of only a limited number of producers in an industry. Since about 1965, however, the emphasis has shifted to the promotion of competition as a means of encouraging greater efficiency and reduction of prices of manufactured goods, and, with few exceptions, the entry of as many producers as want to establish facilities in Mexico has been authorized.

BORDER INDUSTRIALIZATION PROGRAM

Mexico's long border with the United States, extending nearly two thousand miles, poses special problems to the country. The area's sizable population, in excess of five million, has traditionally been economically oriented toward the neighboring territory of the United States and to a large extent has been outside the market for domestically produced goods. While domestic producers are usually protected against competing imports, large amounts of goods are brought into the border region free of the import controls that apply generally, mainly for consumption there, but probably also for smuggling into the interior of the country.[71] These purchases abroad represent a drain on Mexico's foreign exchange reserves and a negative element in its balance of payments. Apparently because of the free-import privileges of the area and because of the noncompetitive prices of many domestic products, owing in part at least to the relatively high shipping costs from the manufacturing centers in the interior of the country, Mexican manufacturers have done little to penetrate and develop the border market.

Furthermore, while the frontier cities have always attracted free-spending North Americans from across the border and partially as a result its residents have the highest per capita income outside the Federal District,[72] realization of the full potential of the tourist industry in the area has been limited by the shabby image and inadequate facilities of many of the border communities.

More recently, the problems of the area have been substantially compounded by the large immigration to the border cities of persons seeking employment, many as seasonal agricultural workers in the United States under the *bracero* farm-workers program. This program at its maximum involved more than 450,000 Mexican workers annually, and upon its effective termination by the United States in 1965[73] many of these persons remained in the border area without employment, either unable financially to return to their homes or hoping for a resumption of the program. Largely as a consequence, unemployment in the area has been enormous—estimated at 40 to 50 percent in some cities.[74]

An attack on some of these problems was initiated by the government in 1961 in the form of the National Border Program (Programa Nacional Fronterizo—PRONAF). Motivated primarily by balance of payments concerns, the program seeks to reduce purchases by border residents in the United States by increasing consumption in the area of domestic products and to stimulate industrial development, principally tourism. Encouragement to domestic producers to expand the distribution of their goods in the area is offered in the form of reductions of 25 to 50 percent in freight rates on shipments to the area and by rebates of the federal portion of the commercial receipts tax on initial sales of domestic goods in the border zone. To stimulate tourism and other industrial development, PRONAF has made substantial investments in infrastructure and physical improvements, rehabilitating municipal facilities and constructing hotels, commercial centers, exhibition and convention halls, housing, schools, and the like, and has promoted the sale of quality Mexican handicrafts and other products.[75]

The results of PRONAF have been encouraging. Firms registered with the program increased their sales in the border zone by more than $88 million (U.S.) from 1961 to the end of 1966, and foreign tourist expenditures rose 48 percent to $540 million in the same period.[76] However, continued insistence by government spokesmen that Mexican manufacturers do more to penetrate the border market and that border residents reduce their United States purchases seems to indicate that there is still much room for import replacement.[77] Also, while the growth of tourism and other industrial development stimulated by

PRONAF has undoubtedly brought increased employment opportunities in the area, unemployment has continued to be a major problem, and the improved conditions of the border communities may even have stimulated immigration from rural areas in the interior and intensified the problem.

To combat the problem of unemployment, Minister of Industry and Commerce Octaviano Campos Salas announced in mid-1965 the initiation of an imaginative program to attract foreign manufacturers to establish plants in the area for the processing of imported raw materials and components into finished and semifinished products for export.[78] Unlike PRONAF, the objective of this program is to increase the utilization of Mexican labor, rather than to promote import substitution and exports of Mexican-made goods. The program was established administratively without special legislation under broad policies set out in an exchange of correspondence between the minister of finance and the minister of industry and commerce.

Under the border industrialization program, as it is often called, approved enterprises are permitted to import, free of duty and under bond, machinery and equipment to establish their plants and raw materials and semifabricated components for further processing or assembly. All goods produced from such raw materials and components must be exported, though not necessarily to the country of origin of the raw materials. Plants established under the program are designated "fiscal zones" or bonded areas, and strict government control is maintained to ensure that goods imported or produced under the program do not find their way into the domestic market. Inasmuch as the program is designed to attract foreign producers of labor-intensive goods, approved companies may be wholly foreign owned, unless, of course, they are engaged in an activity in which foreign investment is restricted by law, and there has been no administrative pressure on foreign firms to associate with Mexican investors. The prohibition against ownership of land in the border zone by aliens and companies having foreign owners does not seem to present any difficulty since most enterprises operating under the program lease their plants or plant sites from Mexican citizens.[79]

While the program has full government support, it has not been adequately implemented. No uniform criteria have been established for qualification under the program, and its administration has not been centralized in one agency. Each proposed plant project is negotiated individually with the Ministry of Industry and Commerce, which administers quantitative control over imports and must authorize the necessary import permits, and the Ministry of Finance, which must approve the waiver of import duties on the applicant's equipment and components. Once the project is approved by those agencies, a Mexican company is formed, for which a permit from the Ministry of Foreign Relations is required, to carry out the project. If foreign personnel are to be employed by the company, their entry must be authorized by the internal affairs ministry. Because of the number of government departments involved and the practical difficulties of co-ordinating their activities, prompt approval of applications has not been common. Since the primary objective of the program is the creation of new sources of employment in the area, the closest thing to a criterion seems to be the number of employees to be used in the new plant, and the procedure has reportedly been expedited for applicants anticipating a sizable labor force. In some cases the industrial development agencies of the northern border states, which offer advice to interested firms and assistance in connection with their applications to the federal government, have been helpful in expediting the approval of plant proposals.

Although it has been in existence only a few years, the program has already met with considerable success. In April, 1968, Campos Salas stated that 100 projects, providing employment for more than 8,400 persons, had been approved under the program, and by early 1969 it was reported that 125 border plants had been established.[80] Because of the relatively low cost of Mexican labor, the program is most attractive for labor-intensive processing, assembling, or finishing operations, and a number of plants have been established for the assembly of electronic components and to perform cut and sew operations for the wearing apparel industry.[81] The great majority of these plants are owned by United States companies, but the program has also begun to attract the attention of Mexican manufacturers, some of whom have established border plants to produce for the export market.

Many observers in Mexico, both in and out of government, feel that the program has vast potential and that it will bring substantial long-term benefits to the border zone and the country. Cities on the United States side of the border are also enthusiastic about the program and have actively promoted it. Not only are the economies of those cities to a large degree dependent upon purchases by Mexican residents,[82] but they hope to attract complementary plants to produce components for the Mexican plants or for final processing of goods produced on the Mexican side. One key to the program's future, as well as an indication of its potential, is the attitude of organized labor in the

United States, which has voiced increasing opposition to the program, charging that it attracts "runaway" plants and results in the loss of jobs in the United States.[83] It is probably out of concern for this reaction that Mexican officials have largely avoided openly promoting the program in the United States and have emphasized that the program seeks to attract to Mexico plants that would otherwise be established in other low-labor-cost areas such as the Far East rather than to lure plants away from the United States.[84]

VI

Entry and Status of Aliens and Foreign Legal Entities

ALIENS

Mexican constitutions have long embodied the principles, with few exceptions, of free entry of aliens and equality between aliens and Mexicans. For many years, however, it has been the policy of the government to discourage the immigration of persons who intend to work in any way in the country, and in recent years it has become increasingly difficult for foreign enterprises in Mexico to obtain authorization for the entry of aliens as permanent employees. The policy is not one of absolute prohibition nor is there an official quota system, but a bias against foreign immigration is evident in the laws. A labor law requirement that at least 90 percent of every company's employees must be Mexicans, a statutory prohibition against the practice of professions by aliens, and provisions in the law governing immigration that only aliens whose services are essential will be admitted and that Mexicans must be trained to replace foreign technicians are examples. More importantly, special authorization of the Ministry of Internal Affairs *(gobernación)* is required for the entry of all aliens to work in Mexico, and the policy to restrict foreign immigration is enforced by the simple refusal to grant many visas for that purpose.

Underlying this policy is a strong nationalistic attitude on the part of government policy makers, backed by the trade unions, that Mexicans should be employed and trained for the technical and professional positions that have in the past been filled to a considerable extent by foreigners. Foreign companies themselves have probably contributed to this attitude by their earlier reluctance to permit Mexicans to advance to responsible positions and what was often, at least in pre-Revolution times, and still is to some extent, outright discrimination against Mexican workers in pay and other conditions of employment.

While most foreign enterprises of today recognize both the legitimate desire of the government to encourage the employment of more Mexicans and the advantages to the companies themselves of employing Mexicans in positions of responsibility, the lack of sufficient numbers of qualified Mexican industrial technicians, supervisors, and management personnel still makes it necessary for many companies to seek the admission of aliens to fill those positions. The government's restrictive policy prevents the use of permanent foreign employees in sufficient numbers to cover the deficiency in trained Mexican personnel, but the government is not entirely unsympathetic to the problem and will in most cases permit the entry of foreign technicians for limited periods of time.

Not only does the government control the entry of foreigners, but also the activities in which they may engage in the country are subject to strict regulation. They may not hold employment or perform acts of a business or economic nature other than those for which their entry is specifically permitted without the authorization of the Ministry of Internal Affairs, and even such occasional acts as the execution of contracts and the attendance of meetings of directors and shareholders of Mexican companies must be specially authorized.

ENTRY OF ALIENS

Article 11 of the Constitution grants to everyone, including aliens, the "right to enter the Republic, leave it, travel through its territory and move his residence without need of letter of security, passport, safe-conduct or other similar requirements," but this right is subject to "limitations imposed by laws on emigration, immigration, and general health" and by laws relating to pernicious aliens. The power to enact laws on immigration and the legal condition of aliens is delegated to the federal Congress by article 73, section XVI, of the Constitution.

The entry of aliens is governed by the population law of 1947 and its 1962 regulations,[1] which confer broad powers on the federal executive, acting through the Ministry of Internal Affairs, over the admission of aliens and establish the purposes for which their entry may be authorized.

Aliens may be admitted to Mexico under either of two general categories—immigrants and nonimmigrants. Immigrants are aliens who enter the country for the purpose of residing there, and persons who enter for temporary visits are classified as nonimmigrants. An alien may not hold more than one type of visa or entry permit simultaneously,[2] but a change in the status under which he was originally admitted may be authorized if he fulfills the requirements for admission under the new classification.[3]

The control of the Ministry of Internal Affairs over the admission of aliens is virtually absolute, and it must directly authorize all immigrant visas and those for nonimmigrants who are permitted to engage in lucrative activities in the country. Under the law the ministry is enjoined to take care that immigrants are "useful elements" for the country, and it may, for reasons of public interest, "suspend or definitively cancel the admission of aliens whose entry may place in danger the economic or social equilibrium of the Republic."[4] It may also deny the entry of foreigners "when it deems it prejudicial to the economic interests of nationals."[5] There are also prohibitions against the entry of indigents, criminals, illiterates, alcoholics, drug addicts, and other persons considered undesirable.[6]

Immigrants

Permits to enter as immigrants may be granted for a variety of purposes, the most important of which for foreign enterprises are to hold management or other positions of responsibility and confidence in companies established in Mexico and to render technical or specialized services in the country. Aliens may also be authorized to enter as immigrants in order to live on foreign-source assets or income, to make certain types of investments, or to engage in a profession, or as family dependents of immigrants or Mexicans.[7]

Application for the admission of managerial and other confidential employees must be made by the employer enterprise itself rather than by the employee, and the legal requirements relate principally to the employer and are designed to ensure that it is a going concern of some importance to the country's economy.[8] The employer must be an established enterprise, institution, or person that has been operating in Mexico for at least two years prior to the date of the application, unless it is considered by the ministry a necessary industry. If it is located in the Federal District or one of the surrounding industrial zones, it must have a paid-in capital of at least 600,000 pesos, or 200,000 pesos if it is located elsewhere in the country. The application must be accompanied by a list of the employer's personnel and their nationalities, positions, and salaries. If it employs more than one hundred workers, they need not be listed, but the total number of foreign and Mexican employees must be stated, and the names, nationalities, and salaries of the confidential employees given. The ministry may request a copy of the employer's most recent balance sheet, but it rarely does so. It does, however, require that a copy of the company's last monthly commercial receipts tax declaration be submitted as evidence of its economic importance.

Technicians and specialized personnel may be admitted as immigrants to render services which, in the judgment of the ministry, cannot be performed by Mexican residents.[9] The entry must be requested by an enterprise, institution, or person domiciled in the country, which must justify to the satisfaction of the ministry the permanent necessity of utilizing the services of the alien. While there are no statutory requirements relating to minimum capital or period of operation as in the case of companies requesting the entry of confidential employees, in practice the same requirements are imposed. The employee need not hold a professional degree when the nature of the work does not require it, but the ministry may and usually does require evidence that he has the necessary capacity and knowledge of his work or specialty. The employee is required to instruct at least three Mexicans in his specialty, and the employer must communicate to the ministry the names of the persons who will receive the instruction within sixty days from the date the alien's employment commences. In special cases the ministry may waive the instruction requirement.

Pursuant to the governmental policy to discourage the entry of aliens for the purpose of working permanently in the country, the ministry is often reluctant to authorize the entry of aliens as confidential employees and technicians. In the case of confidential employees, the law requires that the position for which the alien is sought must be one of responsibility and absolute confidence, in the judgment of the ministry, and it provides that the entry may be authorized only if there is no duplicity of positions in the employing enterprise and if the service involved merits the alien's entry, also in the ministry's judgment. In practice, the employer company must usually convince the ministry that there is a real need for the alien's services because of the high degree of confidence involved in the position, and authorization will be granted only for positions of importance such as company officers, managers, administrators, and superintendents. Considerable weight is also given to the size of the company and the type of business in which it is engaged. Although the ministry's policies vary somewhat from time to time, manufacturing companies, especially the larger ones, do not usually encounter difficulties in bringing aliens to fill managerial positions, but the current practice is not to permit the entry of foreign confidential employees of real estate or insurance companies or Mexican financial institutions, and a highly restrictive policy is followed in the case of companies in hotel, mining, agricultural, and retail and wholesale trade businesses. In the case of foreign technical personnel, the current policy is still more restrictive, and even where the ministry is convinced of the need for foreign technicians, it will not in most cases authorize their entry as immigrants but requires that they enter under temporary visitor permits, discussed below.

Immigrant visas for purposes other than to hold permanent employment in Mexico are more readily granted. Aliens who receive a monthly income from assets brought to Mexico from abroad or from foreign sources of at least 3,000 pesos may be authorized to enter as immigrants under the classification of *rentier (rentista)*.[10] If an alien requests immigrant permits for family dependents, he must have an additional monthly income of 1,000 pesos for each member of the family over fifteen years of age. In the event the immigrant's income is from assets brought to Mexico, he must establish a trust approved by the ministry or make a cash deposit with Nacional Financiera or other financial institution authorized by the ministry of a sum equivalent to the minimum monthly income for five years. If the required income is from foreign sources, evidence of it must be presented to the appropriate official of the Mexican foreign service abroad, who issues a certificate to that effect.

Immigrant permits may also be granted to aliens who wish to make investments in industrial, agricultural, livestock raising, or export trade activities.[11] The amount of the investment must be at least 600,000 pesos if the business is established in the Federal District or a surrounding industrial zone, or 200,000 pesos if the investment is made elsewhere, and a deposit of 10,000 pesos is required to guarantee that the investment will be made. The ministry may authorize a reduction of as much as 50 percent in the amount of the investment required if it is to be made in agriculture in new or little exploited areas or in industries that are considered necessary. These investments may not be made in companies whose capital is represented by shares of stock, that is, stock corporations *(sociedades anónimas)* or limited partnerships with shares *(sociedades en comandita por acciones),* but the ministry may authorize investments in other forms of commercial companies.[12] Since the corporation is the preferred form of business association for most purposes, this restriction is often a substantial impediment to the entry of immigrants under this classification. Immigrants are also, of course, subject to the restrictions on foreign investments contained in other laws and regulations discussed in Chapter III, and the ministry will not authorize investments in violation of those restrictions.

Persons may also be permitted to enter as immigrants for the purpose of investing in certificates, bonds, or other securities issued by the federal government or, provided they are to finance basic activities for the economic development of the country, in securities issued or guaranteed by national credit institutions or issued by decentralized institutions or state participation enterprises.[13] The amount invested must be sufficient to produce the minimum income required for *rentiers*, 3,000 pesos a month, and a guaranty deposit of 10,000 pesos is required. The securities in which the investment is made must be deposited with Nacional Financiera or other financial institution authorized by the ministry as long as the alien retains immigrant status, but he may withdraw monthly the interest and dividends paid on them.

Authority to enter Mexico to practice a profession is rarely granted to aliens, the law requiring that there exist exceptional circumstances, that the alien be eminent in his specialty, and that he comply with the laws and requirements relating to the practice of professions.[14] This does not apply, however, to professional persons employed by Mexican companies whose entry is requested as confidential employees or technicians. Foreign professors may be admitted under special circumstances upon the request of officially recognized educational institutions.

All immigrants are required to be registered in the national register of aliens in the Ministry of Internal Affairs within thirty days after their entry into the country, and they must notify the ministry of all changes in their nationality, civil status, domicile, and business activities within thirty days of the change.[15] Activities in which an immigrant may engage, discussed later in this chapter, are strictly limited to those for which his entry is specifically authorized, and authorization of the ministry is required for any change in employment or business activity during the period of his status as an immigrant.

An alien admitted to Mexico as an immigrant is expected to establish his permanent residence there, and the law imposes limitations on the periods of time he may be out of the country without loss of his status. In each of the first two years of his residence his total absences may not exceed ninety days, and he may not be out of the country for more than a total of eighteen months during the entire five-year period of his immigrant status.[16] No periods of grace are granted, and an alien's immigrant permit is cancelled for any violation of these restrictions.

Immigrant status is normally maintained for a period of five years, but the immigrant's permit must be renewed annually. Renewal is granted automatically by the ministry upon payment of the required fee, provided the conditions under which the alien was admitted have not been violated and his absences from the country do not exceed the maximum allowed.[17]

Upon the expiration of the five-year period, an immigrant may apply for the status of *inmigrado,* under which he may reside permanently in the country.[18] The law provides that the alien's activities must have been "honest and socially positive" during the immigrant period, and in practice the ministry requires evidence of good conduct and denies *inmigrado* status if the alien has been involved in significant legal difficulties or if the restrictions on his activities as an immigrant have been violated. As an *inmigrado,* an alien is permitted to engage in any activity or to hold any job he wishes, with minor exceptions established by the ministry and except for activities closed to foreigners under other laws. The residence requirements are also substantially more liberal for an *inmigrado* than for an immigrant, but he may not be absent from the country for more than two consecutive years or for a total of more than five years in any ten-year period.

Nonimmigrants

Aliens admitted into the country for temporary visits are classified as nonimmigrants. These include tourists, transients, visitors *(visitantes),* political refugees, and students. Of these, only aliens admitted with the status of visitor, and under exceptional circumstances political refugees and students, may be employed or engage in business activities in Mexico.[19]

A distinction is made between persons who enter as visitors to perform services or engage in activities which by their nature are normally regarded as lucrative or remunerative and those who enter to engage in other business activities.[20] Aliens who enter the country for limited periods of time to engage in activities for which compensation is customarily paid, whether or not they actually receive pay for their services in Mexico, such as the installation of machinery, the performance of technical or supervisory services, or the attendance of meetings of the boards of directors of Mexican companies, must be admitted as remunerated visitors. Authorization of the entry must be obtained directly from the Ministry of Internal Affairs by the enterprise that wishes to employ the services of the alien, and it is liable for any penalties that may be incurred by the alien and for the expenses of his repatriation in case of expulsion. The law provides that remunerated visitors will be admitted "only to the degree that the protection of nationals permits," but the ministry is substantially more liberal in authorizing the entry of visitors than in the case of immigrants, and foreign technicians whose entry as immigrants is refused are often admitted with visitor status. While the law imposes no special requirements on the employer enterprise, the ministry often takes into account the amount of its capital and the purposes for which the entry is sought, and visitors are not usually permitted to hold specific positions or offices in Mexican companies. A visitor permit authorizes the holder to remain in Mexico for a period not exceeding six months and may allow multiple entries. The law provides that a permit may be extended for an additional six-month period, and if the alien has been admitted to engage in scientific, technical, artistic, sports, or similar activities, two additional six-month extensions may be granted by the ministry. Under the ministry's current practice, two extensions are allowed for scientists and technicians, and only one for others. Upon the expiration of his visitor permit, however, it is often possible for an alien to leave the country and re-enter under a new permit.

Visitor permits for unremunerative business activities are rarely denied and may be obtained by the alien himself either directly from the ministry or from a Mexican consul abroad without specific authorization of the ministry. Under this type of permit, aliens may enter Mexico for such purposes as to participate in business conferences, negotiate contracts, carry out market or investment studies, or attend meetings of shareholders of Mexican companies. These permits may also allow multiple entries and are issued for a period of six months, which may be extended for one additional six-month period.

Of the other classifications of nonimmigrants, that of tourist is the most common. Aliens who enter Mexico for purposes of recreation or health, or to pursue unremunerated scientific, artistic, or athletic activities, are issued tourist permits for periods up to six months, which may not be extended.[21]

RIGHTS AND OBLIGATIONS OF ALIENS

It has long been a general principle of Mexican law that aliens have the same basic protections against state action as Mexican citizens. Provisions for the protection of the individual, set out in the first 28 articles of the Constitution, are stated in article 1 to apply to "every individual" and are expressly made applicable to aliens by article 33 of the Constitution. These guarantees include such fundamental civil rights as freedom of speech, of the press, and of religion; the right of free assembly and of petition; protection against ex post facto laws and deprivation of life, liberty, property, or other rights without a trial before a duly established court in compliance with law and essential procedural formalities; protection against illegal searches and seizures; and protections concerning detention and criminal trial.[22] Article 29 provides that these guarantees may be suspended only by the president, with the agreement of the Council of Ministers and the approval of the federal Congress or its Permanent Commission if it is in recess, and only in cases of "invasion, grave disturbance of the public peace, or any other that puts society in great danger or conflict." Such suspensions may be only for a limited time and must be of general application and not directed to any specified individual.

Mexico has also ratified the principle of equality of aliens in international treaties. It is a party to the Convention on the Legal Condition of Aliens signed in Havana on February 20, 1928,[23] article 5 of which establishes the obligation of the states to recognize in favor of aliens domiciled or in transit within their territory all individual guarantees that are recognized in favor of their own nationals. As a member of the General Assembly of the United Nations, Mexico is also a signatory of the Universal Declaration of the Rights of Man of December 10, 1948.

The principle of equality has not always been respected in the law, but where a law has operated to deprive aliens of their constitutional rights and has been challenged by legal action, the federal Supreme Court has not hesitated to uphold the Constitution. The issue has on a number of occasions been raised by aliens seeking to practice a profession in Mexico. Article 4 of the Constitution provides that no person may be prevented from engaging in the profession, industry, business, or work that suits him, provided it is legal, and that the exercise of this right may be restrained only by judicial determination when the rights of third persons are infringed or by governmental resolution issued pursuant to law when the rights of society are offended. That article also provides that the law of each state shall determine for which professions a degree shall be required, the conditions that must be fulfilled to obtain it, and the authorities that must confer it. Article 5 contains a prohibition against agreements by which a person temporarily or permanently renounces the right to engage in a determined profession, industry, or business. The law governing the practice of professions in the Federal District and federal territories, enacted in 1944 to implement those articles of the Constitution, denies the right to aliens to engage in any of the professions covered—including law, medicine, dentistry, engineering, various sciences, and others—even though they fulfill the other requirements of the law.[24] This prohibition has been challenged in a number of *amparo* proceedings, and the Supreme Court has consistently held that the protection of articles 4 and 5 of the Constitution are applicable to aliens and that the federal Congress does not have power to prohibit persons from engaging in professional activities on the sole basis of their nationality.[25] Despite the fact that the Court has reached this conclusion in five consecutive decisions and has thus established binding precedent that the nationality requirement is unconstitutional, neither the president nor Congress has acted to amend the law, and consequently the general bureau of professions of the Ministry of Public Education continues to apply it and refuses to issue professional licenses to aliens.[26] The result is that an alien who wishes to practice a profession and who has fulfilled the other requirements of the law must bring an *amparo* suit and have his constitutional right declared by the courts, a burden that does not exist with respect to Mexican citizens.

The constitutional guarantees available to aliens are not unlimited, however. They extend only to the exercise of civil rights, and aliens are strictly prohibited by article 33 to become involved in the country's political affairs and are denied the rights of petition and assembly in connection with domestic political matters under articles 8 and 9. The Constitution also contains prohibitions against aliens serving in the military and police forces, holding certain civil positions of an official nature, and engaging in the ministry of any religious faith.[27] Furthermore, while article 11 guarantees to everyone the "right to enter the Republic, leave it, travel through its territory and change his residence," the president has the important power, under article 33, to expel "immediately and without necessity of a prior decree, any alien whose presence he deems undesirable."[28] The Supreme Court has held that, since this power is exercisable in the discretion of the executive and is for the protection of the public, a restraining order against expulsion is not available to aliens ordered to leave the country under that article.[29]

In accordance with the principle of equal treatment under the laws, no special privileges or rights are granted to aliens, and they are generally subject to the same obligations that apply to Mexicans. They must pay all taxes and other charges that are imposed by law and are applicable to the general population where they live. They are also obligated "to obey and respect the institutions, laws and authorities of the country" and are subject to the judgments and decrees of the courts and may not resort to other recourses than those available under the law to Mexicans. They may appeal to their home government for diplomatic protection only "in cases of denial of justice or wilful and notoriously malicious delay in its administration."[30] Aliens are exempt from military service, but those domiciled in Mexico may be required to perform guard duty when the security of property is threatened or maintenance of order is required in the town where they reside.[31]

RESTRICTIONS ON ACTIVITIES OF ALIENS

The general principle of equality of aliens and Mexicans under the law, contained in the Constitution with respect to protection of the individual against state action, is also found in private Mexican law. The provisions of the Civil Code for the Federal District and Territories relating to the legal capacity of individuals make no reference to nationality or citizenship, and the fact that no distinction between aliens and Mexicans is intended is confirmed by article 12 of the code, which provides that "Mexican laws, including those that refer to status and capacity of persons, apply to all inhabitants of the Republic, whether nationals or aliens, either domiciled in it or transients."[32] The Commercial Code likewise contains no restrictions on aliens' activities and expressly recognizes their right to "exercise commerce"—that is, to engage in what the code defines as "acts of commerce" as their ordinary occupation—"pursuant to what has been agreed to in treaties with their respective countries, and as provided in the laws that govern the rights and obligations of aliens."[33] Mexico is not a party to any treaty that prohibits the exercise of commerce by aliens.

Important limitations on aliens' activities in Mexico are, however, imposed by other laws and by policies followed by various governmental agencies. Restrictions on foreign ownership of land and other property rights under article 27 of the Constitution and limitations on direct foreign investments have been discussed in detail in Chapter III. Other limitations are imposed under the population law, as interpreted and applied by the Ministry of Internal Affairs. The administration of the law has not always seemed entirely consistent, and the absence of clearly applicable legal provisions has given rise to some confusion regarding the validity and effect of acts performed in Mexico by aliens who do not have the required authorization.

Under the population law the activities in which an alien may engage and the acts that he may perform in Mexico are determined by the specific purposes for which he is admitted into the country, and any act not allowed under the conditions stated in his entry permit must be specially authorized by the ministry.[34] Nonimmigrants, with the exception of persons admitted under the classification of visitor and in special circumstances political refugees and students,[35] may not hold employment or engage in any form of business activity. Tourists, for example, are defined in the law as aliens who are admitted "for purposes of recreation or health, or for scientific, artistic or athletic activities, not remunerated or lucrative."[36] This provision is interpreted as an absolute prohibition against any remunerative activity by an alien who is in the country with tourist status. While it does not seem that all acts or contracts could necessarily be considered "remunerated or lucrative," the prohibition obviously applies to any employment for pay, and the ministry construes it to cover most other activities of a business or economic nature. Articles of association of Mexican companies and most commercial contracts may not, for example, be executed by tourists. The ministry also considers the prohibition to include the purchase (though not necessarily the ownership) of shares in Mexican companies and other securities and the attendance of meetings of the boards of directors or shareholders of Mexican companies.

With few exceptions, only aliens admitted as immigrants or nonimmigrant visitors may engage in business activities in Mexico. Of these only confidential or technical employees of established enterprises with immigrant status and persons admitted temporarily as remunerated visitors may hold employment in the country, and they are not permitted to hold any position or perform any act not expressly authorized. Immigrants admitted under the classification of business or industrial investors or investors in securities are authorized only to make the investments specifically designated by the ministry, and immigrant *rentiers* may not engage in any remunerative activity but may be authorized by the ministry to make investments in Mexico under the limitations applicable to investors.[37]

Once an immigrant fulfills the five-year residence requirement and acquires the status of *inmigrado,* the restrictions on his activities are substantially relaxed, and he may engage in any lawful activity not specifically prohibited.[38] While the ministry has the authority to establish limitations on the activities of *inmigrados,* either in individual cases or by general resolution, in practice the only restrictions it has imposed for a number of years have related to work in restaurants, cabarets, and bars, and that is prohibited only to persons not originally admitted to hold employment in those establishments.

No one may employ an alien without first ascertaining that he is in the country legally and is authorized by the Ministry of Internal Affairs to hold the specific employment concerned.[39] An enterprise that employs an alien is also required to notify the ministry within fifteen days of any circumstance, such as discharge, resignation, or change in position, that modifies or contravenes the conditions under which the alien has been admitted into the country, and it is liable for the expenses of his expulsion if that should be ordered.[40]

Furthermore, all governmental authorities, public notaries, certified public accountants, and commercial notaries are obligated to require that aliens who transact business or execute documents before them prove their legal residence in the country and that their status under the population law "permits them to execute the act or contract concerned" or that they have special authorization of the Ministry of Internal Affairs. Powers of attorney and wills are excepted from that requirement "in case of urgency," and on the basis of that exception notaries often certify the execution of those documents by aliens without the necessary status or authorization. In all cases, however, the notary or other official before whom an instrument is executed is required by law to give notice of it to the ministry,[41] though that requirement is often ignored.

The validity of contracts and other acts executed in Mexico by aliens who have not been admitted with the appropriate status under the population law and do not have special authorization of the Ministry of Internal Affairs has apparently never been determined by the courts. A distinction is made in Mexican law between civil capacity *(capacidad de goce)* and functional capacity *(capacidad de ejercicio),*[42] and one view is that, even though aliens have civil capacity under the Civil and Commercial Codes, the effect of the population law is to deprive them of functional capacity except to the extent permitted by that law. Under this view, aliens who do not have the required status or authorization may not enter into valid contracts in view of article 1798 of the Civil Code, which provides that all persons *not excepted by law* have capacity to contract.[43] Capacity to contract, as used in that article, is generally considered to mean functional capacity rather than merely civil capacity. Furthermore, so the reasoning goes, a contract executed in Mexico by an unauthorized alien would fall within article 1830 of the code, which establishes that contracts that are "contrary to the laws of public order or good customs" are unlawful. The population law is a "law of public order" since it implements a provision of the Constitution, article 11. Under article 2225 an act is void whose "object, purpose or condition" is unlawful. Since the term "act" in Mexican legal terminology includes not only contracts but all acts that produce effects under the law, the reasoning necessarily leads to the conclusion that virtually any activity of an unauthorized alien in Mexico is void. Thus, for example, the attendance and vote at a meeting of the directors or shareholders of a Mexican corporation by an unauthorized alien are void, and if there is not a quorum or sufficient vote without his presence or vote, the meeting or resolution itself is void. While this question does not seem to have been resolved by the courts, most Mexican lawyers seek to avoid the risk that this reasoning would be followed by recommending that foreigners who enter the country to attend corporate meetings, especially meetings of boards of directors, obtain visitor permits for that purpose.[44] It is also common practice, where nonresident aliens are elected to the board of directors of a corporation, for Mexican citizens to be elected as alternate directors to act in their absence.

With respect to aliens' contracts, even if they should be considered void, a judicial decree of nullity would be required, and the possibility of a legal challenge may be slight in view of the Civil Code provision that incapacity may be alleged only by the party who lacks capacity and not by the other contracting party.[45] And if a contract is declared void, each party is required to return to the other any consideration he has received under the contract.[46]

Whether or not the Mexican courts would hold that an unauthorized alien's acts are void, it is highly likely that a penalty would be imposed administratively by the Ministry of Internal Affairs if such an act should come to its attention. The population law provides for a fine of 200 to 10,000 pesos for violations of the law or its regulations,[47] and more severe penalties are authorized for certain specified infractions. A person who fraudulently holds himself out as having a status under the law that he does not possess, for example, may be sentenced to imprisonment for six months to five years and expelled from the country.[48] While it is undoubtedly true that many violations do not come to the ministry's attention, that possibility exists in the case of documents certified by a notary in view of the requirement that notaries inform the ministry of all acts of aliens executed before them.

A somewhat anomalous distinction is made between activities of aliens who are in Mexico and those of aliens who are outside the country at the time of the act. In the ministry's view and on the basis of the territorial theory of law, the restrictions on aliens' activities under the population law, with the exception of the limitations on acquisitions of interests in real property,[49] are applicable only to aliens who are physically present in Mexico. Since there is no general limitation on the capacity of aliens except under the population law, aliens who are not in Mexico may enter into valid contracts to be performed in Mexico, purchase shares of Mexican companies, and even appoint agents to act for them in Mexico provided the agent is qualified by nationality or status under the population law to act in Mexico. Consequently, an absent alien may sign a contract, act as incorporator of a Mexican company, or attend a shareholders meeting through a qualified agent, while he may not so act personally in Mexico without the required status or authorization under the law.

FOREIGN LEGAL ENTITIES

Virtually all direct foreign investments in Mexico are made through some form of Mexican business association, and it is very uncommon for foreign companies to engage in any sort of permanent business in the country by qualifying to do business there. Not only are there greater restrictions with respect to the activities in which foreign companies may engage than in the case of foreign-owned Mexican companies, as has been discussed in Chapter III, but it has long been a policy of the government to encourage foreign enterprises to conduct their operations in Mexico through subsidiary companies organized under domestic law. The law does, however, recognize foreign legal entities, and provision is made for their qualification to do business in Mexico. Also, it is quite common, of course, for foreign companies to contract with Mexican enterprises and governmental agencies, and it is important to consider in what circumstances foreign companies are required to qualify under the law and the status and capacity in Mexico of unregistered companies.

A distinction is made in Mexican law between civil and commercial companies, and provisions relating to foreign companies are found in both the Civil Code and the commercial law. The provisions of the Civil Code are applicable only to companies of a civil nature—that is, companies whose purpose is not primarily to engage in a profit-making activity—and consequently are of little concern to foreign business enterprises.[50] Foreign business companies are governed by the Commercial Code and by the 1934 commercial companies law,[51] which repealed and replaced most of the provisions of the Commercial Code relating to business associations and foreign companies.

REGISTRATION REQUIREMENT

Both the Commercial Code and the commercial companies law require that foreign companies be registered in the public commercial register in order to do business in Mexico and establish conditions for registration. The question of whether the registration requirement applies to all foreign companies, regardless of the extent of their activities in Mexico, and is a prerequisite to recognition as a legal entity in the country has been the subject of considerable controversy and uncertainty.

A distinction seems to be made in the law between companies that engage in business in the country on a permanent basis and those that perform only isolated acts, and the registration requirement seems applicable only in the case of the former. Article 250 of the commercial companies law provides that legally constituted foreign companies have "legal personality" in Mexico, while article 251 states that in order to "exercise commerce" such companies must be registered. The intention of the draftsmen of the law that registration should be required only in the case of companies that engage in a continuing business is evident from the statement of purposes accompanying the law:

The problem of foreign companies . . . is resolved by the Law . . . according to whether the company is one that wishes to establish in the Republic an agency or branch, or one that only must undertake the defense before Mexican authorities of rights arising from juridical acts validly effected outside or within national territory, provided that, in the latter instance, they do not imply the exercise of commerce.

The Commission thought that, while it was necessary to establish formal requirements and guarantees for the first of the situations mentioned, for the second it was sufficient to require that the company has been legally constituted, which the authority in each case must determine.

The provisions of the Commercial Code that were not repealed by the commercial companies law, though perhaps not so clear, also suggest this distinction. Article 15 provides that legally incorporated foreign companies "that become established in the Republic or have an agency or branch in it may exercise commerce" by fulfilling the requirements of the code. While article 19 establishes the general requirement of registration for all business associations, article 24 provides specifically for the registration of foreign companies and is limited to those "that wish to become established or to create branches in the Republic." These provisions seem to imply that foreign companies that do not "exercise commerce" are not required to be registered.

Under both the code and the law, therefore, the requirements of registration would seem to depend on whether or not a foreign company is engaged in the "exercise of commerce." No definition of that term is found in either the code or the law, but it has been suggested by Mexican writers that it means the performance in Mexico of commercial acts in such volume and with such continuity as to indicate that the company is engaged in a regular business activity. It should not, it is argued, be construed to cover only occasional acts in Mexico that do not constitute the doing of business on a continuous, permanent basis.[52]

The question of whether a foreign company is engaged in commerce and thus required to be registered appears to have been considered by the Mexican Supreme Court in only one case, decided in 1929.[53] There the Court seemed to consider that the test was whether there existed an intention on the part of the foreign company to establish a permanent agency in Mexico, and such an intention was found to exist from the circumstances that the company had sent agents or representatives to Mexico for the purpose of promoting the sale of its products, had accepted an order for the sale of goods taken by one of its agents in Mexico, and had appointed a general agent in Mexico and instructed him to register the company's trademarks there. This rather extreme view of what constitutes doing business for purposes of the registration requirement has been criticized by some Mexican writers,[54] and whether or not the Court would follow it if the question should arise again is subject to speculation.

The distinction that seems implicit in the law between companies that conduct a permanent business in Mexico and those that do not has not always been recognized by the Mexican Supreme Court. The question has arisen principally in connection with the standing of an unregistered company to sue and be sued in the Mexican courts. Before 1929 the Court's position was that foreign companies not engaged in a permanent business in Mexico were not subject to the registration requirement but had legal personality in the country and were entitled to bring suit and could be sued in the courts.[55] Beginning in 1929, however, the Court's position changed radically, and in a number of decisions it was held that registration was a prerequisite to recognition as a legal entity and that unregistered foreign companies, regardless of the extent of their activities in Mexico, had no legal personality in the country and consequently no standing in the courts. The most widely publicized of this series of cases was a suit brought by The Palmolive Company, a Delaware corporation, against a Mexican company arising out of an alleged infringement of its trademark, "Palmolive." The company had registered its trademark in Mexico but apparently engaged in no other activities in the country and was not registered in the commercial register. The Supreme Court held that registration was obligatory for all foreign companies under articles 19 and 24 of the Commercial Code and, since the company had not fulfilled that requirement, it had no existence in Mexico and consequently no standing to bring suit in the Mexican courts.[56]

The enactment in 1934 of the commercial companies law should have put an end to the question. The draftsmen of the law quite obviously had the recent decisions in mind when they referred in the statement of purposes to the fact that "the imperfection of the relative provisions of the Commercial Code" had given rise to "multiple controversies and uncertainties in the judicial decisions," and it seems clear that they intended to require registration only for the exercise of commerce and not as a prerequisite to recognition as a legal entity or for isolated acts or standing in the courts. The majority of the decisions of the Supreme Court since the enactment of the law have sustained that interpretation,[57] but in at least one case, decided in 1943,[58] the Court reverted to its earlier position and held that registration was required for recognition as a legal entity, even for the purpose of bringing suit. Although the Court has recognized the existence of such companies in its most recent decisions, there has not as yet been a sufficient number of consecutive decisions to that effect to constitute new binding precedent, and references to the earlier decisions continue to appear in the collections of jurisprudence.[59]

It is perhaps premature to conclude, therefore, that the matter has been finally settled. Even the most conservative of Mexican lawyers do not, however, seem to consider that there is much risk that the Court will follow its earlier line of decisions and do not recommend registration of foreign companies that perform isolated acts or enter into occasional contracts in Mexico. They do, nevertheless, usually recommend out of caution that contracts between an unregistered foreign company and a Mexican entity be executed by the foreign company outside Mexico, whether the contract provides for performance in Mexico or abroad.

REGISTRATION PROCEDURE

Both the Commercial Code and the commercial companies law contain requirements that must be fulfilled for the registration of a foreign company. While the registration itself poses no special problems, it must first be authorized by the Ministry of Industry and Commerce, and substantial difficulties may be encountered in obtaining the ministry's authorization. Article 251 of the law sets out three conditions for this authorization: the company must be duly incorporated under the laws of its own country, its articles and other documents of incorporation must not be contrary to the "precepts of public policy established by Mexican laws," and it must be "established" or have an agency or branch in Mexico. Proof of incorporation must be made by an authentic copy of the company's articles and other documents of incorporation and a certificate issued by the Mexican diplomatic or consular representative in the company's home country attesting that it is legally incorporated and authorized. Article 24 of the code provides that those documents, as well as "the inventory or last balance sheet," must be recorded in the public commercial register, and article 25 requires that all foreign documents that are to be recorded must first be authenticated in Mexico.

Compliance with these conditions is often a tedious and time-consuming process. Certified copies of the company's articles, bylaws, and other documents of incorporation, the resolution of the board of directors authorizing the creation of a branch or agency in Mexico, a power of attorney to the company's representative in Mexico, and the company's inventory if it is newly established or its most recent balance sheet if it has been in operation must be obtained and authenticated by the Mexican consul at the company's domicile, whose signature must then be authenticated by the Mexican Ministry of Foreign Relations.

The requirement of a consular certificate often gives rise to a significant problem in practice; in effect, the certifying consul must give a legal opinion that the company is properly incorporated and in good standing under its domestic law, and Mexican consuls are frequently unwilling or at least reluctant to give such an opinion. If the corporate documents are in a language other than Spanish, they must be translated by an authorized translator. They must then be certified by a Mexican notary, for which judicial authorization is required.[60]

In addition to the corporate documents and the certificate of legal incorporation referred to in the law, the Ministry of Industry and Commerce has in practice also required a permit from the Ministry of Foreign Relations authorizing the foreign company to engage in business in the country. This requirement does not appear to be imposed by the provisions of any law, and the only possible justification for it seems to be article 33 of the law of nationality and naturalization, which provides that foreign legal entities may not obtain concessions from or execute contracts with governmental agencies without a permit from the Ministry of Foreign Relations and unless they agree to the terms of the so-called Calvo clause.[61]

The requirement of the law that the foreign company be established or have an agency or branch in Mexico as a prerequisite to the ministry's authorization poses a dilemma. Before a company may engage in business in Mexico it must be registered, but before it may be registered it must take some affirmative step that amounts to creating an agency or branch in Mexico, which may in itself constitute the exercise of commerce for purposes of the registration requirement. To require that a foreign company maintain an agent in Mexico, at least for purposes of service of citation on the company, is, of course, entirely reasonable. But the ministry has not considered the appointment of an agent sufficient to satisfy the requirement of an "agency or branch"; it has in practice required the filing of a lease contract on premises in Mexico or other proof that the company has actually established a place of business in the country.

The meaning of the condition of article 251 that the documents of incorporation of a foreign company must not be contrary to Mexican "precepts of public policy" has never been defined with any degree of certainty. It has been suggested that all mandatory provisions of the commercial companies law that are designed to protect the interests of shareholders and creditors of the company are provisions of public policy.[62] The Ministry of Industry and Commerce has seemed to take advantage of this uncertainty and has decided in its own discretion in each case whether or not Mexican public policy is violated by the articles or bylaws of a foreign company. In at least one instance it has even imposed the condition that the articles and bylaws of a foreign company be amended to incorporate to the greatest extent possible the requirements of Mexican law for domestic corporations.[63]

Even if all the requirements of the law are met, there is no assurance that the ministry will authorize the registration of a foreign company. The language of article 251 of the law, stating that the ministry's authorization "shall be granted" when the specified requirements are fulfilled, seems to indicate that the ministry's function should be limited to ascertaining whether or not those conditions have been met. Mexican authors who have studied the question, however, are of the opinion that the ministry may in its discretion refuse to grant authorization for registration in any case.[64] The number of applications for permission to register has in recent years been so small as to make it impossible to ascertain under what circumstances the ministry might deny entry to a foreign company, but no instance is known in which authorization has been refused without reason based on the law.

EFFECT OF DOING BUSINESS BY UNREGISTERED FOREIGN COMPANIES

The lingering doubt left by the Supreme Court decisions on the status of unregistered foreign companies has been discussed earlier in this chapter. The most recent decisions indicate, however, that foreign companies that are not engaged in a permanent business in Mexico may enter into valid contracts and perform other acts in the country without being registered, and this view is strongly supported by Mexican legal writers and is accepted by most lawyers. The validity and effect of acts of unregistered companies that are engaged in a continuous business in Mexico, on the other hand, have apparently never been decided by the courts, and no clear answer to the question is provided either by the commercial companies law or the Commercial Code. Article 15 of the code states that foreign companies "may exercise commerce" by fulfilling the registration requirement, and it further provides that, with respect to their capacity to contract, they shall be subject to the provisions of the section of the code entitled "Foreign Companies." That section was replaced by the chapter on foreign companies in the commercial companies law, which recognizes their legal personality but provides in article 251 that "foreign companies may exercise commerce only after their inscription in the Register." This language suggests the possibility that it was intended that unregistered companies lack capacity to "exercise commerce," that is, to engage in a permanent business in the country.

At least one Mexican writer has suggested, however, that unregistered foreign companies should be considered the same as defectively incorporated Mexican companies.[65] The commercial companies law originally provided that only companies inscribed in the public commercial register had legal personality distinct from that of their members. This was changed by a 1942 amendment to article 2 of the law,[66] providing that companies not inscribed in the register that have been held out as registered companies to third persons shall have legal personality. Recognition of an unregistered company as a legal entity separate and distinct from its members or shareholders thus depends upon whether or not it has been held out as such, and an act or contract of a company that has been so represented is valid and may be enforced against it. Third persons who deal with such a company are further protected by a provision that persons who act on behalf of a defective company (called an "irregular company") are secondarily liable for obligations incurred in the company's name. Since article 2 is not expressly limited to defectively incorporated Mexican companies, it is argued, it is also applicable to unregistered foreign companies; therefore, a foreign company that has been represented as qualified to do business in Mexico should be recognized as a legal entity and its contracts held valid and enforceable against both the company and persons who act on its behalf.

VII

Business Organizations

It seems customary in studies of doing business abroad to devote some consideration to the question of whether it is preferable for an investor to qualify his foreign corporation or perhaps a foreign subsidiary of it in the country concerned or to organize some form of business association under the laws of that country. Mexican law does establish a procedure for the qualification to do business of foreign companies, which is discussed in Chapter VI. Nevertheless, the question in the case of Mexico is largely irrelevant; the foreign investor who wishes to engage in a continuing business in the country usually has little choice but to operate through a Mexican company. The main reason for this is said to be a deep-rooted governmental policy, based on Mexico's historical experiences with foreign companies, that aliens who engage in business in Mexico must be willing to submit to the domestic laws, accept local customs and social responsibilities, and integrate into and contribute fully to the economic and social progress of the country. It has been made clear that Mexico is not interested in foreign capital that will not make a permanent and stable contribution to its economy. Operation through a qualified foreign company conveys, at least to the Mexican mind, a feeling that the investor is not willing to commit himself more or less permanently to the country and wishes to retain to the greatest extent possible his ties with his home country and the protections it might afford.

The result is that virtually all direct foreign investments in Mexico are channeled through some form of business association incorporated under Mexican law. The formation and operation of Mexican business associations are governed by the commercial companies law, which is a federal statute applicable throughout the country.[1] It is relatively modern, having been issued in 1934, and does not pose substantial difficulties for most foreign investors or their attorneys.

The law provides for five principal forms of association. The *sociedad en nombre colectivo* is similar to the partnership under United States law; its main features are unlimited liability of its members for the debts of the company and restricted transferability of the ownership interests or "parts."[2] The *sociedad en comandita simple,* much like the limited partnership, is managed by the active member or members, whose liability to third persons is unlimited, while the limited or silent members merely contribute capital and have no liability beyond the amount of their contribution.[3] The *sociedad en comandita por acciones* (limited partnership with shares) is an attempt to combine the best qualities of these so-called associations of persons, in which the main factor is the contribution of personal services by the members, and the associations of capital, in which the contribution of capital is the most important aspect. In this form of company, a variation of the limited partnership, the capital is represented by shares of stock, which are more readily transferable than the nonnegotiable "parts" of the simple limited partnership, but the liability of the members is the same as in the case of the limited partnership.[4] None of these forms of association is well suited to the needs of most foreign investors. Limitation of the members' individual liability cannot be achieved except by forfeiture of the right to participate in the active management of the company, and the restrictions on the transfer of ownership interests further detract from their usefulness.

By far the most popular and appropriate forms of association for most investors are the *sociedad anónima* (corporation) and, to a less extent, the *sociedad de responsabilidad limitada* (limited liability company). These, especially the corporation, are sometimes organized in the form of variable capital companies, discussed later in this chapter. The corporation is the only form that offers the advantages of both limited liability and relative freedom of transfer of ownership interests and is the only form in which a large number of persons may participate. Although the members of a limited liability company are not obligated for debts of the company beyond their capital contributions and that type of company is somewhat easier to manage than the corporation, it has not been as widely accepted in Mexico as in some other civil-law countries. The main obstacle to its popularity is the difficulty of transferring ownership interests in the company. Interests are represented by nonnegotiable parts, which may be transferred only with the consent of all other members, except that the articles may authorize transfer with the approval of members representing three-fourths of the capital.

Furthermore, the number of members may not exceed twenty-five.[5] However, in view of the constitutional prohibition against the ownership of agricultural land by corporations, the limited liability company is commonly used by investors who wish to engage in agricultural activities.

All forms of association provided for in the commercial companies law are legal entities and have juridical personality separate from that of their individual owners.[6] For that reason, any type of association may be a member or shareholder in any other association, whatever its nature. The existence of a company as a legal entity arises not by grant from the state, but from the right of association or freedom of contract of its associates.[7] One effect of this concept that the instrument of incorporation is a contract among the associates is that one-man associations are prohibited. Corporations must have at least five shareholders at all times, and other forms of associations may not have less than two members.

Many of the provisions of the law are applicable only in the absence of express provisions in the articles of association or merely establish minimum requirements. Substantial flexibility is therefore allowed in the drafting of the articles, and the parties are often able to create the regime best suited to their needs. This is especially significant in the increasing number of associations between foreign and Mexican investors, and many important protections, such as increased quorum and voting requirements and restrictions on the transferability of shares, may be established in the articles.

Because of the limited usefulness to foreign investors of most of the so-called associations of persons and the relative unpopularity of the limited liability company, only the corporation is dealt with in detail in this chapter. A number of the basic provisions of the law applicable to the corporation, notably those relating to formation, increases and decreases of capital, and distributions of profits, are, however, common to all forms of association.

FORMATION

In almost all cases the act of constitution of a corporation is the execution before a notary of its articles or instrument of association.[8] There must be at least five incorporators, each of whom must subscribe to at least one share. As with other public documents, the original of this instrument is transcribed and remains in the bound books of the notary, and certified copies are issued for the company's records and for other purposes, such as recording. The law also establishes a procedure for incorporation by public subscription of shares, but this method is virtually never used. Not only is it complicated and time consuming, but the Mexican investing public would not likely be receptive to an offer of shares in a company that is not yet in operation, and even if it is anticipated that a public offer of shares will be made, the usual practice is to incorporate before a notary first.

The instrument of incorporation is rather detailed, covering matters that are normally included within the bylaws of a United States corporation. It must identify the incorporators by name, nationality, and domicile, and state the corporate purpose, name, duration,[9] domicile, capital, and number of shares subscribed and amount paid by each incorporator. It should also establish regulations for such matters as management, shareholders meetings, distribution of profits, payment of unpaid balances on shares, and liquidation and dissolution.

Under the emergency decree of 1944, discussed in Chapter III, a permit must be obtained from the Ministry of Foreign Relations for the formation of any Mexican company, which must be inserted by the notary in the articles of incorporation. If foreigners are permitted to own shares—that is, if the articles do not expressly prohibit foreign ownership of shares, as is required when the purpose of the company is to engage in an activity that is completely closed to foreign participation —the articles must also contain the Calvo clause, also discussed in Chapter III, under which any foreigner who acquires shares in the corporation agrees that he will be considered as a Mexican with respect to his shares and that he will not invoke the diplomatic protection of his home government.

The incorporation of companies all or a majority of whose shares are to be owned by foreigners or foreign legal entities poses special problems. Foreign individuals who do not have the status of immigrant, *inmigrado,* or, under some circumstances, visitor, and unregistered foreign companies may not directly perform commercial acts in Mexico, including the execution of contracts of association.[10] For many years it was customary for the Mexican lawyer or law firm representing the foreign investor to furnish the necessary five incorporators, usually members of their staff, who assigned the shares to the real owners upon incorporation. However, the requirement of a permit from the Ministry of Foreign Relations for the transfer of a controlling interest in an existing Mexican company from Mexicans to foreigners[11] and the recently adopted policy of the ministry to deny such permits have limited the usefulness and advisability of this practice. To avoid transfers of shares after incorporation, some attorneys recommend that the foreign investor, whether an individual or a legal entity, appear as an incorporator through an authorized agent. The agent must be either a Mexican national or a foreigner qualified to perform commercial acts in Mexico, and the power of attorney to him must be executed before a Mexican consul abroad and properly authenticated. The prevailing opinion seems to be that a foreign company is not by that act alone doing business in Mexico for purposes of the legal provisions requiring registration of foreign companies and that a foreign individual may validly act as incorporator through a qualified agent. No restriction or permit requirement has so far been imposed on the transfer of shares between foreigners, and in cases in which resident foreigners are available, they sometimes act as incorporators and assign their shares to the beneficial owners after incorporation. It is important to bear in mind, however, that under a 1967 policy decision an application to the Ministry of Foreign Relations for a permit to incorporate submitted in the name of a foreigner is referred to the Ministry of Industry and Commerce for a determination of the amount of foreign ownership in the company that will be authorized.[12]

Once the corporation has been constituted before a notary, its articles of association must be recorded, by judicial order, in the public commercial register. For this purpose a petition together with the corporate documents are filed with the district judge or a judge of first instance at the domicile of the company. The petition is then referred to the public attorney's office, and a hearing is set. The hearing may be waived if the public attorney does not oppose the recordation. If the articles of incorporation contain the essential provisions required by law, the judge orders their recordation.[13] This procedure is rapid, and in the large majority of cases the judicial order is issued and the recordation effected as a matter of routine.

In addition to these requirements, certain obligations are imposed on newly formed companies by various other laws, principally tax laws. Within ten days after the date of initiation of operations the company must make application to the federal finance office having jurisdiction over its domicile for registration in the federal register of taxpayers,[14] and its accounting and minute books must be presented to that office for official authorization. If the company is domiciled in the Federal District, a similar notice must be given to the commercial receipts tax bureau of the Federal District Treasury. Within sixty days after incorporation certified copies of the articles must be filed with both of those offices. Notice is also required to be given for statistical purposes to the statistics bureau of the Ministry of Industry and Commerce. All companies are required by law to join the chamber that represents the branch of industry or commerce in which they operate, and companies engaged in importing or exporting must be registered with the national register of importers and exporters. Finally, within five days after initiation of operations, the company and its employees must be registered with the social security institute.[15]

CAPITAL STRUCTURE AND SHARES

SUBSCRIPTION AND PAYMENT OF SHARES

The minimum capital with which a corporation may be organized is 25,000 pesos. All of the shares must be subscribed and at least 20 percent of the par value of each share payable in cash must be paid in at the time of incorporation. Shares that are paid for in property other than cash must be totally paid upon incorporation.[16] As a safeguard against watered stock, such shares must be deposited with the company for a period of two years in order to guarantee that the value of the property given in exchange for the shares is not substantially less than that at which it is received by the company. If during that period it appears that the value of the property was 25 percent or more less than the value at which it was received, the shareholder is obligated to pay the difference to the company.[17] A shareholder who contributes a chose in action is liable for its existence and legality and the solvency of the obligor at the time of the contribution.[18]

The period for payment of any unpaid balance on shares may be established either in the articles of incorporation or by shareholders' resolution.[19] While the law does not expressly establish a maximum period for payment, it does provide that subscribers and assignees of unpaid shares shall be liable for the unpaid balance for five years from the date of registration of the assignment,[20] and the most widely accepted view among Mexican lawyers, based on that provision, is that shares must be fully paid within five years from the date of incorporation. In practice, payment is customarily required within one year. Dividends and distributions of assets on liquidation are, logically, paid in proportion to the amount actually paid in on the shares.[21]

In view of the underlying principle that a corporation is an association of capital and that each share represents a proportionate part of the capital, and as a guard against possible abuses by promoters, services rendered to the corporation either before or after incorporation do not constitute consideration for shares. Promoters and incorporators may, however, be given the right to receive up to 10 percent of the annual profits, after a 5 percent dividend has been paid to shareholders, for a maximum period of ten years from the date of incorporation. This right is represented by so-called founder's bonds *(bonos de fundador)*.[22] The law also authorizes the issue of "special shares" to persons who render services to the corporation, if expressly provided for in the articles of incorporation. These shares were designed as a device by which companies could give to their workers a participation in profits in compliance with the constitutional requirement of profit sharing,[23] but there would not seem to be any objection to their issuance for promoters' services, provided the services are rendered after incorporation.

PROTECTIONS AGAINST IMPAIRMENT OF CAPITAL

The theory that the capital stock is a fund that represents the shareholders' investment and on which creditors and others dealing with the corporation may rely is reflected in other provisions designed to protect the integrity of paid-in capital. For example, shares may not be issued for a consideration less than the amount of their par value.[24] No-par shares, though authorized by the law,[25] are rarely used in practice, perhaps because of lack of experience and some degree of unsophistication on the part of Mexican lawyers and investors in their use and because the concept of the no-par share is alien to traditional practice.

Furthermore, a corporation may not acquire its own shares except by judicial order in satisfaction of debts to the corporation, and the company must sell shares acquired in that manner within three months. Directors and officers who authorize the acquisition of shares are personally liable for any resulting damage to the corporation and its creditors. The corporation is also prohibited to make loans or advances on the security of its own shares.[26]

A further protective measure is the requirement that every company must set aside at least 5 percent of its annual net profits as a reserve fund, usually called the "legal reserve," until the amount of the reserve equals 20 percent of the stated capital. Dividends may not be paid except out of unreserved profits, and if stated capital is impaired through operating losses, net assets must be restored or capital must be reduced before any distribution of profits may be made.[27] However, the articles of incorporation may provide for the payment of interest on shares, in the maximum amount of 9 percent annually, for a period of up to three years from the date of their issue.[28] Presumably, the payment of this interest would not depend on whether or not the corporation had any profits and consequently might result in an impairment of capital stock.

CLASSES OF SHARES

Shares may be classified according to voting rights and preferential rights in dividends and assets. The law does not use the terms "common" and "preferred" shares, but it does authorize the division of shares into various classes with special rights for each class, and it provides that the articles of incorporation may establish that part of the shares shall confer the right to vote only at extraordinary assemblies, which are those held to amend the articles of incorporation and to deal with certain other matters of fundamental importance. Such limited-vote shares are entitled to a cumulative annual dividend of at least 5 percent of their par value and have preferential rights in assets on the liquidation of the company.[29]

SHARE CERTIFICATES

Share certificates may be registered or issued in bearer form.[30] Besides the fact that the holder of a bearer certificate may remain anonymous for most purposes, the difference between the two types of certificates relates primarily to the method of assignment. Since mere possession of a bearer instrument is evidence of ownership, bearer certificates are transferable by simple delivery. The assignment of registered certificates, on the other hand, requires an endorsement or separate assignment and annotation on the certificate, and is effective as against the corporation only upon the entry of the transfer in the register required to be kept by the corporation for registered shares.[31]

Generally, the incorporators are free to provide in the articles of incorporation for either registered or bearer shares. There are, however, certain situations in which it is important for the corporation to know the identity of its shareholders, and some restrictions on the issue of bearer shares are imposed. For example, shares that are not fully paid and provisional stock certificates, which will eventually be exchanged for definitive certificates, must be registered.[32] Also, companies having variable capital, discussed below, may not issue shares in bearer form. Apart from these limitations, because of the anonymity afforded by bearer shares and as a defense against evasion of restrictions on foreign investment, companies engaged in activities in which foreign investment is prohibited or limited are in most instances required to issue registered shares.[33] Nevertheless, bearer shares are widely used in Mexico, and most shares that are listed on the stock exchanges and traded publicly are in bearer form.

Certificates representing shares must be issued within one year from the date of incorporation or amendment of the articles to increase the capital and must contain a description of the shares covered and basic information on the issuing corporation, including the data of its inscription in the public commercial register. Since there is inevitably some delay in completing the recordation of the articles of incorporation, the law authorizes the issuance of provisional certificates, which in practice usually take the form of typewritten or mimeographed instruments. Dividend coupons are required to be attached to the certificates and may be in bearer form even when the certificate itself is registered.[34]

RESTRICTION OF TRANSFER OF SHARES

As a protection to the shareholders against the admission of unwanted outsiders through a transfer of shares, it may be provided in the articles of incorporation that transfers of registered shares may be made only with the authorization of the board of directors. The law provides that the board may deny authorization by designating a purchaser of the shares at the current market price.[35] Since it is unlikely that there will be an established market value of the shares where such a restriction has been adopted, this provision seems unrealistic. Because of this difficulty, in practice it is often specified that the remaining shareholders have the option to purchase the shares of a selling shareholder at the price that has been offered to him or at some appraised value. On occasion a restriction on the transfer of bearer shares is imposed, but the validity and enforceability of such a provision are doubtful.

INCREASE AND DECREASE OF CAPITAL

Capital may be increased or decreased by amendment of the articles of incorporation. The requirements for an amendment are substantially the same as those for original incorporation. The amendment must be adopted by an extraordinary shareholders meeting and must be executed before a notary and recorded in the public register of commerce, and a permit is required from the Ministry of Foreign Relations authorizing the amendment.[36] An increase of capital may not be made until all previously authorized and issued shares have been fully paid. For the protection of shareholders against dilution of their proportional interests in the corporation, they are given the pre-emptive right to subscribe for shares issued on a capital increase, but this right must be exercised within fifteen days following the date of publication of the resolution increasing capital in the official periodical of the corporate domicile.[37] A capital increase may also be effected through a transfer of retained earnings to capital, in which case new shares are issued as a stock dividend or the par value of the existing shares is increased.

The law provides for reduction of capital either through a redemption of outstanding shares or waiver of unpaid share subscriptions or through the amortization or purchase of shares out of distributable earnings.[38] Since redemption of shares or waiver of unpaid subscriptions has the effect of reducing stated capital, certain protections are provided for creditors. Notice of the reduction must be published three times at ten-day intervals in the official periodical of the federal entity in which the corporate domicile is located, and creditors may bring suit to oppose the reduction within five days following the date of the last publication. The reduction will be enjoined until the corporation pays the opposing creditors or guarantees payment to the satisfaction of the court, or until the opposition is declared unfounded, presumably if the court finds that the capital reduction will not be prejudicial to the creditors' interests. Amortization of shares out of distributable earnings, on the other hand, does not involve a capital reduction, and no publication is required or right of opposition given. Only fully paid shares may be amortized in this manner, and the shares to be amortized are purchased on the open market or, if a fixed price is established, they are selected by drawing before a notary. The articles of incorporation may authorize the issue of so-called "enjoyment" shares (acciones de goce) to the holders of amortized shares. These shares confer the right to receive dividends after a fixed dividend has been paid on unamortized shares, and they may even carry the right to vote. Unless the articles provide otherwise, they participate with unamortized shares in the assets of the corporation on liquidation, after the par value of the unamortized shares has been totally paid.

Although the law does not specifically recognize this method, there is no obstacle to reducing capital through the reduction of the par value of the outstanding shares. That device might be most appropriate where the value of net assets has declined below the amount of stated capital so that the corporation is prohibited to pay dividends. A reduction in the par value of the outstanding shares would have the effect of equalizing the amount of stated capital and the value of net assets and would permit the payment of dividends out of subsequent profits.

VARIABLE CAPITAL COMPANIES

Any type of business association may be organized with what is known as variable capital.[39] The variable capital form of corporation offers several advantages over the fixed capital form and is often used by both foreign and Mexican businessmen. Not only may the capital of such a company be increased and decreased with fewer formalities than in the case of an ordinary corporation, but the corporation may in effect have authorized and unissued shares, which is not possible for a fixed capital corporation in view of the requirement that all of its shares be subscribed upon incorporation. Furthermore, since an amendment of the articles of incorporation is not required for a change in capital, a permit from the Ministry of Foreign Relations is not necessary, and the risk that restrictions on foreign ownership may be imposed is reduced.[40] However, a company having variable capital may not issue shares in bearer form.

The articles of incorporation of a variable capital company must provide for a fixed minimum capital of at least 25,000 pesos, and the authorized capital above the stated minimum is considered the variable portion. No maximum limit on the variable portion of the capital is required to be stated, but in practice this is often done. Within the limits of the variable portion, the capital may be increased and decreased as established in the articles of incorporation or by resolution of an extraordinary shareholders meeting.

Although it is probably the intent of the law to dispense with the requirements of execution before a notary and public recordation of changes in the variable portion of the capital, there is an apparent inconsistency in the law. In the absence of a provision in the articles, a capital increase must be by resolution of an extraordinary shareholders meeting. The chapter of the law dealing with shareholders meetings contains a general requirement that minutes of extraordinary meetings must be notarized and recorded.[41] Consequently, the law might be construed to require those formalities even in the case of a variable capital company.

This interpretation would, it seems, largely defeat the principal purpose of the variable capital form, since substantially the same formalities would be required as in the case of an ordinary corporation, the only difference being that an increase of variable capital would not take the form of an amendment to the articles. Nevertheless, some lawyers take the precaution of notarizing and recording resolutions to increase or decrease variable capital.

A potential problem in a variable capital corporation is the statutory right of shareholders to have their shares redeemed as long as the capital is not thereby reduced below the minimum stated amount. Notification to the corporation of the exercise of this right takes effect at the end of the current fiscal year if it is given before the last trimester of the year, and at the close of the following year if it is given thereafter. In view of the possible consequences to the corporation of the exercise of this redemption right, it is often expressly waived in the articles of incorporation, but the validity of such a waiver is doubtful.

MANAGEMENT

The hierarchy of management of a Mexican corporation consists of the shareholders assembly or meeting, the administrators or directors, and the managers.[42] The *comisario,* an elected representative of the shareholders whose main duties are to safeguard their interests against abuses by the directors, is sometimes included in a discussion of management, but he has no management function and is considered below in connection with rights of shareholders.

The management powers of shareholders extend far beyond the power to elect and remove directors. The general assembly of shareholders is the "supreme organ" of the corporation and "may resolve and ratify all acts and operations" of the corporation.[43] The effect of this provision is to give the shareholders power to initiate any action in connection with corporate management and even to override management decisions made by the board of directors. It is necessary, for example, for the shareholders to decide on the declaration and amount of dividends,[44] though the date and form of payment may be delegated to the board.

Within the limitations imposed in the articles of incorporation and shareholder resolutions, the directors have charge of the active management of the corporate business.[45] A corporation may have one or more directors, as established in its articles. If a corporation has only one director, he is referred to as the "sole administrator" *(administrador único)*; if there are two or more, they constitute a board of administration or board of directors. In order to avoid the necessity of amending the articles for an increase or reduction in the number of directors, it is often provided that the number of directors shall be determined by the shareholders.

The initial directors are customarily named in the articles of incorporation, and thereafter directors are elected by the shareholders for the term established in the articles and until their successors are elected and take office. Since they are general agents of the corporation, their election must be recorded in the public commercial register.[46] Directors are not required to be shareholders.

The requirement that directors must have capacity to exercise commerce[47] raises some question as to whether or not nonresident foreigners may lawfully be directors of Mexican corporations. Resident aliens with immigrant status must have express authority from the Ministry of Internal Affairs to serve as corporate directors. Most Mexican lawyers, however, see no difficulty in the election of nonresident foreign directors, and it is rather commonplace for foreigners to serve on Mexican boards. It is usual for alternates to be elected to serve in the absence of the directors, and Mexicans are often elected as alternates for foreign directors. Furthermore, in most cases in which foreign share ownership is limited by law or by the permit to incorporate issued by the Ministry of Foreign Relations, a majority of the directors must be Mexican citizens. Cautious attorneys also follow the practice of obtaining visitor permits for nonresident foreigners to enter the country to attend board meetings, on the theory that the legal restrictions on the exercise of commerce by foreigners apply only to persons with tourist status.[48]

Unless otherwise agreed, the first director elected holds the office of president of the board. The law does not expressly recognize other officers, but it is customary also to name a vice-president, a secretary, and a treasurer. The board may be given the authority in the articles to elect its own officers. The officers of the board normally also serve as officers of the corporation. Although the appointment of separate corporate officers is somewhat foreign to Mexican practice, there seems to be no reason that this could not be provided for in the articles of incorporation, especially in view of the fact that general and special managers are specifically authorized.

The office of director is by definition revocable, and the shareholders may consequently remove a director at any time for cause or without cause. Most textwriters are of the opinion, however, that removal without cause subjects the corporation to liability to the director for damages, apparently on the theory of breach of contract.[49] This opinion is supported by the argument that article 176 of the commercial companies law, which specifies certain grounds for the removal of a director, would be meaningless if removal without cause and removal for cause had the same legal effect.

In the event of removal of one or more of the directors, the remaining directors continue to act as the board if they constitute a quorum. If the sole administrator is removed or if the remaining directors do not constitute a quorum of the board, the vacancies are filled by appointment by the *comisarios* until the next meeting of shareholders for the election of directors.

Board meetings are held at the times designated in the articles of incorporation or upon the call of the president or other person specified in the articles. At least half of the directors must be present for there to be a quorum, and resolutions are adopted by the affirmative vote of a majority of those present. These are minimum requirements, however, and may be increased in the articles of incorporation. In case of a tie the president has the deciding vote.

Despite the broad powers of the board, it has been held that a corporation is not bound by directors' acts that are beyond the corporate purpose.[50] However, directors are presumed to have full power to represent the corporation in dealings with third persons, and limitations on their authority contained in the articles of incorporation or otherwise are not effective against outsiders.[51]

Directors are jointly liable to the corporation for breach of their duties. Liability is imposed not only for their own improper conduct but also for that of their predecessors in office if they have knowledge of it and fail to report it in writing to the *comisarios*. A director may escape liability only by manifesting his disagreement with the improper action at the time of board deliberation and vote on the matter. Absence from the meeting at which the improper action was taken does not relieve him from liability.

Directors having a personal interest in an act or transaction that conflicts with that of the corporation are required to reveal it to the other directors and may not participate in the discussion or vote on the matter. A director who violates this requirement is liable for damages resulting to the corporation. Furthermore, it seems likely that the vote of an interested director would be void and that, if his vote was necessary to the adoption of the resolution, the resolution itself would be void.

In order to guarantee satisfaction of possible liability to the corporation, directors must post security, usually in the form of a bond or cash deposit, as established in the articles of incorporation or by the shareholders. In practice, probably because the persons responsible for drafting the articles also intend to serve as its directors, this protection is often rendered meaningless by a provision setting the amount of the guarantee at a nominal sum.

Managers, who normally have charge of the daily operations of the company, are appointed by the shareholders or by the board of directors or sole administrator, and their authority must be expressly conferred. Although the wording of the law is not entirely clear, it is understood that only the body which has made the appointment or a higher body in the hierarchy of corporate management may remove a manager, so that one appointed by the shareholders may not be removed by the directors. The requirements as to capacity, guarantee of performance of duty, and recordation of appointment that are applicable to directors also apply to managers.

RIGHTS AND PROTECTIONS OF SHAREHOLDERS

In view of the growing number of cases in which foreign investors in Mexico associate, often in a minority position, with Mexican investors, either because it is required by law or government policy or because the foreign investor considers it advantageous, it is becoming increasingly important to consider the rights and protections available to shareholders, especially minority shareholders. There seem to be few decided cases in this area, probably because Mexican companies have traditionally been closely held by small groups of shareholders who have either actively managed the business or dominated the directors. Only recently has the phenomenon of separation of ownership from control begun to emerge to any significant extent. The law, however, provides certain basic protections to shareholders, and additional rights and protections may often be inserted in the articles of incorporation. Since the articles are considered a contract among the parties, the law allows considerable leeway in the establishment of the rules that govern the corporation. The extent to which the provisions of the law may be waived or changed by contract is not always clear, however. In some cases the law expressly prohibits waiver, and it can probably be said that no provision whose purpose is to protect minority shareholders or creditors of the company may be waived, though the protections established by law may usually be increased by contract.[52]

Certain protections of the proprietary rights of shareholders have been mentioned above in the discussion of capital structure. These include protections against impairment of capital, pre-emptive rights on new issues of shares, and possible contract restrictions on transfers of shares. The most important protection is, of course, that the shareholders are not liable for debts of the corporation once the value of their shares has been paid.[53] Conversely, creditors of a shareholder may not reach corporate assets.[54] There is one exception, however, that should be noted. Under article 23 of the law it is at least implied that a shareholder's creditors may reach profits of the company that correspond to the shareholder according to the financial statements, presumably even when no declaration of dividends has been made. This provision lends support to the view of at least one Mexican textwriter that the shareholders have the right to receive all profits that can be legally distributed and that the corporation may not refuse or postpone the distribution of profits unless otherwise provided in the articles.[55]

SHAREHOLDERS MEETINGS

Shareholders' rights of control and management are exercised through the shareholders assembly or meeting.[56] The power of election and removal of directors and managers and the unusually broad powers derived from the fact that the general assembly is the "supreme organ" of the company have been noted.

Shareholders meetings are classified as general or special. Special meetings are held when a class vote is required by the holders of a special class of shares to approve action that may affect their rights as a class. General meetings are either ordinary or extraordinary. Ordinary meetings must be held at least annually within four months following the close of the fiscal year for the purpose of considering the annual financial statements, electing directors and *comisarios* and fixing their compensation when it is not established in the articles of incorporation, and taking action on any other matters included in the notice of the meeting. Extraordinary meetings are those held to consider amendments to the articles of incorporation and other matters of fundamental importance, such as the issuance of bonds, and any other matters for which the law or the articles require a special quorum. All meetings must be held at the corporate domicile except in case of *force majeure,* or they will be void.

Shareholders meetings are normally called by the sole administrator or board of directors, but the *comisarios* also have this power, and protections are provided for shareholders against the refusal or failure of those persons to call a meeting. Shareholders holding at least 33 percent of the outstanding shares may at any time make a written request for the call of a general assembly to deal with the matters stated in their petition. If the administrator, board, or *comisarios* refuse or fail to call a meeting within fifteen days, the call may be made by a court at the corporate domicile on the petition of those shareholders. All shareholders, regardless of the number of shares they own, have this right when there has been no meeting for two consecutive fiscal periods or when the shareholders have failed to approve the annual financial statements or elect directors and *comisarios* at the meetings held during that period. Furthermore, if for any reason any of the *comisarios* have resigned or been removed, the board is required to call a general meeting within a period of three days to fill the vacancy. If the board fails to make the call, any shareholder may request judicial call of a meeting for that purpose.[57]

Notice of general meetings must be published in the official periodical or a major newspaper at the place of the corporate domicile. If the articles do not specify the time of the notice, publication must be made at least fifteen days before the date of the meeting. Since notice published in this manner may not reach many shareholders, especially nonresident foreigners, it is often important that some form of personal notice be required in the articles, preferably notice by registered mail.[58] This is not practicable, however, when the shares are in bearer form. The notice of meeting must contain the agenda of matters to be presented, called the order of the day, and must be signed by the convening authority. If these requirements are not fulfilled, resolutions adopted by the meeting are void unless all of the shares are represented at the time of voting. The Supreme Court has held that the mere physical presence of shareholders is not sufficient to constitute waiver of notice if they abstain from voting and object to the legality of the meeting.[59]

If the meeting is an ordinary one, holders of shares representing half the stated capital constitute a quorum, and the vote of a majority of those present is sufficient to adopt resolutions. In the case of extraordinary meetings, at least three-fourths of the outstanding shares must be represented for the transaction of business, and the vote of shares representing half the capital is required. If a quorum is not present on the date of the meeting, a second call may be made, and a quorum is deemed to exist for the transaction of the business stated in the agenda regardless of the number of shareholders present. In the case of extraordinary meetings, however, the vote of at least half the outstanding shares is required in any case. Shareholders may be represented by proxies, but neither directors nor *comisarios* may act as proxies.

Holders of 33 percent of the shares represented at a meeting have the right to request postponement for a period of three days of the vote on any matter.

Shareholders who have a personal interest in a transaction adverse to that of the corporation must abstain from the discussion and vote on the matter. The law does not provide that a shareholder's vote in violation of this prohibition is void, but it imposes liability on him for damages to the corporaton if his vote was necessary for approval of the measure. Shareholders who are directors or *comisarios* may not vote on resolutions relating to the balance sheet or to their liability for improper actions. Resolutions adopted in violation of this provision are void if the vote of the director or *comisario* was necessary for adoption. This restriction has the effect of discouraging controlling shareholders from serving personally on the board of directors.

Minutes of shareholders meetings must be kept in the officially authorized minute book and signed by the president and secretary of the meeting and by the *comisarios* who attended. If for any reason the minutes of a meeting cannot be inserted in the minute book, they must be notarized. Minutes of all extraordinary meetings are required to be notarized and recorded in the public commercial register.

RIGHT OF WITHDRAWAL

In the event of an amendment to the articles of incorporation to change the purpose or nationality of the corporation or to transform it into a different form of business association, dissenting shareholders are given the right to withdraw and receive reimbursement of the book value of their shares. This right must be exercised within fifteen days following adjournment of the meeting at which the amendment was adopted.[60]

CORPORATE CONTROL DEVICES AND MINORITY REPRESENTATION

Except for the voting limitations that may be imposed on preferred shares, discussed above, each share is entitled to one vote.[61] Further-more, article 198 provides that "any agreement that restricts the freedom of vote of the shareholders is null." On the basis of this provision, most authorities are of the opinion that voting trusts and pooling agreements, often employed in the United States to obtain control by a combination of voting power, are illegal.[62] Shareholders may, however, achieve the same results of a voting trust or pooling agreement through the use of a separate holding company that would hold title to and vote their shares.

It is also thought that provisions for cumulative voting for the elec-tion of directors are invalid.[63] The law does, however, provide for minority representation on the board of directors. If there are three or more directors, minority shareholders holding 25 percent of the out-standing shares may elect at least one director.[64] The articles of incor-poration may give the minority greater representation on the board, though a provision allowing minority shareholders to elect a majority of the directors would doubtless be invalid. Protection against subsequent removal of the minority's directors by the majority shareholders is afforded by a provision that they may be removed only when all other directors are removed.[65] While no condition is placed on this restriction, it presumably does not apply where removal of the directors elected by the minority is for good cause.

Despite the general view that pooling and voting trust agreements are not enforceable, there are other methods by which minority share-holders may gain effective voting control. Probably the most obvious situation is that in which the majority shares are widely held by a large number of persons who cannot easily be marshaled into a unified group. One of the ways in which foreign-controlled Mexican companies are responding to government pressure to admit Mexican investors into their operations is the public sale of shares, and even if more than half the outstanding shares are sold in this manner, effective voting control may not necessarily be lost.

Another device that has been suggested as a means of obtaining voting control for a particular meeting of shareholders, though it is doubtful that it has been used for this purpose, is the contract of reporto.[66] This contract, apparently intended originally for speculative stock exchange transactions, is in the nature of a purchase with an option to repurchase. The purchaser (reportador) acquires title to shares of stock, obligating himself to sell shares of the same kind to the seller (reportado) at the same price plus a premium. The buyer may make re-purchase mandatory upon the seller, in which case he pays a premium to the seller for the right to hold and benefit from the shares for the period stated. There must always be payment of a money consideration, and in no case may the term of the agreement be more than forty-five days, though it may be extended. Unless the contract expressly provides to the contrary, the right to vote the shares passes to the new holder. This type of agreement would be most useful in the case of bearer shares since there is no requirement of transfer on the books of the corporation as with registered shares.

If it is not possible for minority groups to combine to achieve voting control, the articles of incorporation may usually be drafted to require at least the concurrence of minority shareholders, by imposing greater quorum and voting requirements for shareholders and directors than those established by the law. This possibility is expressly recognized in the case of extraordinary shareholders meetings,[67] and it seems to be universally agreed by Mexican lawyers that greater than majority quorum and voting requirements may be established in the articles of incorporation for ordinary shareholders meetings and directors meetings. It is at least questionable, however, whether a requirement of concurrence of all shareholders may be imposed; this might be considered an invalid restriction on the general right of the majority shareholders to manage the affairs of the corporation.[68]

RIGHT TO INSPECTION AND INFORMATION

The right of a shareholder to examine the books and records of the corporation is recognized by the law in only one situation. During the fifteen-day period immediately preceding a general shareholders meeting or other period of notice provided in the articles of incorporation the shareholders have the right to examine the books and documents relevant to the purposes of the meeting.[69]

Except in that instance, the right of inspection is exercised through the *comisario*.[70] The office of *comisario* is intended as a protection of shareholders against mismanagement and other abuses by the directors, by virtue of his role as an inspector or overseer of the general operation and finances of the company. More specifically, the *comisarios* are obligated to verify the existence of the security that must be posted by directors and managers, require of the directors a monthly balance sheet, examine the books and records of the company and cash on hand at least once a month, examine and report to the shareholders on the annual balance sheet, and generally oversee the operations of the company.

They also have authority to call shareholders meetings and must attend but have no vote at meetings of the board and shareholders. In order to insure their independence from management, they may not be employees of the corporation or related to any of the directors. Minority shareholders have the same right to representation among the *comisarios* as on the board of directors. That is, unless the articles of incorporation provide for greater rights, minorities representing 25 percent of the outstanding shares may elect a *comisario* provided there are three or more.

Despite the laudable theory behind the role of the *comisario,* the protection afforded in practice is often illusory. Since they are elected by the same interests who elect the members of the board, they in fact seldom oppose the directors' operation of the company. The right of the minority to representation among the *comisarios* is rarely exercised because most corporations do not have more than one *comisario.* Therefore, the effect of the requirement of a *comisario* is often merely to impose the burden on the shareholders to find a person who is qualified to exercise commerce to hold the office. Because the duties of the *comisario* relate mainly to the financial aspects of the company's operations, the independent auditor or a member of the accounting firm employed by the corporation is frequently willing to serve in this capacity. Nevertheless, the *comisario* may acquire a key role in struggles for control or in other disputes between shareholders because of his right of inspection, power to call meetings, and right to fill vacancies on the board.

SHAREHOLDERS' SUITS

The shareholders are given a right of action against the directors for damages to the corporation resulting from violations of their duties. Article 161 provides that a demand may be made to enforce a director's liability only upon the decision of a general shareholders meeting. As soon as the shareholders adopt a resolution to bring suit against a director, he ceases to act in his capacity as director and may be reelected only if the court finds the suit against him to be without merit.[71] In the event the shareholders fail to take action against a guilty director, any shareholder or group of shareholders representing at least 33 percent of the outstanding shares may bring suit on behalf of the corporation, pursuant to article 163, provided their suit is for the total amount of the liability to the company and not only for the personal damages of the plaintiff shareholders and provided the plaintiffs did not vote for or approve a shareholders' resolution not to bring an action against the director.

The law makes no provision for a shareholder's derivative suit against third persons, such as defaulting debtors of the corporation, in the event the board of directors should fail or refuse to bring suit. A majority of the shareholders, acting in a general meeting, could undoubtedly resolve to take action on behalf of the corporation by virtue of their broad managerial powers. Also, of course, they have the authority to remove recalcitrant directors from office and replace them with persons who are more willing to abide by the shareholders' wishes. It does not seem possible, however, for a minority shareholder to enforce a corporate right in defiance of the will of the majority.

In cases in which shareholders' resolutions are adopted in violation of the law, as for example where a director improperly votes on the balance sheet or on a measure relating to his liability to the corporation or resolutions adopted at a meeting held on improper or inadequate notice, shareholders representing 33 percent of the capital have the right under article 201 to bring suit to challenge the validity of the resolutions. The suit must be brought within fifteen days following the date of adjournment of the meeting, and the plaintiffs must not have attended the meeting or must have voted against the challenged resolution. It is further provided that such a suit may not be brought against resolutions "relative to the liability of directors or *comisarios*." This provision would seem literally to mean that even resolutions approving directors' actions could not be challenged by this procedure, but in view of the right under article 163 of a 33 percent minority to bring suit against directors in defiance of a contrary decision by the majority, the intent of the law undoubtedly is that the restriction applies only to resolutions to enforce a director's liability. Performance of a challenged resolution may be enjoined by the court if the plaintiffs post sufficient security to cover any damages that might result to the corporation in the event their action is held to be unfounded.[72] The Supreme Court has held that an action under article 201 must be brought against the corporation itself rather than against the persons responsible for the violation.[73]

Apart from the statutory right to challenge the validity of resolutions, the Supreme Court has recognized that any shareholder may bring suit to have an illegal shareholders meeting declared null. This right exists, for example, where a shareholders meeting has been held without a quorum or without notice or at a place other than the corporate domicile. The proper defendants in such a case are the shareholders who have improperly held the meeting and not the corporation itself.[74]

MERGER AND TRANSFORMATION

A merger of two or more companies may be effected upon the resolution of an extraordinary shareholders meeting of each of the companies.[75] The resolutions must be recorded in the public commercial register and published in the official newspaper of the companies' domiciles. Each company must also publish its most recent balance sheet, and the company or companies whose existence will terminate must publish the procedure established for the satisfaction of its or their liabilities.

The merger may not be effected until the expiration of three months from the date of recordation of the resolutions to merge. During that period any creditor of the companies may bring suit to oppose the merger, which may not be carried out until judgment is rendered declaring the suit unfounded. Although the law does not state the grounds on which such a suit may be brought, presumably the court would restrain the merger if it found that satisfaction of the indebtedness would not be adequately guaranteed as a result of the merger.

If all outstanding debts, including term obligations, of the merging companies are paid, or the amount of such debts is deposited with a bank, or the consent of all creditors is obtained, the merger will take effect at the time of recordation of the shareholders' resolutions in the public commercial register. If a deposit is made, the certificate evidencing it must be published.

Upon the merger the surviving company or the new resulting company succeeds to the rights and assumes the liabilities of the company or companies that cease to exist.

Transformation under Mexican law means the change from one form of company to another. A company in any form provided for in the commercial companies law may be transformed into any other legal form, even a civil company.[76] One of the types of partnership or a limited liability company, for example, may be transformed into a corporation, or vice versa. Also, any company organized with fixed capital may be changed to a variable capital company. The requirements and procedure for transformation are the same as those for merger.

DISSOLUTION AND LIQUIDATION

Corporations are dissolved upon any of the following events: expiration of the term established in the articles of incorporation, impossibility to carry out the principal purpose of the corporation, resolution of the shareholders adopted in accordance with the articles and the law, reduction of the number of shareholders to less than five, or loss of two-thirds of the stated capital. Except in the case of expiration of the life of the corporation, dissolution must be recorded in the public commercial register, and suit may be brought by any interested person to compel recordation.[77] In order to avoid the risk of automatic dissolution for reduction of the number of shareholders to less than five, where there are two or more groups of shareholders, it is prudent for each group to apportion its shares among at least four persons.

Upon dissolution, the corporation is placed in liquidation under one or more liquidators elected by the shareholders or as provided in the articles of incorporation. The powers of the liquidators and the procedure for the liquidation may be established in the articles or by shareholders' resolution. In the absence of express provisions, the liquidators wind up the company's affairs, collect debts to the corporation and pay its obligations, and liquidate the assets. Any remaining assets are distributed to the shareholders on the basis of a final balance sheet, which must be published and approved by a general meeting of shareholders.[78]

VIII

Taxation

Mexican taxes take a wide variety of forms and are levied by both the federal and state governments. Federal taxes are by far the more significant. Of these the federal income tax, taxes on foreign trade, and the commercial receipts tax on gross income from commercial sales and services are the most important sources of revenue, but there are also other taxes on domestic transactions, including special excise taxes on the production, manufacture, or first sale of certain products, and taxes on the production of natural resources, notably minerals. Less important is the federal stamp tax, which applies only to noncommercial transactions and documents. Only the general taxes—the income tax and the commercial receipts tax—are covered in detail in this chapter. Import duties are discussed in Chapter V, and social security contributions, a form of taxation, are included in Chapter IX.

State and local governments are largely dependent on federal grants-in-aid and loans and participation in federal taxes, and state revenues from taxes are relatively small. The most significant state taxes are those on real property,[1] but taxes are also levied on commerce and industry, usually on the principal industrial or agricultural products of each state. Although the states do not impose a general income tax, they all tax income from capital received from sources within the state and either participate in the federal commercial receipts tax or levy their own tax on commercial revenues.

Under the Constitution, taxing authority is reserved to the federal government in certain cases, and in others the federal and state governments have concurrent power to tax. Political subdivisions of the states, called *municipios* (municipalities), have no taxing authority.[2] Article 73, section XXIX, of the Constitution gives the federal Congress exclusive power to tax foreign commerce, natural resources, credit institutions, insurance companies, and public utility services rendered by or under concession from the federal government, and to impose excise taxes (called special taxes) on electric energy, production and consumption of processed tobaccos and beer, gasoline and other petroleum products, matches, agave juice *(aguamiel)* and products of its fermentation, and the exploitation of forests. Through the exclusive power to legislate on these matters under article 73, section X, of the Constitution, the federal government also has the sole taxing power over hydrocarbons, mining, the motion-picture industry, commerce, betting and lotteries, credit institutions and electric-power companies, and in labor matters. The taxing power of the federal government is not limited to matters expressly assigned to it, however, since the federal Congress is given the power under article 73, section VII, to exact all contributions necessary to cover the federal budget and because of the general principle that the power to legislate includes the power to tax, and federal excise taxes are imposed on a number of matters not listed in the Constitution.

The states have concurrent authority to levy taxes in areas not within the exclusive jurisdiction of the federal government, but there are substantial restrictions on states' taxing power. Article 73, section XXIX, of the Constitution is interpreted as an exclusive grant of authority to the federal government and as prohibiting state taxation of the matters listed therein. Other fiscal matters are forbidden to the states under articles 117 and 118 of the Constitution, including the issuance of tax stamps and stamped paper; the taxation or the entry, exit, or transit through their territory of persons, merchandise, or other property; the imposition of taxes or fees on the circulation or consumption of domestic or foreign products; and the issuance of fiscal laws or other measures that discriminate against domestic or foreign goods on the basis of their origin. They are also prohibited, under article 118, section I, to impose duties *(derechos de tonelaje)* or other port charges and to impose contributions or fees on imports or exports without the consent of the federal Congress.[3] While there is substantial overlapping of the taxing authority of the federal and state governments, in practice the federal government discourages concurrent state taxes by allocating a portion of the federal tax revenue to those states that renounce their right of taxation in the field covered by a particular federal tax.[4]

Despite the fact that the taxing authority of the federation is virtually unlimited, certain individual rights guaranteed by the Constitution operate to protect taxpayers and may not be invaded by the tax laws or disregarded by the tax authorities. Article 31, section IV, for example, requires that the burden of taxes and other public contributions must be proportional and equitable. Laws that are not of general application and retroactive laws are prohibited by articles 13 and 14. The important right of petition contained in article 8 entitles taxpayers to submit written petitions to public officials and obligates the latter to answer them in writing and without undue delay. The procedural due process guaranteed by article 14 implies that a taxpayer must be informed of administrative decisions that affect him and that an opportunity must be given to him to contest these decisions and to offer evidence in support of his contentions.

Each federal tax is established and regulated by a separate federal statute. However, all federal taxes and other revenues to be collected during a particular fiscal year must be listed in the annual revenue law *(ley de ingresos)*, which is usually promulgated on December 31 immediately preceding the year for which it is effective, and no tax may be collected in a year for which it is not listed in that law even though the tax is imposed by a separate statute. Many of the basic rules that apply to all federal taxes are found in the federal fiscal code of 1966,[5] including provisions on the origin, prosecution, and extinction of tax liabilities; administrative agencies and procedure; litigation before the tax court *(tribunal fiscal);* violations and penalties; and criminal offenses and their investigation.

The administration of the federal tax laws, as well as all matters of fiscal and monetary policy and public credit, are the responsibility of the Ministry of Finance and Public Credit. One of the three subsecretaries of the ministry is in charge of taxes and heads the department of income, which is composed of bureaus for the administration of each major tax or group of taxes. Under the subsecretary of income there is also a federal fiscal attorney, whose office represents the government in tax litigation, prepares rulings on questions of law, investigates tax violations, and imposes civil penalties in connection with violations.

Administrative remedies available to a taxpayer against a determination of the government are provided for in each law imposing a tax. After all available administrative remedies have been exhausted, a taxpayer may appeal to the tax court, which is an administrative court since it is within the executive rather than the judicial branch of government, but is independent of the Ministry of Finance and all other administrative agencies.[6] No provision is made for an appeal by the taxpayer from the tax court, but its decisions may be challenged in direct *amparo* proceedings before the collegiate circuit court of the

Federal District.[7] Tax authorities may request review of an unfavorable decision by the full tax court and in important cases may appeal to the Supreme Court.[8]

INCOME TAX

The income tax was first introduced in Mexico in 1921, and in 1925 it was made permanent and the essential characteristics of the tax which were to survive for some forty years were established. Under the income tax law of 1925 and the subsequent laws of 1941 and 1953 there was no lumping of income into a common taxable mass, but rather income was classified under various schedules according to categories of taxable activity and separate tax rates were applied to each schedule. An excess profits tax on commercial, industrial, and agricultural profits was introduced in 1948 and was incorporated into the law of 1953. Another notable feature of that law was the so-called distributable profits tax, a proportionate tax on the profits of all business entities whether or not they were distributed in the form of a dividend or otherwise.

A major step forward in a tax reform program initiated at the end of 1961 to modernize and simplify the law and to secure a more equitable distribution of the tax burden was taken with the adoption at the end of 1964 of a new law, which became effective January 1, 1965,[9] and radically changed the structure of the income tax. This was the first step toward the establishment of a true personal income tax system. The schedular tax was abolished and replaced by a progressive tax system under which business enterprises are taxed under a single table applicable to their total taxable income and individuals with income exceeding a stated minimum amount are also subject to a global tax on their combined income after specified exemptions, exclusions, and deductions. Vestiges of the schedular system are evident, however, in the separate rates applicable to certain types of income of individuals. Among the other important innovations of the present law, the excess profits tax was abolished and the distributable profits tax was repealed except with respect to profits of branches and agencies of foreign corporations. Amendments to the law were adopted at the end of each of the years 1965, 1966, 1967, and 1968 to clarify doubtful matters and to correct certain inequities that had appeared in its practical application.[10] No regulations had been issued as of early 1970 under this law, and the 1954 regulations are still in effect to the extent they are not inconsistent with the new law.[11]

CLASSES OF TAXPAYERS

The income tax is applicable to all individuals and entities that are citizens or residents of Mexico or that derive income from Mexican sources.[12] Mexican citizens and companies organized under Mexican law, resident aliens, and branches, agencies, or other permanent establishments in Mexico of foreign entities are taxed on all income, both domestic and foreign. Foreign companies that engage in taxable transactions in Mexico through branches or agencies in the country are taxed, however, only on the income from the operations of their Mexican establishments.[13]

Nonresident aliens and foreign entities that do not regularly engage in taxable transactions in Mexico through branches, agencies, or other permanent establishments in the country are subject to tax only on their income from sources of wealth located in Mexico. The law contains no general definition of what constitutes Mexican-source income, but certain rules seem to be well established in practice. Any income from a business activity performed in Mexico or from income-producing capital employed in Mexico is considered to be from Mexican sources. Under administrative practice, income from the sale by a foreign seller to a buyer in Mexico of merchandise or other tangible property is deemed to be from Mexican sources only if the property is located in Mexico at the time of the transaction but not if it is located abroad. However, activities such as advertising or the solicitation of orders on a continuous basis may be considered engaging in commerce under the Commercial Code and subject the profits from the sales to tax even though the goods are not located in Mexico at the time of the sale. Income from personal services rendered to a Mexican resident is considered to be derived from Mexican sources regardless of where the services are performed or where payment for them is made.[14] Income from the following activities is expressly stated to be from Mexican sources when it is received from persons resident in the country: lease of railroad cars; distribution of foreign publications; rendering of technical services paid for by persons or entities subject to the tax on business enterprises; reinsurance and rebonding operations with Mexican companies; licensing of patents, trademarks, and trade names; and loans made by foreign banks and other foreign enterprises.[15]

Exemption from the income tax is provided for certain types of organizations and persons engaged in designated activities, such as public service enterprises owned by the government; chambers of commerce and industry; tenants of communal lands and local agricultural and *ejido* credit associations; producers' and consumers' co-operatives; owners of a single taxicab for hire; educational institutions; charitable, religious, cultural, and other similar organizations; and trust funds for employees' pension plans.[16]

There are two broad catagories of taxpayers, enterprises and individuals, and the rules of taxation are different for each. Enterprises are subject to a graduated global tax on their aggregate taxable income from all sources. Legal entities, individuals, and economic units that are engaged in commercial, industrial, agricultural, livestock raising, and fishing activities are subject to the tax on enterprises.[17] Although the nature of the activities of an enterprise is the principal criterion, legal entities may be subject to the tax because of their form of organization. All business companies organized in one of the forms provided for in the commercial companies law are taxed as enterprises by virtue of the fact that they are classified as "merchants" under the commercial law.[18] Companies and associations formed under the civil law, though not organized for the purpose of obtaining a profit, are taxed as enterprises if they nevertheless engage in commercial activities, that is, activities from which they derive a profit.[19] A combination of individuals or entities that constitutes an economic unit distinct from its members, even though not a separate legal entity, is also taxed as an enterprise when it engages in any of those activities.[20] Individual merchants and unincorporated economic units are subject to the global tax on enterprises only on income from their business activities and from property used in the business.

Individuals are taxed separately on income from personal services and income from the investment of capital.[21] If an individual's total annual income from both sources exceeds 100,000 pesos, after taking into account the deductions and adjustments authorized for the different types of income when taxed separately, he is subject to a global tax on his combined income. However, certain income taxable separately under the tax on income from personal services or the tax on income from capital investments is excludable from combined income. Persons subject to the tax on combined income are allowed certain exemptions and deductions in addition to those allowed under the separate tax systems for personal-service and capital-investment income. An individual whose total annual income from both sources is less than 50,000 pesos is taxed separately on each type of income without the additional exemptions and deductions. Individuals whose total income is between those amounts may elect to be taxed by either method.

FEDERAL REGISTER OF TAXPAYERS

An important feature of the tax system is the requirement that tax-payers be registered in the federal register of taxpayers in the Ministry of Finance.[22] This requirement is applicable to all persons, both individuals and enterprises, that are regularly subject to any type of federal taxes, not only the income tax. Persons who make certain types of payments to others to whom the payments are taxable income are required by law to withhold the amount of tax due and pay it for the account of the recipient, and the registration requirement also applies to persons who regularly withhold taxes even though they are not themselves taxpayers. However, individuals who receive certain types of taxable income from capital investments, such as dividends or other distributions of profits of com-panies and gains from sales of urban real property or securities, are cur-rently exempt from the registration requirement.[23]

Application for registration of an enterprise must be filed with the federal finance office with jurisdiction over the taxpayer's domicile or business establishment within ten business days following the date of initiation of operations. Employers are required to register their em-ployees within ten days after commencement of employment unless they are already registered or have applied for registration.

Nonresidents who are regularly obligated to pay federal taxes, such as nonresident aliens and foreign entities that receive interest, royalties, or fees for technical services from Mexican sources, may be registered by the persons who make payments to the nonresident from which they are required to withhold taxes. For purposes of registration, the nonresident taxpayer's domicile is considered to be that of the payer, and registration must be made within thirty business days after the date of the contract or other document giving rise to the taxpayer's right to receive payment from the payer.

Registered taxpayers are issued a registration number and a card evidencing their registration. Recipients of taxable payments are required to indicate on their invoices and receipts their registration number, and taxpayers who claim such payments as deductible expenditures must furnish the payee's registration number or prove that he has com-municated to the Ministry of Finance the data necessary for making the registration, or the deduction is disallowed.[24]

TAXATION OF INCOME OF ENTERPRISES

"Major" and "Minor" Taxpayers

The law differentiates for some purposes between taxpayers with gross annual income in excess of 150,000 pesos, called "major" taxpayers, and those with gross annual income of 150,000 pesos or less, called "minor" taxpayers. While both classes of taxpayers are taxed on the basis of net income and under the same tax rates, the methods of computing net income are different for each. Taxable income of "major" taxpayers is gross income less the deductions authorized in the law; taxable income of "minor" taxpayers is determined as a statutory percentage of gross income that varies according to the nature of their business. Furthermore, "minor" taxpayers are required to keep only a simple cash book rather than the more complete records required of "major" taxpayers, but they may elect to keep complete accounting records, and if they do they are subject to the same method of taxation as "major" taxpayers.[25]

Taxable Income

The global tax on enterprises is imposed on the aggregate gross income of business enterprises from all sources, with certain exceptions, less the deductions authorized by the law, which include cost of goods sold.[26] Income includes all receipts in cash, in kind, or in credits that change the net worth of the taxpayer, derived from capital, from labor, or from a combination of both. When income is received in the form of property other than money, the amount of the income is the market or appraised value of the property in Mexican currency as of the date of receipt. Transactions in foreign currency must be recorded and reported in Mexican currency at the official exchange rate on the date of the transaction.[27]

Dividends and other distributions of profits received by Mexican companies from companies that operate in Mexico or from Mexican companies that operate abroad are exempt from the tax on enterprises but are subject to tax at the rates applicable to dividend income of individuals, which are proportionate rates that vary from 15 to 20 percent. However, the tax is not payable by enterprises on such dividend income to the extent that it is used to pay normal business expenses, distributed to shareholders or workers, invested during the fiscal year in which it is received or the following year for industrial, agricultural, or similar purposes, or used to pay the principal amount of debts incurred in order to pay for shares of Mexican companies constituted for those purposes.[28]

Taxpayers are not generally permitted to report sales of goods or services at cost or less. If this is done, the value of the goods or services is estimated by the Ministry of Finance and the difference between that value and the price actually received is deemed income, unless the taxpayer establishes that the sale was made at the market price, that the property had depreciated in value, or that there were circumstances that required the sale at the price received. Likewise, when goods are purchased by the taxpayer at a price that is not the true market value, the ministry makes an independent determination of the value, and the difference is includable in income.[29]

Gains and losses from the sale of capital assets are treated differently according to the type of property involved. Gains from the sale of real property that is part of the fixed assets of the taxpayer and gains from the merger or liquidation of companies in which the taxpayer is a shareholder or partner are included in income in a percentage depending upon the period of time elapsed between the dates of acquisition and sale of the property. In the case of property held for two years or less, the total amount of the gain is taxable; thereafter, the taxable amount is reduced by 20 percent for each additional two years the property has been held, and the full amount of the gain is exempt if the holding period is more than ten years. Regardless of the holding period, such gains are exempt if, within one year following the sale and with the prior authorization of the Ministry of Finance, they are invested in fixed assets for industrial, agricultural, livestock raising, or fishing activities.[30] This rule does not apply to reinvestments in commercial activities. Losses from the sale of real property or on mergers or liquidations are not deductible from ordinary income but may be offset against gains from similar transactions in the year in which the loss is incurred or in the five succeeding years, unless the property was acquired more than ten years before the date of the loss.[31] The total amount of gains from the sale of other capital assets, such as machinery and equipment, is taxable income, and losses incurred on sales of such property are fully deductible.

In the case of installment sales in which not more than 50 percent of the sales price is paid at the time of the sale, the taxpayer may elect either to report the total sales price as income in the year of the sale or to report only the amounts actually received. If he elects to report on the installment basis, a proportionate part of the cost of the goods sold is deductible in the taxable year in which installments are received. A taxpayer who makes an installment sale of real property that is part of his fixed assets has the same election. Once an election of the method of reporting installment sales has been made, it may not be changed without the authorization of the Ministry of Finance. Repossessed merchandise must be returned to inventory at the original cost less actual deterioration, plus the value of any improvements made after the sale.[32]

Income from occasional acts of commerce is subject to the tax on enterprises, with the exception of gains from occasional sales or other dispositions of real property, which are taxed under the rules covering income of individuals.[33] An occasional act of commerce is defined in the regulations as one carried out by a person who does not make commerce his usual occupation.[34] For this purpose, the term "commerce" is used in a broad sense, and transactions of enterprises that are regularly engaged in commerce, industry, agriculture, livestock raising, or fishing are not considered occasional acts of commerce even if the particular transaction is unusual in the taxpayer's business. It follows that occasional acts of commerce may be performed only by an individual outside his business sphere, a civil company, or a foreign company that does not regularly engage in taxable transactions in Mexico.

The Ministry of Finance may determine gross income by estimate if the taxpayer fails to file a return or fails to produce his books of account, documentary evidence supporting a return, or other data requested by the tax authorities; if certain irregularities are found in the taxpayer's books; or in the case of individuals who reported gross income of less than 500,000 pesos for their last fiscal year and who do not present the books of account and supporting documents required by the law. Gross income in these cases is determined from the taxpayer's records or estimated from other sources of information, and taxable income is computed as a statutory percentage of gross income according to the nature of the taxpayer's business.[35]

Deductions

General Principles.—The deductions applicable to gross income of enterprises are listed in article 20 of the law, and no deductions other than those specifically enumerated are allowed. The authorized deductions are returns, discounts, rebates, and allowances; cost of goods sold; depreciation and amortization; operating losses incurred in prior years; casualty losses; bad debts; reserves for employee retirement plans;

and other ordinary and necessary business expenses. Taxpayers engaged in livestock raising may also deduct the difference between their opening and closing inventories if the opening inventory is larger.

All deductions must be ordinary and necessary for the taxpayer's business and reasonable in relation to his operations. Generally, the deductions must be equal to the expenses shown in the taxpayer's books as either paid or accrued in the period for which they are claimed and for which the return is filed. However, expenses paid or accrued in the immediately preceding taxable year and not claimed as deductions for that year may be deducted in the current year if they affect the income of the current year rather than the income of the prior year. In addition to these general requirements, each deduction must meet the specific requirements established for it by the law at the time the expense was incurred or no later than the due date of the return.[36]

If the taxpayer is required to withhold income tax from payments made to other persons and pay it for the account of the recipient, such payments may not be deducted by the taxpayer as business expenses unless the withholding and payment obligations have been met or unless the taxpayer receives documents from the recipient showing that the tax has been paid.[37] This withholding obligation applies with respect to salaries and other compensation paid to employees, including commissions and reimbursement of traveling and representation expenses; occasional commissions; interest on bonds and other obligations issued by the enterprise; and certain payments to nonresident aliens and nonresident foreign entities such as technical service fees, royalties, and interest.[38] Furthermore, if a deduction is claimed for payments made to persons who are required to be registered in the federal register of taxpayers, the taxpayer must furnish the payee's registration number or prove that he has communicated to the Ministry of Finance the data necessary for making the registration.[39]

Purchases of raw materials, supplies, and merchandise, and payments for services must be substantiated by invoices, receipts, or other documents fulfilling the requirements of the regulations.[40] On certain types of payments received by individuals or civil companies, the recipient is required to pay all or part of the tax due by canceling revenue stamps on receipts issued for the payments, and a taxpayer that claims the deduction of such payments must obtain stamped receipts. This requirement applies in the case of fees paid to professional persons, artisans, and artists, interest and other income from capital, and rentals paid for urban real property.[41]

Cost of Goods Sold.—Enterprises engaged in mercantile trade determine the cost of goods sold by adding the cost of merchandise bought during the taxable year to the inventory at the beginning of the year and deducting the year-end inventory from that total. The cost of merchandise bought is determined by adding to the net purchase price the expense of premiums paid on foreign exchange; freight, transportation, and hauling charges; insurance; fees of agents and commission agents; and import taxes, customs duties, and consular fees. Taxpayers that deal in real property or engage in the construction of buildings for sale determine the cost of sales in the same manner, and amounts paid for materials and labor in additions to or improvements of the properties are included in cost.[42]

In the case of imports, if the purchase price declared by the taxpayer is different from the actual market value, the Ministry of Finance will fix the cost, taking into account the invoice price, the official price, or the current domestic or foreign market price.[43]

Mexican branches of foreign entities that receive goods from their home office must take the cost of manufacture and may add only transportation expenses, taxes, and other expenses incurred in connection with the importation of the goods. If the taxpayer fails to comply with this rule, it will be deemed that he has not proved his cost, and the tax is assessed on the basis of an estimate made by the Ministry of Finance.[44]

The unit cost of goods of the same type, bought at different prices and in different lots, is determined by using the average cost method, the first-in, first-out method, or the last-in, first-out method. Once one of these methods has been adopted, the taxpayer may not change it without the ministry's express consent.[45]

These rules for the computation of cost of goods sold are also applicable to enterprises engaged in manufacturing, assembling, or extractive industries, but they are further subject to specific requirements set out in the regulations. In the case of manufacturing and assembling enterprises, cost of production is determined by adding to the cost of raw materials, parts, power and fuel, the cost of direct labor and other direct manufacturing expenses. The total production cost obtained is then increased or decreased, as the case may be, by the difference between the beginning and closing inventories of goods in process.[46]

Taxpayers engaged in extractive industries determine cost of production by adding the expenses of exploration, development, and operation directly connected with the extraction of the minerals, to the cost of materials, fuel, power, and direct labor. Taxpayers that convert the mineral products they extract compute production cost as stated above and manufacturing cost according to the rules applicable generally to manufacturing enterprises.[47]

In the case of taxpayers engaged in agriculture, cost of goods sold is determined by adding the cost of products grown or purchased during the year to the inventory at the beginning of the year and deducting from the total the closing inventory. Cost includes seeds, plants, depreciation and amortization, salaries, fuels, fertilizers, insecticides, transportation, and other expenses.[48]

Depreciation and Amortization.—Depreciation of fixed tangible assets and amortization of intangible assets and deferred expenses are subject to the same general rules.[49] With few exceptions, only the straight-line method of depreciation and amortization is allowed. Maximum annual rates are established in the law and must be computed on the original cost of the asset or the actual amount of the deferred expense. In the case of assets acquired as a return of capital, a distribution of profits in kind or a contribution in kind to the capital of a company, the basis for depreciation or amortization may not exceed the undepreciated or unamortized balance on the books of the enterprise from which it was acquired.

The maximum annual amortization and depreciation rates are as follows:

1. Amortization of fixed intangible assets and deferred expenses — 5%
2. Depreciation of buildings and constructions — 5%
3. Depreciation of machinery, equipment, and other movable property not included in 4 — 10%
4. Depreciation of vehicles, rolling stock, ships, airplanes, machinery used in the construction industry, and barrels used in the wine or distilling industry — 20%

A taxpayer may apply a lower rate than that allowed by the law, but the rate initially selected must be applied consistently and may not be changed except with the consent of the Ministry of Finance. Depreciation and amortization may be first deducted in the year in which the asset is placed in service or in the following year at the taxpayer's election. He may also postpone claiming the deduction to a subsequent year, but if he does so he loses the right to deduct the amounts corresponding to the years for which no deduction was claimed.

Exceptions to the general rules on amortization are provided in the law for certain types of expenditures. Discounts, premiums, commissions, and other expenses incurred in connection with the issuance of obligations must be amortized over the life of the issue. Leasehold improvements that become the property of the lessor upon the termination of the lease and improvements to fixed assets of which the taxpayer has the use under a governmental concession must be amortized over the term of the lease or concession. Separation payments to employees may be amortized only if the separation results from a necessary readjustment incident to a reorganization of the business; such payments are amortizable over a period of up to five years. The expense of repairs and adaptations of installations is subject to amortization if the expenditure adds to the value of the fixed assets. The cost of goodwill, originally deductible under the law, may no longer be deducted or amortized.[50] Special rules are also established for the amortization of the cost of motion pictures produced in Mexico. The depletion deduction and special depreciation and amortization rates allowed mining enterprises are discussed separately below.

Depreciation and amortization at rates higher than those fixed in the law may be authorized by the Ministry of Finance upon application of the taxpayer and for adequate reasons.[51] The law further provides that, for purposes of economic development, the ministry may authorize accelerated depreciation of machinery and equipment by industrial, agricultural, livestock raising, and fishing enterprises. Commercial enterprises are not covered by this rule. Although the law expressly contemplates the issuance of general resolutions specifying the types of businesses, the applicable depreciation methods, and other criteria for the application of accelerated depreciation rates, no regulations for the implementation of this provision have been issued, and specific criteria have been established in each case in which accelerated depreciation has been authorized.

Depreciation and amortization for book purposes need not be the same as for tax purposes. If, however, the taxpayer is authorized by the Ministry of Finance to apply rates of depreciation or amortization in excess of the statutory rates, he may not charge lesser amounts in his books than those used for tax purposes.

Transactions involving fixed assets and payments of deferred expenses and charges made in foreign currency must be registered in the taxpayer's books in Mexican currency at the official rate of exchange prevailing on the date of the transaction, regardless of the date of payment.

Business Losses and Bad Debts.—The 1964 income tax law provided for the first time for the carry-forward of net operating losses. A loss incurred after the effective date of the law, January 1, 1965, may be deducted over the five taxable years following the year in which the loss is sustained.[52] To be deductible, a loss must be both a book loss and a tax loss, and if they are different, only the lower amount may be deducted. An operating loss deduction must be charged as a loss on the taxpayer's books. Losses resulting from any of the following are not deductible: operations that eliminate or tend to eliminate competition, write-offs of bad debts, and provisions for employee pension funds not provided for by law, regulations, or collective labor contracts.

The right to deduct an operating loss is a personal right of the taxpayer who sustains the loss. It may not be transferred *inter vivos* or by virtue of a merger, but the heirs or legatees of an individual taxpayer may deduct a loss if they continue the operation of the business in which the loss was incurred.

Losses of movable property, including machinery and equipment, sustained by the taxpayer by reason of fortuitous circumstances, an act of God, or the wilful act of another are deductible to the extent that the loss is not recovered by insurance, bond, or the enforcement of civil liability for the damage.[53] Losses that are reflected in the taxpayer's inventory for purposes of determining the cost of goods sold are not deductible as casualty losses. Losses that affect buildings that are part of the fixed assets of the taxpayer are treated the same as losses from the sale of real property; they are not deductible but may be offset against gains from the disposition of similar property in the same year or in the five succeeding years, except in the case of a loss sustained more than ten years after the property was acquired.

In the event that merchandise on hand has become worthless in the taxpayer's judgment because of deterioration or for other reasons, its value may be deducted if the Ministry of Finance either authorizes its destruction and it is actually destroyed in the presence of a representative of the ministry or authorizes its donation to an educational institution.

Losses from bad debts may be deducted when the limitation period for collection of the debt has expired or sooner if the taxpayer can prove that collection is impossible.[54] Reserves for bad debts, not recognized under the current law, were formerly deductible in a limited blanket amount, and a taxpayer who had a reserve for bad debts computed as a deduction for income tax purposes before January 1, 1965, must charge actual losses against the reserve until it is exhausted before he may claim additional deductions.[55] If the taxpayer recovers a bad debt for which he claimed a deduction in a prior year, he must include the amount recovered in income for the year of recovery.

Employee Pension Plans.—Contributions to employee pension or retirement plans to supplement social security pensions are deductible under certain conditions.[56] The amounts contributed to the plan must be calculated on the basis of actuarial principles and must be apportioned equally over a period of years, without regard to profits or losses, in accordance with a plan approved by the Ministry of Finance. Contributions must be deposited in an irrevocable trust administered by a credit institution authorized to operate in Mexico. At least 30 percent of the fund must be invested in Mexican government bonds, and the balance must be invested in securities approved for the investment of technical reserves of insurance companies, in the purchase or construction of houses for the taxpayer's workers, or in loans for workers' houses. Assets of the fund may be disposed of only for the purpose of paying pensions to employees, and if the taxpayer makes any other use of them, he is subject to tax at the rate of 42 percent on the amount so used.

Payments for Technical Services.—Under the 1968 amendments to the income tax law, payments to persons or companies domiciled abroad for technical services or assistance are deductible by the taxpayer only if it is proved to the satisfaction of the Ministry of Finance that the person or company to whom the payments are made has technical facilities of its own, as distinguished from those of third persons, to render the services; that the services are rendered directly by the recipient of the payments and not through third persons; and that the services are actually received by the taxpayer.[57]

Although no maximum limit is imposed by the income tax law on the amount deductible for payments for technical services, under the "ordinary and necessary" limitation applicable to all deductions discussed above, the tax authorities seem to follow the rule of thumb that the deduction should not exceed 3 percent of the taxpayer's sales, and deductions claimed for amounts substantially in excess of that have been disallowed.

Other Business Expenses.—Special requirements are established in the law for the deduction of certain other business expenses.

Real property rentals are deductible by the lessee if the property is used for the specific purposes of the business. The Ministry of Finance may order an appraisal of the property by a credit institution, and if it does so, the amount deductible annually as rental may not exceed 12 percent of the appraised value.[58]

Social welfare expenses are deductible if the benefits are granted generally to all workers of the taxpayer. Under the regulations, such expenses qualify as deductions only if they are made in accordance with a labor contract or government regulation, and the following expenses are listed as deductible: payments to savings plans; payment of rentals for employees' houses; medical services; compensation for labor accidents; payments for schools, libraries, and employee scholarships; relief funds; payments for the promotion of athletics; employees' share of social security contributions paid by the employer; and insurance premiums paid for the benefit of employees, provided the annual payment for each employee does not exceed his salary for three months.[59]

Premiums paid on insurance of key personnel under which the employer is beneficiary are deductible if certain conditions are met. Any amounts received by the taxpayer under such a policy are taxable income in the year received.[60]

In all cases, premiums on insurance and for bonding must be paid to Mexican companies in order to qualify as deductions.[61]

No general deduction of interest is permitted under the law, but interest paid on borrowed capital used for the purposes of the taxpayer's business is deductible.[62]

Contributions for public works or services or for beneficial or cultural purposes may be deducted with specific authorization of the Ministry of Finance. The ministry may grant annual authorizations for the deduction of contributions for welfare purposes or for officially recognized schools.[63]

Special Deductions for Mining Enterprises.—The law contains special rules for mining enterprises concerning the deduction of depletion, depreciation and amortization, certain exploration expenses, and reserves for employee separation pay.[64]

A deduction for depletion of mineral deposits is allowed. The rate of depletion is determined by dividing the expenses of exploration, preparation, and development incurred before the beginning of extractive operations by the known or computed tonnage or volume of the deposit upon the commencement of regular extractive operations. This rate is then applied to each ton or cubic meter of recovered mineral for the taxable year to determine the depletion allowance for that year. The Ministry of Finance may authorize a different depletion allowance for cause.

The depreciation of tangible property and the amortization of intangible property used in direct connection with or as a direct consequence of the extraction of the mineral, not included in costs for purposes of computing the depletion allowance, are computed at a rate determined by dividing the total investment in those assets by the total tonnage or volume of the mineral deposit known at the time of commencement of extraction. Assets not used directly in the mining operations are depreciated or amortized at the rates established for enterprises generally. Different rates of depreciation and amortization may be authorized by the Ministry of Finance in individual cases.

Exploration expenses incurred in prospecting for new deposits after commencement of mining operations are currently deductible and are not required to be amortized.

Reserves for separation payments to employees upon their dismissal after the exhaustion of the mineral deposits are deductible if the conditions for employee retirement plans, discussed above, are met.

Nondeductible Expenses.—Deductions are not allowed for the following: [65]

1. Payments of income tax of the taxpayer or third persons, or payments of other taxes for the account of third persons.

2. Payments representing profit participations or conditioned on the realization of profits by the taxpayer.

3. Interest paid by a company on its shares during the initial period of its existence. [66]

4. Expenses paid abroad pro rata with entities that are not subject to the tax on income of enterprises.

5. Provisions for liability reserves charged to costs or expenses of the taxable year, unless expressly authorized by the Ministry of Finance, with the exception of reserves for specific demand obligations.

6. Reserves for severance, disability, seniority, or similar payments to employees.

7. Amounts paid in excess of par value for the redemption of shares issued by the taxpayer.

8. Losses resulting from the merger or liquidation of companies in which the taxpayer has shares or ownership interests.

9. Losses from the sale of real property that is part of the taxpayer's fixed assets.

10. Losses from the sale of assets acquired at a cost other than actual value.

11. Cost of goodwill, even though purchased.

12. Losses from the sale of shares, bonds, and other securities, unless their acquisition and sale are made pursuant to requirements established by the Ministry of Finance.

Computation and Payment of the Tax

With certain exceptions discussed below, the income tax of enterprises is computed by applying to total net income for the taxable year the tax rates set out in article 34 of the law and summarized below in table 9.[67] In the case of taxpayers engaged in agriculture, livestock raising, or fishing, the income tax is reduced by the following percentages: if the taxpayer's total income is from one or more of those activities, 40 percent; if the taxpayer processes its products or engages in other commercial or industrial activities that account for not more than 50 percent of its gross income, 25 percent. Taxpayers engaged exclusively in the publication of books receive a reduction in the income tax of 50 percent.[68]

Certain types of income of nonresident aliens and nonresident foreign entities from Mexican sources are taxed at fixed proportionate rates applied to gross income rather than at the graduated rates generally applicable to enterprises. Mexican enterprises making payment of these types of income are required to withhold tax on the payments and file a return and pay the tax within the month following the withholding, unless a different filing and payment requirement is specifically provided in the law. Income from the lease of railroad cars, distribution of foreign publications, interest on loans made by nonresident foreign banks, and interest on loans made by other foreign entities when, in the judgment of the Ministry of Finance, the proceeds of the loan are used for purposes of general interest are taxed at a fixed rate of 10 percent. Income from reinsurance and rebonding operations with Mexican companies is subject to a uniform tax of 4 percent. Fees for technical services or assistance paid by taxpayers subject to the tax on enterprises are taxed at the rate of 20 percent. However, royalties received from the licensing of patents, trademarks, or trade names are subject to the grad-

Table 9
Tax Table—Income of Enterprises
(In pesos)

Annual Taxable Income		Tax Calculation	
Lower limit	Upper limit	Fixed rate	Percentage of amount exceeding lower limit
$ 0.01	$ 2,000.00	$	Exempt
2,000.01	3,500.00		5.00
3,500.01	5,000.00	75.00	6.00
5,000.01	8,000.00	165.00	7.00
8,000.01	11,000.00	375.00	8.00
11,000.01	14,000.00	615.00	9.00
14,000.01	20,000.00	885.00	10.00
20,000.01	26,000.00	1,485.00	11.00
26,000.01	32,000.00	2,145.00	13.00
32,000.01	38,000.00	2,925.00	16.00
38,000.01	50,000.00	3,885.00	18.00
50,000.01	62,000.00	6,045.00	19.00
62,000.01	74,000.00	8,325.00	20.00
74,000.01	86,000.00	10,725.00	21.50
86,000.01	100,000.00	13,305.00	22.50
100,000.01	150,000.00	16,455.00	24.10
150,000.01	200,000.00	28,505.00	26.76
200,000.01	300,000.00	41,885.00	29.64
300,000.01	400,000.00	71,525.00	34.00
400,000.01	500,000.00	105,525.00	38.00
500,000.01	1,500,000.00	143,500.00	48.65[a]
1,500,000.01		630,000.00	42.00

a. Tax calculation for this bracket has been computed from the statutory formula: 42% of total taxable income, less 6.65% of the difference between total taxable income and 1,500,000 pesos.

uated tax rates applicable to enterprises generally. Nonresident aliens and foreign companies that receive interest, dividends, rentals, or other income from capital investments in Mexico are taxed under the provisions applicable to income of individuals from capital investments.[69]

Taxable income from occasional acts of commerce is subject to the graduated tax rates set out in table 9, but the tax is computed separately for each transaction. A return must be filed and the tax paid within fifteen days after the transaction.[70] Income from occasional commissions is taxed at the fixed rate of 20 percent, and the tax must be withheld and paid by the person paying the commission.[71]

Taxpayers who receive taxable income from foreign sources are entitled to credit foreign income taxes paid on the income against their Mexican income tax. The credit is limited to the amount of the Mexican tax computed separately on the foreign income. If the taxpayer has an income tax exemption in the foreign country, credit is given for the foreign income tax that would be payable but for the exemption; this rule does not apply, however, in the case of exemptions covering income from capital.[72]

Taxpayers are required to make three payments of estimated income tax during the first fifteen days of the fifth, ninth, and twelfth months of the current taxable year, except in the first year of operation or if the operations of the preceding year resulted in a loss. Payments of estimated tax are calculated on estimated taxable income determined by applying the ratio of taxable income to gross income of the preceding year to the gross income of the current year. The Ministry of Finance may authorize a different method of computing the estimated tax in individual cases for good cause. Taxpayers engaged in livestock raising make estimated tax payments by canceling revenue stamps in the amount of 1 percent of gross receipts on invoices they issue.[73]

An annual income tax return must be filed with the federal tax office that has jurisdiction over the taxpayer's domicile within three months following the close of the taxable year, and the amount of the tax due after deducting current prepayments must be paid at the time of filing. If prepayments exceed the amount of the tax, the taxpayer may request a refund of the excess or apply it against future taxes.[74] Together with the annual return the taxpayer is required by the regulations to file comprehensive financial information, including copies of the balance sheet and profit-and-loss statement for the year; a classified inventory; summaries or descriptions of assets subject to depreciation and amortization, leases, agreements covering concessions from the government, patents used under license, and all contracts giving rise to a deduction; a statement of salaries paid to employees; lists of persons to whom payments for professional services and interest on borrowed capital were made; a reconciliation of book income and taxable income; and copies of the declarations accompanying estimated tax payments.

Representatives in Mexico of nonresident aliens and nonresident foreign entities that engage in activities that give rise to tax liability are required to file the necessary returns and statements for their principals and must withhold and pay the tax for their account.[75]

All persons who withhold tax from payments made to others are required to file a return showing the reason for the withholding and the amount withheld and pay the tax collected within the month following the withholding, except in certain cases in which the law provides other requirements. Persons required to withhold tax or to obtain proof that the tax has been paid are jointly liable with the taxpayer for the tax.[76]

If a tax is not paid on time or within a grace period of ten days after the tax is due, the law provides that a penalty will be applied not exceeding 8 percent per month or three times the amount of the deficiency.[77]

"Minor" Taxpayers.—"Minor" taxpayers—those with gross income for the taxable year of 150,000 pesos or less—compute taxable income as a proportion of gross income, ranging from 3 percent to 30 percent according to the nature of the taxpayer's business. If a specific rate is not established for the type of business in which he is engaged, taxable income is computed as 15 percent of gross income.[78] The tax rates applicable to "major" taxpayers are applied to taxable income so determined to arrive at the amount of the tax.

If a "minor" taxpayer elects to keep complete accounting records, he computes the income tax in the same manner as "major" taxpayers. Commercial entities—companies organized under the commercial companies law—are required to keep full accounting books and records regardless of the amount of their income and consequently are never taxed as "minor" taxpayers.[79] A taxpayer who has once computed his tax as a "major" taxpayer must continue to do so, even if his gross income for the taxable year is less than 150,000 pesos, unless he obtains authorization from the Ministry of Finance to change.[80]

The "minor" taxpayer must make one prepayment of estimated tax in July of the current taxable year, in the amount of 50 percent of the tax for the preceding year, except in the first year of operation. An annual return must be filed and the balance of the tax paid on or before the last day of February following the taxable year.[81]

TAXATION OF INCOME OF INDIVIDUALS

Income from Personal Services

Taxable Income.—The tax on income from personal services is imposed on all income earned in the calendar year, with certain exceptions, from services rendered as an employee, agent, or in the independent practice of a profession, art, trade, or technical, athletic, or cultural activity, after deducting the allowable deductions.[82] Individuals regularly engaged in commerce, industry, agriculture, livestock raising, or fishing are taxed as enterprises, and those activities must be distinguished from independent professional and similar services of an individual.

Included in income are all forms of remuneration, such as wages, salaries, fees, commissions, prizes, bonuses, workers' profit participations, and separation pay, pensions, retirement pay, and subsidies derived from personal services. Payments for travel and representation expenses are taxable income unless they are actually incurred in the employer's business and are supported by receipts that meet the requirements of the law and regulations.[83] Persons who render professional or similar services through a professional organization, association, or civil company are taxed on their respective shares of the net taxable income of the organization.[84]

The Ministry of Finance may determine by estimate the gross income of persons engaged in an independent professional, technical, artistic, or similar activity in the event the taxpayer fails to file a return or keep the required accounting books and records or when information obtained by the ministry shows that the average gross income received exceeds by 3 percent the gross income declared.[85]

Certain types of income and income of specified foreign individuals are exempt from the tax. Excludable from taxable income are wages not exceeding the amount of the general minimum wage and dismissal or separation pay based on the minimum wage; social welfare benefits; annual bonuses not exceeding one month's salary paid generally to employees whose wages do not exceed 2,000 pesos per month and annual bonuses to government employees; industrial accident and illness benefits paid pursuant to law or a labor contract; pensions and allowances for disability, unemployment, old age, or death; payments for funeral expenses; and properly documented travel and representation expenses incurred in the employer's business.[86] The income of foreign diplomatic and consular personnel, representatives of international organizations, members of official foreign delegations and scientific and humanitarian delegations, and under certain circumstances foreign technicians contracted by the Mexican government is also exempt from tax, in some cases on the condition that the foreign country grant reciprocal exemptions to Mexicans.[87]

Deductions.—No deductions are allowed from income from personal services as an employee. Persons who receive income from the independent practice of a profession, art, trade, or technical, athletic, or cultural activity; agents of banking, insurance, and bonding institutions; and customs brokers are allowed to deduct from gross income the normal and appropriate expenses of the taxpayer's income-producing activity.[88]

All deductions must be ordinary and necessary for the taxpayer's activity and must be reasonable in relation to his operations. Taxpayers are required to keep a cash book and a record of their amortizable and depreciable assets and deferred expenses, and deductible expenditures must be shown in the taxpayer's books and supported by documentary evidence. If the taxpayer is required by the law to withhold income tax from payments made to other persons, such payments are not deductible as expenses unless he complies with the withholding and payment requirements, and in the case of a deduction claimed for payments made to persons who are required to be registered in the federal register of taxpayers, he must furnish the payee's registration number or show that he has furnished to the Ministry of Finance whatever data he has for making the registration. Purchases of raw materials and supplies and payments for services must be substantiated by invoices, receipts, or other documents that meet the requirements of the law and regulations, or by other methods prescribed by the ministry. Rentals are deductible only for premises in which the taxpayer's activities are carried on. Contributions must be specifically authorized by the Ministry of Finance in order to be deducted. The maximum annual rates of depreciation and amortization are the same as those applicable to taxpayers subject to the tax on income of enterprises, unless specific authorization of different rates is obtained from the Ministry of Finance.

In lieu of claiming itemized deductions, the taxpayer may at his election deduct a fixed amount of 20 percent of gross income. If gross income is determined by estimate by the Ministry of Finance, only the fixed 20 percent deduction is allowed.[89] Special fixed deductions in lieu of itemized deductions are required for motion picture and theater actors and performers, bullfighters, and athletes, ranging from 60 percent of gross income of 96,000 pesos or less to 24 percent of gross income exceeding 312,000 pesos.[90]

Computation and Payment of the Tax.—The basis of the tax is determined by adding all income earned in the calendar year from personal services, deducting the allowable deductions, and reducing the balance by

20 percent of the first 150,000 pesos.[91] The income tax is computed by applying to the resulting balance the rates of the table set out in article 75 of the law and reproduced below in table 10.

Table 10
Tax Table—Income of Individuals from Personal Services and Capital
(In pesos)

Annual Taxable Income		Tax Calculation	
			Percentage of amount exceeding lower limit
Lower limit	Upper limit	Fixed rate	
$ 0.01	$ 4,800.00	$	Exempt
4,800.01	5,760.00	114.00	3.88
5,760.01	6,720.00	151.25	3.95
6,720.01	7,680.00	189.17	3.99
7,680.01	8,640.00	227.47	4.09
8,640.01	9,600.00	266.73	4.47
9,600.01	14,400.00	309.64	5.67
14,400.01	19,200.00	581.80	6.88
19,200.01	24,000.00	912.04	8.06
24,000.01	28,800.00	1,298.92	9.44
28,800.01	38,400.00	1,752.04	11.62
38,400.01	48,000.00	2,867.56	13.57
48,000.01	57,600.00	4,170.88	15.25
57,600.01	67,200.00	5,634.28	16.72
67,200.01	76,800.00	7,239.40	18.15
76,800.01	86,400.00	8,981.80	19.50
86,400.01	96,000.00	10,853.80	20.81
96,000.01	115,200.00	12,851.00	22.90
115,200.01	150,000.00	17,247.80	22.92
150,000.01	180,000.00	25,223.96	24.06
180,000.01	240,000.00	32,441.40	27.50
240,000.01	300,000.00	48,941.40	31.65
300,000.01		67,931.40	35.00

In the case of individuals who receive taxable income from services as an employee, the employer is required to withhold estimated tax on the employee's compensation every month and to pay it to the tax collection office at the employer's domicile by the fifteenth day of the following month. The amount of the withholding is determined from a table set out in article 56 of the law, and the rates are progressive. The employer must also compute the employee's income tax on his salary for the entire year and withhold and pay any deficiency. If the tax has been overpaid, the amount of the overpayment is credited to the employee by the employer against future withholdings. The employee is not required to file a return if he received compensation from only one employer during the year, but the employer must file during March of each year a return showing the computation of the annual tax, payments made, and tax withheld for each employee during the preceding year.[92]

In the case of an individual who receives compensation for services as an employee from two or more employers during the calendar year, each employer must withhold the estimated tax on the compensation paid by him, but the total tax for the year is computed, at the employee's election, either by the employee himself or by his last employer, if he held two or more jobs successively, or the employer paying the highest compensation, if he held two or more jobs simultaneously. The employee must notify his employers of his election by January 31 following the taxable year, and if he elects to have the employer compute the tax, the employee must inform him of all other compensation received during the year and the amounts withheld and notify the other employers of the name of the employer who will make the computation. If he elects to compute the tax himself, he must file an annual return. Any deficiency is payable at the time of filing of the employee's return or in nine consecutive monthly installments withheld by the employer.[93]

Employees who receive taxable remuneration for services in foreign embassies, legations, or consulates accredited in Mexico and residents of Mexico who receive compensation from abroad for personal services as employees must report their income every month and pay the estimated tax thereon within the first fifteen days of the following month. They are also required to compute the tax on their total income for the year and file an annual return.[94]

Individuals who are engaged in an independent professional, technical, artistic, or similar activity, and members of professional organizations or associations are required to make prepayments of the tax by canceling revenue stamps on their receipts in the amount of 4 percent (5 percent of 80 percent) of the fee or other remuneration. All persons who receive income from such activities during the year must file an annual return of total personal-service income from all sources.[95] Professional partnerships, associations, and civil companies must file an information return in March of each year for the preceding calendar year showing their total income and authorized deductions and the share of each partner or member in the net income and prepayments of the tax.[96]

Individual income tax returns are filed during the month of April following the calendar year in which the income is received with the tax collection office having jurisdiction over the taxpayer's domicile. Any deficiency in the tax due after deducting taxes withheld and prepaid must be paid at the time of filing, except that deficiencies of employees may be withheld and paid by the employer.[97]

Income from Capital

Income derived from the investment of capital without the contribution of labor or other form of personal services is taxed separately from personal-service income. The method of taxation varies somewhat according to the type of income from capital. While certain types of income are taxed at the progressive rates applicable to income from personal services, other income is taxed at special proportionate rates. In the case of income to which the progressive rates of the tax table are applied, the taxpayer is required to compute the tax on his total annual income, but where proportionate rates are applied the tax is computed separately on each type of income and in some cases on each transaction. In the case of most types of income from capital, the tax is based on gross income with no deductions. In addition to the specific types of income from capital discussed below, the tax is applicable to income from investments or transactions of any kind unless it is taxed under other provisions of the law or is expressly exempted.[98]

Interest.—Interest arising from any kind of account, contract, or agreement, such as interest on debts, loans, current accounts, bonds, and other obligations, is taxable as income from capital.[99] Certain types of interest are, however, completely exempt from income tax—interest paid on deposits by banks of deposit and savings institutions and interest on employee savings accounts; interest on bonds and obligations issued by international credit institutions of which the Mexican government or a national credit institution is a shareholder; interest on bonds issued by the federal government in a foreign currency if the exemption is established in the bonds; and amounts, called dividends or interest, paid or credited by an insurance company to its policy holders as adjustments of premiums. Interest on bonds, debentures, certificates issued by credit institutions, mortgage certificates *(cedulas hipotecarias),* and participating certificates issued by mutual funds is exempt when the annual rate of simple interest does not exceed 7 percent of the face value of the security or when compound interest does not exceed 7.2 percent per annum.[100]

The law establishes rules for determining the existence of interest income upon constructive receipt, payment or release of a debt, and transfers of property in satisfaction of a debt.[101] Interest income is not imputed, however, as it was under the prior law, where no interest or unusually low interest is provided for in a loan agreement or other contract.

The income tax is computed at the rates contained in table 10 above on the combined total of income from interest and other income from capital investments to which the progressive rates are applicable received in the calendar year, without deductions.[102]

The taxpayer must make prepayments of the tax by canceling revenue stamps on receipts that are required to be issued for each payment of interest. The amount of the prepayment is computed from the tax table, but may not be less than 10 percent of the amount of the interest received. An annual return must be filed and any deficiency paid in April following the year of receipt.[103]

Certain types of income are taxed at fixed proportionate rates rather than at the progressive rates of the tax table. Interest received from credit institutions, auxiliary credit organizations, and nonresident foreign banks, and interest received by nonresident foreigners on loans considered by the Ministry of Finance to be in the general interest of the country, are subject to a fixed rate of 10 percent, which the payer of the interest must withhold and pay.[104]

The tax payable on total taxable interest income from bonds, debentures, certificates issued by credit institutions, mortgage certificates, and participating certificates issued by mutual funds is determined by applying fixed proportionate rates ranging from 2 percent on annual interest not exceeding 8 percent to a maximum of 10 percent on annual interest of more than 15 percent. If the net yield on such securities after taxes is less than 7 percent simple interest or 7.2 percent compound interest, a reduction in the tax is allowed. The payor of the interest must withhold and pay the tax.[105]

Dividends and Other Distributions of Profits by Entities.—Profits actually distributed by Mexican companies as dividends or otherwise, including participations in profits of bondholders and holders of other obligations and distributions in liquidation or capital reduction in excess of contributions to capital, are taxable income to the recipient. Stock dividends and increases in members' capital accounts through capitalization of reserves or profits are not taxable income but are not considered contributions to capital for purposes of determining the tax on distributions in liquidation or capital reduction.[106] Workers' participations in profits, which are taxed as income from personal services, and dividends paid by duly licensed mutual funds are exempt from the tax on income from capital.[107]

Profits of branches and agencies in Mexico of foreign entities, on the other hand, are subject to tax as income from capital whether or not the profits are actually distributed. The tax is imposed on their aggregate taxable income for the year after deducting the amount of the tax on enterprises.[108]

The rates of the tax, which are proportionate and are applicable to the total taxable income of the taxpayer for the calendar year, are as follows:

180,000 pesos or less	15%
180,000.01 to 270,000 pesos	17.5%
270,000.01 pesos and over	20%

Entities that pay dividends or other profit distributions must withhold the amount of the tax and pay it during the month following the distribution. For purposes of computing the tax, the payor is required to keep a cumulative record of the amounts paid to each shareholder or member. No tax is withheld when the recipient of the distribution reinvests it in capital stock or as a capital contribution in the same company within thirty days after the distribution or when the distribution is made to a credit or insurance institution or mutual fund authorized to operate in the country, in its capacity as shareholder or member of the payor entity. Mexican branches and agencies of foreign entities must pay the tax within three months following the date of their annual balance sheet.[109]

Rents.—Rental income is subject to tax only if it is derived from the lease or sublease of urban real property.[110] The tax is computed on the monthly rental on each unit, apartment, dwelling, or premises, without regard to the form of payment or the number of co-owners. A fixed deduction of 30 percent of gross rental income is allowed for local taxes, depreciation, repairs, and other expenses. No deductions are allowed from rental income from a sublease other than the amount of rental paid by the lessee to the lessor. The rates of the tax are as follows:[111]

Rental on property subject to rent regulation   0.14%
Nonregulated monthly rentals from 1 peso to
    700 pesos   0.75%
Nonregulated monthly rentals exceeding
    700 pesos   5%

Gains from Sales of Real Property and Securities.—The income tax law provides that gains from the sale or other disposition of urban real property and securities are taxable as income from capital.[112] Since the law specifies *urban* real property, gains of individuals from the sale of rural property are not taxable unless the recipient is engaged in business and is thus subject to the tax on enterprises. Furthermore, the federal revenue law for each year since the enactment of the 1964 income tax law through 1969 has expressly exempted from the tax gains of individuals from the sale of public and private securities issued in Mexico.[113]

The gain from a sale of urban real property is the difference between the sale price or current market value, whichever is higher, and the value of the property at the time of acquisition or on January 1, 1962, if the property was acquired before that date. Value as of January 1, 1962, is determined by appraisal made by a credit institution authorized for that purpose by the Ministry of Finance.[114]

The following items are deductible from the gain for purposes of determining taxable income: taxes and notarial fees and expenses paid by the taxpayer in connection with deeds to the property executed after January 1, 1962; local taxes and assessments on the property for planification or public works paid between the date of acquisition or January 1, 1962, whichever is later, and the date of sale; investments in buildings, additions, and other improvements to the property, not including maintenance expenses, during the same period; and losses incurred by the taxpayer in the current taxable year or during the five immediately preceding years on the sale of other urban real property.[115]

The gain so determined is further reduced by a percentage depending upon the period of time the property was held by the taxpayer. In the case of property held two years or less, 80 percent of the gain is taxable, and this percentage is reduced for each additional two-year holding period; gains from property held more than ten years are completely exempt from the tax. A gain from the sale of property used by the taxpayer as his residence during the preceding two years is not taxable if he invests the proceeds in the acquisition or construction of another residence within one year after the sale, provided he obtains authorization from the Ministry of Finance before the sale to treat the gain as nontaxable.[116]

The tax is computed separately on each transaction by applying the rates of table 10 above to the net taxable income. If transfer of title is in the form of a public instrument—that is, a deed executed before a notary—payment of the tax must be made within thirty days after the conveyance; otherwise, the tax is payable within fifteen days. Although the purchaser is not required to withhold the tax, he is jointly liable for payment of the seller's tax, and it is therefore advisable for him to determine at the time of the sale that the seller's tax has been paid.[117]

Income from Copyrights.—Royalties and other consideration received by a copyright holder for the exploitation of the copyright are taxed under the rules applicable to interest income. An exemption from the tax is granted to authors of scientific, artistic, literary, or other cultural productions on their income from such work, but this exemption does not extend to other holders of rights in those productions.[118]

The tax is based on gross income for the calendar year and is computed at the rates set out in table 10 above. The recipient of the income must make prepayments of the tax by canceling revenue stamps on receipts in an amount computed from the tax table or 10 percent of the royalty or other payment, whichever is higher. The taxpayer must file an annual return and pay any deficiency in April following the year in which the income was received.[119]

License or Transfer of Governmental Concessions and Subsoil Rights.— Income from the license or transfer of concessions and income under mining contracts is taxed at the same rates and under essentially the same rules as apply to interest income. Included in this are royalties from the license and gains from the transfer of a governmental concession, permit, authorization, or contract; royalties and other income under any contract or other transaction with the owner of the land for exploitation of the subsoil; and income of a person other than the concessionaire, mining operator, or landowner from a participation in the products of the subsoil.[120]

The tax is imposed on gross income, except that in the case of a transfer of a governmental concession, permit, authorization, or contract, the taxable gain is the difference between the taxpayer's cost and the sales price or value if the transfer is made as a contribution to the capital of a corporation or other legal entity. If machinery, equipment, or other tangible movable property used for purposes of the business is sold, rented, or contributed together with the exploitation rights, the income is taxed as income of enterprises rather than as income from capital.[121]

Tax on Combined Income of Individuals

Taxable Income.—Individuals whose total net income from personal services or capital or both exceeds 100,000 pesos in a calendar year are subject to a global tax on their combined income in lieu of the separate taxes on each type of income. Persons whose annual net income is between 50,000 pesos and 100,000 pesos may elect to compute and pay the tax on their combined income, but once they elect that method of taxation, they must follow it as long as their total annual income is at least 50,000 pesos. For purposes of this tax, net income is all income, with certain exceptions, received from personal services and capital, reduced by the deductions and adjustments authorized under the rules for determining the tax separately on each type of income.[122]

The following types of income are excludable from income for purposes of the tax on combined income but are taxed separately according to the nature of the income: old age, retirement, or separation pay received by an employee; gains from the sale of urban real property and securities; and rental income not exceeding 700 pesos monthly per unit from the lease or sublease of urban real property. In the case of monthly rentals exceeding 700 pesos, 50 percent of the rental after the authorized 30 percent deduction is includable in income.[123] The annual revenue laws for 1965 through 1969 have further authorized the exclusion from income, for purposes of this tax, of dividends and other distributions of profits paid by legal entities established in Mexico and distributable profits of Mexican branches or agencies of foreign entities, interest on securities issued by Mexican residents, and interest on loans to or deposits with credit institutions operating in Mexico.[124]

Personal Exemptions.—Deductions from combined taxable income are allowed in the amount of 6,000 pesos for the taxpayer, 3,000 pesos for the taxpayer's dependent spouse, and 1,500 pesos for each dependent parent, grandparent, child, and grandchild. No deduction is allowed for a dependent who has income of more than 6,000 pesos in the calendar year.[125]

Deductions.—Taxpayers subject to the tax on combined income are entitled to deduct the following expenses from income after taking personal exemptions into account, provided they have not been deducted for purposes of computing the tax on income from personal services or the tax on income from capital:[126]

1. Medical, dental, and funeral expenses, provided the taxpayer or his dependents are not entitled to receive such benefits from an institution or enterprise, such as the social security institute or an employer. Only that amount of the expenses that exceeds 3 percent of total income after deducting personal exemptions is deductible, and the deduction may not exceed 10 percent of total income or 20,000 pesos, whichever is lower.

2. Contributions made by the taxpayer to public institutions of social security.

3. Interest paid on indebtedness incurred for purposes of investments producing income subject to the tax on combined income. Deductible interest may not exceed the maximum interest rate authorized by the Banco de México to be charged by mortgage banks.

4. Premiums on insurance policies covering property that produces income subject to the tax on combined income.

5. Premiums on life insurance on the taxpayer, health and accident insurance on the taxpayer and his dependents, and property insurance not included in 4 above. The amount of the deduction may not exceed 5 percent of total income after deducting personal exemptions or 5,000 pesos, whichever is lower.

6. Contributions to charitable or cultural institutions or for public works or services, provided the deductions are authorized by the Ministry of Finance.

7. Federal and local taxes, except the federal income tax, on income subject to the tax on combined income.

8. Reasonably necessary expenses paid for salaries, fees, and commissions to obtain income subject to the tax on combined income.

In lieu of itemizing the deductions allowed, the taxpayer may take a standard deduction in the amount of 10 percent of total income after deducting personal exemptions or 20,000 pesos, whichever is lower.[127]

Computation and Payment of the Tax.—Net taxable income remaining after the deduction of personal exemptions and deductible expenses is taxed at the progressive rates set out in article 86 of the law and reproduced in table 11 below. Income taxes paid through withholding or otherwise on items of income included in combined income are deducted from the total tax due.[128]

Table 11
Tax Table—Combined Income of Individuals
(In pesos)

Annual Taxable Income		Tax Calculation	
Lower limit	Upper limit	Fixed rate	Percentage of amount exceeding lower limit
$ 0.01	$ 1,200.00	$	13.00
1,200.01	2,400.00	156.00	13.20
2,400.01	3,600.00	314.40	13.25
3,600.01	4,800.00	473.40	13.45
4,800.01	6,000.00	634.80	13.70
6,000.01	7,200.00	799.20	13.80
7,200.01	8,400.00	964.80	14.10
8,400.01	9,600.00	1,134.00	14.15
9,600.01	10,800.00	1,303.80	14.20
10,800.01	12,000.00	1,474.20	14.65
12,000.01	18,000.00	1,650.00	14.95
18,000.01	24,000.00	2,547.00	15.70
24,000.01	36,000.00	3,489.00	17.00
36,000.01	48,000.00	5,529.00	18.55
48,000.01	72,000.00	7,755.00	20.70
72,000.01	96,000.00	12,723.00	23.45
96,000.01	120,000.00	18,351.00	25.45
120,000.01	150,000.00	24,459.00	26.90
150,000.01	180,000.00	32,529.00	29.00
180,000.01	240,000.00	41,229.00	31.35
240,000.01	300,000.00	60,039.00	33.90
300,000.01		80,379.00	35.00

Taxpayers whose combined income in the first six months of the calendar year exceeds 50,000 pesos must make one prepayment of the tax during the month of August, computed at the rates of the tax table. Taxpayers whose only income is from personal services are exempt from this requirement.[129]

Persons subject to the tax on combined income of individuals file only one annual return, covering their total taxable income for the calendar year, and are not required to file separate returns of income from personal services or income from capital. Returns must be filed and any deficiency in the tax paid in April following the calendar year in which the taxable income was received.[130]

COMMERCIAL RECEIPTS TAX

The most important of the federal transactions taxes is the commerical receipts tax, sometimes called the gross sales tax or commercial revenues tax. Introduced in 1948 to replace the existing large number of local taxes on commerce, the tax is at present imposed under the federal commercial receipts tax law of December 30, 1951, which has been amended in important respects since its enactment.[131]

The tax is essentially a gross receipts tax on commercial and industrial businesses and is levied on receipts from most commercial sales and services. The tax is imposed at a federal rate of 1.8 percent and an additional rate of 1.2 percent for the benefit of states that agree to forego their own taxes on commerce and industry, with certain exceptions, for a participation in the proceeds of the tax collected in their territory. The Federal District, both federal territories, and about half the states have entered such agreements with the federal government.[132] Most of the non-participating states, which include such important states as Mexico, Jalisco, Nuevo León, Veracruz, and Tamaulipas, impose gross receipts taxes similar to the federal commercial receipts tax, generally at rates of 1.2 percent or less.

In 1968 a draft of a proposed law establishing a new tax, called the federal tax on payments *(impuesto al egreso),* to replace the federal portion of the commercial receipts tax, was prepared and distributed to representatives of private industry. It was the intention of the executive branch to submit the draft to Congress for study and approval, but because of the complications of its regulation it has not yet been submitted, and the administration of President Gustavo Díaz Ordaz has apparently abandoned the proposal or will leave it for the next administration. The proposed tax would be levied on each buyer of goods or services and would be wholly absorbed by the last purchaser. The rate of the tax was not revealed, but it appeared likely that there would be a general rate of 5 percent and special rates on certain types of products and services.

THE TAXPAYER

All individuals and entities that habitually realize receipts from taxable transactions that are either carried out or take effect in Mexican territory are subject to the commercial receipts tax. Receipts are realized at the place where the taxpayer's business is located, which is also where his business must be registered and his books kept.[133]

Taxpayers may pass the tax on to the buyer of goods or user of services, but if they do so they must set forth separately on the invoices or sales slips the amount of the transaction and the amount of the tax.[134] It is not customary in business practice, however, to charge the tax expressly to the buyer, except in the case of certain products subject to price regulation, such as automobiles and tractors. Also, companies that have been granted an exemption from the commercial receipts tax under the law for the promotion of new and necessary industries and enterprises that receive a tax subsidy on export sales are prohibited to charge the tax to the buyer, under penalty of loss of the exemption or subsidy.

TAXABLE RECEIPTS

With certain exceptions discussed below, the tax is imposed on all receipts from commercial sales, rentals, and services. Taxable services include those of commercial agents, commission agents, consignees, brokers, distributors, and other representatives who perform commercial acts for the account of another or who bring together the parties to a commercial transaction.[135] Receipts from sales of real property and fixed assets are exempt from the tax, with the result that receipts from sales are taxed only if the property sold is stock-in-trade of the seller. The tax is levied, however, on each sale of merchandise, whether at the manufacturing, wholesale, or retail level.

In general, the tax applies to the total amount of the consideration, including overprices, interest, and other additions to the sales price. Liability for the tax arises at the time the agreement is entered into regardless of when payment is actually received; there is no deferral in the case of installment sales or other sales on credit. The consideration received by the taxpayer may take any form, such as cash, securities, credit instruments, other property, services, or book credits.[136]

The taxable receipts of consignees, agents, commission agents, brokers, distributors, and other representatives are the amount of the commissions received by them, provided two formal requirements are met. There must be a written contract in which the amount of the commission is stipulated either as a fixed amount or as a percentage of the price, and the taxpayer must submit to the tax authorities at their request evidence supporting the accounts rendered by him to his principal and the amount of commissions received. If these requirements are not met, it will be presumed that the taxpayer has acted for his own account and the tax is imposed on the total sales price. Expenses charged by agents and brokers to their principals, including traveling and office expenses, are considered taxable receipts. They may deduct the amount of commissions that they pay to other agents, but no other deductions are allowed.[137]

In the case of receipts from certain types of transactions, the tax is imposed on the difference between the purchase price and the sales price or on the commission realized, whichever is applicable. The transactions covered by this rule include exchanges of currencies, sales of gasoline and National Lottery tickets, and under certain conditions sales of cigarettes and wholesale sales of medicines.[138]

The following are not considered taxable receipts: the actual amount of expenses incurred by the seller and charged to the buyer in connection with the shipment of merchandise for insurance, cartage and freight, packing, crating, containers, taxes, fees, and other similar expenses, unless the agreed sales price is free of expenses to the buyer; discounts and allowances granted by the seller to the buyer; and repayments of the sales price, in whole or in part, by the seller upon rescission of the contract. Reimbursements of expenses for auxiliary services incurred by a person who renders taxable services are not considered taxable receipts of the person rendering the principal service if he does not add a profit to his actual cost and if the auxiliary services are performed by another.[139]

EXEMPT RECEIPTS

Numerous exemptions from the tax are provided in order to alleviate the tax burden on consumers of basic necessities, to further social or cultural purposes, to prevent the imposition of both the commercial receipts tax and a federal excise tax on receipts from the same goods or services, or for reasons of commercial policy.[140]

Receipts of a wide variety of tradesmen and others are exempt, including establishments that are limited to the sale of certain basic items of food and other necessities, sellers in public streets or markets, itinerant vendors, small general stores and eating establishments, small craftsmen and repair shops, farmers and ranchers with respect to receipts from the first sale of their products if they have not undergone any industrial processing, and sellers of agricultural products and industrial by-products that are used as raw materials in the preparation of animal feeds. Enterprises and labor unions that sell necessary consumer goods to their employees and members are exempt with respect to the receipts from such sales if certain conditions are met.

Persons engaged in the publication, printing, sale, or rental of books, newspapers, magazines, geographical maps, or anatomical or artistic illustrations are exempt with respect to receipts from the production, distribution, and sale of their own publications. The exemption also applies to printed music but not to phonograph records or tapes.

Receipts from contracts for the construction of immovables, such as buildings, highways, and bridges, with the federal or a state or local government or with a decentralized entity are exempt, but this does not apply to receipts of subcontractors or to sales of goods or services even though they are related to the construction of public works.

Certain other designated industries and trades are exempt from the tax, including motion picture studios and laboratories and producers of Mexican films and carriers of persons or goods. Industries considered new or necessary may be granted an exemption from the federal portion of the tax, as discussed in Chapter V.

Important to some producers and manufacturers is an exemption covering receipts from the first sale of a product that is subject to a special federal tax imposed either on the manufacture or production of the product or on the first sale thereof. This exemption applies to mining enterprises that are subject to the federal production tax and to producers of products on which a federal excise tax is levied, such as bottled fruit juices, mineral water, and soft drinks, tobacco products, electric energy, cement, salt, and matches. The exemption does not, however, apply to sales of automobiles or trucks assembled in Mexico or to receipts of laboratories that produce medicines, medical supplies, pharmaceuticals, or cosmetics.

Since the commercial receipts tax is applicable only to commercial transactions, receipts from noncommercial activities are not taxable. Expressly exempt are receipts from professional services, except receipts of associations of professional persons that are organized in the form of a commercial company, receipts of nonprofit organizations from membership dues, and receipts of consumers' co-operatives from sales to their members.

Finally, most receipts from investments and other financial activities are exempt from the tax. These include receipts from sales of real property or fixed assets, from contributions to the capital of a company, from sales of partnership shares, and from distributions in liquidation; receipts from the lease of real property or of an entire business;[141]

receipts from sales of securities or credit instruments; receipts of banks and other credit institutions and of insurance companies and bonding companies realized in the regular course of their business; and receipts of stock exchange brokers, dealers in securities, and of agents of banks, capitalization banks, insurance companies, and bonding companies realized in the regular course of their business.

COMPUTATION AND PAYMENT OF THE TAX

With few exceptions, the tax is imposed on the total amount of taxable receipts at the combined rate of 3 percent in the Federal District, the federal territories, and the participating states, and at the federal rate of 1.8 percent in nonparticipating states.[142]

Certain types of receipts are subject only to the federal rate of 1.8 percent. These include receipts for telephone and telegraphic services rendered under a federal concession; receipts from the sale of gasoline, greases, lubricants, and other petroleum derivatives; and receipts from the operation of billiard tables, bowling alleys, and music machines.[143] Receipts from sales of certain necessities and receipts of various service establishments and small general stores, formerly subject to tax at one-half of the full rate, are now either taxed at the full rate or are entirely exempt from the tax.[144]

Returns are filed and the tax is paid monthly within the first twenty days of each month on the receipts of the immediately preceding calendar month. Filing and payment are made at the tax collection office at which the taxpayer is registered. Branch offices and other establishments of the taxpayer, which are required to be registered separately, pay the tax on their receipts at the collection office where they are registered. Unless the taxpayer proves the contrary, it is presumed that his taxable monthly receipts are not less than 600 pesos. Taxpayers who have not realized any taxable receipts during the preceding month must nevertheless file a return, with an explanation of the reasons for the lack of receipts.[145]

Taxpayers who have only exempt receipts are not required to file monthly returns, but in some cases they must report their annual receipts in January of each year.[146] Monthly returns are, however, required of taxpayers who have exemptions under the law for the promotion of new and necessary industries.[147]

A taxpayer who has both taxable and nontaxable receipts must keep separate accounts for each and report his total receipts and deduct therefrom the exempt receipts and any discounts, returns, and allowances. If he fails to keep separate accounts or fails to file a return and pay the tax, the tax is imposed on both taxable and nontaxable receipts.[148]

In the case of individuals who have realized total receipts of less than 500,000 pesos during their last fiscal year and who fail to present the books of account and supporting documents required by the law, the Ministry of Finance may determine taxable receipts by estimate. In that case, the tax is computed on the estimated receipts for the twelve months preceding the month in which the estimate is made, the balance of the current year, and the next succeeding calendar year. If total receipts realized in a period exceed the estimated receipts by more than 20 percent, the taxpayer must pay the tax on the actual receipts.[149]

Certain persons who make payments that represent taxable receipts to the recipient are required to withhold and pay the tax for the account of the taxpayer. This requirement applies to users of technical services, lessees of railroad cars, and payors of royalties when payments are made to nonresident taxpayers and are derived from transactions that are either carried out or take effect in Mexican territory, and to residents of Mexico who pay commissions or other compensation for services to agents, commission agents, or representatives abroad.[150]

In some cases persons who represent or act on behalf of a taxpayer are personally liable for the tax owed by the person they represent. This liability is imposed on legal representatives, commission agents, and holders of a power of attorney. Administrators of a company who authorize its manager, director, or attorney to file the monthly returns without their express prior approval thereby assume full responsibility for all consequences if the returns are false or incorrect. Administrators of a company are jointly liable with their predecessors in office for irregularities committed by their predecessors if they have knowledge of them and fail to report them in writing to the competent authorities. Accountants who sign the financial statements of a taxpayer or render an opinion thereon must state whether the taxpayer's receipts are reported in accordance with the law, and they become personally liable for penalties if their certification is false.[151]

REGISTRATION AND BOOKS OF THE TAXPAYER

All persons subject to the commercial receipts tax must register with the federal tax office for their district within ten days from the commencement of operations. Branch offices and other establishments must be registered separately.[152] A metallic plate bearing the registration number is issued to each registered taxpayer and must be displayed in his establishment.[153] Certain taxpayers who have only exempt receipts must also register and must submit their claim for exemption to the Ministry of Finance.[154]

Taxpayers whose annual receipts are 300,000 pesos or more must keep an inventory and balance sheet book, a general journal, and a ledger or register of current accounts. Taxpayers with annual receipts of less than 300,000 pesos, and agents, brokers, and other representatives regardless of the amount of their receipts are required to keep only a cash receipts and disbursements book. These books must be authenticated by the federal tax office.[155]

IX

Labor and Social Security

The labor laws of a foreign country, provided they are not a source of undue economic burden, are not often high on the list of factors influencing the decision of whether or not to invest in that country, and the fact that a large number of foreign-owned enterprises operate successfully in Mexico is a good indication that its labor laws are not overly burdensome. It is true that concern arose over the 1962 amendments to the law giving workers the right to participate in their employers' profits, and a few private foreign investors may have delayed or canceled their investment projects in Mexico as a consequence. But their fears were centered mainly on uncertainty as to how the profit-sharing law would be implemented and were largely allayed when the resolution on the percentage of profits to be distributed was issued. Nevertheless, it is important to foreign businessmen and their lawyers to be aware of their obligations under the labor code and the possible problems they may encounter once the decision to invest is made.

Important also are considerations of the availability and cost of labor. Although there is no shortage of manpower and unskilled labor is actually in oversupply, there is a notable shortage of trained workers, from semiskilled factory workers to supervisory and managerial personnel. The government has for some time been making great efforts to improve education generally in the country and particularly to increase technical and vocational training, but the country's needs are not yet being satisfied, and most skilled workers must still be trained on the job. Some persons feel that the insufficient supply of trained personnel is potentially the most important handicap to the continued industrialization of the country. Many foreign-owned enterprises find it necessary to import aliens to fill some technical, supervisory, and managerial positions, but because of the increasing difficulty of obtaining entry permits for foreign personnel and the obvious public and government relations advantages, many companies prefer to hire Mexicans, at least at levels below the chief executive officers. As a result, Mexicans with ability and experience in management are highly sought after and there is a substantial amount of raiding among the larger enterprises.

The Mexican industrial worker has no aversion to working for a foreign-owned enterprise and in fact often prefers to work for such a company because of its relative size and stability and because he can usually count on fair treatment and conscientious compliance with the law. Furthermore, union leaders have no antipathy toward foreign-owned companies, and foreign employers probably have fewer labor difficulties than domestic employers because their wage scales are often higher.

It is difficult to make a general assessment of labor costs. Wage rates vary considerably among geographic areas, industries, and even companies within an industry, and benefits in addition to wages are usually substantial. In almost all companies of any size, including foreign-owned companies, employment conditions are covered by collective contracts that typically provide for benefits well above the legal minimum wages. The minimum wage scales are, however, an indication of the relative wage rates in different parts of the country, and on that basis it appears that labor costs are higher in the Federal District and the industrialized states that adjoin it and in the northern border areas, especially the State of Baja California, than in other areas.

Although conditions of employment and workers' rights are usually established by collective bargaining, to a substantial extent the formulation of labor policy rests ultimately with the federal and local governments. Overt government interference in labor disputes is not frequent, but the government often plays a key role in mediating the settlement of controversies in important industries. Also, since the government representatives on the tripartite boards of conciliation and arbitration, to which many labor disputes are submitted, have the deciding vote in case of disagreement between the representatives of labor and management, the government has at least potential power to dictate the terms of settlement. In the heady days of President Lázaro Cárdenas, it seemed that labor could do no wrong and that a disproportionate number of disputes were resolved in favor of labor, but administrations since that time have been dedicated to rapid industrialization of the country as the key to economic progress and have been more concerned with maintaining a reasonable balance between labor and industry.

The influence of the government in labor matters is also facilitated by the extremely close ties between organized labor and the PRI, the dominant political party. The government receives the apparently unconditional support of some 90 percent of the organized industrial workers in the country, and the support of labor is undoubtedly a necessary element in the broad base on which the power of the PRI rests. In return, the government may not be overly unmindful of the demands of labor, but the extent of labor's actual influence is difficult to assess. On the surface at least, this influence appears to be substantial. One of the three sectors of the PRI is the labor sector, represented principally by the Confederación de Trabajadores de México (CTM), the largest trade-union confederation. As a sector of the PRI organized labor has a voice in the selection of the party's candidates for the federal Congress and is also influential in the nomination of candidates to the state legislatures. Its participation in the selection of candidates for state governorships and for the presidency is much more subtle and difficult to ascertain. It is perhaps of some significance that President López Mateos rose to the presidency in 1958 from the position of minister of labor and that the nomination of Gustavo Díaz Ordaz as the presidential candidate of the PRI in 1964 was made known publicly by the CTM even before it was announced by the party itself. Whether or not labor plays a major role in the selection of the president, it can probably be said at least that the candidate must not be a person offensive to the labor sector.

Mexicans are highly proud of their labor law and the fact that Mexico was the first country to incorporate basic protections of labor in its Constitution. A progeny of the Revolution, the constitutional provisions on labor have been described as a declaration of social rights on a par with the French Declaration of the Rights of Man of 1789.[1] Article 123 of the 1917 Constitution laid down broad standards for the protection of the laboring class, at a time when no labor movement of importance existed, dealing in detail with such matters as hours of work, rest days and vacations, minimum wages and other benefits, occupational risks, discharge, labor unions, collective bargaining, strikes, and dispute settlement. As originally adopted, the Constitution left to the individual states the power to enact labor legislation, and within ten years most states had adopted implementing laws. These laws varied considerably, and no law was enacted for the Federal District, where the greatest number of industrial workers were concentrated. The need to unify labor legislation in the country resulted in a 1929 amendment to the Constitution to give exclusive legislative jurisdiction in labor matters to the federal Congress. The first federal labor law was enacted on August 18, 1931,[2] and was in effect for nearly thirty-nine years. Amendments to the law were adopted from time to time, the most recent being the important changes made at the end of 1962 under the administration of President Adolfo López Mateos incorporating compulsory profit sharing, changing the system for setting minimum wages, increasing the protections to workers unjustifiably discharged, and providing increased protections for employed women and minors.[3]

Toward the end of 1969 a new labor law was enacted on the initiative of the president, effective May 1, 1970.[4] While this law follows the basic scheme of the 1931 law, it represents a substantial improvement in form and organization and contains some important innovations, such as a requirement that employers furnish housing for their workers, provisions for the payment of annual bonuses and a seniority bonus, and other additional benefits for workers.

With the exception of civil servants, the federal labor law governs the rights and obligations of all workers in the country, including employees of public enterprises. The protections of article 123 were extended to civil servants by a 1960 constitutional amendment, but they are covered by separate legislation.[5] Special rules are provided in the law for certain classes of workers—confidential workers, seamen, aircraft crews, railroad and autotransport workers, employees in public service operations in zones of federal jurisdiction, rural workers, commercial agents, professional athletes, actors and musicians, workers in home and family industries, domestic servants, and hotel and restaurant employees. Confidential workers are defined as those who perform general functions of management, inspection, supervision, and auditing, and functions related to personal work of the employer within the enterprise or establishment.[6]

The law applies in all cases in which a person renders a personal service to another under his direction and control and for an agreed compensation.[7] This language has led the courts to hold that agents, commission agents, attorneys, doctors, professors, and even managers are protected by the law when the person or company they serve exercises control and direction over their activities.[8] The obligations imposed by the law apply independently to "enterprises" and to "establishments." An enterprise is defined as an economic unit of production or distribution of goods or services, and an establishment is a technical unit in the form of a branch, agency, or other similar form that is an integral part of and contributes to the achievement of the purposes of an enterprise.[9]

The enforcement of the law has been deficient in many respects. Provision is made for federal and state labor inspectors, whose function is to see that the requirements of the law are fulfilled, but this system has not been very successful in practice. Enforcement against a particular employer often depends upon whether or not the workers are represented by a union. It is the unions that bear the real responsibility for enforcing employees' rights, and they have done much to create in the industrial laboring class a consciousness of their position and rights under the law. Outside of industry, notably in smaller commercial enterprises, and in small factories, employee groups have not always been receptive to organization attempts. In the absence of a union, workers are likely to be ignorant of the laws and procedures or lacking in sufficient power to enforce their rights, and violations of the minimum wage and other requirements are regularly reported.

CONDITIONS OF EMPLOYMENT

HIRING

The employment relationship exists when one performs personal work under the subordination of another for a salary or wage. The existence of an employment relationship and a contract of employment is presumed when those conditions exist, and the worker is entitled to all the benefits and protections of the law.[10]

The conditions of employment are required to be in writing when they are not established in a collective labor contract.[11] The absence of a writing is deemed the fault of the employer and does not deprive a worker of his rights under the law. A written contract is always advisable because of the difficulties of proof by the employer of the terms of an unwritten contract in the event they are disputed by the worker. The employment contract must specify the name, nationality, age, sex, marital status, and domicile of each party; whether the employment is for a specific piece of work, a fixed period of time, or an indefinite period; the services to be performed; place or places or work; compensation; time and place of payment of wages; and such other conditions as rest days, vacations, and other matters agreed between the parties. Attention to drafting of the contract, especially the description of services, is important. Under the law disobedience of orders of the employer is grounds for discharge only if the orders relate to the work contracted, and the

Supreme Court has held discharge to be unjustified where the employer's orders did not relate to the work for which the worker was employed.[12]

An employment contract is deemed to be for an indefinite term unless it is expressly provided that it is for a fixed term or for the performance of a specific job.[13] However, a contract for a specific job is allowed only when the nature of the work so requires, and a fixed term may be provided only when the work is by its nature temporary, when the employment is to fill the temporary absence of another worker, or in other cases permitted by the law. Also, employment contracts for the mining of unprofitable mineral reserves or for the restoration of abandoned or closed mines may be for a fixed term or a specific job or for the investment of a specified amount of capital. In no case may a worker be bound by an employment contract for more than one year.

While the law does not expressly recognize a probationary period in contracts of employment, the employer is given the right to cancel a contract without incurring liability if he finds within thirty days of the date of employment that the worker does not possess the skills that he or the union claimed.[14] On the basis of a similar provision in the 1931 labor law,[15] the practice developed of providing in individual contracts for a trial period of up to thirty days, and this practice has been upheld by the Supreme Court. The Court has also recognized that collective contracts under which the union supplies new workers may provide for a trial period for skilled workers in excess of thirty days. However, the 1969 law provides that one of the means that may be established in collective contracts to prove that a worker has the knowledge and aptitude necessary for a specific job is a trial period not exceeding thirty days,[16] and this provision may be intended to prohibit longer trial periods.

The employment of foreigners is somewhat more restricted under the 1969 law than under the prior law. Except for directors, administrators, and general managers, at least 90 percent of all workers in each enterprise and establishment must be Mexicans. An employer may hire foreigners in technical and professional categories only if there are no Mexicans available in a specific specialty and then only temporarily and in a number not exceeding 10 percent of the employees in that specialty. If foreign workers are employed, they and the employer are jointly obligated to train Mexicans in their specialty.[17]

Most enterprises of any importance have collective contracts providing for a closed shop through an "exclusion clause" prohibiting the employer from hiring nonunion workers.[18] In the absence of a collective contract or an exclusion clause, the employer must give preference in hiring, under equal circumstances, to Mexicans over non-Mexicans, to those who have worked satisfactorily for the employer for the longest time, and to organized over nonunion workers whether or not a collective contract exists between the employer and the union to which the worker belongs. Promotions to fill vacancies or new jobs are required to be made on the basis of seniority in the category immediately inferior to that in which the vacancy exists, and if there are two or more workers with the same seniority, the selection is made on the basis of competence. The 1969 law provides, however, that collective contracts shall establish the method by which the worker who has the right to promotion proves that he has the necessary knowledge and aptitude for the job, either by a certificate of completion of vocational training courses furnished by the employer or an independent school or institute, by an examination, by a trial period not exceeding thirty days, or other means agreed.[19]

Although discrimination by reason of sex or age, as well as race, religion, political beliefs, or social condition, is prohibited, the law contains special provisions for the protection of women and minors.[20] Women may not be employed in dangerous or unhealthful activities, industrial night work, or commercial establishments after 10:00 P.M. Minors under fourteen years of age are not permitted to work, and those over fourteen and under sixteen must have completed their required education and must have parental or other specified authority and present a medical certificate to be employed. Those under sixteen may not be employed in such things as bars, work that may affect their morals or good behavior, underground or underwater work, dangerous or unhealthful activities or those that might retard their normal physical growth, or nonindustrial establishments after 10:00 P.M. Those under eighteen may not be employed in industrial night work.

HOURS OF WORK AND VACATIONS

The maximum legal working day is eight hours in the case of day work, seven hours for night work, and seven and one-half hours for mixed working days.[21] Day work is work performed between 6:00 A.M. and 8:00 P.M., and work during other hours is considered night work. If a mixed working day includes three and one-half hours or more of night work, the entire work period is considered night work. Workers are entitled to a rest period of at least one-half hour during the work period. When a worker cannot leave the place of work during the periods of rest or meals, those periods must be counted as work time.

Overtime work may not exceed three hours in a day and overtime may not be worked more than three days in a week. Overtime work must be compensated at twice the rate fixed for normal hours of work, and for any overtime exceeding nine hours a week the employer must pay three times the normal wage and is subject to fine.

For each six days of work, workers are entitled to at least one day of rest with full pay, which should be on Sunday if possible.[22] For work on Sunday an additional 25 percent of the pay for a normal work day must be paid.[23] Workers may not be required to work on their rest day, and if they do the employer must pay three times the normal wage. The maximum of forty-eight hours for the six-day work week may be distributed over less than six full days by agreement between the workers and the employer. Collective contracts often provide for a work week of forty-five hours, distributed among five days, leaving the workers two days of rest.

Seven paid holidays must be given to workers annually, and every six years an additional holiday is given for the presidential inauguration. Most collective contracts provide for additional national and religious holidays with pay.

After one year of service workers have the right to six days of vacation with pay, which is increased by two days for each additional year of service to a maximum of twelve working days. Following the fourth year of service the vacation period is increased by two days for each five years of service. Vacations must be granted within six months after the completion of the year of service, and at least six days of the vacation period must be consecutive. Vacation time may not be paid in cash, but if a worker's employment is terminated before the year of service is completed, he is entitled to compensation for the portion of the vacation period earned. Workers are also entitled to a bonus of 25 percent of their normal wages during their vacation time.[24]

The periods of work of women and minors under sixteen are subject to special limitations.[25] Women may not perform any overtime work, and if they do work overtime, they are entitled to be compensated at three times their normal pay. During pregnancy they may not perform work dangerous to their health of that of their child. Employed women have the right to a paid leave of six weeks before and six weeks after childbirth. This period may be extended for a term of not more than sixty days at half pay if the employee is unable to work because of the pregnancy or childbirth and up to one year from the date of birth without pay after the expiration of the sixty-day extension. Women who are nursing their infants must be given two special rest periods daily of half an hour each with full pay.

Minors under sixteen may not be employed for more than six hours per day, divided into two three-hour periods with an intermediate rest period of one hour. They may not work overtime or on Sundays or legal holidays, and if they do they are entitled to compensation equal to three times their normal rate of pay. They must be given an annual paid vacation of eighteen working days.

PAY

Wages are set by agreement but must be compensatory in the judgment of the board of conciliation and arbitration and may not be less than the officially established minimum rates.[26] It is further required that the quantity and quality of work must be considered in fixing wages and that equal compensation must be paid for the same work under similar conditions. No discrimination in pay may be made on the basis of age, sex, or nationality. Wages in most major industries are governed by collective contracts and are well above the minimum rates, but the government has resisted union attempts to tie wages to the cost of living through a sliding scale.

Before the 1962 amendments to the 1931 labor law, minimum wage rates were fixed by local boards for individual states or municipalities, with the result that hundreds of different and often irrational rates were in effect in the country. The method of establishing minimum rates was substantially improved in 1962, and the procedure in effect since that time has been retained in the 1969 law.[27] Rates are now established for geographical economic zones. A general minimum wage for urban workers and a separate schedule for rural workers are established in each zone. In addition, minimum occupational wages may be fixed for special occupations, trades, or jobs in specific branches of industry or commerce within one or more economic zones. The law provides that occupational minimums shall be fixed when there does not exist any other legal procedure for establishing them and the majority of the workers of specific occupations or trades in the zone involved are not covered by collective contracts.

Minimum rates are fixed every two years by a regional commission in each economic zone and must be approved by the national minimum wage commission.[28] Each regional commission is made up of a representative of the government, appointed by the labor ministry, and an equal number of representatives of union workers and employers. The national commission is composed of a chairman appointed by the president of the republic, two nonvoting government advisors, and an equal number of representatives of union workers and employers, and it is assisted by a technical advisory board. The only guideline established in the law is that the minimum wage must be sufficient to meet the normal material, social, and cultural needs of the head of a family and to provide for the required education of his children.[29]

Under this system the country has been divided into 109 economic zones. For the biennium 1970-71, the general daily minimum wage rates for urban workers ranged from a low of 15.75 pesos in a few less-developed areas to a high of 46.00 pesos for northern Baja California, wth 32.00 pesos for the Federal District. Minimums for rural workers were slightly lower, ranging from 13.75 pesos to 36.00 pesos for that period. Minimum occupational wages have been set for a number of occupations and trades, mainly in service and commercial establishments, in most of the major cities. In each biennium from 1954-55 through 1970-71 the average increase in minimum wages for urban workers was less than 19 percent, and the increase was held to 15.5 percent in 1968-69 and again in 1970-71.[30]

These minimum rates are for an eight-hour workday, but in view of the requirement that workers be paid for one day of rest for each six days of work, the minimum wage for a six-day work week is the equivalent of seven days' pay.

One of the innovations of the 1969 labor law is an obligation of employers to pay to their workers, before December 20 of each year, an annual bonus equivalent to at least fifteen days' wages.[31] Workers who have not completed one year of service are entitled to an amount proportional to the period of their service. Annual bonuses have long been commonly paid to employees in addition to wages and have often been provided for in collective contracts. However, the profit-sharing requirement imposed in 1963, discussed below, to some extent replaced this practice and companies that have gone into business since the adoption of profit sharing have not customarily paid bonuses.

Wages must be paid in cash and at least every week in the case of manual workers or every fifteen days in the case of other workers. Wages are paid at the place of work unless otherwise agreed but may not be paid at places of amusement, restaurants, taverns, bars, or stores, except to employees of those establishments.[32]

Wages are also protected againt attachments by creditors and excessive deductions by the employer.[33] Fines may not be imposed on a worker for any reason, and deductions from his wages are authorized only for certain specified payments and in limited amounts. Debts contracted by the worker to his employer for wage advances, excess payments, errors, losses, damages, or purchases of articles produced by the enterprise may be deducted but not in an amount exceeding 30 percent of the amount of his wages over the minimum wage. In no case is an employee liable for debts contracted to his employer in excess of the equivalent of one month's wages. Rent on employer-furnished housing not exceeding 15 percent of the worker's wages and agreed installments on the purchase of a house are also deductible. Ordinary union dues and, if the worker expressly consents, contributions to co-operatives or savings funds up to 30 percent of his wages over the minimum wage may also be deducted. Amounts ordered by competent authorities to be paid for food allowances to family dependents are likewise deductible. Under the social security law, the employer may withhold the amount of the worker's social security contributions,[34] but in a few instances collective contracts require the employer to pay a part or all of the workers' share of social security contributions. Wages may not be assigned and are not subject to attachment by a worker's creditors, except for payment of food allowances ordered by a competent authority in favor of his wife, children, ascendants, or grandchildren. In case of bankruptcy or receivorship of the employer, workers are preferred over all other creditors, incuding secured creditors and tax authorities, to the extent of unpaid wages earned in the last year and any compensation owed by reason of unjustified discharge.

PROFIT SHARING

The right of workers to participate in the profits of their employers has been enshrined in the Mexican Constitution since its promulgation in 1917.[35] The original scheme was that special commissions in each municipality would establish the workers' share of profits. In several state laws, notably that of Veracruz, rudimentary provisions for profit sharing were enacted, but the federal labor law of 1931 failed to implement the constitutional requirement, and it lay dormant for forty-five years. What demand there was on the part of labor to enforce the constitutional right was not strong, and attempts to enforce it in the courts met with failure. The Supreme Court consistently held that the right could not be enforced against an employer until implementing legislation was enacted and the amount of participation established by local commissions,[36] which were never created.

The government's procrastination continued until the latter half of the López Mateos administration. The lack of any strong demand on the part of labor had long before led the Mexican business community to assume that the exemption would continue indefinitely, and the move to implement the law was the source of some alarm and concern. In November, 1962, the Constitution was amended to provide for the establishment of profit sharing by a national commission under certain guidelines, and the following month implementing provisions were incorporated into the federal labor law.[37] The national commission for the participation of workers in profits of enterprises, composed of representatives of labor, employers, and the government, was created on February 23, 1963. The task of the commission and its technical department was monumental. In a major effort the Confederación Patronal, representing employers, made exhaustive legal and economic studies for the commission's guidance, and valuable studies were also made by the government. The contribution of labor to the effort was not substantial. The commission's resolution was approved unanimously on December 12, 1963, and was published the following day.[38] The fact that it was the source of neither jubilation in the ranks of labor nor consternation on the part of the business community was probably indicative that the commission had succeeded in laying the basis for a desirable improvement in the conditions of labor without endangering the continued industrial development of the country.

The scheme of the profit-sharing requirement was preserved in the 1969 labor law with a few changes favoring labor,[39] and the commission's 1963 resolution continues in effect.

The requirement applies generally to every employer, whether a sole proprietorship or a legal entity. There are, however, certain exemptions: newly established concerns during the first year of their operations, newly established concerns that manufacture a product considered as new during the first two years of their operations, new extractive enterprises during the exploration period, public and private welfare institutions recognized by law, sole proprietorships whose annual gross income for income tax purposes does not exceed 120,000 pesos, and legal entities with less than 25,000 pesos capital stock and annual gross income not exceeding 125,000 pesos.[40]

The amount of profit to be distributed to workers was fixed by the commission at 20 percent of annual "net distributable profits." For purposes of determining net distributable profits, the commission established five categories of taxpayers and a separate formula of computation for each category. These categories were based on and followed the divisions of taxpayers under the 1953 income tax law then in effect, and even though they were abolished under the subsequent income tax law of 1964, they were retained for purposes of the profit-sharing computation. The categories are: legal entities, physical persons with annual income over 300,000 pesos, physical persons with annual income under 300,000 pesos, branches and agencies of foreign enterprises operating without their own capital, and professional persons, technicians, artisans, and artists.

The formulas for computing net distributable profits vary to some degree among these categories of employers, but the provisions for legal entities are the most important and are indicative of the general scheme. The starting point is the annual taxable income of the enterprise calculated in accordance with the income tax law but without deduction of any losses from prior years. The fact that an enterprise is exempt from paying income tax does not necessarily mean, however, that it is relieved of the profit-sharing obligation. From the taxable income, normal income tax for the year and any additional taxes that may have been assessed for prior years are deducted. Of the resulting amount 30 percent may then be subtracted for what is termed "reasonable return on invested capital and an incentive to favor the reinvestment of profits."[41] Finally, from the resulting balance there is deducted a percentage determined by the ratio of invested capital to labor force. For this purpose, labor force is the total amount of wages, salaries, and other compensation to labor paid during the year. Invested capital is defined in the income tax law and generally includes stated capital, reserves, and retained earnings from prior years. The theory behind this deduction is that the share of profits allocated between capital and labor should vary according to their relative roles in the enterprise. Once the "comparison factor" is determined by dividing the invested capital by labor force, the amount of the variable deduction is found from the schedule contained in article 5 of the resolution. These deductions range from 10 percent for enterprises with twice as much capital as labor force to a maximum of 80 percent for enterprises having a ratio of invested capital to labor force of thirty or more. The amount resulting from this deduction is the "net distributable profit," 20 percent of which is distributed among the employees. The formula operates to limit the amount of the distribution to a maximum of 12.6 percent of taxable income, and it may be as low as 2.8 percent, depending upon the amount of invested capital in relation to labor cost.

For purposes of determining the amount to which each individual worker is entitled, the total amount of the workers' participation is divided into two equal parts. One part is distributed equally among the workers on the basis of the number of days worked by each during the year. The other part is divided in proportion to the total wages earned by each worker in the year. For this purpose wages means only the amount received by the worker as his basic daily pay rate and does not include bonuses, allowances, overtime pay, or other benefits such as rent-free housing. Employers who had a voluntary profit-sharing plan in effect at the time of the 1962 amendments to the law may credit their profit distributions against the amount they are obligated to distribute under the law, unless the employer charges them as a business expense or cost on his books, in which case they are considered a salary supplement and not a distribution of profits.[42] Directors, administrators, general managers, domestic help, and temporary workers who have been employed less than sixty days during the year are not entitled to participate in profits. Confidential employees other than those named are entitled to share in profits, but if the salary of a confidential employee is greater than that of the highest paid plant worker, the amount of the plant worker's salary plus 20 percent is considered the salary of the confidential employee for purposes of computing the distribution. There is a maximum limit of one month's pay on the amount to which workers are entitled where the employer's income is derived exclusively from their services and in the case of workers engaged in caring for income-producing properties or the collection of debts.

The computation of the amount due each worker is made by a commission composed of an equal number of representatives of the workers and the employer, and the projected distribution schedule must be posted. If the commission is unable to reach an agreement, the controversy is resolved by the official labor inspector. The workers may file objections with the commission within fifteen days, and if no objections are raised, the projected distribution becomes final. The amount of the workers' participation must be distributed to them within sixty days following the date the employer's annual income tax is payable. Any amount not claimed by workers in the year in which it is payable is added to the amount distributable for the next year.

Under the 1969 labor law the employer is required to deliver to the workers, within ten days after filing, a copy of the annual income tax return of the employer and to make the attachments filed with the return available for their inspection for thirty days. During the next thirty days the union or a majority of the workers may file with the Ministry of Finance any observations concerning the return they consider appropriate. The workers are enjoined not to reveal data from the return or its attachments to third persons, and it is further provided that the workers' right to participate in profits does not entitle them to interfere in the management of the employer.

Profits distributed to workers may not be considered an expense or cost of the employer and consequently are not deductible from annual earnings for purposes of determining the amount of net distributable profit and may not be deducted by the employer for income tax purposes.[43]

A procedure is established for the review of the percentage of profits distributable to workers upon the application of the unions, federations, or confederations of workers or the employers. Once an application for review is made by one of those groups, it may not file a new application for ten years.[44] The commission's resolution now in effect may not be revised until the expiration of ten years from its effective date, December 13, 1963.[45]

OTHER BENEFITS

Housing

One of the most important new requirements of the 1969 labor law is the obligation of employers to provide, under certain circumstances, housing for their workers.[46] Article 123 of the Constitution calls for the enactment of such an obligation,[47] and the 1931 law provided that the president should issue special regulations for workers' housing. However, regulations issued by President Avila Camacho in 1941 and 1942[48] were declared unconstitutional by the Supreme Court on the ground that only Congress has the power under the Constitution to legislate in labor matters. The 1969 law contains the first congressional implementation of the constitutional mandate on housing.

The obligation extends to two types of employers: those located outside a city or town if the distance between their place of business and the town is more than three kilometers or if, regardless of the distance, there is no ordinary and regular passenger transportation service from the town, and those located within a city or town which employ more than 100 workers. Permanent employees of such enterprises with at least one year of service are entitled to be furnished housing but must notify the employer, either directly or through the union, of their desire to exercise their right. Employers that have sufficient houses to satisfy the workers' requirements must so inform the union or the workers. If the employer does not have a sufficient number of houses and is not able to acquire them, it must notify the union or the workers of that fact, and within a period of three years from the effective date of the law or, in the case of new enterprises, three years following the first year of operation, agreements must be reached between the employer and the workers, including confidential workers, for compliance with the housing obligation. The agreements must specify the number of workers who have a right to receive houses and those who have exercised that right, the method and term for compliance with the employer's obligation to furnish houses, the specifications of houses to be constructed by the employer, and the number of houses to be constructed periodically and the dates for the construction of new houses until all the workers' requirements are satisfied. If the houses are to be rented to the workers, the employer may charge annual rent in an amount not exceeding 6 percent of their tax appraisal value. If they are to be acquired by the workers, the agreement must specify the amount to be contributed by the employer and the method of financing the balance to be paid by the workers. Enterprises that enlarge their installations or increase their personnel must likewise enter agreements with the workers for the construction of new houses. Employer-furnished houses may be single- or multiple-family dwellings.

In the assignment of houses workers with greatest seniority have preference, and among those with equal seniority, heads of family and union members are preferred in that order. If a worker already owns a house furnished pursuant to article 123 of the Constitution or a collective labor contract, he is not entitled to another house even if his house was provided by a different employer. If he acquired a house independently, he has the right to receive a new one from his employer but only after the requirements of the other workers have been satisfied.

Until houses are furnished by the employer, the workers are entitled to receive a monthly compensation in an amount provided for in the agreement between the employer and the workers or the union. If the amount is not specified, the compensation must be determined according to the type of houses the employer is obligated to furnish and the difference between the rental value of such houses and the amount of rent the workers are required to pay for similar houses.

Seniority Bonus

Another innovation of the 1969 law is the requirement that employers pay to their permanent workers a seniority bonus *(prima de antigüedad)* in the amount of twelve days' wages for each year of service.[49] For purposes of computing the bonus, the maximum daily wage of a worker is considered to be double the amount of the minimum wage for the economic zone in which he works or fifty pesos, whichever is higher. The bonus is paid to workers who resign voluntarily from their employment provided they have completed at least fifteen years of service. It must also be paid to those who resign for justified cause and to those who are discharged for any reason, regardless of the length of service. In case of a worker's death, the bonus is paid to his surviving dependents named in the law, irrespective of the period of his service. If more than 10 percent of the total number of workers in an enterprise or establishment or in a specific category voluntarily resign within a period of one year, payment of the bonus to those exceeding 10 percent may be deferred until the following year. In that event, preference in payment is given to those who resign first or, if more than 10 percent resign simultaneously, to those with greatest seniority.

Education

The labor law imposes various obligations on employers aimed at improving the education and training of their employees and their families. They must collaborate with the labor and education authorities in literacy programs for their workers.[50] Employers are also required to offer permanent or periodic vocational and technical training courses or programs pursuant to plans agreed upon with the unions or the workers, of which the Ministry of Labor or the local labor authorities must be notified. These courses may be given in one or more enterprises, establishments, or departments or sections, either by the employer's own personnel, by technical teachers specially contracted, through specialized schools or institutes, or in some other form.[51]

Employers with more than a hundred and fewer than a thousand workers must provide a full scholarship for one worker or child of a worker for technical, industrial, or practical studies either in Mexico or abroad. Employers with more than a thousand workers must provide three such scholarships. Recipients of scholarships are selected by the workers and the employer on the basis of aptitude, personal qualities, and dedication, and they must remain in the employer's service for at least one year following the completion of their studies.[52]

The labor law further imposes the obligation on employers to establish and maintain "Constitutional Article 123" schools as required by law and the Ministry of Public Education.[53] This obligation is implemented by the 1942 organic law of public education and its regulations, which require that businesses located more than three kilometers from the nearest town must provide primary schools for their workers' children if the number of primary-school age children is more than twenty.[54]

An additional obligation of employers is to contribute to the promotion of cultural and athletic activities among their workers and to furnish the necessary equipment for that purpose.[55]

TERMINATION OF EMPLOYMENT

Of substantial difficulty to employers and the source of most litigation are the provisions of the labor law relating to job security and discharge. The Constitution and the law embody the principle that the employment relationship is permanent and may be terminated without payment of indemnity only for reasonable cause.[56] As an exception to this principle, contracts for a fixed period or for piece work are allowed but, as pointed out above, only when the work is by its nature temporary. Furthermore, the written employment contract must expressly provide that it is for a fixed term or specific job and describe the work to be performed during the term or the specific job. Otherwise, it is considered a contract for an indefinite term.[57]

The law lists fourteen specific reasons for which an employer may discharge a worker without incurring liability for severance pay and further provides that reasons similar to those listed are justified cause for discharge.[58] Among the most important of these are discovery within thirty days that the worker does not possess the skills or talent that he or the union claimed; failure in the performance of his duties or dishonesty, violence, or threats to a superior or the employer; wilful or negligent damage to premises, equipment, machines, or other property related to the work; immoral conduct at the place of work; disclosure of trade secrets; jeopardizing the safety of the workplace; intoxication at work; unjustified absence from work more than three times within a thirty-day period; and disobedience of the employer in connection with the work contracted for. A confidential employee may be discharged if there exists a reasonable cause for loss of the employer's confidence in him. If he was promoted from a plant position, he must be returned to it unless cause exists for his discharge.[59]

In many cases the question of whether there was justifiable cause for dismissal is challenged by the worker before the board of conciliation and arbitration, and if the employer fails to discharge the burden of proof on this issue, the worker is entitled, at his option, to be reinstated in his job or to receive compensation in the amount of three months' wages. In either event the employer is also required to pay full wages from the date of dismissal until compliance with the final decision.

The worker's right to receive full pay until the employer's obligation is discharged has in some cases led labor lawyers, who usually accept employees' claims on a contingent fee basis, to delay filing a petition to contest the grounds for discharge until the latest possible time and to employ dilatory tactics to prolong the litigation and thus increase the amount of the recovery if the claim is successful. To avoid this, an employer wishing to discharge a worker either without cause or where grounds might be difficult to prove often takes the initiative by negotiating a settlement with the worker.

Although the optional right to reinstatement has long been contained in the Constitution, the Supreme Court held before 1962 that compulsory reinstatement could not be specifically enforced.[60] Under this decision an employer could freely discharge a worker without reason upon payment of the required compensation. However, the 1962 amendments to the Constitution and the 1931 labor law restored to the worker the right to choose between reinstatement and compensation, and this right is preserved in the 1969 law. Under the existing law, the employer may refuse to reinstate certain classes of workers only: those with less than one year of service, those in direct and permanent contact with the employer where the board of conciliation and arbitration finds that it is not possible for a normal employment relationship to exist, confidential employees, domestic help, and temporary workers.

When the employer is exempt from the reinstatement requirement, he is obligated to pay, in the case of an employment contract for an indefinite term, an indemnity equal to twenty days' wages for each year of service. If the employment contract is for a specific period of time less than one year, the severance pay is equal to wages for one half the period during which services were rendered. If the specified contract term is over one year, the employer is obligated to pay an amount equal to six months' wages for the first year and twenty days' wages for each subsequent year during which services were rendered. Regardless of the type of contract involved, the employer must also pay three months' wages and all wages from the date of dismissal until the indemnity has been paid.

A worker may terminate his contract for certain specified improper conduct on the part of the employer, such as misrepresentation of the conditions of the job offered, dishonesty, violence or mistreatment to the worker or his family, or reduction of the worker's wages. In the event of termination by the worker for cause, he is entitled to receive an indemnity in the same amount provided for workers discharged without cause who are not entitled to reinstatement.[61]

In addition to rescission for cause, an employment contract may be terminated by mutual consent, the worker's death or incapacity, or completion of the work or expiration of the term provided for in a piecework or fixed-term contract. If the worker's incapacity is not the result of a work-related illness or injury, he is entitled to one month's wages and the seniority bonus earned, and if possible and if he wishes, he should be furnished another job compatible with his ability. Labor relations may also be terminated, either under an individual employment contract or upon the shutdown of the employer's enterprise or establishment or a permanent reduction of work,[62] for the following reasons: *force majeure* or a fortuitous event not imputable to the employer or the employer's death or incapacity if it necessarily results in termination of the work, evident unprofitability of the operation, exhaustion of the mineral substance in an extractive industry, or bankruptcy or judicial liquidation of the enterprise if the competent authority or the creditors decide that the business should be closed or its operations permanently reduced. In the event of termination by reason of the closing of the employer's business or a permanent reduction of work for any of those reasons, the authorization or approval of the board of conciliation and arbitration must be obtained pursuant to procedures established in the law, and the workers discharged are entitled to receive three months' wages and the seniority bonus earned. If the employer reopens the enterprise or establishes a similar business, he is subject to the obligations relating to preference in hiring, discussed above. An employer may reduce his work force as a consequence of the installation of machinery or the adoption of new work methods with the authorization of the board of conciliation and arbitration, but he must pay compensation to the dismissed workers in the amount of four months' wages plus twenty days' wages for each year of service and the seniority bonus earned.

The obligations under an employment contract may be temporarily suspended without liability of either party in certain events,[63] such as the contracting of a contagious disease by the worker, temporary incapacity resulting from a nonwork-related illness or injury, arrest, compliance with certain civic responsibilities, or the appointment of the worker to a labor board or commission. An employer may also temporarily suspend work without incurring liability for the following reasons: *force majeure* or death or incapacity of the employer requiring a suspension of work, lack of raw materials not resulting from the employer's fault, excessive production in relation to the employer's financial condition and the state of the market, evident temporary unprofitability of the business, lack of funds and impossibility to obtain them for the normal operation of the business, or failure of the government to pay for materials or services that have been contracted for with the employer provided the amounts payable are indispensable to the business. The employer must obtain authorization or approval of the suspension from the board of conciliation and arbitration, which determines the indemnities to be paid to the workers.

A worker may not be deprived of his employment by a sale of the enterprise in which he is employed The law provides that the substitution of one employer for another does not affect existing employment contracts and that the former employer is jointly liable with the new employer for obligations under contracts or the law arising before the date of the substitution. This joint liability continues for six months from the date on which notice of the substitution is given to the union or the workers, after which the new employer becomes solely responsible.[64] A similar requirement in the 1931 labor law has been interpreted to apply where an entire business or enterprise, or even part of an enterprise if it constitutes an economic and legal unit, is sold or assigned to another. Machinery and equipment are not in themselves, however, an economic and legal unit, so that a purchaser of part of the equipment of an enterprise does not necessarily become a substitute employer. Also, attaching creditors of a business are not considered substitute employers.[65]

COLLECTIVE BARGAINING

The right of workers to organize for the defense of their interests is provided for in the Constitution and the labor law,[66] and in almost every company of any importance the workers are represented by a union. Directors, managers, and other persons who perform management functions are considered employers' representatives and may not belong to workers' unions; confidential employees may belong to unions but not to those of other workers.[67] Though union membership may not be required under the law, most collective contracts contain an "exclusion clause" under which union membership is a condition of employment.

The labor law provides for various types of unions—craft unions *(gremiales)*, plant unions *(de empresa)*, industrial unions composed of workers in two or more enterprises in the same industry, national industrial unions made up of workers in one or more interstate enterprises in the same industry, and mixed trade unions *(de oficios varios)* formed by workers of various occupations where there are fewer than twenty workers of one trade in a municipality. The industrial union is the most common form of organization, but craft unions are also important.

A union may be formed with at least twenty workers and must register with the appropriate board of conciliation and arbitration or, in the case of unions in enterprises under federal jurisdiction, with the Ministry of Labor. The law recognizes the right of unions to form federations and confederations, the largest and most powerful of which is the Confederación de Trabajadores de México (CTM).

All enterprises employing workers who belong to a union are required to enter a collective contract with the union at its request.[68] There is no condition as to the number of workers that must be organized for purposes of this requirement, but if more than one industrial or plant union exists within the same enterprise, the collective contract is executed with the union having the largest membership. If there are two or more craft unions, a contract is executed jointly with a majority of them if they agree; otherwise, a separate contract is entered into with each. A collective contract covers all workers in the enterprise, whether members of the union or not, and extends to confidential employees unless the contract expressly excludes them.[69] However, a contract may not be applied to the detriment of nonunion workers who were employed before execution of the contract was requested. By law a collective contract must establish wage rates, working hours, and rest days and vacation periods, and contracts usually cover such other matters as the filling of vacancies, transfers, promotions, and industrial health and safety, and many provide for such fringe benefits as bonuses, pensions, sickness and accident benefits, life insurance, and savings plans.

Collective contracts are subject to renegotiation every two years upon the request of either party, and most contract negotiations take place in even-numbered years. The request for renegotiation, which is automatically made by unions in virtually all cases, must be presented at least sixty days before the expiration of the two-year period or the date of expiration of the contract.

An industry-wide collective contract, called a contract-law *(contrato-ley),* may be executed between one or more unions and several employers or one or more employers' associations.[70] A request for the execution of a contract-law may be made by a union or unions that represent at least two-thirds of the organized workers in a specific industry in one or more states, in one or more economic zones that cover one or more states, or in the entire country. The request is presented to the Ministry of Labor in the case of interstate industries and industries of federal jurisdiction or to the governor of the state or territory or the head of the Federal District Department in the case of industries of local jurisdiction. If the execution of a contract-law is considered opportune and beneficial for the industry by the authority to whom the request is made, a convention of the unions and employers is called to negotiate a contract, which may be for a maximum term of two years. The contract must be approved by a majority of the workers represented by the unions that made the request and a majority of their employers. It is then published by decree of the president of the republic or state governor and declared binding on all enterprises or establishments in the industry in the geographic area covered. If a collective contract has been executed by at least two-thirds of the union workers in an industry, it may be elevated to the status of a contract-law upon application by the unions or the employers to the same authorities to which a request for the execution of a contract-law is made. A contract-law is renegotiated every two years upon the request of either of the parties made at least ninety days before the expiration of its term. If renegotiation is not requested and the workers' right to strike is not exercised, it is automatically extended for a period equal to its original term, unless it is terminated by mutual consent or by failure of the parties to reach an agreement during the renegotiation. There are now eight contract-laws in existence, six covering various branches of the textile industry and the other two covering the sugar and alcohol industry and the manufactured rubber products industry.

DISPUTES

Both individual and collective labor disputes over compliance with the law or a labor contract are submitted, if other means of settlement fail, to boards of conciliation and arbitration. Responsibility for administration of the labor law is divided between the states and the federal government, and there are both state and federal boards. At each of those levels of government there are two types of boards— boards of conciliation and boards of conciliation and arbitration. A federal board of conciliation sits in each state capital, and there are local conciliation boards, often called municipal boards *(juntas municipales),* in the municipalities or in economic zones determined by the state governor. There is one federal board of conciliation and arbitration, which sits in Mexico City, and at least one local board of conciliation and arbitration, often called a central board *(junta central),* in each of the states and territories and in the Federal District.[71]

The federal boards have exclusive jurisdiction over enterprises that operate in federal zones and territorial waters, labor disputes that affect two or more states or a state and the Federal District or a federal territory, collective contracts that have been decreed obligatory in more than one state, and disputes involving enterprises that operate under a federal contract or concession and connected industries. The law further provides for federal jurisdiction over certain specified industries —the mining, hydrocarbon, petrochemical, metallurgical and steel, electric power, textile, motion picture, rubber, sugar, cement, and railroad industries, and enterprises that are administered directly or in a decentralized form by the federal government. The states are responsible for enforcing the law in other industries in matters wholly within their boundaries.[72]

The federal and local boards of conciliation are either permanent or *ad hoc* and are composed of a representative of the government, appointed by the state government in the case of local boards and the Ministry of Labor in the case of federal boards, and one representative each of labor and employers. The federal board of conciliation and arbitration is permanent and is composed of a representative of the government and representatives of labor and employers for each industry or group of related industries as classified by the Ministry of Labor. The federal board sits by groups if only one industry is involved and otherwise *en banc*. The local boards of conciliation and arbitration are also permanent and tripartite and are likewise divided into various special groups that handle disputes arising in different industries. The central board for the Federal District, for example, has eight special industrial groups.

Both individual and collective disputes are dealt with by these boards, but separate rules of procedure are established for collective disputes of a legal nature and those of an economic nature.[73] Individual disputes, involving such allegations as improper discharge or other violations of a worker's legal or contractual rights, are submitted either to the proper board of conciliation or to the appropriate board of conciliation and arbitration, which have concurrent jurisdiction at the conciliation stage. The boards of conciliation have no judicial authority and can only attempt to bring the parties to a voluntary settlement, except in disputes involving claims for amounts not exceeding three months' wages, in which they act as boards of conciliation and arbitration. If the parties fail to agree at the conciliation stage, the proceedings enter the arbitration phase before the board of conciliation and arbitration. One or more hearings are held for the presentation of evidence and written arguments. The arbitration proceedings are notable for their informality and the broad authority of the board to gather evidence it considers necessary to determine the facts, though because of the volume of litigation this authority is rarely exercised. The judgment of the board is final and binding and is not subject to appeal. However, it may be attacked in the courts in *amparo* proceedings upon an allegation that the constitutional guarantees of the losing party were violated by the board through incorrect application of the law to the case in dispute, and this recourse is often used. The same procedure is followed in collective disputes of a legal nature.

Most collective disputes are of an economic nature, involving union demands for increased benefits and better working conditions at the time of renegotiation of collective contracts. While such disputes may be resolved on the merits by the boards of conciliation and arbitration after a somewhat lengthy procedure, they are not normally called on to do so. But they do perform functions that are essential to the means of their settlement in the event the workers resort to a strike.

One of the basic rights of labor guaranteed by the Constitution and the law is the right to strike provided certain conditions are met.[74] A strike may be called only with the approval of a majority of the workers of the enterprise and must be for one of six purposes specified in the law: to obtain "equilibrium" between the various factors of production by "harmonizing" the rights of labor with those of capital, to force the employer to enter into a collective contract or to obtain renegotiation of a collective contract upon its termination, to obtain the execution of a contract-law or its renegotiation, to demand compliance with an existing collective contract or contract-law, to force the employer to comply with the statutory provisions on profit sharing, and to support a strike called for any of these purposes. The concept of "equilibrium" is obviously open to broad interpretation and has been the subject of considerable discussion by the courts and the text writers.[75] Some guidelines have been laid down by the boards and the courts; the Supreme Court has stated, for example, that the disequilibrium must be between the economic conditions of the workers involved and those of their employer and not in relation to the general cost of living.[76]

Before a strike may be called, written notice of the workers' grievances and their intention to strike must be filed with the appropriate board of conciliation and arbitration and served on the employer at least six days before the date set for the strike or ten days in the case of a public service enterprise. The employer is required to answer the workers' demands within forty-eight hours, also through the conciliation and arbitration board, but there is no sanction for failure to answer and in practice the employer often fails to answer the demands. If the employer refuses to meet the workers' demands, the board may attempt to mediate a settlement, but in practice it is more often the Ministry of Labor or the state director of labor that tries to obtain a settlement. Failing an agreement, the red and black strike flag may be raised.

If the requirements for filing notice of the workers' grievances have not been met, if less than a majority of the workers have approved the strike, or if the purpose of the strike is not one of those recognized by the law, the workers, employer, or interested third parties may request, within seventy-two hours from the commencement of work stoppage, that the board of conciliation and arbitration declare the strike to be nonexistent. If no such request is made, the strike is considered in existence for all legal purposes. If the strike is declared nonexistent, the workers must return to their jobs within twenty-four hours, and if they fail to comply with that requirement the employer is free to terminate their contracts and employ new workers to replace them without liability.

A strike is limited to the act of suspending work, and if a majority of the strikers commit acts of violence against persons or property or if, during wartime, the striking workers are employed in government-operated enterprises or services, the strike is declared unlawful by the board of conciliation and arbitration, and the employment contracts of the strikers are terminated. If the strike is lawful, all workers must stop work even if they voted against the strike, and the employer may not hire substitute workers except for certain essential work where the board of conciliation and arbitration has ordered a continuation of work and the strikers have refused to comply.[77]

Although the majority of strikes are terminated by private agreement between the parties, usually with the mediation of the Ministry of Labor or the state director of labor, the parties may also agree to submit the dispute to formal arbitration by any person or commission, or the striking workers may submit it to the board of conciliation and arbitration for resolution. If it is submitted to the board and the board finds that the reasons for the strike are imputable to the employer, the employer is ordered to satisfy the workers' demands and, except in the case of a sympathy strike, to pay all wages accrued to the workers during the period of the strike.

ACCIDENT AND ILLNESS COMPENSATION

The law imposes on employers liability to compensate their workers for personal injuries resulting from both accidents and illnesses suffered by reason of, or in, the performance of their work.[78] This liability exists regardless of any fault on the part of the employer, and it is no defense that the worker assumed the risks of his occupation, that the accident was caused by the negligence of a fellow worker or a third person, or that it resulted from the negligence or lack of intelligence of the worker himself. Workmen's compensation is provided for under the social security system, and an employer whose workers are covered by social security is relieved of the liability to pay compensation. Since the social security system has been extended to most industrial and commercial enterprises in urban areas, few concerns of importance are now affected by the workmen's compensation provisions of the labor law. Nevertheless, employers must report all accidents within seventy-two hours to a labor board or labor inspector, and giving notice to the social security institute does not relieve them of this obligation.

The amount of compensation payable for occupational injuries and diseases is calculated on the basis of the daily wage of the worker at the time of the accident or illness and varies according to whether the injury results in death, total or partial permanent disability, or temporary disability. However, the daily wage used for computing workmen's compensation may not be less than the legal minimum wage, but it is limited to a maximum of double the amount of the minimum wage for the economic zone in which the worker works or 50 pesos, whichever is higher.

In case the accident or illness results in death, the amount of compensation is equal to 730 days' wages, plus two months' wages to cover funeral expenses, apart from any amount that may have been paid to the worker during the time of disability. Death benefits are payable to the worker's wife, husband if he was financially dependent on the worker and has an incapacity of 50 precent or more, children under sixteen years of age and those over that age who are incapacitated, and dependent parents and grandparents. The compensation for total permanent disability is an amount equal to 1,095 days' wages. For partial permanent disability the compensation is a percentage of the amount payable for total permanent disability, calculated on the basis of a table of values for disabilities contained in the law. Compensation for permanent disability is payable in full without any deduction for wages paid during the period of treatment. In case of temporary disability, the worker is entitled to receive his wages for the period of time he is unable to work. Three months after the date of the disability and at three-month intervals thereafter, the worker or the employer may request that a determination be made of whether the same medical treatment should be continued and wages continued to be paid to the worker or whether the worker should be declared permanently disabled and entitled to receive compensation for permanent disability. In the event the worker's injury resulted from inexcusable fault of the employer, as defined in the law, the amount of the compensation may be increased by 25 percent in the discretion of the board of conciliation and arbitration.

In addition to the compensation provided for in the law, the worker is entitled to receive medical and surgical treatment, rehabilitation, hospitalization when necessary, medications and other pharmaceutical needs, and necessary prostheses and orthopedic devices.

All employers are required to keep medicines and equipment for first-aid treatment at the place of work. Those who employ over one hundred workers must have an infirmary for emergency medical and surgical treatment attended by competent personnel under the supervision of a medical doctor. Employers of over three hundred workers must provide a hospital with the necessary medical and other personnel. If the workers agree, an employer may satisfy these requirements by contracting for the services of a hosiptal or sanitarium located at or near the place of work. However, if the employer is covered by social security, he is relieved of the obligation to provide an infirmary or a hospital.[79]

SOCIAL SECURITY

Among the protections of labor incorporated in article 123 of the Constitution of 1917 was a rather vague provision calling on the federal and state governments to promote the organization of "popular insurance funds for disability, life insurance, involuntary unemployment, accident, and other similar purposes."[80] Efforts to enact implementing legislation, which became more serious following a 1929 amendment to the Constitution clearly calling for the enactment of a social security law,[81] were unsuccessful, however, until 1942, when the existing social security law was adopted.[82] The social security program established in this law is intended to provide broad coverage of all social hazards— not only occupational injuries and illnesses of workers, but also non-occupational sickness, disability, old age, death, and involuntary unemployment at an advanced age—and also to provide benefits for marriage and maternity expenses.

Realistically, the framers of the law did not attempt to bring into immediate existence a full-blown program of social insurance covering the whole country and all workers. On the contrary, the coverage of the law was to be extended geographically by the president on the recommendation of the social security institute on the basis of industrial development, location, density of insurable population, and the possibility of establishing the services provided for in the law.[83] Beginning with the Federal District in 1944, the obligatory coverage of the law was gradually extended to other industrial centers and to selected rural areas as it became possible to provide hospital and medical services in those areas. Agricultural workers were covered for the first time in 1961. The system now extends to all economically important urban areas and many rural areas. The coverage of agricultural workers is still limited, however, and the law has not yet been extended to domestic help, persons who perform work at home, and family enterprises.

The system is administered by the Instituto Mexicano del Seguro Social (Mexican social security institute—IMSS), a decentralized institution in which the employer and labor sectors as well as the government have representation.[84] The IMSS is governed by a tripartite general assembly and technical board and a director general appointed by the president. Decisions of the technical board, which is the legal representative and administrative body of the IMSS, are subject to the veto power of the director when he considers that they are contrary to the law or its regulations or are harmful or undesirable for the institute. There is also a supervisory committee composed of two representatives of each sector and the government, whose function is to make an annual report to the assembly on the financial statements submitted by the board.

Insurance coverage under the social security system is obligatory for all workers of the type and in the geographical areas to which the system has been extended and for apprentices and members of producer cooperatives. Only the employer's wife, parents, and children under sixteen years of age are excepted from compulsory coverage.[85] Employers must register themselves and their workers with the social security institute and give notice of any reductions in personnel and changes in wages. They are also responsible for the payment of contributions, but may deduct workers' contributions for their wages provided they are not reduced below the legal minimum wage. Each type of insurance, the benefits provided, and the required contributions are covered by a separate chapter of the law.

Under the program of insurance covering occupational accidents and illnesses[86] an insured worker has the right to receive necessary medical attention and compensation in the full amount of his wages for a maximum period of seventy-two weeks. If the disability is total and permanent, his is entitled to a pension based on the amount of his wages. A pension is also payable for a partial permanent disability, calculated as a percentage of the pension for a total permanent disability on the basis of the seriousness of the physical impairment. In the event of death resulting from an occupational accident or illness, one month's wages are paid for funeral expenses and a monthly pension is paid to the widow and children of the deceased worker or to his dependent parents if he had no wife or children.

Since the employer is obligated to provide medical services and compensation for occupational injuries and illnesses under the federal labor law, the program of insurance against these risks is entirely employer financed. The employer's contributions are based on the amount of wages paid and the class and degree of risk of the business in which he is engaged, pursuant to a schedule prepared by the technical board of the IMSS. Under the current regulations,[87] for example, an enterprise classified in group I, such as a retail sale business, pays a weekly contribution for each worker, depending upon his daily wage, of .11 to 1.42 pesos. An enterprise in group V, such as a construction firm, pays a weekly contribution per worker of 2.78 to 35.44 pesos.

The program of insurance against occupational injuries and illnesses covers only the employer's obligations under the labor law. If the employer is obligated under a collective labor contract to pay additional benefits, they must be paid by the employer.[88] The social security law provides that additional insurance may be contracted for with the IMSS upon the payment of additional contributions in an amount established in each case by the institute. However, because of lack of necessary technical data and personnel, the institute has not made any determination of the amount of contributions for additional coverage, with the result that it has not been possible in practice for employers to obtain additional insurance.

In the event of nonoccupational illnesses and injuries,[89] insured workers, their immediate families, and persons receiving pensions for total or at least 50 percent partial permanent disability have the right to medical attention for a fifty-two-week period, which may be extended for an additional twenty-six weeks. Insured workers are also entitled to compensation for the same period in an amount based on their wages. Insured women workers, wives of insured workers, and wives of pensioners receive medical attention during pregnancy and childbirth and financial aid for milk if they are physically unable to nurse their children. Insured women workers also have the right to compensation for forty-two days before and forty-two days after childbirth. If a nonoccupational injury or illness results in death, one month's wages are paid for funeral expenses.

The cost of insurance against these risks is shared by the employer, the worker, and the government. The worker's contribution is equal to one-half the amount of the employer's contribution, and the government pays 20 percent of the amount paid by the employer. The employer's weekly contribution for each worker is based on the amount of the worker's daily wage and ranges from 2.20 pesos to a maximum of 28.36 pesos.

Benefits are also provided for invalidity, old age, involuntary unemployment, and death of covered workers.[90] A person is considered an invalid when because of some physical or mental condition he is unable to obtain suitable work for a remuneration of more than 50 percent of the customary pay of a healthy worker in the same conditions in the same area. An old-age pension is payable to covered workers at age sixty-five. Invalidity and old-age pensions are from 866.32 to 11,138.40 pesos annually, depending upon the worker's wages, and are increased if the worker paid more than five hundred weekly contributions, if he requires nursing care or if he has children under sixteen years of age. Workers who are unable to find employment at age sixty, even though not invalid, are entitled to a reduced old-age pension.

Upon the death of a covered worker or a pensioner, his wife or concubine is entitled to a pension of 50 percent of the amount of the invalidity pension until she remarries. Children of the deceased worker or pensioner receive 20 to 30 percent of the amount of the pension payable to the worker until they reach sixteen years of age, but if they are incapacitated or are students, this may be extended to age twenty-five.

Finally, a covered worker who marries is entitled to receive a payment toward the expenses of marriage in the amount of 30 percent of one year's invalidity pension.[91]

The contributions for this insurance are also shared by the employer, the worker, and the government in the same proportions as in the case of insurance against nonoccupational illnesses and injuries. The employer's weekly contribution is from 1.48 to 18.90 pesos for each worker, depending upon the amount of his daily wage.

X

Secured Transactions

Foreign firms have for many years been involved in, and are increasingly concerned with, credit transactions in Mexico, both as lenders and as sellers of goods. The relatively high rate of return on loan capital, coupled with stability of the Mexican currency and lack of restrictions on conversion and export of funds, has attracted substantial amounts of loan capital from abroad. Foreign companies or their Mexican subsidiaries or affiliates are also called on to finance purchases of their products at both the wholesale and the retail levels. In all of these situations it is important to the foreign financier and seller to know what types of property are available as collateral and what security interests may be created.

Mexican security law has traditionally centered upon the mortgage *(hipoteca)* of real or immovable property and the pledge *(prenda)* of personal or movable property. Perhaps because land was for centuries the principal repository of wealth and because the industrial development of the country, with the concurrent need for large amounts of credit secured by personalty, is a relatively recent phenomenon, nonpossessory interests in chattels are still somewhat suspect in the view of Mexican law, and independent security devices have not developed to the extent they have in some other countries. It is often bewildering to the foreign businessman and his attorney to discover, for example, that the chattel mortgage, with minor exceptions, is not recognized in Mexican law. There are, however, three security devices in use in addition to the pledge, and to some extent they fill the needs of business to use personal property as collateral for loans: the *habilitación o avío* credit, a uniquely Mexican institution inherited from colonial times; the "refectionary" *(refaccionario)* credit, which was once a priority (that is, a preferential right of payment given by statute) and has been transformed into a contractual security; and the trust *(fideicomiso),* which is used as a security device though it also has many other uses. The contract of sale is sometimes used for the purpose of securing payment of a debt, but the Mexican courts have held such a sale void on the ground that it is "simulated" and have even refused to recognize it as a mortgage.

These security interests are most useful as protection for the lender. The seller has other devices at his disposal which afford him better protection—the sale with retention of title *(venta con reserva de dominio)* and the sale subject to rescission *(venta con cláusula rescisoria)*. Although they are often referred to in English as conditional sales, these contracts do not serve the same function as the common-law conditional sale. Their purpose is not to secure payment of the purchase price but rather to make it possible, by virtue of recordation, to recover the property sold from bona fide purchasers in case of rescission for nonpayment of the price.

None of these devices is entirely satisfactory for inventory financing for the wholesale distributor or retailer of goods, who is left with only the field warehouse, an adaptation of the pledge, to satisfy his needs. Since he is not a producer of goods, the refectionary credit is not available to him, and apart from that there is no such thing as a floating lien or chattel mortgage with after-acquired property clause.

MORTGAGE

Mortgages of real property are widely used as security by commercial and industrial establishments, as well as by private homeowners and farmers. Banks consider a mortgage loan to be a secure investment, and the amount of bank funds that may be devoted to that purpose is much higher than the amount available for loans secured by interests in movables. Mortgages, even on property located within the so-called prohibited zone, may also be executed in favor of foreign companies and individuals, and some banks in the United States have on occasion taken mortgages to secure payment of loans to Mexican borrowers. A permit from the Ministry of Foreign Relations is required for the foreign mortgagee to acquire title to the property upon a foreclosure, and it has been the practice of the ministry to grant such permits upon the condition that title be conveyed to a qualified person within two years.[1]

Legal rules relating to the mortgage are found in the civil codes of each of the states. The provisions of most of the codes are identical or similar to those of the Civil Code for the Federal District and Territories, which has federal application in the case of commercial mortgages because of the silence of the Commercial Code.[2] The requirements are well known to most lawyers, and the transaction is thought to involve few legal risks. The property covered must be specifically described, but the mortgage also extends to certain interests not expressly designated, such as improvements and fixtures.[3] When the amount of the mortgage loan exceeds 500 pesos, the mortgage must be executed before a notary; mortgages securing smaller loans may be executed before two witnesses.[4] All mortgages must be recorded in the public register of property of the municipality where the property is located in order to be effective against third persons.[5]

There exists one important difficulty in the Civil Code provisions relating to the extent of the property covered by a mortgage, in case the mortgage contract fails to deal with the question. Article 2896 states that the mortgage covers, among other things, "movable objects permanently attached to the property by the owner which cannot be separated therefrom without damage to such property or objects." A problem is posed, therefore, when a person has mortgaged his land and buildings and later attaches thereto a machine that is free and clear of liens: Can he validly create a pledge or other movable property security interest in the machine which is prior to the mortgage? The answer to this question seems to be that as long as the machine is attached to the soil it is subject to the mortgage as an immovable but that once it is detached from the soil it ceases to be an immovable, is no longer covered by the mortgage, and can therefore be freely subjected to any valid security interest.[6]

The same problem may arise in connection with agricultural implements, which are not immovables by material incorporation as are machines, but are so classified by destination if they are devoted to a particuar farm or ranch. If a tractor has been destined for use at a farm on which a mortgage has been executed, the owner of the farm cannot subject it to a special lien since, it would seem, the tractor has become an immovable and thus is covered by the mortgage.[7] These uncertainties arise only when the machine or tractor comes under the mortgage before an attempt is made to create a special lien upon it. If it is purchased under a purchase money security agreement or is already subject to some other security interest, that interest prevails over the mortgage, provided it was recorded before the object became attached to the immovable by incorporation or destination.

The mortgage of movable property is not expressly prohibited by law, but in practice the chattel mortgage is not utilized because it cannot be recorded and hence is not effective against third persons.[8] However, special security interests in ships and airplanes are provided for in the law of maritime and navigation commerce and the law of general means of communication.[9] The communications law also provides for a general mortgage covering all the properties, movable and immovable, belonging to an air transport enterprise. These special security interests are not regulated completely in those laws, and the use of the word "mortgage" should probably be taken as a reference to the rules on mortgages contained in the Civil Code to fill the gaps.

Finance companies *(sociedades financieras)* are specifically authorized to make loans to industrial, agricultural, and stockraising enterprises on the security of a special type of mortgage, often known as an industrial mortgage, which covers all the property of the enterprise, immovable as well as movable, including goods produced and on hand, except property expressly excluded.[10]

PLEDGE

The pledge of personal property is very commonly used in both civil and commercial transactions. For historical reasons reaching back to Roman law, under which it was considered a real contract, the pledge is linked to the idea of dispossession. This type of interest could be created only by physical delivery by the debtor to the creditor of the object that secured payment of the debt. To a very considerable extent, delivery of the property pledged is still required under Mexican law for the creation of a pledge.

The very fact of dispossession gives rise to certain problems during the life of the pledge. The debtor may wish to replace some of the goods he has pledged with other goods without entering into a new pledge contract so as to avoid the risk that it will be held invalid in bankruptcy as a security interest created to guarantee an antecedent debt. The creditor holding shares of stock or negotiable instruments pledged in his favor must know what to do when dividends or interest are payable, when a shareholders meeting is called, or when the instrument matures or is redeemed. Finally, problems often arise in connection with the sale of the security for payment of the debt.

CREATION OF THE PLEDGE

Provisions relating to the pledge are found both in the Civil Code and in the law of credit instruments and operations.[11] A pledge is governed by one or the other depending upon whether it is civil or commercial in nature, but there is no legal provision that clearly establishes when a pledge is commercial and when it is civil. Two rules are followed to determine the nature of a pledge. If commercial instruments—that is, negotiable or nonnegotiable instruments or investment securities—are given in pledge, the pledge is always commercial, regardless of the parties or their intent, because all operations relating to such instruments are commercial.[12] Also, if the intent of the borrower is commercial, that is, if he intends to invest the borrowed money in the accomplishment of commercial acts, the pledge is commercial because it is accessory to a commercial loan.[13]

Distinguishing between the civil and the commercial pledge is especially important in the formative stage of the contract. Indeed, it is at this point that the most important difference between the two types of pledge arises. While the civil pledge can be created by means of constructive or "juridical" delivery of the object pledged, the commercial law does not authorize the creation of a commercial pledge except by means of actual delivery.[14]

There has been much discussion of this point, and most Mexican lawyers feel that the civil rules on creation of the pledge should be applied by analogy to the commercial pledge. That approach is appealing from a business point of view, both for the borrower, who may need to use the property that he has available as collateral for the debt, and for the lender, who may not have the facilities for storing it. However, the Mexican Supreme Court has on two rather recent occasions indicated that a commercial pledge may be created only in accordance with the law of credit instruments and operations, which provides for actual delivery, and that this law is complete in its regulation of the subject and does not contain gaps that must be filled by application of the provisions of the Civil Code.[15]

The possibility of creating a pledge without dispossession in civil law, but not in commercial law, is paradoxical. The rules should of course run the other way in each case. In civil matters the pledge without dispossession is almost never used; the creditor would not feel secure if his debtor could at any time dispose of the object that guaranteed payment of his debt. When the civil pledge without dispossession is used, there is often a fraudulent intent. The person appearing as creditor is in reality a friend or relative, and a pledge to him is used to obstruct collection attempts by other creditors.

In business circles, on the other hand, the pledge without dispossession would be very useful, so much so that it is often created with the wishful thought that it will stand judicial scrutiny. The business lender is not so much afraid of the bad faith of his business borrower; what he fears most of all is his insolvency. That being the case, he is usually not interested in having possession of the borrower's goods; he prefers that the borrower keep them and use them in his business.

The decisions of the Supreme Court declaring null commerical pledges created in the civil form with constructive delivery reflect the differences of outlook between the draftsmen of the Civil Code and those of the law of credit instruments and operations. Both statutes were written during the same period, and they came into force at an interval of only two weeks. Yet the Civil Code reflects the modern trend of allowing personal property security interests without dispossession, while the commercial law follows the pattern set by statutes of the late nineteenth century, especially the French law of 1863 on commercial pledges, as expanded and somewhat liberalized by French decisions. In short, the tradition of dispossession still weighs heavily in Mexico, but it leans the wrong way.

A problem often facing the parties to a commercial pledge, therefore, is how to get around the requirement of dispossession of the borrower. In many cases, it is possible to use the *habilitación o avío* or the refection-ary credit, discussed below. These security interests do not require delivery of possession, but they can be used only for the purpose of financing the acquisition of raw materials and capital goods. Since their purpose is to stimulate production, it is doubtful that they can be used by a wholesale distributor or retail merchant or by persons providing a public service. Those persons are left with the pledge.

There is, however, a partial means of escape through a field ware-housing arrangement. The law expressly allows the commercial pledge to be created by deposit of the goods in a storage room, which may be located on the debtor's premises, the keys to which are in the possession of the creditor.[16] The theory of dispossession is kept intact by this scheme, but the needs of the parties are also to some extent taken into account. This provision poses some nice problems: May the debtor also have a set of keys without rendering the pledge void? Is the security valid even though the storage room is unlocked, assuming that the creditor has the only set of keys and could lock it at any time? These questions become particularly acute in connection with the provision that the debtor may substitute fungible goods for other goods of the same kind without affecting the continuity of the pledge.[17] A merchant may wish to avail himself of both advantages simultaneously. He might in such a case pledge the goods he holds ready for sale, storing them on his own premises. He would give a key to the storage room to his creditor, or to an employee of the creditor, who would allow him to remove goods and replace them with others. There is no rule of constructive fraud, as there was in the United States prior to the passage of the Uniform Commercial Code, which would render void the whole arrangement if the debtor were allowed to diminish the stock of merchandise without repaying a part of the loan, but the arrangement would always have to be such as to imply full dispossession of whatever part of the stock remained in storage. Giving a key to the debtor for the purpose of allowing him freely to take out and add merchandise would negate the theory of a pledge.

Pledged goods can also be delivered to a third party, who holds them in lieu of the creditor.[18] Where the borrower is a commercial company, it is quite common in practice for a manager or shareholder of the company to be designated as depositary for the pledged goods. Deposit may also be made in a public warehouse, in which case the certificate of deposit may be pledged. It is also possible to obtain from the warehouseman a pledge certificate *(bono de prenda)*, which indicates that the goods are pledged. When both documents are issued, the existence of the pledge is noted on the deposit certificate and both documents are required to withdraw the property from the warehouse.

A pledge of intangibles, such as securities and negotiable instruments, is subject to the same requirement of transfer of possession.[19] Bearer instruments are merely delivered to the creditor or to a third party who holds them for the creditor. Instruments payable to order are endorsed to him, but the debtor may protect himself against a fraudulent assignment of the instrument by the creditor by inserting the words "in guarantee" *(en garantía)* or "in pledge" *(en prenda)* in his endorsement.[20] When registered shares are pledged, it is necessary not only to endorse the certificates to the creditor but also to have the pledge noted in the stock register of the issuing company.

RIGHTS IN PLEDGED PROPERTY

Certain problems may arise relating to the rights of the parties in pledged property or the proceeds from it after the pledge has been created but before the debt matures. Who, for example, is entitled to receive the proceeds of insurance on pledged property that is destroyed? The law on the contract of insurance provides that the existence of any security interest obligates the insurance company to pay to the creditor a part of the proceeds equal to the amount of the secured indebtedness even if he does not appear as beneficiary under the policy, but the insurance company must of course be notified of the security interest.[21]

Furthermore, the insurance company must notify the creditor before canceling the policy for any reason in order to give him an opportunity to be subrogated to the debtor's rights under the policy.[22]

Most problems, however, have to do with negotiable instruments and other securities. A question often arises concerning to whom payment should be made if interest comes due or dividends are declared on pledged securities. The Civil Code provides that the income from pledged property belongs to the debtor and requires that, if it is received by the creditor, it be credited against interest and principal owing on the debt after the creditor's expenses are reimbursed.[23] The commercial law also specifies that such income received by the creditor be applied against the debt but permits the parties to change this rule by agreement.[24] If the lender is not required to credit the income from the pledged paper against the amount due on the loan and the total sum received by the creditor is far above the normal rate of interest, the loan may become usurious, and a court may equitably reduce the amount of the interest.[25] A criminal action may also lie in this case against the usurious lender.[26]

If the debtor is entitled to the interest or dividends on the instrument he has pledged, there may be a problem of collection since possession of the instrument is often the only evidence of ownership and possession has been given to the creditor. In the case of corporate securities carrying coupons against which interest or dividends are paid, the debtor can detach the coupons before giving possession to his creditor. If registered shares are involved and notice of the pledge has been given to the issuing company, it must pay the dividends directly to the debtor. In many cases, however, there is no other solution than to let the creditor collect payment on behalf of the debtor.

Another possible difficulty may arise if the pledged property is converted into money during the life of the pledge. Unlike the disposition of insurance proceeds, which are paid to the creditor only to the extent of the debt, when an instrument is paid or shares are redeemed the whole proceeds go to the creditor, who may keep the money in pledge.[27] Only when the principal debt matures must he pay the excess over to the debtor. This seems unfair to the debtor since he is exposed to the risk of his creditor's insolvency or bad faith and is deprived of his money at a time when he may need it badly.

The question of whether the debtor may vote shares he has pledged has been much discussed in Mexican legal commentaries.[28] There is no specific statutory provision dealing with it, but the weight of opinion is inclined to give the right to vote to the pledgor as owner of the shares.

That seems the best solution since the debtor is normally entitled to the dividends and should be allowed to vote in favor of their distribution. It is arguable also that the debtor cannot be bound by an agreement to let his creditor vote his shares since any agreement limiting a shareholder's right to vote is void under the commercial companies law.[29]

FORECLOSURE OF THE PLEDGE

If the debtor does not pay the secured debt upon its maturity, the creditor may seek to pay himself by selling the pledged property or by having it sold judicially. But he is not required to do so; if he wishes to wait in the hope of being paid later, he is free to take that course, and the debtor may not regain possession of the property. If it is worth much more than the amount of the debt, and if the creditor would have to seek a judicial sale, he is likely to sit back and let the debtor take the next step. The debtor has no choice. If he wishes to realize some value from the object he has pledged and cannot pay the debt, he must sell it to the creditor or agree with him on a sale to a third party. Such a sale is valid.[30]

On the other hand, the debtor may be content to take no action and let the creditor look to the pledged property for satisfaction of the debt. The question then arises as to whether the creditor must bring an action in order to obtain the sale of the object pledged or whether he may sell it without court authority. Under the Civil Code, the answer to this question is clear: Judicial action is required unless there is an express agreement that the property may be sold in a nonjudicial sale.[31] In the case of a commercial pledge, with respect to which there is no express provision dealing with the validity of such an agreement, one may reason either that the civil law provision is applicable to fill the gap or else that the agreement is valid because it is not specifically prohibited. In the opinion of most Mexican lawyers, however, such an agreement is not valid in a commercial pledge since the law provides only for judicial sales.

If the creditor is a bank, there is a right of nonjudicial sale even in the absence of an agreement. The commercial law provides that credit institutions may sell property pledged to them through a commerical notary *(corredor público)* or two local merchants.[32]

If the creditor is not a bank and the contract of pledge does not contain a clause permitting nonjudicial sale, the creditor must seek a court order if he wishes to sell the property. In the case of a commerical pledge he does not have to go through a trial on the merits of his claim but can have the sale ordered within three days from the time the debtor is notified. In case of great urgency, as where the goods are perishable, the court may even authorize the sale immediately, before notice is given to the debtor. If the debtor appears in the proceedings before the sale has taken place, he may not present his defenses, not even the defense of payment. He may avoid the sale only by paying the full amount of the debt into court.[33]

The commercial law further provides that after the sale the creditor shall hold the proceeds of the sale in pledge.[34] The proceeds are not taken as payment by the creditor, however. The effect of the sale is merely to substitute money for the merchandise, which might perish during a long trial and would in any case require storage; hence the pledge continues on the money. Any defenses of the debtor may be presented after the sale. If he successfully defends against the creditor's claim, he can recover the proceeds of the sale, though obviously not the object initially pledged.

This rapid system of judicial sale seems to fulfill the needs of commerce in the absence of an agreement for nonjudicial sale. There is, however, an additional consideration that makes a nonjudicial sale clause advisable for the creditor. The small amount of judicial intervention before the sale is sufficient ground for a petition for *amparo* challenging the sale order, under which the order may be suspended until the *amparo* litigation is resolved. Under this recourse the debtor may achieve a lengthy postponement of the sale since the case may reach the Supreme Court before the goods can be sold.

FORECLOSURE ON BANKRUPTCY

Creditors holding pledged property as security have priority over most unsecured creditors, but they do not generally have the right to foreclose on the pledge outside the debtor's bankruptcy proceedings and consequently must share in the administration expenses of the bankruptcy.[35] There are two exceptions to this rule. Banks and other credit institutions that are pledgees are given special protection in the event of bankruptcy of the pledgor. They have the right to "separate" the pledged property from the bankruptcy estate but are required to sell the pledged goods within one month from the date of bankruptcy and pay any excess into the bankruptcy estate.[36] In practice, this right of separation has amounted not only to a right of immediate and separate payment but to a preference over other creditors as well, including the debtor's workers, whose claims for unpaid wages should have priority over that of any other creditor under Mexican law.[37]

A nonbank creditor has the same privilege of separation enjoyed by banks if his contract of pledge is in a public instrument[38]—that is, executed before a notary—and a sale may be made immediately if the contract contains a provision for nonjudicial sale. Although no special form is required in order for a commercial pledge to be valid, this right makes the use of a public instrument nonetheless advisable, at least when the creditor is not a bank. Another reason for using a public instrument is the judge-made rule that all contracts that transfer title to property (and probably also those that create real rights, of which the pledge is one) must have a "date certain" in order to be valid as against the creditors of the transferor.[39] A date certain may be established most readily by the certification of the date by a notary, who is endowed with public faith. It is by no means clear that this rule would be applied to the commercial pledge, but this very uncertainty may make it advisable to put the contract in a public document even when bankruptcy of the debtor does not seem likely.

HABILITACION O AVIO *AND REFECTIONARY CREDITS*

Since the basic requirement of the pledge is dispossession of the debtor, complementary securities are necessary to satisfy the needs of business when delivery is not possible or practicable. The refectionary *(refaccionario)* and *habilitación o avío* credits[40] fill this need to some extent since they may be secured by personal property that remains in the possession of the borrower. But they have a particular purposes, to stimulate production, and it is doubtful that they can be used by persons not engaged in a productive activity. Furthermore, they are substantially limited to the financing of acquisitions of raw materials, equipment, and capital goods, though the *habilitación o avío* credit may also be used to pay other direct costs of production. There are, therefore, two important limitations on these secured transactions—the purposes for which the money borrowed may be used and the property that may be covered by the security interest.

The *habilitación o avío* credit may be used for the acquisition of raw and other materials and for the payment of wages and direct expenses of production required for the purposes of the borrowing enterprise.[41] Security for the loan consists of the materials purchased and all products obtained by the use of the borrowed funds.[42] The security thus follows the materials throughout the process of production and attaches to the finished products. It is not, however, a floating charge—that is, no substitution of after-acquired goods takes place when end products are sold and new materials are purchased. If the loan is used to finance the purchase of seeds and fertilizers, it is secured by the crop produced.

The refectionary credit is somewhat more flexible than the *habilitación o avío,* with respect to both the property that may be used as security and the purposes for which the proceeds of the loan may be used by the borrower. The object of the refectionary loan being to stimulate agricultural and industrial production, it may be invested in virtually any type of equipment or permanent improvement—the acquisition of implements, tools, fertilizer, or livestock, the planting of crops or clearing of land for cultivation, the purchase and installation of machinery, and the construction of facilities or performance of other works for the enterprise. The parties may also agree that part of the loan shall be used to pay tax liabilities of the enterprise existing at the time of the contract and further that part shall be applied to discharge outstanding debts of the borrower incurred within one year before the date of the contract for purchases or expenses of the type for which the loan funds may be used directly.[43]

Security for the debt is not limited to property purchased with the loan proceeds. The security extends to the land, buildings, machinery, implements, tools, and other chattels of the enterprise and its existing and future production.[44] Only raw materials seem to be omitted from the security, perhaps because they were intended to be reserved as collateral for the *habilitación o avío.* Because of the flexibility of the refectionary credit, it can be used as a means of mortgaging a whole business enterprise or farm, covering in a single contract both its immovables and its movables. As in the case of the *habilitación o avío,* however, the loan contract must specifically designate the property in which the security interest is created,[45] and for that reason the security is not a floating charge.

Under both types of credit the lender is required to supervise the use made by the debtor of the proceeds of the loan. If they are used for any purpose other than that specified in the loan agreement, with the creditor's knowledge, the security interest is lost. The lender may designate a representative to oversee the expenditures made by the borrower, but his salary and expenses are borne by the lender unless the parties otherwise agree. The creditor also has the right to rescind the contract and declare the entire debt due and payable if the debtor uses the funds for improper purposes or fails to attend to his business with due diligence.[46]

The lender is further exposed to some risk by the fact that his lien does not attach to the proceeds of a sale of property covered by the security. However, he has the right to recover the goods themselves from the debtor's direct vendee, who is deemed to be on notice of the security interest by virtue of its recordation in the public register, and from subsequent purchasers with actual notice.[47] In practice this protection may be meaningless if the creditor is unable to locate the property, but in some instances innocent purchasers have been seriously prejudiced by this rule. Loan contracts are recorded in the mortgages section of the public register of property where the property is located if the security includes immovables or in the appropriate commercial register if only movables are covered.[48]

Though Mexico has no general bulk sales law,[49] it is provided in the law governing these transactions that if the property or business for the development of which a refectionary or *habilitación o avío* loan has been made is transferred without the creditor's consent, he has the right to rescind the loan contract or to declare the debt immediately due and payable.[50] This rule may help the creditor reach his debtor before he escapes, but it does little else. The creditor does not lose his security interest in the property of the enterprise because of his rights as against the first purchaser, but he has no interest in the proceeds of the sale and is not even entitled to notice of the sale.

If an *habilitación o avío* and a refectionary credit should be secured by the same property, which would seem to be possible only with respect to finished products, the *avío* creditor would prevail over the refectionary creditor even if his security interest had been recorded later.[51] This rule permits an enterprise that has placed all its property under a refectionary credit to obtain an *habilitación o avío* loan to finance further purchases of raw materials. Both types of security have preference over subsequently recorded mortgages but not over previously recorded mortgages.

Since no special procedure is provided for the foreclosure of the *avío* and refectionary credits, ordinary commercial procedure is applicable. The creditor must request that the secured property be sold judicially, and the debtor may present his defenses to the claim before the issuance of a sale order. The creditor has a right of preference over other creditors, except prior mortgagees,[52] but he cannot attach the property at the outset of the trial. Hence, the debtor can conceal or sell it insofar as it is movable, and the creditor is defenseless if he cannot locate it.

If, however, the debt is represented by a special type of promissory note authorized by law,[53] which contains a reference to the lien and states the place where it is recorded, a summary action is available to the holder of the note. The plaintiff in such a suit may obtain an attachment of the goods covered by his security interest at the inception of the trial. The attachment allows him to place the goods in the hands of a bailee of his choice and prevents their fraudulent transfer by the debtor. These instruments also have the advantage of easy transferability—when immovables are involved, the creditor need not follow the troublesome procedure established in the civil law for the assignment of mortgages;[54] he may transfer the credit along with its security merely by endorsing the promissory note.

THE SIMULATED CONTRACT OF SALE AS A SECURITY DEVICE

Lenders are often dissatisfied with the pledge and other conventional securities because they do not want to have to sell the property that secures their credit in case of default; they would rather simply keep it. In the conventional security transactions, this result cannot normally be achieved. A clause in a pledge agreement under which the lender becomes owner in case of default, called a *pacto comisorio*, is void under the Mexican civil law.[55] This agreement is allowed, however, in the case of a commercial pledge if it is executed after the pledge itself.[56] Commercial lenders often take undue advantage of this exception, and borrowers are sometimes forced to sign such an agreement, in postdated form, before the loan is made. Its effect often is to give the lender a windfall in case of default, if the value of the pledged property exceeds the amount of the debt.

In civil transactions an outright sale is sometimes used to attain this result. The borrower purports to sell the property to the lender, who agrees to return it if the debt is fully and promptly paid. Such a sale contract has been held by the Mexican courts to be "simulated" and therefore void under the Civil Code. The courts have even refused to treat the sale as a mortgage in disguise and have held the transaction to be a mere loan without security.[57] Some recent decisions have upheld the transaction as a trust arrangement on the ground that the parties really intended to make a transfer of title, even though the purpose was one of security.[58] Although the decisions of the Supreme Court on this question have not been consistent in recent years, the prevailing tendency seems to be to declare such sales void.

The risk that the sale may be declared void does not concern the typical lender, however. When the object is movable, the debtor does not usually find it profitable to bring suit; the object might be fraudulently transferred or concealed by the lender, and the borrower would be entitled only to a money judgment for the difference between its value, assuming he can prove it, and the amount of the debt. For this reason, most cases in which the question has been litigated have involved immovables where a fraudulent transfer is impossible once the fact that the property is subject to litigation has been recorded.

THE TRUST AS A SECURITY DEVICE

The trust was introduced into Mexican law in 1926, but the original trust statute was inadequate and was replaced by a chapter of the law of credit instruments and operations enacted in 1932.[59] That law, together with the provisions on trust institutions contained in the law of credit institutions and organizations of 1941,[60] now governs the field of trusts.

Although the idea of the trust seems to have been taken mainly from the practices of trust and savings banks in the United States, it was soon put to a different use. Trust institutions, which have a legal monopoly on the management of trusts and are almost always ordinary commercial banks as well, began using the trust as a device to secure their own loans. Lending banks took title to immovables or commercial paper of the borrower and held it in trust for their own benefit, the bank acting as both trustee and beneficiary. If the borrower did not pay his debt, the trust department of the bank either declared that the items placed in trust had become the absolute property of the bank, if such was the agreement, or else sold them privately, paid the amount owed to the loan department, and turned over any balance to the borrower. This arrangement was doubly advantageous to the bank. In the first place, it was highly profitable since the borrower paid not only the usual interest on the loan but fees for the management of the trust as well, and these fees were, and still are, rather high. In the second place, the bank could foreclose on the security and recover the amount of the unpaid loan without any formality. For these reasons, the law was amended in 1933 to prohibit the creation of a trust under which the trustee is also a beneficiary.[61]

Once this rule was put into effect, the use of the trust as a security device declined sharply, and it came into use for a variety of other purposes as well. Foundations for the preservation of works of art and passive investments in immovables and commercial paper sometimes take the form of trusts. Especially difficult financing arrangements are also often cast in that form, particularly in connection with subdivisions of land. For example, a subdivider may not be able to pay the full price of the land he wishes to subdivide. The landowner is not willing to surrender title until he has been paid. He therefore transfers title in trust to a bank, which gives a deed to the purchaser of a lot once he has completed paying the purchase price; the price is then divided between the subdivider and the original owner, the bank having received its fee in advance. Tax considerations are also a factor, since a transfer of title to land in trust does not give rise to a transfer tax.

The trust is also a useful device for the acquisition by foreigners of land in the so-called prohibited zone. Although direct ownership by foreigners in the coastal and border areas is forbidden, the policy of the Ministry of Foreign Relations since March, 1967, has been to permit the acquisition by Mexican trust institutions of title to such land in trust for foreign beneficiaries, who have the beneficial interest in and use of the land for the term of the trust.[62]

The trust as a security for a loan is still very useful when the loan is made by a private lender. It is often used rather than a mortgage where the security is immovable property, and under the policy of the Ministry of Foreign Relations, title to realty, even in the prohibited zone, may be conveyed in trust to secure a foreign lender, such as a foreign bank. The expenses of a trust are considerably higher than those involved in the creation of a mortgage, but the trust has the advantage to the lender that no action need be brought to effect a sale of the property in case of default. The trustee bank may sell it privately and pay the creditor from the proceeds. Usually the trust agreement stipulates that in case of default the bank must convey title to the lender. This clause is favored by banks, since they avoid the trouble of finding a buyer, and by lenders, who like to keep the property on default in the hope of making an extra profit on its resale. But the validity of this clause is doubtful since it has the same effect as the *pacto comisorio,* which is void in the pledge and mortgage.

A trust agreement must be in writing and must fulfill the formal requirements of the civil law for transfer of title to the type of property involved.[63] Only specially authorized and regulated trust institutions may act as trustees.[64] To be effective as against third parties, a conveyance in trust of immovable property must be recorded in the appropriate public register of property. Notice of transfers of movable property must be given by delivery of possession in the case of chattels and bearer instruments, endorsement and transfer on the books of the issuer in the case of registered securities, and notice to the debtor in the case of nonnegotiable instruments and accounts receivable.[65]

The legal assumption on which the trust as a security device rests is the transfer of title from the settlor to the trustee. However, both the original law of 1926 and the existing law failed to provide for the essential element of transfer of title to the trustee. This gave rise to a misunderstanding by the courts and writers of the nature of a trust, and initially it was considered merely an irrevocable mandate to the trustee to dispose of the trust estate and the income from it as agreed by the settlor. Since 1950 the Supreme Court has corrected the vagueness in the law by interpretation and has consistently held that the trust does operate as a transfer of title.[66]

The fact that a trust agreement is a transfer of title to the trustee has had one unusual consequence. Because the debtor no longer has title, his employees and the tax authorities are unable to reach the property to satisfy unpaid wages and delinquent taxes, even if the trust was meant only as a security. Thus, the creditor secured by the trust prevails over other creditors who are normally entitled to preference.[67]

Despite this advantage to the creditor, the use of the trust as a security device is limited mainly to large or complicated transactions. Primarily, this is because of the high fees charged by trust institutions. Also, many banks have discovered that trusts breed litigation, especially in the case of real property, and have found themselves caught in the midst of it. Not only is the trustee caught in the conflict between debtor and creditor, which becomes very acute at the time of default, but it is also under attack by the debtor's unsecured creditors, who still hope that the trust will be held void or considered ineffective as a transfer of title.

CONDITIONAL SALES

While the seller of goods or land on credit may use one of the security devices available to lenders, he usually prefers a form of conditional sale. The sale with retention of title (venta con reserva de dominio) and the sale subject to rescission (venta sujeta a cláusula rescisoria) are more advantageous to the seller because he can either recover the property sold on the purchaser's default or bring suit on the promissory notes that usually accompany the sale contract to recover the purchase price. Under a title retention contract, as its name implies, title to the property sold does not pass to the buyer until he has fulfilled the requirements of the contract, usually merely payment of the purchase price. On the other hand, title immediately passes to the buyer under a sale subject to rescission, but the seller may rescind the contract and recover the property upon the buyer's failure to pay one or more installments of the price.[68]

Both forms of contract are effective against third parties if they are recorded in the public register. Sales of chattels, however, are not always susceptible of recordation. Only contracts covering objects that can be unmistakably identified, usually by means of a serial number, such as automobiles, motors, pianos, and sewing machines, may be recorded.[69] Chattels that are not identifiable in this fashion may be sold under conditional sale contracts, but these agreements are not effective against third parties who acquire the property in good faith from the purchaser.[70]

The secret of the popularity of these types of contract, however, does not lie in the seller's protection against third parties; it lies in the rapid procedure for repossession or enforcement. Repossession by self-help is not recognized in Mexican law and a contract provision permitting it would doubtless be held invalid, but the Code of Civil Procedure for the Federal District and Territories allows the seller to bring a summary action to recover the property sold under either form of contract, provided it has been recorded.[71] Upon the filing of suit to rescind the contract, the seller may have the property attached and placed in the custody of a person chosen by him pending a final judgment. Even though the seller may effect quick repossession, the buyer is entitled to recover and the seller must deposit with the court all payments the buyer has made on the purchase price, less compensation to the seller for the use of the property and any deterioration it may have suffered in his hands.[72] However, in most cases once the buyer loses possession, he fails to defend the suit. If land or a valuable machine is involved, there may be a trial, but typically consumer goods are sold in this fashion, and the defaulting purchaser does not find a lawsuit worth the small amount he could recover. Hence the real value to the seller of the title retention contract and sale subject to rescission, in consumer sales at least, is the probability that the buyer will not defend the suit and that what was initially an attachment will in fact become a final disposition.

The right to bring a summary action to recover the property sold stems from an inconsistency between the substantive law and the law of procedure. For an action to be summary, that is, preceded by an attachment, a sum certain of money must be involved. In the case of rescission under a rescissory clause or title retention contract, the amount involved is undetermined; it depends upon the rental value of the property and its deterioration. To overcome this doctrinal obstacle, the draftsmen of the procedure code allowed the parties to stipulate in advance what the amount of the deterioration of the property would be in case of default.[73] In practice it is usually agreed that the amount attributable to deterioration will be equal to whatever the buyer may have paid to the time of default. This clause exempts the seller from the requirement of the procedure code that he deposit with the court the amounts he has received, less the amount of the deterioration as calculated in the contract.

An advance agreement on the amount attributable to rental and deterioration has nevertheless repeatedly been held void under substantive civil law by the Mexican Supreme Court.[74] Sellers have tried a number of devices to avoid this result, such as a contract provision that the clause in question is a penal clause and hence valid under article 1840 of the Civil Code[75] or a provision that experts agreed upon by the parties have determined the amount of the rental and deterioration in advance as set forth in the contract, but these provisions have not convinced the Court.

Repossession is not, however, the only remedy of the seller in case of default by the buyer. He may, in lieu of rescission and repossession, bring a summary suit either on the promissory notes that are normally given by the buyer for the installments on the price or on the sale contract itself after it has been ratified before a notary. Upon filing the suit the seller may levy attachment on the property sold and on other property of the buyer to guarantee satisfaction of his claim. A suit on the notes or the contract avoids the problems of a determination of the amount of rental and deterioration and for that reason is often faster and easier than a repossession. Consequently, it is often used instead of repossession, unless the buyer's default occurs very soon after the sale is made or unless the buyer is in bankruptcy.

In the event of bankruptcy of the purchaser, the situation of the seller is essentially the same as it is otherwise. The seller is given a right of separation—that is, the right to recover the property sold—but this is subject to the performance of his obligations to the bankrupt on rescission of the contract. The bankruptcy law provides that he must return the purchase price,[76] but he may deduct an amount for rental and deterioration of the property.

For most purposes the sale subject to rescission and the title retention contract are parallel legal institutions. There are some differences between them, however, resulting from fortuitous divergencies in the drafting of certain statutes. The federal labor law and fiscal code allow

the owner of an object being attached by workers or by the tax authorities to intervene in the proceedings in order to recover his property.[77]
These provisions permit the seller under a title retention contract to
assert his property right, but the position of the seller under a rescissory
clause is unclear. If the buyer fails to pay his installments, as is likely to
be the case, the seller may claim that the property reverted to him under
the clause; but if the payments are continued until the property has
passed into the hands of a third party in a forced sale, the security would
probably disappear.

For this reason, one might conclude that the retention of title is a
better security than the rescissory clause. In practice, however, the title
retention contract has given rise to some difficulties. In the first place,
title carries with it not only advantages but also responsibilities. The
conditional seller of a tract of land, for example, has been held liable
for the payment of land taxes; and the conditional seller of an automobile has been found liable, under the strict liability theory, for
damages caused by the automobile to a third person.[78] These results do
not follow from a sale subject to rescission since title passes to the buyer
under the contract.

But the most difficult problem in connection with the title retention
sale stems from a statutory provision under which, as long as the buyer
has not paid the price in full, he is considered a lessee of the property.[79]
This provision was intended to answer the question, arising under the
law of possession, of by what right the buyer is in possession. Obviously,
he is not the owner, nor is he in possession under any other title for that
matter; to fill this void, he was by law made a lessee.

One positive effect of this provision is to resolve the problem, inade-
quately covered elsewhere in the code, of who bears the risk of loss of
the property. Since the purchaser is considered a lessee, the rules
established in the section of the code regulating leases are applicable.
It is there clearly provided that the risk of loss or deterioration is "always presumed to be for the account of the lessee, unless he proves that
it occurred without his fault, in which case it shall be for the account of
the lessor."[80] Despite this provision, the risk of loss from all causes,
including *force majeure,* is customarily imposed on the buyer by contract, at least in installment sales of consumer goods, and in many cases
the buyer is obligated under the contract to insure the property in favor
of the seller.

A number of practical problems, however, arise from the provision
that the purchaser under a title retention contract is considered a lessee.
If the seller wishes to rescind, must he ask for rescission of a sale or a

lease? If the buyer loses the property to a third person claiming under the seller, must he ask for damages for breach of his warranty of peaceful use and enjoyment, given to lessees, or for breach of the warranty against eviction, given to buyers? If the property has a hidden defect, must he ask for redhibition, an action given to buyers, or for rescission for defects in leased property?[81] The weight of judicial opinion on these questions has been in favor of application of the rules relating to leases. Otherwise, the Supreme Court has reasoned, the provision treating the conditional purchaser as a lessee would be rendered meaningless.[82] Therefore, when either party frames his petition in the form of an action under a sale contract, he is likely to lose the suit.

In one recent case,[83] however, the merits of the controversy proved to be stronger than the force of logic. The owner of a tract of land sold it under a title retention contract and thereafter executed a mortgage on it to a friendly creditor. The creditor then brought a foreclosure action against the owner-seller, who gladly confessed. Upon the buyer's attempt to intervene, the question was presented as to whether or not he had a legal interest giving him the right to intervene. If he was considered a lessee, he lacked such an interest. A tenant does not lose his rights under a lease if the leased property is sold judicially, and he cannot prevent the sale. But the Supreme Court held that the buyer should be considered a buyer and not a lessee. It reasoned that the code reference to the lease was meant only to explain the fact that the seller is entitled to rental value as a part of the restitution; it was not meant to transform the buyer's rights into those of a defenseless lessee. His legal interest thus established, the buyer argued successfully that the seller had no right to mortgage the property since the sale had been recorded.

This novel theory, which seems correct, did not outlast the decision for which it was fashioned, however. Two months later, the Supreme Court reverted to its traditional position. It held that the seller must request payment from the buyer under the code provisions relating to lease contracts before bringing suit against him.[84]

The case law on this question is not conclusive. The Court has attempted to furnish some guide by saying that the rules relating to leases will not be applied if they are inconsistent with the legal nature of the sale. Under such a vague standard, however, it seems extremely difficult to predict whether or not the statutory provisions on leases will be applied to a particular case.

There is at least one situation in which the title retention contract seems clearly a better security than the sale subject to rescission—where the buyer purchases a chattel intending to incorporate it into an immovable, either by material incorporation (as in the case of a machine that is bolted to the ground) or by destination (as in the case of a tractor used on a farm). In that case, the object sold becomes an immovable when the sale is made under a rescissory clause, but not when it is made under retention of title, because it can become a fixture only when the person who incorporates or destines it to an immovable is the owner of both the immovable and the chattel. The rescissory clause would be effective as between the parties despite the immobilization, but third persons, in particular the buyer's creditors, could treat the object as a part of the immovable, and the buyer could even sell it with the immovable to a third person, whose title would be superior to the rights of the seller even if the secured sale had been recorded.

Use of the title retention contract is not limited to sales where there is a possibility that a chattel will become a fixture; it is employed in the great majority of secured sales in preference to the rescissory contract despite the potential problems that have been mentioned. While it is true that this form of contract gives the seller clearer protection against the claims of certain creditors of the purchaser—notably labor creditors and tax creditors—this preference on the part of sellers can be attributed primarily to two other factors. In the first place, the body of case law relating to the lease-sale dilemma is generally unknown. Even though the seller and his lawyer are often aware of the code provision under which the buyer is considered a lessee, this is usually considered to have the effect of reducing the buyer's rights and seldom gives rise to any objections on the part of the seller. Furthermore, the word "title" has an undeniable emotional content. When the seller knows that his buyer will not have title to the property until he has fully paid the purchase price, he feels more secure than he would otherwise.

This emotional attachment to the notion of property title as something secure also explains the persistent use of two other means of guaranteeing the seller, lack of form of the sale contract and the promise to contract after the price has been paid.

LACK OF FORM AND PROMISE OF CONTRACT AS SECURITY DEVICES

When an immovable is sold, the seller can secure his interest by using the title retention contract or sale subject to rescission discussed above. But these contracts must be recorded to be effective against subsequent purchasers of the land, and recordation cannot be accomplished unless the contract is in notarized form. This requires payment of the notary's fees and the land transfer taxes. When the seller fears that there is a risk that his buyer may default in payment of the purchase price, he may seek a way to avoid or at least postpone these expenses.

There are two ways in which sellers have attempted to accomplish these objectives. The first is to draw up a private sale contract, with an agreement that the seller will execute it before a notary once he has been paid. The second is to sign a promise to contract or precontract of sale containing a provision that the final sale contract will be executed upon payment of the price. In practice, however, both of these devices have failed to provide effective security to the seller.

Lack of form—that is, the unnotarized sale contract—has fared even worse than the promise to sell. The Civil Code provides that when a contract is lacking in form, either of the contracting parties may request a judge to "elevate" it to the proper form, provided the intention of the parties can be proved beyond doubt.[85] In the case of an unnotarized contract to sell land, the buyer may present his copy of the contract as proof of the intention of the parties. Once the court has put it in the required notarized form, the buyer may record the sale, and since the seller has no security interest in the land, the buyer can sell it to a third person and disappear with the proceeds.

The device of using a contract lacking in form has often been even more disadvantageous for the seller than a formal unsecured sale would have been. In some instances where the seller has sought rescission on the ground of breach by the purchaser without first requesting that the contract be put in proper form, the Supreme Court has refused to grant relief on the ground that validity of a contract is a prerequisite to its rescission.[86]

The rules relating to the promise of sale are somewhat more complex. According to the Civil Code the promise to contract and the actual contract are two different things.[87] The promise, or precontract, is an agreement by which the parties promise to execute a contract at some time in the future. It is enforceable, but it must contain all essential provisions of the final contract. If the purchaser refuses to sign the contract at the time specified in the precontract, the seller may seek specific performance and the judge must sign it in his place.[88]

If that were all the law on the subject, the promise could indeed be used as a security device, since it could be made unenforceable until full payment of the price. But the Supreme Court very early superimposed a judge-made rule on this set of code provisions, and it has not deviated from its position. When the buyer has been put in possession of the property and has paid a part of the price, the Court has held that the actual intent of the parties was not to execute a promise to sell but to effect an actual sale.[89] The Court's reasoning is that, since the parties have actually performed obligations "to give," they could not have meant to enter into a mere promise, which creates only obligations "to do," consisting of the signing of the final contract.[90] It is true that in some early cases the Supreme Court stated that such a sale was "perhaps under reservation of title," but these doubts never crystallized into an actual holding. Hence, there is a sale; the sale is lacking in form, but that does not prevent the buyer from recording it if he obtains a judicial elevation of the contract to the proper form. The promise to sell therefore affords no security against third persons, including the buyer's creditors. It is in reality a simple sale on credit.

For this reason, the promise of sale as a security device is in steady decline. During the 1920's and 1930's it was in constant use by land development companies, but the stream of unfavorable judicial decisions has greatly reduced its utilization.

XI

Patents, Trademarks, and Licensing Agreements

The protection of industrial property rights is of vital concern to foreign enterprises that conduct business in Mexico, whether it consists merely of export sales of their products or domestic manufacture through subsidiary or affiliated companies. Large numbers of Mexican companies, both foreign and Mexican controlled, manufacture and sell goods under licenses for the use of foreign-owned patents and trademarks and with technical services and information furnished by foreign enterprises. The Mexican government is well aware that the continuing supply of advanced industrial technology, which domestic capital and human resources are inadequate to furnish, is required if an acceptable rate of industrial development is to be maintained and if its program to promote the export of manufactures is to succeed. This need is one of the most important reasons the government continues to promote foreign direct investments, and foreign enterprises that are best able to bring with them new technology are those that are most welcome. The channeling of foreign know-how to domestically owned enterprises is also encouraged by the government, and domestic companies are encouraged to seek licensing agreements with foreign companies that are able to furnish the technical assistance that will enable them to produce and sell competitively in international markets.

The Mexican law governing patents, trademarks, trade names, and commercial slogans generally affords adequate protection to foreign and domestic proprietors. The present federal industrial property law and its regulations became effective January 1, 1943,[1] and there have been few and rather insignificant amendments to the law since its enactment. A draft of new law, designed to modernize Mexican practice and to correct certain inadequacies that have appeared under the present law, has been prepared by the Asociación Mexicana de la Propiedad Industrial, an association of patent and trademark attorneys and agents, but there is no certainty that it will be enacted within the near future. Mexico is a party to the Convention of Paris for the Protection of Industrial Property of 1883, as revised at Lisbon in 1958, and the Arrangement of Lisbon for the Protection of Appellations of Origin and their International Registration of 1958.

The industrial property law contains provisions governing licensing of patents and trademarks, but agreements for the furnishing of technical services and information are subject only to the provisions of the Commercial Code and the Civil Code for the Federal District and Territories covering contracts generally. The most important consideration in connection with licensing and technical service agreements is the tax treatment of royalties and fees, and the last section of this chapter is devoted primarily to a discussion of that aspect of licensing.

PATENTS

PATENTABLE PROPERTIES

The basic requirements for patentability are that an invention be both novel and susceptible of industrial exploitation. The law does not contain a comprehensive definition of patentable inventions but rather lists the types of properties that may be patented and those that are not patentable.[2] Patentable properties are divided into three general classifications: inventions, improvements, and industrial models and designs. Invention patents may be issued on new industrial products and new compositions of materials, with the exception of chemical products; and uses of new means or new applications of known means to obtain an industrial product or result. Improvement patents are those covering improvements in an invention already patented or within the public domain, provided they produce an industrial result. Patentable industrial models or designs are defined as new forms of industrial products, machines, tools, statuary, or reliefs that form new and original industrial products because of their new artistic use or new uses of materials; and new designs used for purposes of industrial ornamentation that give a distinctive and unique appearance to the industrial products on which they are used.

Patents may not be issued on a discovery or invention that merely reveals something that already existed in nature, even though it was previously unknown to man; theoretical or purely scientific principles of a speculative nature; ideas or concepts that do not involve a new industrial adaptation; a discovery or invention whose use is contrary to law, public safety or health, good customs, or morals; chemical products; commercial, accounting, financial, or advertising systems or plans, the application or use in an industry of an invention already known or used in another industry, and procedures that consist solely in the use of a device, machine, or apparatus that functions according to known principles even though such use is new; and the juxtaposition or change of form, dimensions, or materials of known inventions, unless the combination is such that the known inventions cannot function separately or their qualities or functions are modified in such a manner as to produce a novel industrial result.

Of special interest is the prohibition against the issuance of patents on chemical products, which was imposed in order to avoid discouraging the discovery of new methods of producing pharmaceuticals and other chemical products and to prevent scarcities and other evils that might result from monopolies on medicines and other products important to the public welfare. However, the law provides that new industrial processes to produce chemical products and new industrial applications of such products are patentable, and Mexican patent examiners generally accept the use of new starting compounds or new reactants to obtain new products or compounds as a patentable process even if the reactant itself is aready known but involves other compounds. Since chemical products are patentable under the laws of some parties to the Paris Union Convention, notably the United States, problems may arise when a right of priority is claimed in Mexico under the Convention for a patent application filed in another country. In order to avoid rejection of the application, in practice it is often filed under the denomination of a new process, which is patentable, rather than the product in itself.[3]

An invention is not considered novel and is thus not patentable when it has previously been covered by a Mexican or foreign patent, when it has been published in such form as to permit its execution, or when it has been exploited commercially or industrially in Mexico or abroad.[4] However, a period of one year is granted to the inventor for filing from the date of publication or first exploitation of the invention if a patent is applied for first in Mexico, and the novelty of an invention is protected under certain conditions when it has been published by exhibition at an industrial exposition.[5]

Patents issued on nonpatentable inventions, on those that lack novelty, or on two or more inventions that should be patented separately are void.[6] Furthermore, a patent may be subjected to an "extraordinary examination of novelty" at any time upon the request of anyone or by judicial order, and if it is found that the patented invention does not meet the requirements of novelty, it is declared to be within the public domain.[7]

PROTECTION OF FOREIGN PATENTS

The novelty of an invention for which a patent application has been filed in another country is also protected and certain rights of priority granted, either in accordance with the provisions of the Convention of Paris or on the basis of reciprocity in the case of applications filed in countries that are not parties to the Convention. In either case a priority period of twelve months for invention and improvement patents and six months for industrial model or design patents is granted for filing in Mexico, and if application is filed in Mexico within those periods after the original filing, the effective date of the Mexican filing is considered to be the same as the date of the first foreign filing. This right of priority is also subject to the conditions that proof of the country and date of first filing be given, that the Mexican patent grant no greater rights than the original foreign patent, and that the other requirements of the law, its regulations, and the Convention be fulfilled within ninety days of the filing. Furthermore, the date of the foreign publication or first exploitation must be no more than six months before the effective date of the Mexican filing.[8]

The law also grants a right of priority to holders of foreign patents that have been published, for a period of six months from the date of publication, provided the country concerned grants reciprocal rights to Mexicans.[9]

APPLICATION FOR PATENT

Patent applications are filed with the bureau of industrial property of the Ministry of Industry and Commerce and must be made by the individual inventor or his assignee.[10] The application must be accompanied by a detailed description of the invention containing a clear specification of what the applicant considers to be a novelty. Only one invention may be covered by a patent, and two or more independent inventions included within one application must be separated.[11] If the applicant is represented by an agent, his power of attorney, executed before two witnesses if the applicant is an individual or before a notary if the applicant is a legal entity, must be filed with the ministry.

Once an application has been filed, an administrative examination for compliance with the formal legal requirements is made, and in case an irregularity is found a period of two months is customarily granted for the applicant to replace defective documents or to file omitted material. A technical examination is then made to determine that existing patents or applications are not infringed and that the invention otherwise fulfills the requirement of novelty. If a patent is denied for lack of novelty, an administrative reconsideration may be requested within two months. Following the formal examination, the applicant is required to present within two months printing blocks or electrotypes necessary for publication and a copy or model of the invention for the patent museum of the ministry.

Patents are issued in the name of the president by the minister of industry and commerce and must state the number and classification of the patent, the names of the person to whom it is issued and the inventor, its term, the title or name of the invention, the effective date or date of priority, and the date of issue. Publication of patents is made in the monthly *Gaceta de la Propiedad Industrial,* the official publication of the bureau of industrial property.

RIGHTS AND OBLIGATIONS OF PATENT HOLDERS

The term of a patent is counted from the date and hour of filing of the application, except where a date of priority is claimed under the international conventions to which Mexico is a signatory or as otherwise provided in the law. Patents of invention and improvements are issued for a period of fifteen years, and industrial model or design patents for a period of ten years. These terms may not be extended, but they are reduced to twelve and seven years, respectively, when a patent has not been industrially exploited in Mexico during those periods, unless material impossibility of exploitation is proved to the ministry's satisfaction. Annual fees, which are nominal, are payable beginning with the fourth year following the effective date of the patent. A period of grace to July 1 of the year following the year for which payment is due is granted for payment of the annual fees, but if payment is not made within that period, the patent lapses and becomes public domain.[12]

The holder of a patent has the exclusive right to exploit it, either personally or by licensing third persons, during the life of the patent. He may bring suit against those who infringe his right either by the manufacture of the patented product, by the industrial employment or use of the patented procedure or method, or because they have in their possession, place on sale, sell, or introduce into the country for a commercial purpose a patented product produced without his consent.[13]

The holder's protection does not, however, extend to products similar to the patented product which are transported across national territory or are in its territorial waters in transit, nor is he protected against a third person who exploited or had made preparations to exploit the patented process or product before the date of filing of the patent application, or against a third person who produces an object or employs a process like that covered by the patent for purposes of experimentation, study, or recreation that do not amount to industrial or commercial exploitation.[14]

A potential problem for the owner of a chemical process patent is whether or not the law affords protection against the importation into Mexico of products manufactured abroad by the patented process. The prevailing view seems to be that the only way a chemical process patent can be infringed is by the use in Mexico of the patented process and that the importation and sale of a chemical product manufactured abroad, by whatever process, is not an infringement since chemical products are not themselves patentable.

In case of an alleged infringement of a patent by the illegal use, exploitation, or importation by a third person without the consent of the patent holder, an administrative determination must be made by the Ministry of Industry and Commerce on the petition of the patent holder. The administrative action is limited to a factual determination of whether or not the process, product, model, or design is the same as or similar to that covered by the patent and thus constitutes an invasion. The ministry has no authority to impose sanctions, but its resolution is published in the *Gaceta de la Propiedad Industrial,* and where an infringement is found, notice is given to the federal attorney general for criminal action. The criminal penalties provided for in the law range from one month to three years imprisonment or 100 to 3,000 pesos fine, or both, for industrial manufacture of patented products or commercial or industrial use of patented methods or processes, to three days to one year imprisonment or 10 to 1,000 pesos fine, or both, for lesser violations. The patent holder may also bring civil action, regardless of the results of the administrative determination, and if successful he has the right to recover damages and the objects illegally produced and the instruments used for their production.[15]

In order to prevent the existence of "umbrella patents," "patent pools," "bottleneck patents," and the like that might impede the industrial development of Mexico, the law establishes the obligation of the owner of a patent to exploit it.[16] Notice must be given to the ministry within thirty days after initiation of exploitation and proof made that the patent is being exploited. If a patent of invention or improvements is not exploited in the country within twelve years after its effective date, or an industrial model or design patent within seven years, its term is reduced to twelve or seven years. Furthermore, failure to exploit within three years of the effective date of the patent, "improper or insufficient" exploitation, or subsequent suspension of exploitation for more than six months gives the ministry the right to grant licenses to third persons. The requirement of proper and sufficient exploitation is considered to mean that all aspects of the patent must be exploited and in sufficient quantities to fulfill the domestic market requirements. These compulsory licenses may be requested by any interested person and are granted only after notice and opportunity are given the patent holder to present proof of the reasons for nonexploitation, except where he has failed to notify the ministry of commencement of exploitation. A compulsory licensee must exploit the patent within six months and may not suspend exploitation for more than three months. He is also required to pay a royalty to the patent owner of 50 percent of his net profits, but the term "net profits" is not defined in the law. Compulsory licenses are not exclusive, and the patent owner may request cancellation of a license after two years from its issue if he or his licensee has begun industrial exploitation. The royalty and cancellation provisions make compulsory licenses relatively unattractive, and no requests for such licenses are known to have been made.

Patented products must carry a legend, either on the products themselves or on their packaging, that they are patented, and the number and date of the patent should also be stated. Failure of compliance with this requirement deprives the patent holder of the right of action for damages for infringement of the patent and relieves the infringer of criminal liability.

ASSIGNMENT AND LICENSING

There are no restrictions on the assignment of patents or the execution of licensing agreements for their exploitation.[17] While no formal requirements for assignments or licenses are established in the law, they must be registered in the Ministry of Industry and Commerce in order to be effective against third persons, and in practice the ministry requires as a condition for registration that they be executed before a notary. This may be somewhat complicated if the assignor or licensor is a foreign company; the notary must certify not only that the company's agent is authorized to sign the contract on its behalf but also that the company is legally incorporated and has the power, as evidenced by its corporate purposes, to execute patent assignments or licenses. If the notarial certification is made in a foreign country, the notary's signature and official capacity must be certified by a Mexican consul, whose signature must then be authenticated by the Ministry of Foreign Relations. The Mexican assignee or licensee must likewise execute the agreement before a notary, whose certificate is similar to that of the foreign notary. A foreign licensor or assignor may execute a power of attorney authorizing an agent in Mexico to sign the contract before a Mexican notary, but since the same formalities are required for the power of attorney as for the contract itself, it is usually simpler for the foreign company to execute the contract abroad.

TRADEMARKS

AVAILABILITY OF REGISTRATION

The owner of a trademark may secure the right to its exclusive use on the goods he produces or sells by registering it with the Ministry of Industry and Commerce. In the case of manufacturers or producers, a trademark may consist of a proper name in a distinctive form, a term, or generally any material means that distinguishes the objects to which it is applied from others of the same kind or class. Merchants and merchandising enterprises may register as trademarks their corporate or business names, provided they are not descriptive of the products they sell or the line of business in which they are engaged; they may also register the distinctive emblems of their establishments. For the registration by a merchant of a trademark that he intends to use on goods in addition to that of the producer, however, he must have the producer's consent.[18]

Not registrable as trademarks are proper, technical, or common names of the products on which they are used, generic terms, or names that are commonly used in Mexico; containers that are within the public domain, are in common use in Mexico, or lack originality; figures, names, or phrases descriptive of the products covered; colors in themselves unless they are combined or used together with distinctive signs or terms; anything contrary to law, morals, or good customs; Mexican national coats of arms, seals, or emblems, or those of foreign countries or Mexican or foreign political subdivisions without their consent; personal names, signatures, seals, or pictures without authorization of the person or his heirs; the emblem or name of the Red Cross; words in modern foreign languages that are applied to articles produced only in Mexico or another Spanish-speaking country; geographic names when they merely indicate origin or may cause confusion or error concerning origin; terms or signs that may mislead the public as to the nature, origin, or qualities of the products covered; the emblem of the International Olympics Committee, its component elements, or the terms Olympics, Olympiad, or Olympic Games; or those that are like or deceptively similar to previously registered trademarks covering the same products.[19]

Mexican law does not provide for the registration of service marks or certification marks.[20] Registration of service marks was allowed in practice by the bureau of industrial property in the past and a number are found in the trademark register, but all applications for their registration since 1966 have been systematically denied. Applicants in some cases have attacked resolutions of denial in *amparo* proceedings, and several federal district courts have held that registration should be granted. The ministry has appealed these judgments to the Supreme Court, which has reached no decision on the merits of the question as of this writing. Ministry officials have informally indicated, however, that the international classification, under which the registration of service marks is recognized, will be adopted in Mexico within the near future. Until the law is changed, the proprietor of a service mark in many cases may be protected by registering it as a trademark on the goods related to his service operation.

REGISTRATION PROCEDURE, TERM, AND RENEWAL

The registration of a trademark may be requested by individuals or legal entities.[21] If the applicant is a legal entity, its agent must be authorized by a power of attorney executed before two witnesses and ratified before a notary. An application must be accompanied by a description of the trademark, stating the reservations that are made, a printing block or electrotype of the mark with twelve prints in black and white, and a statement of the date of first use in Mexico of the trademark if it has been used. When the trademark is in color and use of the colors is reserved, twelve color prints must also be filed.

A single trademark registration may be made only for coverage of products belonging to one class within the formal classification of goods established in the regulations to the law, and the products to be covered must be specified in the application. The formal classification consists of forty-nine classes of specific types of goods and a fiftieth class for products that do not fall within any of the other classes. Class heading coverage or a claim of all goods of a class is also permitted, except for class fifty.

Applications are subjected first to an administrative examination for formal sufficiency. If the application or accompanying documents are not in order, a period is granted to the applicant to correct or complete them. An examination of novelty is then made to determine that the trademark does not infringe the rights of a previously registered trademark owner. If the ministry finds that an infringement exists, notice is given to the applicant, who may contest the finding in an administrative proceeding. An unfavorable administrative resolution may be attacked through an *amparo* suit in the appropriate federal district court.[22]

If a trademark registration has been requested in a foreign country, it is considered to have been registered in Mexico as of the date of the foreign application, provided registration in Mexico is requested within six months following the date of the foreign application and provided further that the foreign country involved grants the same right to Mexicans.

A trademark registration is valid for a period of ten years and is renewable indefinitely for ten-year periods upon application filed within six months before its expiration and payment of the appropriate fees. Delay in filing of the renewal application does not result in loss of rights in a mark, however, if renewal is requested within a grace period of two years following the date of expiration and the required fees plus a penalty of 2 percent per month are paid. Nevertheless, criminal action for infringement may not be brought if timely renewal has not been made, and no assignment of the mark may be registered during the grace period.

Independently of ordinary renewals, trademarks that have not been used or whose use has been suspended for five consecutive years may be renewed only in a special manner provided for in the law and upon application made before the end of the five-year period of nonuse or suspension.

USER REQUIREMENTS

While prior use is not a requirement of Mexican law, some use of a trademark is required after filing, and if no use is made for a period of more than five years, the registration will become ineffective unless a special renewal application is filed before the expiration of the five-year period of nonuse. It is presumed that use has been suspended when the establishment with which the trademark is related is removed from its location without notice of the change having been given to the Ministry of Industry and Commerce.[23] The law does not, however, specify what constitutes use for purposes of this requirement. The bureau of industrial property takes the position that use must be continuous and in a volume considered appropriate for the products covered and the market conditions. Furthermore, use must be made on products sold in Mexico, for which sales invoices are required as proof, and mere advertising of the products is not considered use of the trademark.

The cancellation of a registration for nonuse is not automatic but must be declared by administrative resolution, either upon the bureau's own motion or upon the petition of another person. In either case, notice and opportunity for a hearing must be given the owner of the registration.[24]

Use of a trademark is effective for purposes of the user requirement if it is made by either the proprietor of the registration or his licensee. A question that has given rise to considerable controversy is whether or not the license or authority of a user must be recorded in the trademark register in order for his use to be effective for this purpose. The question has arisen on a number of occasions when cancellation of a registration for nonuse has been requested on the initiative of a third person or as a defense to an action for infringement brought by the registration owner. The law does not provide a clear answer to the problem; registration of licenses is required for most purposes, but article 162 provides merely that "authorized use" shall be considered the same as use by the owner for purposes of the user requirement, without specifying that the user's authorization must be registered. Reversing the position of the bureau of industrial property, the Mexican Supreme Court held in 1959 that registration of a user's authorization is not required for that purpose, and the bureau has followed that interpretation since.[25] There has not, however, been a sufficient number of decisions by the Supreme Court to that effect to constitute binding precedent. The lingering possibility that the judicial or administrative interpretation of the law will be modified and the requirement of strict proof of the effective date of a challenged authorization, which may be difficult to establish in the absence of registration, make it advisable for foreign owners of Mexican trademark registrations to record their licenses to Mexican users, even though they are subsidiaries or affiliates of the owner.

The ministry has the authority under the law to require the use of trademarks, whether registered or not, on necessary consumer goods, domestic raw materials and manufactured products, pharmaceuticals, and generally any articles that are closely related to the national economy and public needs.[26] Several type of products have been subjected to this requirement, including travel goods and other products made totally or partially of leather; articles of silver, silver plate, or white metal; clothing and thread; and hosiery of nylon or other synthetic fibers.[27]

A trademark must be used in the same form in which it is registered.[28] If any portion of it is altered or modified, a new registration must be made. However, modifications that do not alter or affect the identity of a trademark and changes in dimensions or in the material on which the mark is reproduced are excepted.

Registered trademarks used on goods must contain the term "MARCA REGISTRADA" or its abbreviation "MARCA REG." No other legend may be used except "MARCA IND. REG.," for trademarks registered under laws in effect before 1928. In the case of domestically produced goods, the location of the factory must also be stated. Omission of these two requirements does not affect the validity of the trademark registration, but it does deprive the proprietor of the right to recover damages for an infringing use of the mark and relieves an infringing user of criminal liability.

All domestically made products on which trademarks are used, whether registered or not, must also carry the legend "HECHO EN MEXICO," "ELABORADO EN MEXICO," or "PRODUCIDO EN MEXICO," as appropriate. Failure of compliance with this requirement is punishable by prison sentence of three days to one month or a fine of 10 to 500 pesos, or both. If the nature of the goods is such that they cannot be marked with these legends, these requirements can be fulfilled by marking the containers in which they are sold to the public.

Indications of registration in other countries and legends in foreign languages may not appear on domestic products, on the ground that they tend to mislead the public with respect to the origin of the products. Also prohibited are false statements as to the origin of products, that is, the designation of any place where the product is falsely stated to have been manufactured, produced, or obtained; an indication on domestically manufactured goods that a factory exists abroad, even when this is true; and an indication that there exists an industrial or commercial establishment owned by the proprietor of the trademark, when this is untrue. Legends in foreign languages may not be used on products made in Mexico, nor may foreign-made goods be sold under a trademark falsely stated to be registered in Mexico. Violation of any of these prohibitions is punishable by imprisonment of three days to two years or a fine of 10 to 2,000 pesos, or both.

Before any change in the name of the holder of a trademark or in the location of his establishment may be stated on products covered by the mark, notice of the change must be given to the Ministry of Industry and Commerce. Persons who violate this requirement are subject to the penal sanctions applicable in the case of false statements of origin.

INFRINGING REGISTRATION AND USE

The proprietor of a registered trademark is protected against infringing registrations and use of the mark, and under some circumstances a prior user may also obtain protection against the registration of his trademark. Infringing applications are, in the great majority of cases, rejected at the stage of the administrative examination of novelty, either upon the bureau's initiative or upon the petition of the owner. If there is doubt as to whether or not the second trademark is sufficiently similar to registered marks as to constitute an infringement, the owners must be notified and given an opportunity to be heard.[29]

If an infringing trademark is registered, its registration is subject to cancellation upon the bureau's motion or upon the petition of the owner, provided cancellation proceedings are brought within three years following the date of publication of the infringing registration in the *Gaceta de la Propiedad Industrial*. There is no limitation period, however, in the case of infringing registrations made in bad faith. Bad faith is presumed when the agent or representative in Mexico of the owner of a foreign trademark registers the mark in his name without the owner's consent.[30]

The law denies registration only to identical or similar marks that cover the same goods as registered marks, and generally the registration of a trademark to cover a different class of goods may also be denied.[31] The bureau of industrial property has in a number of cases denied applications for the registration of well-known trademarks covering different classes of products than those for which application is made, and such registrations have been denied even where the prior trademark was not registered or used in Mexico, implicitly on the ground of possible public deception.[32] The bureau has likewise not hesitated to protect well-known trademarks registered in Mexico in administrative proceedings for the cancellation of registrations covering different goods, on the theory that the second registration constitutes a type of unfair competition or gives rise to possible confusion, and the bureau's position has been upheld by the federal courts.[33] The question as to whether or not the registration of another's well-known mark that is not registered or used in Mexico is subject to cancellation has apparently never arisen, and there seems to be considerable uncertainty that the law would be interpreted to protect such marks, the only provisions in the law on which a cancellation order might be based being the prohibitions against registrations that are contrary to good customs and those that might deceive the public. Some Mexican lawyers are of the opinion, however, that cancellation may be obtained on the basis of article 6 bis of the Paris Union Convention, provided the marks cover identical or similar goods.

The owner of a trademark that is not registered in Mexico also has the right to obtain cancellation of an infringing registration, provided he initiated use of the mark in Mexico before the effective date of the registration and has used it continuously for three years and provided further that he files a registration application within three years of the date of publication of the first registration. Similar protection is given to users abroad of foreign registered trademarks if the owner's country of origin grants reciprocal rights to Mexicans, but the Mexican filing must be made within six months rather than three years of publication of the first registration.[34]

A person who makes infringing use of a registered trademark is subject to both civil and criminal liability. Infringement consists of falsification, imitation, or illegal use.[35] Before a criminal action may be brought, an administrative determination of infringement must be made upon the bureau's own motion or upon the petition of the owner or his registered licensee or the attorney general's office if the federal government has an interest in the matter.[36] These determinations are made only from a technical standpoint and are not binding in subsequent civil or criminal litigation. An unfavorable administrative determination may be challenged in an *amparo* suit. Criminal penalties provided for in the law are from three days to two years imprisonment or a fine of 10 to 2,000 pesos, or both, in the case of unauthorized use of a registered trademark or a deceptive imitation of it on products similar to those covered by the registration and for the fraudulent production or sale of trademarks or imitations. A somewhat lesser penalty of three days to one year imprisonment or 10 to 1,000 pesos fine, or both, is provided for the fraudulent sale of illegally marked goods. The owner of an infringed trademark not only may recover damages from the infringing user, but he also has the right to be awarded all products illegally marked and illegally produced trademarks and instruments used for their production.[37]

LICENSING AND ASSIGNMENT

Licensing of trademark use is permitted when equality of the products covered is assured by employment of the same production procedures and technical formulas.[38] Goods produced by a trademark licensee must carry the name of the registered user and the address where they are manufactured or produced.

Registration of licenses is required for most purposes and, as discussed above, is advisable in all cases. The law does not establish any formal requirements for license agreements, but the practice of the ministry is to require, as a condition for registration, execution before a notary in the same form as patent licenses. The application for registration must state the name, domicile, and location of the establishment of the licensee; the industrial or business relations that exist between the owner and the licensee and information on the degree of supervision or control the owner will exercise over the use of the trademark; whether or not the license is exclusive; the products with respect to which registration of the license is requested; any limitations or restrictions relating to the characteristics of the products or the manner or place of use of the mark; and the term of the license.

The Ministry of Industry and Commerce, following a hearing of the parties, may cancel the registration of a license when the licensee has used the trademark in an unauthorized manner or one that gives rise to public error or confusion, when the owner of the trademark or the licensee has furnished false information or omitted important facts in the application for registration, or when there has been a change of circumstances such that the reasons for allowing registration of the license no longer exist.

Assignments of trademarks must be registered with the ministry in order to be effective as to third persons.[39] No formalities are established in the law other than those required by the Civil Code for contracts generally, but in practice registration is made by the ministry only if an assignment is executed before a notary in the form required for assignments of patents.

COMMERCIAL SLOGANS

Original slogans used to advertise a commerical establishment, business, or particular products may be protected by registration, which is effective for ten years and may not be renewed. The requirements and procedure for registration and the protection available are substantially the same as for trademark registration.[40]

TRADE NAMES

Every person, whether an individual or a legal entity, engaged in manufacturing or commerce has the exclusive right to use his trade name, which is protected within the area of the effective clientele of the business without any requirement of deposit or registration. A procedure is established for the publication of trade names in the *Gaceta de la Propiedad Industrial,* but the only effect of publication is that fraudulent intent of an unauthorized user, required for criminal liability, is presumed if the name has been published. Except to the extent the law makes special provisions for trade names, they are governed by the same provisions that apply to trademarks.[41]

LICENSING AGREEMENTS

Agreements between foreign and Mexican companies for the use of patents, trademarks, slogans, and trade names, for manufacturing, and for the furnishing of technical services and information are very common and, as such, are subject to no special requirements or restrictions. Except for the legal and practical requirements relating to licenses for the use of patents, trademarks, slogans, and trade names, discussed above, there are no formal requirements for such agreements and they may take the form of ordinary written contracts. There is, however, an important practical consideration that makes it advisable to obtain a notarial certification of the execution of a contract, the foreign licensor making an acknowledgement before a notary in his home country and the Mexican licensee ratifying his signature before a Mexican notary. Mexican tax authorities are often suspicious, sometimes with reason, that deductions will be claimed by Mexican taxpayers for fictitious payments for licenses and technical services, and notarial certification is usually the best possible evidence that a license agreement was executed on the date and in the form claimed.

In view of the different tax treatment of payments under patent, trademark, and manufacturing licenses on the one hand, and those under technical service agreements on the other, it is customary and usually advisable to have separate contracts when both types of agreement are involved in the same licensing arrangement. If the foreign company is also to furnish management services to the Mexican licensee, the management agreement is normally included within the contract for technical services and covered by the same royalty or fee. For the protection of the foreign company's rights under a management agreement, especially one with a Mexican company in which it has a minority stock interest, provision is often made for termination of the technical services agreement upon breach by the Mexican company of the management agreement.

Of special importance is the tax treatment of royalties and fees paid and received under licensing and technical service agreements.[42] In the case of licenses for the manufacture of goods or for the use of patents, trademarks, slogans, or trade names, payments received by the licensor as royalties or other form of compensation are subject to the global income tax on enterprises and are taxed at progressive rates of from 5 percent to 42 percent, without deduction. The Mexican licensee must withhold and pay for the account of the licensor the amount of the tax on each payment made, which is determined by applying the rate schedule to each payment. The licensor is required to file a tax return for each taxable year and to pay any excess that results from applying the rate schedule to the total income received as royalties during the year. The licensee is jointly obligated for the filing of returns and for the payment of taxes.

Income received under technical service contracts is taxed at a fixed rate of 20 percent of the gross amount thereof, and the amount of the tax must also be withheld from each payment and paid by the Mexican company that pays the fees.

Both royalties and technical service fees are subject to the commercial receipts tax, which in the Federal District is 3 percent of gross income and which the Mexican payer must also withhold and pay for the account of the recipient.

Even though there are no legal restrictions on the amounts that may be contracted as royalties or technical service fees, there are considerations that must be taken into account by the contracting parties that do, in fact, constitute limitations. Under the income tax law only necessary and ordinary business expenses are deductible for purposes of determining taxable income, and royalties or technical service fees that are considered excessive may be disallowed as deductions. In practice, total payments under licenses and technical service contracts of 5 percent of net sales have not been considered unreasonable. However, in cases in which tax exemptions have been granted to Mexican companies under the law for the promotion of new and necessary industries, the tax authorities have followed the practice of limiting the amount that may be paid as technical service fees and royalties to a maximum of 3 percent of net sales, as a condition for the exemption.[43]

In addition to royalties and fees, it is not unusual for licensing and technical service agreements to provide that the Mexican licensee will reimburse the licensor for certain expenses incurred in connection with the services contracted, such as salary and travel expenses of the licensor's personnel assigned to render services to the licensee and expenses of special research or other work requested by the licensee. These payments, even though they are reimbursement of expenses actually incurred by the licensor, are considered income of the licensor and are taxable as royalties and fees and are also regarded as compensation for purposes of the 3 percent limitation on the amount that may be paid for licenses and technical services by tax-exempt companies.

Although compensation is customarily fixed as a percentage of net sales, it is becoming increasingly common, especially where the licensee or service recipient is a wholly or partially Mexican-owned company, to calculate fees and royalties as a percentage of net profits. This practice seems more reasonable and affords protection to Mexican shareholders in the case of companies that have large sales but low profit margins and is encouraged by the Mexican government.

While government policy encourages the use of foreign technology and recognizes that payment must be made for it, the large amounts paid to foreign enterprises under licenses and technical service contracts— over $100 million (U.S.) to United States companies alone in 1967 —are a significant item in Mexico's balance of payments and, understandably, the government wants assurance that payments sent abroad are for services actually rendered and are reasonable in amount and that profits are not being taken out of the country at low tax rates under the guise of royalties and fees. As a consequence, the income tax authorities are paying increasingly close attention to such payments and often require substantial evidence that claimed services have been rendered and that the amounts paid for those services are reasonable.

XII

Conclusions

Foreign investment has played a vital role in the development of Mexico, but its evolution over the past hundred years has seen drastic change. During the Porfirian era, the foreign investor was regarded as the only productive force available in the private sector and was given a free hand to develop the country's natural resources, build its railroads, and install public utilities and communication facilities, and, in the process, to acquire control of an enormous amount of the country's wealth.

Following the Revolution of 1910, the country's efforts to reduce the participation of foreign capital in the economy and to regain control of its own economic destiny resulted in a drastic decline in the relative role of foreign investment. One by one, industries that were developed by foreign capital and technology—petroleum, railroads, public utilities, and mining—were closed entirely or partially to foreigners.

The 1940's saw the beginning of a new era of influx of substantial amounts of foreign capital, but of a different sort. Attracted by the growing domestic market and stimulated by the government's import-replacement policy, foreign firms scrambled to establish facilities for the production of consumer goods for the domestic market. Industrial development was the clarion call and, though lip service was sometimes paid to the desirability of associations with Mexican capital, foreign investment was welcomed to contribute to the development process and few obstacles were placed in the way of new investment projects.

Though domestic capital formation has progressed rapidly and the great bulk of total investment—probably 90 percent—is financed from domestic sources, the impact of foreign companies has probably seemed disproportionately large because of their size and dominant position in many industries and constant reminders of their presence on billboards, radio, and television. This has resulted in periodic emotional cries against foreign investment from some quarters, but the concerns in more responsible segments of the community are more subtle and have revolved around such questions as the effects of foreign investment on Mexico's balance of payments and the limits on Mexico's capacity to absorb foreign capital, and whether foreign companies' purchasing and hiring policies impede further industrialization and training of Mexicans.

Out of these concerns and the legitimate desire of the government to keep for Mexico the lion's share of the fruits of its development, Mexicanization of industry, once a timid suggestion, has become entrenched as permanent policy. One of the facts of economic life which foreign companies that wish to enter the country must accept as the price of admission, with few exceptions, is the requirement that they accept the participation of Mexican equity capital, often in a majority position. There is now substantial consensus in support of this policy in the private sector in Mexico, and in fact, it has sometimes been Mexican businessmen seeking to participate in good investment opportunities who have pressed the government to extend the Mexicanization requirement.

More controversial have been the government's efforts to impose Mexicanization on foreign-owned enterprises that were established before the policy existed and without any suggestion that they would eventually be required to surrender to Mexican investors part of their ownership. Though these pressures have subsided in the late 1960's under stiff resistance, this may be only a temporary lull in a long-range policy. Perhaps the main consideration behind the government's insistence on associations with Mexican capital is the balance-of-payments argument—for a number of years more capital has left the country in the form of distributions of profits and royalty payments than has entered the country as new investments. The Mexicanization of existing foreign-owned enterprises theoretically represents a net loss of capital to the economy, and whether or not the country can afford this disinvestment seems an important question. The commitment of the government to continuing the industrialization process and to maintaining what it considers an adequate rate of growth should have higher priority than the Mexicanization of foreign-owned companies.

While the government is confident of the country's ability to continue to provide most of the financing necessary for its development, it does not deny that large amounts of foreign capital are essential if the development process is to continue at an acceptable pace. In particular the government recognizes the need for advanced technology that only the highly industrialized countries can supply. And, while it encourages the acquisition of foreign technology through technical service and licensing arrangements, it probably realizes also that it is not the same for a Mexican manufacturer to buy foreign technology as it is for him to be in business directly with a foreign partner who can supply it.

But Mexico has become more selective in the type of investment that it considers acceptable, and this trend will no doubt continue. It is clear, for example, that the country does not want foreign-controlled enterprises in the extractive industries or other industries that it considers basic to the economy. And in areas in which it is felt that foreign enterprise has little to offer in the way of advanced technology and know-how, such as retail merchandising, it is not likely to be receptive to new foreign ventures.

In other areas, too, there are increasingly severe restrictions on the freedom of operation of private industry that affect foreign-controlled as well as Mexican-owned companies. The installation of assembly operations to produce consumer goods, which often resulted from the government's protectionist policies in the 1940's and into the 1950's, is no longer feasible. The requirement of industrial integration, forcing manufacturers to produce or purchase domestically the majority of their intermediate products and components, has become a goal of high priority in the government's efforts to keep the industrialization process going. While this has encouraged new investment in industry, both foreign and domestic, it has amplified the problem of high cost of production of Mexican manufactured goods and has given rise to new problems of quality control and delivery schedules.

A significant problem facing businessmen in Mexico and an impediment to the continued industrialization of the country is the limited size of the market for domestic manufactures. One possible solution would be to increase the domestic market at a faster pace than is now occurring. While the total population of the country is approaching 50 million, a large percentage of its people are outside the market for many modern-day products. Not only is at least 40 percent of the population classified as rural, most of whom are ejidal and small subsistence farmers, but there are large numbers of urban poor, and even the average industrial worker probably does not earn enough to enable him to buy very much more than the essentials of life. The government's efforts at tax reform and the increased benefits to labor under the profit-sharing law and the 1969 labor law are helpful but perhaps seem timid when measured against the scope of the problem. However, any aggressive move by the government toward effecting a significant redistribution of wealth in order to raise living standards and increase the domestic market would undoubtedly be taken by the private sector as antibusiness and would not be easy under a political system in which consensus is considered highly desirable and in which every effort is made not to offend any source of power in the country.

The other possible line of attack on the problem is to develop an export market for Mexican manufactured products. The foreign market for Mexico's traditional exports of fibers, food, and minerals is not flexible enough to fulfill the country's requirements of foreign exchange earnings, and it is universally agreed that Mexico must increase its exports of manufactures if it is to sustain its economic growth. The government has made real efforts to create an export consciousness on the part of Mexican businessmen, and its efforts have had some effect. The real obstacle to the creation of an export market for Mexican manufactures is the high cost of production. This is the result of several factors. The limited size of the domestic market restricts production and in many cases the market is divided among too many producers. In the automobile industry, for example, there are numerous producers when one manufacturer could satisfy the country's needs and still have excess capacity. The cost of domestically produced raw materials is high, again because of the limited market and short production. Furthermore, the high cost of utilities, transportation, port handling charges, and similar overhead expenses adds to the burden.

The government is fully cognizant that the country's products must be competitive in international markets, and its earlier attitude that the Mexican consumer had to pay the price of industrialization by bearing the high cost of production has changed. Various measures have been taken to force domestic producers to reduce their production costs. For one thing, increased domestic competition has been permitted. Before 1965 the number of producers in a particular line of production was often strictly limited, apparently on the theory that the domestic market could not support more than a few producers. The administration of President Díaz Ordaz has reversed this policy and has permitted the entry of new producers in fields that were formerly closed to them. This has, of course, further divided the market and compounded the problems of many companies. Furthermore, one of the conditions consistently imposed on the approval of new manufacturing programs by the Ministry of Industry and Commerce is that the manufacturer's products may not be sold at more than 25 percent above the foreign cost of the products.

High production costs have also been attacked by restricting somewhat the tariff protection granted to new manufacturers and by permitting greater competition of imports. Tariff protection is no longer being granted for an indefinite period but is limited to a specified term, usually three to seven years. Thus, a decision on the future role of protectionism is being postponed to the next presidential administration, and presumably protection will not be automatically renewed but will be re-examined in the light of conditions at that time. Furthermore, import licenses for products for which there is a domestically produced substitute are no longer automatically denied in all cases. The policy announced in 1965 that prices, quality, and delivery terms would be taken into account has at least given importers a basis on which to make a case for imports. Of course, there has been no across-the-board policy to permit foreign imports to compete with domestic goods, but in some cases where the quality and price of a domestic product are at substantial variance from international standards, the licensing of imports of foreign goods has been used as a pressure tactic to force domestic producers to improve the quality and reduce the cost of their production. At the same time, there has gradually developed a trend to define "substitutability" with greater precision. Formerly, there were many complaints that there was no real understanding within the import-licensing apparatus of what was substitutable and what was not, and a product produced in Mexico was often considered to be a substitute for all similar products, without much regard for whether or not it actually fulfilled the same requirements. More recently, more careful consideration is being given to importers' arguments that domestically produced goods are not substitutes for the products they seek to import.

Also significant in the effort to reduce costs and increase exports has been the decision to permit imports of raw materials and component parts, even if they are produced domestically, when the end product is to be exported and the use of domestic components would make the product noncompetitive internationally.

The practical result of these policies is that there has been some degree of liberalization of foreign trade, at the same time that foreign investment has been subjected to greater limitations. Although it will be many years before Mexico is able to export substantial quantities of manufactured products, there are probably a number of existing producers that could develop an export capability by cutting their production costs. Some observers think that exports of manufactures can be increased to 25 or 30 percent of total exports within the next five to ten years. And it may not be too optimistic to predict that, as the volume of exports increases, the process of trade liberalization will continue and that at some time in the future Mexico will have a liberal trade policy.

The lawyer observing the Mexican regulatory system is struck by the fact that the restrictions on the conduct of enterprises in Mexico are not often reflected or even suggested in the legislation. While Mexican private law—the law governing relations between private persons—has been notably stable, sufficiently detailed, and readily ascertainable, the same cannot be said of its public law. The laws governing relations between private persons and the state have seen frequent and substantial changes, which have tended to give to the executive branch of the federal government, first, increasingly greater powers of intervention in the economic life of the country and, secondly, ever greater discretion in the exercise of those powers. Furthermore, powers of control under existing legislation have sometimes been exercised to achieve goals for which the powers were not intended. This has permitted the government to formulate and enforce policies with only the vaguest of statutory guidelines or no guidelines at all. The result is that, more and more, relations between private persons and the state are governed by a policy system rather than a statutory system. Consider, for example, the broad discretionary powers of governmental agencies over the life of a corporation. The Ministry of Foreign Relations, theoretically at least, controls its very birth and parentage through its power to grant or deny a permit to incorporate and its authority to limit foreign ownership of the company. The Ministry of Internal Affairs has almost unlimited freedom to refuse or permit the entry of foreign technicians and managerial personnel to operate it. The Ministry of Industry and Commerce may, as it sees fit, grant or deny licenses for the import of its plant equipment and raw materials or afford it protection or not against competing imports. So pervasive is its power over imports that the Ministry of Industry and Commerce has been able, through it, to assume the authority to restrict new foreign investments, force industrial integration, and impose price controls on industry, despite the fact that there is no general law on foreign investment and only a handful of statutory restrictions on its entry, no mention of integration is found in the statutes, and the price-control law is aimed at basic consumer goods and not at the great majority of manufactured products.

This system has, of course, afforded the government great flexibility to shape its policies to meet changing needs and circumstances, but the absence of statutory standards also has meant that there is less predictability in every-day dealings with the government and greater opportunity for favoritism and discrimination in the government's treatment of private investors. Nevertheless, it must be said in all fairness that the government has not frequently abused these powers and that, on the whole, its policies have proved to be constructive. The restrictions on the entry of foreign investment and the Mexicanization policy have stimulated the growth of domestic savings and investment. Without limitations on the entry of foreign employees, the training of skilled Mexican workers would not have progressed as it has and most technical personnel would probably still be foreigners.

There is no doubt that Mexico deserves the reputation it has as a highly attractive country for foreign investment. Its long history of political and monetary stability and its record of economic growth are achievements envied by many other developing nations. Foreign enterprises that are sympathetic to Mexico's problems, goals, and aspirations and possess an understanding of the limits within which foreign participation in the country's economy is acceptable have an opportunity to contribute to and benefit from her further development.

Notes

CHAPTER I

1. Many of the data in this section are taken from or based on Nacional Financiera, *Statistics on the Mexican Economy* (Mexico, D.F.: Nacional Financiera, 1966), especially tables 5 and 10. Extensive data on the Mexican economy are also found in Banco Nacional de Comercio Exterior, *Mexico 1968: Facts, Figures and Trends* (Mexico, D.F.: Banco Nacional de Comercio Exterior, 1968), and in the annual reports of Banco de México and Nacional Financiera. Useful recent studies include Raymond Vernon, *The Dilemma of Mexico's Development* (Cambridge: Harvard University Press, 1963); Robert J. Shafer, *Mexico: Mutual Adjustment Planning* (Syracuse, N.Y.: Syracuse University Press, 1966); Howard F. Cline, *Mexico: Revolution to Evolution, 1940-1960* (London: Oxford University Press, 1962); Raymond Vernon, ed., *Public Policy and Private Enterprise in Mexico* (Cambridge: Harvard University Press, 1964); James W. Wilkie, *The Mexican Revolution: Federal Expenditure and Social Change since 1910* (Berkeley and Los Angeles: University of California Press, 1967); *México: Cincuenta años de revolución*, Vol. I, *La economía* (Mexico, D.F.: Fondo de Cultura Económica, 1960).

2. Computed from *Mexican Economy* (above, n. 1), table 4; and *Mexico 1968* (above, n. 1), chart 3-2.

3. *Mexico 1968* (above, n. 1), chart 3-6.

4. For data on population trends, see *Mexico 1968* (above, n. 1), pp. 47-60.

5. A recent survey of the population and economy of the Federal District is found in Oliver Oldman et al., *Financing Urban Development in Mexico City* (Cambridge: Harvard University Press, 1967), pp. 4-25.

6. On problems of population and industrial concentration, see Paul Lamartine Yates, *El desarrollo regional de México*, 2d ed. (Mexico, D.F.: Banco de México, 1962), pp. 118-19. This is by far the best study on regional development in Mexico.

7. A recent study of Nacional Financiera is Calvin P. Blair, "Nacional Financiera: Entrepreneurship in a Mixed Economy," in Vernon, ed., *Public Policy* (above, n. 1), pp. 191-240.

8. See Vernon, *Dilemma* (above, n. 1), table 2; Gustavo Romero Kolbeck, "Government Involvement in Business," in *Business/Mexico* (Mexico, D.F.: American Chamber of Commerce of Mexico, 1968), p. 35.

9. *Mexican Economy* (above, n. 1), table 11.

10. Useful studies of Mexican politics and government include Robert E. Scott, *Mexican Government in Transition*, rev. ed. (Urbana: University of Illinois Press, 1964); William P. Tucker, *The Mexican Government Today* (Minneapolis: University of Minnesota Press, 1957); Vernon, *Dilemma* (above, n. 1); Frank Brandenburg, *The Making of Modern Mexico* (Englewood Cliffs, N.J.: Prentice-Hall, 1964); Cline (above, n. 1), chaps. 14-17; Pablo González Casanova, *La*

democracia en México, 2d ed. (Mexico, D.F.: Ediciones Era, 1967); *México: Cincuenta años de revolución,* Vol. III, *La política* (Mexico, D.F.: Fondo de Cultura Económica, 1961). For an academic treatment by a leading Mexican scholar, see Felipe Tena Ramírez, *Derecho constitucional mexicano,* 6th ed. rev. (Mexico, D.F.: Editorial Porrúa, 1963).

11. Constitution, art. 40.

12. Constitution, art. 76 § V, empowers the Senate to make a finding that "the constitutional powers of a State have disappeared" and to appoint a provisional governor from a list of three names proposed by the president.

13. Constitution, art. 49. Constitutional provisions relating to Congress are found in arts. 50-79; those on the executive in arts. 80-93; and those on the judiciary in arts. 94-107.

14. Ministries and departments are governed by the *Ley de secretarías y departamentos de estado,* 1958 (D.O., Dec. 24, 1958). The ministries are: internal affairs *(gobernación),* foreign relations, national defense, navy, finance and public credit, national properties, industry and commerce, agriculture and livestock, communications and transportation, public works, hydraulic resources, public education, health and welfare, labor and social welfare, and the presidency. The departments are: agrarian affairs and colonization, tourism, and the Federal District Department.

In the footnotes to this book the practice is followed of citing a law or decree by the year of promulgation and the date of the *Diario Oficial* (cited as D.O.) in which it was published. Although the *Diario Oficial* is organized by volumes and numbers, each number being paginated independently, a reference to the volume and page at which a law appears does not materially aid in its location and, following the practice of Mexican legal publications, the citations to laws in this book do not include them. Apart from the federal publication, each state has its own official gazette in which state laws are published.

15. Evidence of this is a 1963 amendment to the Constitution, art. 54 (D.O., June 22, 1963), to increase the representation of opposition parties in Congress by giving any party that obtains 2.5 percent of the total national vote the right to name five "party deputies" to the lower house, plus an additional one for each additional 0.5 percent of the vote received. In the 1964 elections only the PAN received a large enough share of the vote to entitle it to appoint party deputies, but seats were nevertheless assigned to two other opposition parties.

16. Constitution, art. 71.

17. Of the private editions of laws, the most useful are the loose-leaf publications of Antolín Jiménez and Ediciones Andrade, S.A., which are kept current by periodic supplements. Editorial Porrúa, S.A., publishes many of the codes and laws in its series "Leyes y Códigos de México."

18. Constitution, art. 89 § I. On presidential regulations and other executive enactments, see Andrés Serra Rojas, *Derecho administrativo,* 3d ed. rev. (Mexico, D.F.: Librería de Manuel Porrúa, 1965), pp. 209-30.

19. Full discussions are found in Tena Ramírez (above, n. 10), pp. 199-227; Sam G. Baggett, "The Delegation of Legislative Power to the Executive under the Constitution of Mexico," 8 *Southern California Law Review* 114 (1935).

20. This decree is discussed in detail in Chapter III, p. 101.

21. Import tariffs and controls are discussed in Chapter V, p. 164.

22. A classic study emphasizing corruption in the Mexican government is Lucio Mendieta y Núñez, *La administración pública en México* (Mexico, D.F.: Imprenta Universitaria, 1942). See also Frank Tannenbaum, *Mexico: The Struggle for Peace and Bread* (New York: Alfred A. Knopf, 1960), p. 79, who, writing in

the mid-1940's, classified governmental corruption as "now perhaps the greatest single impediment both morally and politically to good government and economic progress" and further stated that "the extortions for the privilege of staying in business, organizing any economic activity, or securing the necessary legal permission for carrying on the work of the day have become so burdensome as to weaken the economy and the moral substance of the nation."

23. See the candid statement on dishonesty in Mexican government made by Ramón Beteta, former minister of finance, quoted in Wilkie (above, n. 1), pp. 8-9. An excellent discussion of conflicts of interest in the public sector is found in Vernon, *Dilemma* (above, n. 1), pp. 149-53.

24. Constitution, art. 104.

25. Constitution, art. 103.

26. Constitution, art. 104 § I.

27. The law governing the federal court system is the *Ley orgánica del poder judicial de la federación,* 1935 (D.O., Jan. 10, 1936), most recently amended by decree of Jan. 3, 1968 (D.O., Apr. 30, 1968).

28. Constitution, arts. 20 § VI, and 111, 5th para.; *Ley orgánica del poder judicial* (above, n. 27), art 62.

29. Decree of Dec. 28, 1950 (D.O., Feb. 19, 1951), arts. 2 and 3.

30. Data on the work of the Supreme Court are published in the annual reports of the president of the Court. The figures are staggering; in 1968, for example, it appears that the Court decided over eight thousand cases. *Informe rendido a la Suprema Corte de Justicia de la Nación por su presidente . . . al terminar el año de 1968* (Mexico, D.F.: Imprenta de Murguía, 1968), annex 11.

31. Supreme Court judges receive a monthly salary of 15,000 pesos and are furnished an automobile with chauffeur and some expense allowances.

32. *Ley orgánica del poder judicial* (above, n. 27), art. 92, as amended by decree of Dec. 30, 1950 (D.O., Feb. 19, 1951), provides that vacancies on the circuit and district courts and in certain other positions within the judicial branch shall be filled by promotion, taking into account such things as ability, conduct, and seniority, but "in exceptional cases" vacancies may be filled by persons who have previously served in the federal judiciary or other persons of honesty, competence, and prior good record.

33. *Ley orgánica del poder judicial* (above, n. 27), arts. 84 and 85.

34. Ibid., art. 74.

35. The law governing the courts of the Federal District and territories is the *Ley orgánica de los tribunales de justicia del fuero común del distrito y territorios federales,* 1932 (D.O., Dec. 31, 1932), most recently amended by decree of Dec. 27, 1965 (D.O., Jan. 4, 1966).

36. Jurisprudence is provided for in *Ley de amparo, reglamentaria de los artículos 103 y 107 de la constitución política de los Estados Unidos Mexicanos,* 1935 (D.O., Jan. 10, 1936), arts. 192-97, as amended by decree of Jan. 3, 1968 (D.O., Apr. 30, 1968). See generally Helen L. Clagett, *The Administration of Justice in Latin America* (New York: Oceana Publications, 1952), pp. 123-26. This law is discussed more fully below under Judicial Protection against Governmental Acts—The *Amparo,* p. 28.

37. The dates covered by the six series (*épocas*) of the *Semanario Judicial de la Federación* are: 1st ser.: 1871-76; 2d ser.: 1881-90; 3d ser.: 1891-99; 4th ser.: 1898-1910; 5th ser.: 1917-55; 6th ser.: 1957-date (in progress). Since volumes of the sixth series are divided into five separate parts, each of which is paginated independently, citations to decisions reported there contain both the series number and the number of the part. In the footnotes to this book such decisions are

cited by the name of the complaining party, the volume number of the *Semanario* (abbreviated S.J.F.), the series number, page number, part number, and year, as follows: *Hemenegildo Moreno González,* 38 S.J.F. (6th) 177 (4th pt.) (1960). Volumes of the fifth series are not divided into parts and are paginated continuously, so no reference to a part number is found in citations to decisions in that series.

38. These rules are applicable to the sixth series and are contained in "Bases que regirán la sexta época del Semanario Judicial de la Federación," 1 S.J.F. (6th) 7-8 (1st pt.) (1957). A substantially larger number of opinions were published in full or abbreviated form in the fifth series than are being published in the sixth series. *Ley de amparo* (above, n. 36), art. 197, provides that *amparo* decisions and separate dissenting opinions of Supreme Court justices and collegiate circuit court judges shall be published in the S.J.F. if they are necessary to constitute jurisprudence or to reverse it, or when those courts so direct. It does not appear, however, that circuit court opinions are being published.

39. While the *Boletin* is not an official organ of the Court, it is published under its auspices and that of the Asociación Nacional de Funcionarios Judiciales.

40. *Jurisprudencia de la Suprema Corte de Justicia, en los fallos pronunciados en los años de 1917 a 1954,* 3 vols. (Mexico, D.F.: Imprenta Murguía, 1955); *Jurisprudencia de la Suprema Corte de Justicia de la Nación de los fallos pronunciados en los años de 1917 a 1965,* 6 vols. (Mexico, D.F.: Imprenta Murguía, 1965).

41. The most comprehensive compilation of decisions from 1935 to 1955 is Salvador Chávez Hayhoe, *Prontuario de ejecutorias de la Suprema Corte de Justicia de la Nación* (Mexico, D.F.: C. Velasco, 1935-55), which digests all Supreme Court decisions during the period of its publication. A good compilation covering the 1955-63 period is Francisco Barrutieta Mayo, *Jurisprudencia y tesis sobresalientes . . . de la Suprema Corte de Justicia de la Nación, 1955-1963,* 5 vols. (Mexico, D.F.: Mayo Ediciones, 1964-65).

42. There are numerous studies on the Mexican suit of *amparo.* Probably the best is Hector Fix Zamudio, *El juicio de amparo* (Mexico, D.F.: Editorial Porrúa, 1964). A good short work by the same author is "Síntesis del derecho de amparo," in *Panorama del derecho mexicano,* 2 vols. (Mexico, D.F.: Universidad Nacional Autónoma de México, Instituto de Derecho Comparado, 1965), 2:103-59. Studies in English include Kenneth L. Karst, *Latin American Legal Institutions: Problems for Comparative Study* (Los Angeles: University of California, Latin American Center, 1966), pp. 614-46, which contains translations of many of the pertinent constitutional and legal provisions and a number of decisions of the Mexican Supreme Court; Lucio Cabrera and William Cecil Headrick, "Notes on Judicial Review in Mexico and the United States," 5 *Inter-American Law Review* 253 (1963); Helen L. Clagett, "The Mexican Suit of 'Amparo'," 33 *Georgetown Law Journal* 418 (1945).

43. *Ley de amparo, reglamentaria de los artículos 103 y 107 de la constitución política de los Estados Unidos Mexicanos,* 1935 (D.O., Jan. 10, 1936), most recently amended by decree of Jan. 3, 1968 (D.O., Apr. 30, 1968).

44. *Ley orgánica del poder judicial de la federación,* 1935 (D.O., Jan. 10, 1936), most recently amended by decree of Jan. 3, 1968 (D.O., Apr. 30, 1968).

45. Examples are the emergency decree of 1944, discussed fully in Chapter III, p. 101 and the law of professions, discussed below in this chapter under The Legal Professionals, p. 43, and in Chapter VI, p. 205.

46. See Clagett (above, n. 42), p. 435, quoting from the work of the great Mexican jurist Ignacio Vallarta, *El juicio de amparo y el writ of habeas corpus* (1881).

47. *Constitución política de los Estados Unidos Mexicanos,* 1917 (D.O., Feb. 5, 1917), cited throughout this book as Constitution. The Constitution as amended to date, with original texts of amended articles and all amendments, is found in Manuel Andrade, comp., *Constitución política mexicana* (Mexico, D.F.: Ediciones Andrade, loose-leaf), which is kept current with loose-leaf supplements. An English translation is *Constitution of Mexico 1917* (Washington, D.C.: Pan American Union, 1968).

48. On the importance of the distinction between public and private law in Italy, see Mauro Cappelletti, John Henry Merryman, and Joseph M. Perillo, *The Italian Legal System* (Stanford, Cal.: Stanford University Press, 1967), pp. 206-12; in France, René David and Henry P. deVries, *The French Legal System* (New York: Oceana Publications, for Parker School of Foreign and Comparative Law, Columbia University, 1958), pp. 45-46.

49. *Código civil para el distrito y territorios federales, en materia común, y para toda la república en materia federal,* 1928 (D.O., May 26, 1928), cited throughout this book as Civil Code. An English translation is Otto Schoenrich, trans., *The Civil Code for the Federal District and Territories of Mexico* (New York: Baker, Voorhis & Co., 1950).

50. See "Motivos del código civil," in *Código civil para el distrito y territorios federales,* 7th ed. (Mexico, D.F.: Editorial Porrúa, 1961), pp. 8-9.

51. Civil Code, art. 16.

52. See, for example, Civil Code, arts. 840, 2453, 2751.

53. Civil Code, art. 836.

54. Civil Code, art. 832.

55. Civil Code, arts. 17, 2398-2496.

56. Civil Code, art. 831.

57. Civil Code, art. 951, as amended by decree of Nov. 30, 1954 (D.O., Dec. 15, 1954); *Ley sobre el régimen de propiedad y condominio de los edificios divididos en pisos, departamentos, viviendas o locales,* 1954 (D.O., Dec. 15, 1954).

58. See, for example, Civil Code, art. 17 (rescission for *lesión*), arts. 2236-37 (annulment of contract), art. 2262 (rescission of certain sale contracts).

59. *Ley federal sobre derechos de autor,* 1956 (D.O., Dec. 31, 1956).

60. For discussions of this distinction, see Cappelletti, Merryman, and Perillo (above, n. 48), pp. 231-33; F. H. Lawson, *Introduction to the Law of Property* (Oxford: Clarendon Press, 1958).

61. The trust and other security interests are discussed in Chapter X.

62. Another institution common in civil law, the forced inheritance, under which certain relatives of a property owner have the right to inherit from him on his death, does not exist in Mexican law.

63. This section also contains provisions on civil instruments payable to order or bearer, arts. 1873-81. These articles are considered to have been repealed by the *Ley general de títulos y operaciones de crédito,* 1932 (D.O., Aug. 27, 1932), trans. art. 3, and all documents payable to order or to bearer are now regarded as commercial instruments and are governed by that law. See Manuel Andrade, comp., *Nuevo código civil para el distrito y territorios federales* (Mexico, D.F.: Ediciones Andrade, loose-leaf), pp. 477-78, quoting opinion of Manuel Borja Soriano.

64. The provisions on the public register, Civil Code, arts. 2999-3044, were amended by decree of Dec. 31, 1951 (D.O., Jan. 18, 1952), which also modified certain provisions relating to holographic wills, installment sales, judicial bonds, and pledges, but this decree has not yet taken effect.

65. *Reglamento del Registro Público de la Propiedad del Distrito Federal,* 1940

(D.O., July 13, 1940). New regulations were published in 1952 (D.O., Dec. 15, 1952), but by subsequent decree of June 3, 1953 (D.O., June 20, 1953) their effective date was postponed to a date to be determined by the president, and they have not yet been put into effect.

66. For example, Civil Code, arts. 840, 845, 851, 853.

67. Civil Code, art. 2688, defines the civil company (sociedad civil) as one whose purpose is "predominantly economic in character, but does not amount to commercial speculation." The fact that "commercial speculation" means an activity for the purpose of obtaining a profit is demonstrated in Pares y Compañía, Sociedad Civil, 32 S.J.F. (6th) 155 (4th pt.) (1960). The civil association (asociación civil) is defined in the Civil Code, art. 2670, as an agreement to associate for a purpose that is not preponderantly economic and is commonly used for sports clubs, charitable organizations, professional and scientific associations, and the like.

68. Código de comercio, 1889, cited throughout this book as Commercial Code. A good compilation of the Commercial Code as amended, together with the supplementary statutes, is Manuel Andrade, comp., Código de comercio reformado, 2 vols. (Mexico, D.F.: Ediciones Andrade, loose-leaf).

69. Commercial Code, art. 2: "In the absence of provisions of this Code, those of the common law shall be applicable to commercial acts." The term "common law" refers to the general law contained in the Civil Code.

70. To this effect, art. 1 of the Civil Code for the Federal District and Territories provides: "The provisions of this Code shall apply in the Federal District and in the Federal Territories in matters of common order, and in all the Republic in matters of federal order."

71. There are no entirely adequate studies in English of Mexican legal education. Perhaps the best is Richard C. Maxwell and Marvin G. Goldman, "Mexican Legal Education," 16 Journal of Legal Education 155 (1963).

72. The program of study and course descriptions at the Faculty of Law of the Universidad Nacional Autónoma de México are published in its annual catalogue.

73. Ley reglamentaria de los artículos 4°. y 5°. constitucionales relativos al ejercicio de las profesiones en el distrito y territorios federales, 1944 (D.O., May 26, 1945), art. 30, hereinafter cited as law of professions; Reglamento de la ley reglamentaria de los artículos 4°. y 5°. constitucionales relativos al ejercicio de las profesiones en el distrito y territorios federales y en materia federal, 1945 (D.O., Oct. 1, 1945), arts. 51-52.

74. See note 73.

75. Law of professions, arts. 15, 25.

76. Ibid., arts. 16, 18-20.

77. For citations to cases, see Chapter VI, note 25.

78. The arguments are summarized in an article based on an interview with Lic. Virgilio Domínguez, then president of the Barra Mexicana, published in Excelsior, Mar. 26, 1963, p. 1. The issue was the main subject of debate at the third convention of the Barra Mexicana, Mar. 27-30, 1963.

79. Martindale-Hubbell Law Directory (Chicago: R. R. Donnelley & Sons Co., 1969) 4: 2701B-33B, lists five firms in Mexico City with ten or more lawyers, two of which have over thirty, and one in Monterrey with ten or more.

80. The law governing notaries in the Federal District and federal territories is the Ley del notariado para el Distrito Federal y territorios, 1945 (D.O., Feb. 23, 1946), as amended by decree of Feb. 11, 1969 (D.O., Feb. 18, 1969), increasing

the number of notarial offices in the Federal District from 134 to 150. It is the model for most state laws, and the discussion in this section is based on it.

81. *Ley del notariado* (above, n. 80), art. 75; see also *Código de procedimientos civiles para el distrito y territorios federales,* 1932 (D.O., Sept. 1 and 21, 1932), arts. 327 § I, 411.

82. Notarial fees are set out in the *Arancel de notarios para el distrito y territorios federales,* 1947 (D.O., Dec. 31, 1947).

CHAPTER II

1. On foreign investments prior to the Porfirian era see J. Fred Rippy, *British Investments in Latin America, 1822-1949* (Minneapolis: University of Minnesota Press, 1959), pp. 95-104; J. N. Tattersall, "The Impact of Foreign Investment on Mexico, 1879-1920" (Master's thesis, University of Washington, 1956).

2. For the history of this debt see William H. Wynne, *State Insolvency and Foreign Bondholders,* 2 vols. (New Haven, Conn.: Yale University Press, 1951), 2:3-13, 31-40; Edgar Turlington, *Mexico and Her Foreign Creditors* (New York: Columbia University Press, 1930), pp. 16-48. Interest alone on the public debt represented one-fifth of the total federal income in 1867. Daniel Cosío Villegas, ed., *Historia moderna de México,* vol. 2, *La república restaurada: La vida económica* (Mexico, D.F.: Editorial Hermes, 1955), p. 24.

3. Decree of Oct. 7, 1823, Manuel Dublán and José María Lozano, *Legislación mexicana o colección completa de las disposiciones legislativas expedidas desde la independencia de la república,* 34 vols. (Mexico, D.F.: Imprenta del Comercio, á cargo de Dublán y Lozano, hijos, 1876-1904), 1:681. Foreign ownership of mines was prohibited under Spanish law. The 1823 decree allowed foreigners to contract to rehabilitate old mines but not to register new ones. In 1842 and 1843 foreigners were permitted to acquire mining properties on almost the same terms as Mexicans.

4. *Científicos* was the name given to the group of young lawyers and intellectuals who gave the Díaz administration an economic philosophy borrowed from French Positivism and English social Darwinism. See Henry Bamford Parkes, *A History of Mexico,* rev. ed. (Boston: Houghton Mifflin Co., 1950), pp. 299-300.

5. This estimate was made in 1911 by U.S. mining engineer William H. Seamon, submitted to Washington by Consul Marion Letcher, and published in U.S. Dept. of Commerce and Labor, Bureau of Foreign and Domestic Commerce, *Daily Consular and Trade Reports No. 155* (July 18, 1912), p. 316. Though Seamon's estimates have been widely cited and are probably the basis for statements that U.S. interests controlled half the total wealth of Mexico, e.g., *México: Cincuenta años de revolución,* vol. I, "El financiamiento del desarrollo económico, in *La economía,* by Alfredo Navarrete R. (Mexico, D.F.: Fondo de Cultura Económica, 1960), p. 513, they are probably much too high and cannot be reconciled with what appear to be more reliable estimates. Cleona Lewis, *America's Stake in Foreign Investments* (Washington, D.C.: Brookings Institution, 1938), p. 606, estimated total U.S. investment, both direct and portfolio, at $672 million in 1908 and $853.5 million in 1914. A summary of various early estimates is contained in Tattersall (above, n. 1), table 26, pp. 115-17.

6. The Seamon-Letcher estimate (see note 5, above) placed the total wealth of Mexico in 1911 at $2.43 billion, of which $1.64 billion, or 67 percent, was said to be owned by foreigners. The most complete account of foreign investment during the Porfirian era, from which the data in table 3 are taken, is Daniel Cosío Villegas, ed., *Historia moderna de México* vol. 7, "Las inversiones ex-

tranjeras," in *El Porfiriato: La vida económica,* by Luis Nicolau D'Olwer (Mexico, D.F.: Editorial Hermes, 1965), pp. 973-1185. A recent study of British investment and enterprise during this period is Alfred Tischendorf, *Great Britain and Mexico in the Era of Porfirio Díaz* (Durham, N.C.: Duke University Press, 1961).

7. The foreign debt incurred during the period 1888-1910 is described in Wynne (above, n. 2), pp. 47-57; Turlington (above, n. 2), pp. 171-244.

8. Mexican railway securities—bonds and preferred stock—acquired in exchange for common stock in railroads and guaranteed in part by the Mexican government are classified as direct investment rather than public debt in table 3. As Cleona Lewis points out (above, n. 5), pp. 320, 346-49, nationalization of the two major lines before 1910 shifted a large part of the railroad investment from a "direct" to a "portfolio" status.

9. The 1884 law, the *Código de minería de la República Mexicana,* was the first federal mining law. Under the 1857 constitution jurisdiction over mining was left to the states, but the Mexican Congress federalized mining legislation in 1883. The 1892 law was the *Ley minera y ley de impuesto a la minería* (D.O., June 7, 1892).

10. For a detailed account of foreign investment in mining during this period, see Marvin D. Bernstein, *The Mexican Mining Industry, 1890-1950* (Albany: State University of New York, 1964), pp. 17-26, 49-77.

11. *Ley del petróleo,* 1901, in *Legislación petrolera* (Mexico, D.F.: Secretaría de Educación Pública, 1922), pp. 12-16.

12. Eyler N. Simpson, *The Ejido: Mexico's Way Out* (Chapel Hill: University of North Carolina Press, 1937), pp. 32-33; Frank Tannenbaum, *Mexico: The Struggle for Peace and Bread* (New York: Alfred Knopf, 1950), p. 141; Raymond Vernon, *The Dilemma of Mexico's Development* (Cambridge: Harvard University Press, 1963), p. 49.

13. Also known as the *Ley Lerdo* for its author, Miguel Lerdo de Tejada. Dublán and Lozano (above, n. 3), 8:197. This law and subsequent land laws of the nineteenth century are discussed in Lucio Mendieta y Núñez, *El problema agrario de México,* 8th ed. (Mexico, D.F.: Editorial Porrúa, 1964), pp. 109-37.

14. An account of the effect of the liberal laws of the 1850's on land ownership is contained in Andrés Molina Enríquez' classic, *Los grandes problemas nacionales,* first published in 1908 and republished in 1964 by the Instituto Nacional de la Juventud Mexicana. This work is also extremely interesting for its review of the social aspects of Mexico's history.

15. *Ley de nacionalización de bienes eclesiásticos,* July 12, 1859, Dublán and Lozano (above, n. 3), 8:680; also published in Felipe Tena Ramírez, ed., *Leyes fundamentales de México 1808-1967,* 3d ed. rev. (Mexico, D.F.: Editorial Porrúa, 1967), pp. 638-41. This law and the series of laws and decrees that followed it limiting the power of the Church are known as the Laws of the Reform.

16. *Ley sobre ocupación y enajenación de terrenos baldíos,* July 20, 1863, Dublán and Lozano (above, n. 3), 9:637.

17. On the formation and organization of the hacienda, see Nathan L. Whetten, *Rural Mexico* (Chicago: University of Chicago Press, 1948), pp. 90-107; and Frank Tannenbaum, *The Mexican Agrarian Revolution* (New York: Macmillan Co., 1929), pp. 102-33, pointing out the lack of material contribution of the hacienda system to the economic development of Mexico.

18. These laws are discussed in Mendieta y Núñez (above, n. 13), pp. 123-30. On the Díaz colonization policy and its results see Fernando González Roa, *El aspecto agrario de la revolución mexicana* (Mexico, D.F.: Poder Ejecutivo Fed-

eral, Departamento de Aprovisionamientos Generales, Dirección de Talleres Gráficos, 1919), pp. 125-33.

19. *Ley sobre ocupación y enajenación de terrenos baldíos de los Estados Unidos Mexicanos,* Mar. 26, 1894, also known as the *Ley Vallarta,* Dublán and Lozano (above, n. 3), 24:35.

20. A good survey of foreign landholdings is found in Tannenbaum (above, n. 17), pp. 358-69, stating that foreigners owned 25.2 percent of Mexico's total land area in 1910 and at least 16.2 percent in 1923, and that about half the total rural land owned by foreigners was owned by North Americans. On land acquisitions by U.S. interests, see also J. Fred Rippy, *The United States and Mexico* (New York: Alfred A. Knopf, 1926), pp. 311-17.

21. An excellent discussion of the Mexican laborer in about 1900 is found in Walter E. Weyl, "Labor Conditions in Mexico," 38 *Bulletin of the Department of Labor* 12-22 (1902). See also Tattersall (above, n. 1), pp. 172-85. For an interesting account of the conditions of mine workers, pointing out that mine operators were responsible for raising the general wage level in the country but were often callous in their treatment of Mexican laborers, see Bernstein (above, n. 10), pp. 84-91. Simpson (above, n. 12), pp. 33-41, describes the conditions of farm workers.

22. For a description of the criticism of the position of foreigners in Mexico during this period, see Daniel Cosío Villegas, ed., *Historia moderna de México,* vol. 4, *El Porfiriato: La vida social,* by Moisés Gonzáles Navarro (Mexico, D.F.: Editorial Hermes, 1957), pp. 153-60; and Rippy (above, n. 20), pp. 320-31.

23. Turlington (above, n. 2), pp. 237-40; Fred Wilbur Powell, *The Railroads of Mexico* (Boston: Stratford Co., 1921), pp. 4, 175-77.

24. Bernstein (above, n. 10), pp. 78-83.

25. At 1950 prices. Ernesto Fernández Hurtado, "La iniciativa privada y el estado como promotores de desarrollo," in *México* (above, n. 5), p. 599. Parkes (above, n. 4), p. 308, reports that the real wage of a peon in 1910, as measured by the price of corn, was one-quarter of what it had been in 1800.

26. There are numerous works on the Mexican Revolution. An interesting summary, emphasizing Mexican–United States relations during that period, is contained in Howard F. Cline, *The United States and Mexico,* rev. ed. (New York: Atheneum, 1963), pp. 113-213.

27. U.S. interference during this period is vividly described in Arthur S. Link, *Wilson: The New Freedom* (Princeton, N.J.: Princeton University Press, 1956), pp. 347-416. A recent detailed account of the Veracruz incident is Robert E. Quirk, *An Affair of Honor: Woodrow Wilson and the Occupation of Veracruz* (Lexington: University of Kentucky Press, 1962).

28. Estimates of losses to United States mining companies during this period range from $115 million to over $500 million. Bernstein (above, n. 10), p. 105.

29. Tannenbaum (above, n. 12), pp. 114-15, makes the point that there was no significant trade-union movement or labor problem in Mexico at that time and that the aim of art. 123 was to create an organized national working class to counterbalance the power of the foreign industrialists.

30. Well-documented and objective accounts of the controversy over subsoil petroleum rights during this period are Lorenzo Meyer Cosío, "El conflicto petrolero entre México y los Estados Unidos (1917-1920)," 6 *Foro Internacional* 425 (1966); Charles P. Howland, ed., *Survey of American Foreign Relations* (New Haven, Conn.: Yale University Press, published for the Council on Foreign Relations, 1931), pp. 121-64; Frederick Sherwood Dunn, *The Diplomatic Protection*

of Americans in Mexico (New York: Columbia University Press, 1933), pp. 332-66.

31. The leading case is *The Texas Company of Mexico, S.A.,* 9 S.J.F. (5th) 432 (1921).

32. The official U.S. record of these conferences is U.S. Dept. of State, *Proceedings of the United States–Mexican Commission Convened in Mexico City, May 14, 1923* (Washington, D.C.: GPO, 1925). For a Mexican scholar's view, see Antonio Gómez Robledo, *The Bucareli Agreements and International Law,* trans. Salomón de la Selva (Mexico, D.F.: National University of Mexico Press, 1940).

33. *Ley reglamentaria del artículo 27 constitucional en el ramo del petróleo,* 1925 (D.O., Dec. 31, 1925), arts. 14, 15. The regulations to this law contained similar provisions. *Reglamento de la ley del petróleo de 26 de diciembre de 1925,* 1926 (D.O., Apr. 8, 1926), arts. 150-56.

34. Decree of Jan. 3, 1928 (D.O., Jan. 10, 1928), provided for the confirmation of rights in land on which petroleum exploitation works had been begun before May 1, 1917, and rights under contracts executed before that date with the surface owner for purposes of oil exploitation. The relevant articles of the regulations were amended by decree of Mar. 27, 1928 (D.O., Mar. 28, 1928), which defined exploitation works as the execution of some "positive act" expressing the intent of the owner to use or obtain the petroleum in the subsoil.

35. On the work of these commissions through 1930, see Howland (above, n. 30), pp. 264-81. Special claims of U.S. nationals for personal or property damage attributable to the Revolution, of a net total of $206.7 million, were settled in 1934 for $5,448,020, or 2.6 percent of the amount claimed; general and agrarian claims of North Americans were settled in 1941 for $40 million. Wynne (above, n. 2), pp. 87-92.

36. Bernstein (above, n. 10), p. 105.

37. Navarrete (above, n. 5), p. 521.

38. The 1936 estimate is from Paul D. Dickens, *American Direct Investments in Foreign Countries, 1936,* U.S. Dept. of Commerce, Bureau of Foreign and Domestic Commerce, Economic Series, no. 1 (Washington, D.C., 1938), p. 46, and is based on "the net investment of Americans in the foreign company as shown on the books of that foreign company." Since it is substantially lower than the value placed on their properties by the oil companies at the time of the 1938 expropriation, it apparently does not include any amount for subsoil petroleum deposits. Bryce Wood, *The Making of the Good Neighbor Policy* (New York: Columbia University Press, 1961), p. 203, says that the U.S. oil companies estimated the value of their lands at about $200 million and their investments in drilling and other equipment at about $60 million; the value of oil lands under concession to all foreign companies was near $500 million.

39. Sanford A. Mosk, *Industrial Revolution in Mexico* (Berkeley: University of California Press, 1954), pp. 53-57.

40. *Ley de expropiación,* 1936 (D.O., Nov. 25, 1936), art. 1, sec. 9. Among the purposes for which expropriation is authorized are the satisfaction of collective requirements in case of war or domestic disturbance; the equitable distribution of wealth monopolized or controlled for the exclusive benefit of one or more persons to the prejudice of either the collective society in general or a particular class; the creation, development, or preservation of an enterprise for the collective benefit; and to carry out measures necessary to avoid destruction of natural elements and damage to property to the prejudice of the collective society. Expropriated property is to be paid for in the manner determined by the expropriating

authority within a maximum period of ten years and in the amount of the real property tax valuation.

41. Bernstein (above, n. 10), pp. 188-89; Cline (above, n. 26), pp. 226-27. For a contemporary account of worker control of industry, see Nathaniel and Sylvia Weyl, *The Reconquest of Mexico: The Years of Lázaro Cárdenas* (New York: Oxford University Press, 1939), pp. 253-78.

42. The 1937 expropriation affected primarily the railroad bondholders, who had acquired their securities as a consequence of the prerevolutionary nationalization of the major lines and their consolidation into the government-controlled National Railways of Mexico. The government took over the operation of the system in 1914, but it was returned to private management in 1926. See Wendell C. Gordon, *The Expropriation of Foreign-Owned Property in Mexico* (Washington, D.C.: American Council on Public Affairs, 1941), pp. 137-39.

43. The story of the oil expropriation has been told many times and from varying viewpoints. A well-documented summary is contained in Gordon (above, n. 42), pp. 104-21. An account from the Mexican viewpoint has been written by Jesús Silva Herzog, a member of the commission appointed by the federal board of conciliation and arbitration, *Historia de la expropiación de las empresas petroleras,* 3d ed. (Mexico, D.F.: Instituto Mexicano de Investigaciones Económicas, 1964).

44. Wood (above, n. 38), p. 203, states that "Cárdenas told [U.S.] Ambassador Josephus Daniels that the [expropriation] decree would not have been issued if the companies even at the last moment had been willing to abide by the decision." Wood concludes, p. 204, that "although the expropriation was consistent with his [Cárdenas'] administration's vigorous prosecution of social reforms, the timing of the decree seems to have been due more to anger and exasperation at the oil companies' policies than to the climax of a calculated course of action."

45. English versions of the official documents relating to the expropriation, including the expropriation decree, Cárdenas' message to the nation, report of the expert commission, and award of the federal board of conciliation and arbitration, are collected in the Mexican government publication, *Mexico's Oil* (Mexico, D.F., 1940).

46. Navarrete (above, n. 5), p. 522.

47. On the growth of manufacturing during this period, see Raymond Vernon's excellent study of the Mexican economy (above, n. 12), pp. 83-86.

48. See John J. Johnson, *Political Change in Latin America* (Stanford, Cal.: Stanford University Press, 1958), p. 144, pointing out that between 1939 and 1946 the share of national income going to wages, salaries, and supplements dropped from about 30 percent to 22 percent; labor boards, on which the government held the balance of power, increasingly sided with management; and labor was told, in effect, that since domestic capital had largely replaced foreign capital in industry, the working man could not expect the same public support he had received when he served as the "protagonist against foreign rapacity."

49. For a survey of the principal industries in Mexico in the 1940's, see George Wythe, *Industry in Latin America,* 2d ed. (New York: Columbia University Press, 1949), pp. 302-17.

50. Settlements of foreign claims and adjustments of the external debt during this period are discussed in Wynne (above, n. 2), pp. 87-105.

51. The major controversy between the Mexican government and the oil companies on calculating the indemnity had been whether or not to include the value of subsoil petroleum deposits, and it is generally believed that the amount of the settlement included nothing for subsoil rights, pursuant to Mexico's position that

they belonged only to the nation. The settlement with the U.S. companies opened a new era of good relations between Mexico and the United States. For a detailed account, see Wood (above, n. 38), pp. 251-59.

52. The 1944 decree is discussed in detail in Chapter III, below, p. 101.

53. Combined Mexican Working Party, *The Economic Development of Mexico* (Baltimore: Published for the International Bank for Reconstruction and Development by the Johns Hopkins Press, 1953), pp. 81-82. Some of the principal U.S. manufacturing firms that entered Mexico in the 1940's are listed in Wythe (above, n. 49), p. 296.

54. Combined Mexican Working Party (above, n. 53), pp. 15, 81-82. This excellent study points out that foreign loans and investments increased total investment in Mexico by more than their own amounts by stimulating an increase in domestic savings and that foreign capital helped to finance investment projects of vital importance for the country's economic development and introduced important technical and administrative services.

55. These percentages are based on data published in 1958 by Banco de México in its annual report for 1957. In 1947 the bank made its first study of foreign investments, going back to 1938, and published detailed estimates of total foreign investment in its annual reports for 1947 through 1957. The publication of these estimates was discontinued after 1957 because of doubt as to their accuracy and reluctance to focus attention on them. The published figures should therefore be taken with some caution, but the relative amounts of investment in the various sectors of the economy are probably reliable enough to give a general picture.

56. Navarrete (above, n. 5), p. 529.

57. Navarrete (above, n. 5), p. 531.

58. A trend toward joint foreign-Mexican investments as early as the mid-1940's was noted in the classic study by Mosk (above, n. 39), pp. 136-38, but the majority of foreign firms undoubtedly preferred to operate through wholly owned Mexican subsidiaries. Less than 11 percent of foreign direct investments made in the period 1950-57 were in association with Mexican capital, and almost 94 percent of the mixed investments were foreign controlled. Manuel Sánchez Lugo, *Las inversiones extranjeras: Un régimen jurídico* (Thesis for Licenciado en Derecho, Universidad Nacional Autónoma de México, 1960), p. 39.

59. Restrictions on foreign investment in the petrochemical industry are discussed in Chapter III, below, p. 128.

60. The following account is based largely on the excellent study by Miguel S. Wionczek, "Electric Power: The Uneasy Partnership," in Raymond Vernon, ed., *Public Policy and Private Enterprise in Mexico* (Cambridge: Harvard University Press, 1964), pp. 19-110.

61. Finance Minister Antonio Ortiz Mena, reporting the takeover of the Mexican Light & Power properties, stated on September 27, 1960, that generating facilities would have to be doubled within the next eight years to keep pace with increasing demand. A similar statement was made by President López Mateos as the primary reason for the nationalization in his second annual report to Congress on September 1, 1960. The texts of both speeches were published in full in Mexico City dailies on the following days.

62. Wionczek (above, n. 60), p. 94; Robert Peter Wolfangel, "The History and Development of Private Electric Power Interests in Mexico" (Master's thesis, Mexico City College, June, 1961), p. 68.

63. A discussion of other and more subtle considerations leading to the nationalization is contained in Wionczek (above, n. 60), pp. 94-100. Though

not mentioned by Wionczek, it was rumored in Mexican circles that one consideration was the government's desire to exert greater control over the aggressive
electrical workers' unions, which had been infiltrated by Communist elements.
See Frank Brandenburg, *The Making of Modern Mexico* (Englewood Cliffs, N.J.:
Prentice-Hall, 1964), pp. 115-16.

64. The mining law and its Mexicanization provisions are discussed in detail
in Chapter III, p. 133. The public reactions of foreign mining company officials
varied from accusations of expropriation to acceptance of the development as
inevitable and one that would stimulate the long-term growth of the industry. See
New York Times, Apr. 21, 1961, p. 47.

65. The removal from foreign hands of control of two important chains of
movie theaters by the government's purchase of their exhibition contracts is sometimes cited as another example of official policy to oust foreign investment in
certain fields. It seems generally accepted, however, that the motives were entirely different and unrelated to the foreign ownership. Finance Minister Antonio
Ortiz Mena stated in a speech before the 1961 national banking convention that
the reasons for the purchase were to end a monopoly in the exhibition of motion
picture films and to stimulate the Mexican film industry, "La política del gobierno
y la situación económica de México," 21 *El Mercado de Valores* 206-7 (1961).

66. The development and operation of this clearing process are discussed in
Chapter IV, p. 156.

67. The industrial integration policy is discussed in Chapter V, p. 170.

68. In 1959 private investment increased by only 1.6 percent over the prior
year, compared to an increase in 1956 of 19.2 percent over 1955. Ortiz Mena
(above, n. 65), p. 210. Raymond Vernon noted the acceleration of capital flight
in 1960 and 1961 (above, n. 12), p. 122.

69. This plan, submitted to Alliance for Progress experts to fulfill Mexico's
commitment under the Charter of Punta del Este and the first national investment
program covering both the public and private sectors, is discussed in Miguel S.
Wionczek, "Incomplete Formal Planning: Mexico," in Everett E. Hagen, ed.,
Planning Economic Development (Homewood, Ill.: Published for the Center of
International Studies, Massachusetts Institute of Technology, by Richard D.
Irwin, Inc., 1963), pp. 169-77; and Robert Jones Shafer, *Mexico: Mutual Adjust-
ment Planning* (Syracuse, N.Y.: Syracuse University Press, 1966), pp. 110-15.

70. In 1963 Wionczek (above, n. 69), p. 171, pointed out that by 1960-61
service on the external public debt had increased to 16 percent of Mexico's
foreign exchange earnings and warned of the burdensome drain on the country's
balance of payments. Dwight S. Brothers and Leopoldo Solís M. also warned of
the risks in further heavy reliance on foreign borrowing in *Mexican Financial
Development* (Austin: University of Texas Press, 1966), pp. 188, 194.

71. Statements of this attitude appeared in the following speeches of Díaz
Ordaz: acceptance of the presidential nomination, Nov. 17, 1963; campaign speech
at Reynosa, Tamps., Feb. 27, 1964; inaugural address, Dec. 1, 1964.

72. "Mexicanization and Present Policy in Mexico," speech by Luis Bravo
Aguilera, director general of industry of the Ministry of Industry and Commerce,
at Ixtápan de la Sal, Mexico, May 11-12, 1967, published in "Report on the
Seminar for Foreign Executives Residents of Mexico," mimeographed (Mexico,
D.F.: Arte y Cultura, A.C., affiliated to Confederación Patronal de la República
Mexicana, 1967), pp. 101-2. It has been reported that, of the 114 important
industrial projects approved in 1965 alone, all were for enterprises with mixed
foreign and domestic capital and in 83 percent the controlling interest was held

by Mexican investors. Alfredo Navarrete R., "La inversión extranjera directa en México," 26 *El Mercado de Valores* 1083 (1966).

73. Industrial integration and price control are discussed in Chapter V, pp. 170, 176.

74. For a popular account of the company's history to 1960 see Robert Sheehan, "The 'Little Mothers' and Pan American Sulphur," *Fortune*, July 1960, p. 96.

75. *Excelsior*, Apr. 27, 1965, p. 6.

76. *Wall Street Journal*, Oct. 5, 1966, p. 4.

77. *Wall Street Journal*, Dec. 15, 1966, p. 6.

78. Finance Minister Antonio Ortiz Mena stated at the time of the sale that the government had not sought the transaction, but that it had been offered to it, and that it had never exerted the slightest pressure on the company to make the sale. *Excelsior*, July 1, 1967, p. 1.

79. For another account of the Mexicanization of the sulphur industry, see Miguel S. Wionczek, *El nacionalismo mexicano y la inversión extranjera* (Mexico, D.F.: Siglo Veintiuno Editores, 1967), pp. 171-309.

80. See, e.g., *New York Times*, Nov. 8, 1966, p. 55; *Barron's National Business and Financial Weekly*, Oct. 10, 1966, p. 1; *Wall Street Journal*, June 17, 1965, p. 1. But see Edmund K. Faltermayer, " 'We're Bullish on Mexico'," *Fortune*, Sept. 1965, p. 149.

81. The trend to associate with domestic investors was not limited to Mexico and was increasingly accepted by foreign investors in many capital-importing countries. See *Wall Street Journal*, Mar. 30, 1965, p. 1.

82. These amendments are discussed in Chapter III, p. 147.

83. The estimates for 1940 are based on figures published by Banco de México in its annual report for 1947, which should be taken with some caution (see note 55, above). U.S. Department of Commerce estimates, shown in table 7, place U.S. direct investment in manufacturing in 1940 at 10 percent of the total. The 1967 estimates in the text are based on U.S. Department of Commerce figures for U.S. direct investments (see table 7) but undoubtedly reflect the trend of investments from other countries as well. The director of Nacional Financiera, Alfredo Navarrete R., has estimated that 56 percent of total direct foreign investment in 1960 was in manufacturing and 20 percent in the traditional activities (above, n. 72), p. 1082, but subsequently foreign investment in electric power was eliminated and that in mining was reduced.

84. Navarrete (above, n. 72), p. 1104.

CHAPTER III

1. *Ley orgánica de la fracción I del artículo 27 de la constitución general,* 1925 (D.O., Jan. 21, 1926), art. 2; *Reglamento de la ley orgánica de la fracción I del artículo 27 de la constitución general de la república,* 1926 (D.O., Mar. 29, 1926), arts. 2-4, as amended by decree of Aug. 1, 1939 (D.O., Aug. 19, 1939).

The clause is also required in powers of attorney granted by foreigners for the acquisition of the property rights and concessions covered by art. 27 of the Constitution. Reservation made by Mexico to the *Protocolo sobre uniformidad del régimen legal de los poderes,* ratified by Mexico June 12, 1953 (D.O., Dec. 3, 1953), reproduced in Manuel Andrade, comp., *Nuevo código civil para el distrito y territorios federales* (Mexico, D.F.: Ediciones Andrade, loose-leaf), pp. 618-24. Execution of the Calvo clause is further specifically required for concessions for the use of federal waters, *Ley de aguas de propiedad nacional,* 1964 (D.O., Aug.

31, 1964), art. 9; *Reglamento de la ley de aguas de propiedad nacional,* 1936 (D.O., Apr. 21, 1936), art. 44, and for permits to engage in fishing, *Ley de pesca,* 1949 (D.O., Jan. 16, 1950), art. 6; *Reglamento de la ley de pesca,* 1933 (D.O., Feb. 1, 1933), arts. 19, 29.

2. *Ley de nacionalidad y naturalización,* 1934 (D.O., Jan. 20, 1934), art. 33; see also presidential accord, Apr. 30, 1926, quoted in Circular no. 294 of the Ministry of Finance and Public Credit, May 31, 1926, supplemented by presidential accord, July 28, 1926, quoted in Circular no. 318 of the Ministry of Finance and Public Credit, Aug. 28, 1926, both reproduced in Manuel Andrade, comp., *Constitución política mexicana* (Mexico, D.F.: Ediciones Andrade, looseleaf), pp. 255-58.

3. The most specific Calvo clause language found in Mexican law is contained in the two presidential accords cited in the note above, which shed light on the meaning of the more general language usually employed. The accord of April 30, 1926, requires the foreign contractor (or concessionaire) to agree that "for all purposes of this contract (or concession)" he will "be considered a Mexican, and that consequently he will not have, with respect to the validity, interpretation and performance of said contract, more rights or recourses than those that the Mexican laws grant to citizens of the Republic. Therefore, he renounces all rights he may have as a foreigner and he specially undertakes not to request, for anything relative to this contract (or concession), the diplomatic intervention of his country." The supplemental accord of July 28, 1926, provides that foreign members or shareholders of Mexican companies that contract with or obtain concessions from the government "shall be considered Mexicans in everything relating to the company," "may never allege, with respect to the shares or affairs related to the company, rights of alienage under any pretext," and "shall have only the rights and means of enforcing them that the laws of the Republic grant to Mexicans." For a discussion and analysis of various elements of the Calvo clause, see K. Lipstein, "The Place of the Calvo Clause in International Law," 22 *British Yearbook of International Law* 131-34 (1945).

4. For treatments of the historical evolution of diplomatic protection see Frederick S. Dunn, *The Protection of Nationals* (Baltimore: Johns Hopkins Press, 1932), especially pp. 53-66; and Edwin M. Borchard, *The Diplomatic Protection of Citizens Abroad* (New York: Banks Law Publishing Co., 1915), pp. 349-54.

In other underdeveloped areas, such as Asia, the Middle East, and parts of Africa, protection was afforded through the system of extraterritorial jurisdiction, whereby the alien remained under the jurisdiction and subject to the laws of his home state, rather than those of the foreign country. See Charles Cheney Hyde, *International Law Chiefly as Interpreted and Applied by the United States,* 2d ed. rev., 3 vols. (Boston: Little, Brown & Co., 1945), 2:849-71.

5. Emmeric de Vattel, *The Law of Nations,* trans. Charles C. Fenwick (Washington, D.C.: Carnegie Institution of Washington, 1916), 3:136, *The Classics of International Law,* 22 vols., ed. James Brown Scott.

6. For a review of early uses by Mexico of Calvo-clause type stipulations in contracts and concessions, pointing out that they were used at least as early as 1849, see Charles P. Howland, ed., *Survey of American Foreign Relations* (New Haven, Conn: Yale University Press, published for the Council on Foreign Relations, 1931), pp. 284-86. A good recent treatment, on which this section substantially relies, is Donald R. Shea, *The Calvo Clause* (Minneapolis: University of Minnesota Press, 1955).

7. Claims Commission, United States and Mexico, *Opinions of Commissioners under the Convention Concluded September 8, 1923, between the United States*

and Mexico, February 4, 1926 to July 23, 1927 (Washington, D.C.: GPO, 1927), 1:21-34. An extensive analysis of this decision and the decisions following it is contained in Shea (above, n. 6), pp. 194-257.

8. See note from Mexican Foreign Minister Saenz to U.S. Secretary of State Kellogg, October 7, 1926, U.S. Department of State, *American Property Rights in Mexico* (Washingon, D.C., 1926), p. 14. Article 32 of the *Ley de nacionalidad y naturalización,* 1934 (D.O., Jan. 20, 1934), provides in part: "They [foreigners] may appeal to diplomatic means only in cases of denial of justice or voluntary and notoriously malicious delay in its administration." See Shea (above, n. 6), pp. 33-61, for a summary of governmental positions on the Calvo clause.

9. The eminent legal scholar Charles Cheney Hyde has defended the right of the local government to rescind the contract in case of breach of the foreign grantee's agreement, "Concerning Attempts by Contract To Restrict Interposition," 21 *American Journal of International Law* 298-99 (1927).

10. *Decreto que establece la necesidad transitoria de obtener permiso para adquirir bienes a extranjeros, y para la constitución o modificación de sociedades mexicanas que tengan o tuvieren socios extranjeros,* 1944 (D.O., July 7, 1944), hereinafter cited as emergency decree of 1944.

11. The inflow of "refugee" capital also contributed to the inflation experienced by Mexico during the war. Sanford A. Mosk, *Industrial Revolution in Mexico* (Berkeley: University of California Press, 1954), pp. 275-76

12. Decree of June 1, 1942 (D.O., June 2, 1942).

13. Emergency decree of 1944, arts. 1 & 2.

14. Decree of Sept. 28, 1945 (D.O., Dec. 28, 1945), art. 1.

15. See Circular of the Consejo de Notarios del Distrito Federal, Feb. 17, 1945, quoting a ruling of the bureau of legal affairs of the Ministry of Foreign Relations to that effect, in Andrade (above, n. 2), p. 262 bis 4a. vta.

16. The requirement of a permit for the acquisition of real property and concessions is largely repetitious of the regulations to the law implementing article 27, section I, of the Constitution. That law and the application of the 1944 decree to acquisitions of real property are discussed in the next section of this chapter.

17. Emergency decree of 1944, art. 3 § I, provides that, except in cases of acquisition by inheritance, foreigners must have their principal source of business or investments in Mexico and a residence sufficient to evidence their settlement in the country. This is interpreted to require *inmigrado* or immigrant status, discussed in Chapter VI. See also the discussion in the section of this chapter on Real Property, p. 121.

18. Decree of May 29, 1947 (D.O., June 23, 1947). A representative of the Ministry of Communications and Public Works was added to the commission by decree of Dec. 1, 1949 (D.O., Apr. 3, 1950). Luis Creel Carrera, *México ante la inversión extranjera* (Thesis for Licenciado en Derecho, Escuela Libre de Derecho, 1966), p. 74, reports on the basis of information from a member of the commission that creation of the commission resulted largely from insistent requests from private Mexican interests, motivated by fear of competition, that the president adopt measures to restrict foreign investments.

19. The texts of these rulings were not generally available before April, 1968, when they were published, together with other legislation relating to foreign investment, by the Centro de Estudios Económicos del Sector Privado in *La legislación mexicana en materia de inversiones extranjeras.*

20. Secretaría de Relaciones Exteriores, Oficio no. 716074, Sept. 27, 1949, quoted in Circular of the Consejo de Notarios del Distrito Federal, Oct. 14, 1949, in Andrade (above, n. 2), p. 262 bis 8a.

21. The April, 1945, written instructions from the minister to the legal department of the ministry did not include the two last-named industries. These were added, apparently at the same time the written instructions were given or shortly thereafter, by verbal instructions from the minister.

22. On June 24, 1947, President Alemán instructed the ministry to continue to apply the rules it had theretofore been applying until the commission issued new rules.

23. As stated in the text, no publicity has been given when an industry has been added to the restricted list by policy decision. It is possible, therefore, to ascertain the existence of a restriction and the year in which it was adopted only by an examination of permits issued by the Ministry of Foreign Relations.

24. These requirements were established in the eleventh general ruling of the interministerial commission, adopted Feb. 6, 1951, reproduced in *Legislación mexicana* (above, n. 19), p. 36. The distinction between registered shares and bearer shares is discussed in Chapter VII under Capital Structure and Shares, p. 225. While voting rights of the majority shareholders may not be limited, as pointed out in Chapter VII under Rights and Protections of Shareholders, p. 237. quorum and voting requirements for shareholders and directors meetings may usually be increased above the statutory minimums so as to require the concurrence of minority shareholders.

25. Variable capital companies are discussed in Chapter VII, p. 228.

26. Ninth general ruling of the interministerial commission, adopted Mar. 24, 1949, reproduced in *Legislación mexicana* (above, n. 19), pp. 35-36.

27. Emergency decree of 1944, arts. 1(a) & 2 § III.

28. The legal department of the ministry has on at least one recent occasion ruled that a permit is not required for the acquisition by a foreign-controlled Mexican company of a minority interest in another Mexican company. Secretaría de Relaciones Exteriores, Dirección General de Asuntos Jurídicos, Oficio no. 704258, Exp. VII/567.1/113911, Mar. 18, 1966.

29. Probably the most forceful protest was a letter addressed to the president and various ministers by the Mexican bar association on July 12, 1955, "Carta dirigida por la Barra Mexicana al C. Presidente de la República," 11 & 12 *El Foro* (4th) 45 (1956), submitting a 1950 study made by F. Jorge Gaxiola, an eminent attorney and former president of the bar association, attacking the validity of the decree, "El artículo 27 constitucional y disposiciones reglamentarias," 11 & 12 *El Foro* (4th) 35 (1956).

30. See Carlos Minvielle M., *Intervención de la Secretaría de Relaciones Exteriores en las sociedades mercantiles* (Thesis for Licenciado en Derecho, Universidad Nacional Autónoma de México, 1960), pp. 60-64, citing an unpublished study of Roberto Mantilla Molina.

31. 66 S.J.F. (6th) 25 (3d pt.) (1963).

32. The *amparo* suit is discussed in Chapter I under Judicial Protection against Governmental Acts—The *Amparo*, p. 28.

33. This debate arose as a result of the 1960 amendment of art. 71 of the population law, decree of Dec. 29, 1960 (D.O., Dec. 30, 1960), and adoption of art. 14 of its regulations, *Reglamento de la ley general de población,* 1962 (D.O., May 3, 1962), requiring foreigners to obtain a permit from the Ministry of Internal Affairs for the acquisition of real property. The positions of the bar associations are reflected in communications of the Ilustre y Nacional Colegio de Abogados de México, the Colegio de Notarios del Distrito Federal, and the Barra Mexicana—Colegio de Abogados, and especially in a detailed study of Victor Manuel Ortega. The government position, at least that of the legal depart-

ment of the Ministry of Internal Affairs, is expressed in the reply of May 29, 1961, of the director of that department to the Ilustre y Nacional Colegio de Abogados. All of these communications are quoted in full in Enrique Sanabria Armendáriz, *El control de la Secretaría de Gobernación en la adquisición de bienes inmuebles por extranjeros* (Thesis for Licenciado en Derecho, Universidad Nacional Autónoma de México, 1966), pp. 56-94. The commentaries of the Barra Mexicana were also published in that association's periodical, 33 *El Foro* (4th) 13 (1961). See also José Luis Siqueiros P., *Las sociedades extranjeras en México* (Mexico, D. F.: Imprenta Universitaria, 1953), pp. 143-44.

34. The Ministry of Foreign Relations is authorized to permit acquisitions by inheritance and acquisitions by judicial decree based on pre-existing rights acquired in good faith, but the property must be conveyed to a qualified person within a period not exceeding five years, usually two years. *Ley orgánica de la fracción I del artículo 27 de la constitución general,* 1925 (D.O., Jan. 21, 1926), art. 6, hereafter in this section cited as organic law of article 27; *Reglamento da la ley orgánica de la fracción I del artículo 27 de la constitución general de la república,* 1926 (D.O., Mar. 29, 1926), art. 11, hereafter in this section cited as regulations to organic law of article 27. Foreign colonizers are also permitted to acquire land in the prohibited zone under certain conditions. Ibid., art. 17.

35. Organic law of article 27, art. 1; regulations to organic law of article 27, arts. 1, 8, as amended by decree of Aug. 1, 1939 (D.O., Aug. 19, 1939). This prohibition must also be contained in the company's articles of incorporation and stock certificates. Ibid., art. 8.

36. Prohibitions against foreign ownership of land in border and coastal states were contained, for example, in the following laws: decree of Aug. 18, 1824, art. 4, Manuel Dublán and José Maria Lozano, *Legislación mexicana o colección completa de las disposiciones legislativas expedidas desde la independencia de la república,* 34 vols. (Mexico, D.F.: Imprenta del Comercio, á cargo de Dublán y Lozano, hijos, 1876-1904), 1:712; decree of Mar. 11, 1842, arts. 9, 10, in ibid., 4:130-32; decree of Feb. 1, 1856, art. 2, in ibid., 8:95; *Ley sobre ocupación y enajenación de terrenos baldíos,* July 20, 1863, art. 2, in ibid., 9:637.

37. Organic law of article 27, art. 8; regulations to organic law of article 27, arts. 8, 16.

38. Emergency decree of 1944, arts. 5, 7.

39. Emergency decree of 1944, art. 1(d).

40. Regulations to organic law of article 27, art. 1, as amended by decree of Aug. 1, 1939 (D.O., Aug. 19, 1939).

41. Emergency decree of 1944, art. 6.

42. Regulations to organic law of article 27, art. 8, requires an agreement that "no foreign person, individual or legal entity, may have any participation or be a shareholder in the company." Permits of the ministry have at times provided that "no foreign person, individual or legal entity, *as well as Mexican companies that do not have a clause of exclusion of foreigners authorized by the Ministry of Foreign Relations,* may have any participation or be a shareholder in the company." (Italics added.) The wording of the regulations has appeared in the ministry's permits since about August, 1966.

43. There is a conflict in the law on this point. Emergency decree of 1944, art. 1, and *Ley de nacionalidad y naturalización,* 1934 (D.O., Jan. 20, 1934), art. 49, both provide that a lease of *more than ten years* is considered an acquisition. A 1930 ruling of the Ministry of Foreign Relations, still followed by the ministry, states that permits are required for leases of *ten years or more.* Secretaría de Relaciones, Oficio no. 1811, Exp. IIIA/567.7(04) (S-4)/1, Feb. 6, 1930, re-

produced in Andrade (above, n. 2), p. 260. Some attorneys cautiously provide terms of slightly less than ten years.

44. Secretaría de Relaciones Exteriores, Dirección General de Asuntos Jurídicos, Oficio no. 7-3600, Exp. VII/025/287772, Mar. 17, 1967, reproduced in full in the Asociación de Banqueros de México's Circular no. 1142, Apr. 4, 1967. Under this resolution trust institutions may act as trustees even though they are permitted by the terms of their articles of incorporation to have foreign shareholders, provided their articles have been amended to prohibit stock ownership by foreign governments or official agencies, foreign financial entities and groups of foreign individuals or legal entities, as required by the *Ley general de instituciones de crédito y organizaciones auxiliares,* 1941 (D.O., May 31, 1941), art. 8 § II bis, as amended by decree of Dec. 27, 1965 (D.O., Dec. 30, 1965), discussed below under Banking, Finance, and Insurance, p. 145. Under the emergency decree of 1944, art. 1, trust agreements covering land in the prohibited zone under which the beneficiary is a foreigner or a Mexican company permitted to have foreign owners are considered acquisitions and require a permit. The execution of such agreements was at one time authorized, and some land titles in the prohibited zone are still held in trust for foreign beneficiaries, but the practice of issuing those permits was discontinued in the early 1950's.

45. Trusts under which the beneficiary is a legal entity may not exceed a term of thirty years. *Ley general de títulos y operaciones de crédito,* 1932 (D.O., Aug. 27, 1932), art. 359 § III, as amended by decree of Apr. 11, 1945 (D.O., May 8, 1945).

46. The requirement that a foreigner who acquires an interest in a Mexican company that owns land must agree to the terms of the Calvo clause and that such a company must obtain a permit for the acquisition of land is not expressly stated in article 27 of the Constitution, but it is clearly imposed by the organic law of article 27, art. 2, and regulations to organic law of article 27, arts. 2 & 3, as amended by decree of Aug. 1, 1939 (D.O., Aug. 19, 1939), and was amplified by the emergency decree of 1944, art. 1. Notaries and other officials are required, under threat of severe penalties, to insert these permits in instruments of conveyance that they authorize or record. Regulations to organic law of article 27, art. 3; emergency decree of 1944, art. 6.

47. Emergency decree of 1944, art. 3.

48. Ninth general ruling of the interministerial commission, adopted Mar. 24, 1949, reproduced in *Legislación mexicana* (above, n. 19), pp. 35-36.

49. Constitution, art. 27, 6th para., § IV.

50. *Código agrario de los Estados Unidos Mexicanos,* 1943 (D.O., Apr. 27, 1943), arts. 138-40, hereinafter cited as Agrarian Code.

51. Agrarian Code, arts. 146, 278-81.

52. *Reglamento para la planificación, control y vigilancia de las inversiones de los fondos comunes ejidales,* 1959 (D.O., Apr. 23, 1959), art. 16. This requirement was adopted in order to put a stop to the practice of acquiring suburban *ejido* land through exchange and subdividing at a huge profit for residential or commercial purposes.

53. The provisions governing expropriation are contained in arts. 187-95 and 286-91 of the Agrarian Code. A request for expropriation is made to the agrarian department either by the interested private person or, preferably, by the government of the state in which the land is located. In addition to the agrarian department, the following officials and agencies must approve or at least give an opinion on the request before it goes to the president: state governor, Ministry of Agriculture, Banco Nacional de Crédito Ejidal *(ejido* credit bank), Cuerpo Con-

sultivo Agrario (agrarian consultation group), and Comité Técnico y de Inversión de Fondos of the Fondo Nacional de Fomento Ejidal (technical and investment committee of the *ejido* development fund). Agrarian Code, arts. 287-88; *Reglamento para la planificación* (above, n. 52), art. 11. Appraisals to establish the amount of compensation are made by the Ministry of National Properties. In some instances it is possible to obtain possession of the land even before the expropriation is formally decreed, subject, of course, to final approval.

54. See Siqueiros (above, n. 33), pp. 143-46, and authorities there cited. This interpretation would seem to make art. 34 of the *Ley de nacionalidad y naturalización, 1934* (D.O., Jan. 20, 1934), superfluous: "Foreign legal entities may not acquire ownership of lands, waters and their accessions, or obtain concessions for the exploitation of mines, waters or combustible minerals in the Mexican Republic, *except in those cases in which the laws expressly so provide.*" (Italics added.)

55. See note 34 above.

56. Constitution, art. 27, 6th para, § I; regulations to organic law of article 27, art. 3; emergency decree of 1944, arts. 1, 3.

57. *Ley general de población, 1947* (D.O., Dec. 27, 1947), art. 71, as amended by decree of Dec. 29, 1960 (D.O., Dec. 30, 1960), hereinafter cited as population law. The debate over this amendment is discussed in the text at note 33.

58. *Reglamento de la ley general de población, 1962* (D.O., May 3, 1962), art. 14 § A VII, hereinafter cited as regulations to population law.

59. The status of foreigners is discussed in Chapter VI. Under a 1934 presidential accord, permits to acquire real property are denied to persons born in Mexico of foreign parents and who have not acquired Mexican citizenship and women who have lost their Mexican citizenship by marriage to a foreigner, since those persons have the right to acquire Mexican nationality. Accord of Dec. 24, 1934, reproduced in Andrade, (above, n. 2), p. 261.

60. Emergency decree of 1944, art. 3 § Ia.

61. First general ruling of the interministerial commission, adopted Sept. 3, 1947, reproduced in *Legislación mexicana* (above, n. 19), p. 31.

62. Regulations to population law, art. 14 § A IV. Although the ministry "has the power to impose limitations on the activities of *inmigrados,*" ibid., art. 67 § I, the restrictions normally imposed would not concern most investors; they relate to such activities as gambling establishments and houses of ill repute.

63. Regulations to population law, art. 14 § A III: "They [immigrants] may also be authorized to acquire other real properties, shares or real rights, provided such transactions do not contradict their immigration status."

64. Regulations to population law, art. 14 § A I; emergency decree of 1944, art. 3 § Ia. Permits may be issued by the Ministry of Internal Affairs "in exceptional cases" to political refugees and students, who are classified as non-immigrants, ibid., art. 14 § A II, but in practice neither ministry issues permits to students.

65. First general ruling of the interministerial commission, adopted Sept. 3, 1947, reproduced in *Legislación mexicana* (above, n. 19), p. 31.

66. Regulations to population law, art. 14 § A I.

67. Regulations to population law, art. 14 § A V, provides that the Ministry of Internal Affairs may issue a permit to formalize an acquisition "when for reasons beyond the control of the foreigner property rights are created in his favor in real properties or shares or real rights," with the requirements "that it considers appropriate in accordance with the general interest." The Ministry of Foreign Relations is authorized to grant a permit for the acquisition by inheritance of property rights with the condition that they be conveyed to a qualified person

within five years, but in practice conveyance within two years is usually required. Organic law of article 27, art. 6; regulations to organic law of article 27, art. 11. Emergency decree of 1944, art. 3 § Ia, also makes an exception for acquisition by inheritance.

68. Regulations to organic law of article 27, art. 3; emergency decree of 1944, arts. 5, 6.

69. Regulations to population law, art. 14 § B I.

70. Population law, art. 109.

71. Secretaría de Gobernación, Dirección General de Asuntos Jurídicos, Oficio no. 1462, Sept. 24, 1962, quoted in Creel Carrera (above, n. 18), p. 118.

72. Constitution, art. 27, 6th para., § IV. This prohibition was incorporated in the Constitution of 1917 to put an end to violations of the laws of the reform prohibiting ownership of land by the Church through the use of companies whose shareholders were anonymous and to prevent the use of such companies by foreigners and Mexican landowners to conceal the real ownership of land. Pastor Rouaix, *Génesis de los artículos 27 y 123 de la constitución política de 1917*, 2d ed. (Mexico, D.F.: Instituto Nacional de Estudios Históricos de la Revolución Mexicana, 1959), pp. 157-58. The constitutional prohibition would seem to render meaningless art. 7, § II, of the regulations to organic law of article 27, as amended by decree of Aug. 1, 1939 (D.O., Aug. 19, 1939), requiring stock companies incorporated for the purpose of acquiring rural property for agricultural use to issue only registered shares.

73. The various types of Mexican business associations are discussed in Chapter VII.

74. Organic law of article 27, art. 3; regulations to organic law of article 27, art. 7 § I.

75. The maximum areas of land and improvements protected against expropriation are set out in Constitution, art. 27 § XV, as amended by decree of Dec. 31, 1946 (D.O., Feb. 12, 1947); Agrarian Code, arts. 104-14; *Reglamento de inafectabilidad agrícola y ganadera*, 1948 (D.O., Oct. 9, 1948), arts. 1-5. A discussion of these provisions is found in Lucio Mendieta y Núñez, *El problema agrario de México*, 6th ed. (Mexico, D.F.: Editorial Porrúa, 1959), pp. 235-42, 361-86.

76. *Reglamento de inafectabilidad* (above, n. 75), arts. 9-41. Foreign applicants for inaffectability must establish that they are registered in the Registro Nacional de Extranjeros (national register of aliens) of the Ministry of Internal Affairs and that they have the necessary permit to acquire the land from the Ministry of Foreign Relations. Ibid., art. 16.

77. Ibid., arts. 42-47. Major livestock includes cattle and horses; minor livestock includes sheep, goats, and pigs.

78. Agrarian Code, arts. 115-26, 295-301; *Reglamento de inafectabilidad* (above, n. 75), arts. 8, 48-97.

79. Petróleos Mexicanos was created and its functions established by decree of June 7, 1938 (D.O., July 20, 1938), amended several times, most recently by decree of Dec. 30, 1952 (D.O., Dec. 31, 1952).

80. Constitution, art. 27, 6th para., as amended by decree of Dec. 27, 1939 (D.O., Nov. 9, 1940).

81. *Ley reglamentaria del artículo 27 constitucional, en el ramo del petróleo*, 1925 (D.O., Dec. 31, 1925), art. 14, as amended by decree of Jan. 3, 1928 (D.O., Jan. 10, 1928).

82. *Ley reglamentaria del artículo 27 en el ramo de petróleo*, 1941 (D.O., June 18, 1941), trans. art. 1.

83. *Ley reglamentaria del artículo 27 constitucional en el ramo del petróleo,* 1958 (D.O., Nov. 29, 1958), trans. art. 1, hereinafter cited as petroleum law.

84. Constitution, art. 27, 6th para., as amended by decree of Jan. 6, 1960 (D.O., Jan. 20, 1960).

85. Petroleum law, arts. 2-4; *Reglamento de la ley reglamentaria del artículo 27 constitucional en el ramo del petróleo,* 1959 (D.O., Aug. 25, 1959), art. 3, hereinafter cited as regulations to petroleum law.

86. Petroleum law, art. 6.

87. Regulations to petroleum law, arts. 31-35.

88. Ibid., art. 25.

89. *Reglamento de la distribución de gas,* 1960 (D.O., Mar. 29, 1960), arts. 7, 8, 10.

90. *Ley reglamentaria . . . del petróleo* (above, n. 83) art. 3.

91. *Reglamento de la ley reglamentaria . . . del petróleo* (above, n. 85).

92. Accord of Jan. 13, 1960 (D.O., Apr. 9, 1960).

93. On the legal concepts of the nature of the state's rights in the subsoil, see Marvin D. Bernstein, *The Mexican Mining Industry, 1890-1950* (Albany: State University of New York, 1965), pp. 150-52; Fernando González Roa, *Las cuestiones fundamentales de actualidad en México* (Mexico, D.F.: Imprenta de la Secretaría de Relaciones Exteriores, 1927), p. 38; Oscar Morineau, *Los derechos reales y el subsuelo en México* (Mexico, D.F.: Gráfica Panamericana, 1948), pp. 251-71; Alberto Vásquez del Mercado, *Concesión minera y derechos reales* (Mexico, D.F.: Porrúa Hnos. y Cía, 1946), pp. 9-11.

94. Constitution, art. 27, 4th & 6th paras.

95. For a brief historical review of the mining laws see José Campillo Sainz, "Los recursos naturales no renovables," in *México: Cincuenta años de revolución,* Vol. I, *La economía* (Mexico, D.F.: Fondo de Cultura Económica, 1960), pp. 78-81. See also Chapter II at p. 55.

96. *Ley de industrias mineras,* 21 *Boletín Minero* 325-43 (1926). For a good summary see E. M. Burton, "Provisions of the Mexican Mining Law of 1926," 123 *Engineering & Mining Journal* 486-87 (1927). The reaction to this law is discussed in Bernstein (above, n. 93), pp. 152-55.

97. *Ley minera de los Estados Unidos Mexicanos,* 1930 (D.O., Aug. 30, 1930). The implementing regulations were *Reglamento de la ley minera de los Estados Unidos Mexicanos,* 1930 (D.O., Oct. 18, 1930). The law is summarized in Frederick F. Barker, "Mexican Mining Concessions," 5 *Southern California Law Review* 1 (1931).

98. *Ley reglamentaria del artículo 27 constitucional en materia de explotación y aprovechamiento de recursos minerales,* 1961 (D.O., Feb. 6, 1961), as amended by decree of Dec. 29, 1965 (D.O., Jan. 4, 1966), hereinafter cited as mining law. The first implementing regulations were issued Feb. 26, 1962, but were replaced by the 1966 regulations, *Reglamento de la ley reglamentaria del artículo 27 constitucional en materia de explotación y aprovechamiento de recursos minerales* (D.O., Dec. 7, 1966), hereinafter cited as regulations to mining law.

99. Mining law, art. 1; regulations to mining law, arts. 1, 2, 4.

100. Mining law, art. 2.

101. Ibid., art. 4; regulations to mining law, arts. 43-56.

102. Mining law, art. 5.

103. On the acquisition of the sulphur companies, see Chapter II, beginning at p. 87. Perhaps the most important association in a new company has been Azufres Nacionales Mexicanos, S.A., 66 percent owned by the government and private Mexican investors and 34 percent owned by a Canadian company.

104. Mining law, arts. 6, 10, 12.

105. Ibid., arts. 24-49; regulations to mining law, arts. 57-149.

106. Mining law, arts. 50-58; regulations to mining law, arts. 150-73.

107. Mining law, arts. 71-75; regulations to mining law, arts. 214-16.

108. Decrees incorporating minerals and zones into the national mining reserves are required to be published in the *Diario Oficial*. Regulations to mining law, art. 214. Decrees of disincorporation are also published. These decrees are compiled in Manuel Andrade, comp., *Leyes y reglamentos sobre aguas, bosques, colonización, minas y petróleo* (Mexico, D.F.: Ediciones Andrade, loose-leaf), p. 643 *et seq.*

109. Mining law, arts. 76-83; regulations to mining law, arts. 217-23.

110. The forms of business association under Mexican law are discussed in Chapter VII.

111. Regulations to mining law, art. 29.

112. Mining law, art. 8; regulations to mining law, art. 30.

113. Mining law, arts. 46 § IV, 57 § III; regulations to mining law, art. 149.

114. Mining law, art. 109 § VII.

115. Ibid., trans. art. 1.

116. *Ley de impuestos y fomento a la minería*, 1955 (D.O., Dec. 31, 1955), arts. 52, 56, as amended by decree of Jan. 3, 1961 (D.O., Feb. 6, 1961); regulations to mining law, art. 279, trans. art. 1.

117. See statement of Eduardo Bustamante, minister of national properties, reported in *Excelsior*, Dec. 11, 1963, p. 1.

118. *Ley forestal*, 1960 (D.O., Jan. 16, 1960), hereinafter cited as forestry law; *Reglamento de la ley forestal*, 1960 (D.O., Jan. 23, 1961), hereinafter cited as regulations to forestry law.

119. In September, 1965, a commission was created to revise the law, and its work lasted over a year. The draft of new law was published in *Excelsior*, July 17 and 18, 1967. The draft was opposed by the Confederación Nacional Campesina, *Excelsior*, Aug. 10, 1967, p. 1, and as of this writing no further action seems to have been taken.

120. Forestry law, arts. 1, 6.

121. Regulations to forestry law, art. 198. General rules on exploitation are contained in arts. 84-93 of the forestry law.

122. The forms of business association provided for by Mexican law and the distinction between associations of persons and associations of capital are discussed in Chapter VII.

123. This announcement was made by Noé Palomares Navarro, subsecretary for forestry and fauna of the Ministry of Agriculture, and was reported in *Excelsior*, Aug. 6, 1966, p. 1.

124. The constitutional arguments are found in Creel Carrera (above, n. 18), pp. 95-97.

125. *Ley de pesca*, 1950 (D.O., Jan. 16, 1950), art. 3. Regulations have not been issued since the enactment of this law, and the applicable regulations are those issued under the prior law, *Reglamento de la ley de pesca*, 1933 (D.O., Feb. 1, 1933). The federal government has exclusive legislative jurisdiction in matters relating to fishing by virtue of the constitutional delegation of power to Congress to issue laws on the use of waters of federal jurisdiction. Constitution, art. 73 § XVII.

126. *Ley de pesca* (above, n. 125), art. 21.

127. The requirement of citizenship by birth is probably in violation of art. 27,

8th para., § 1 of the Constitution, which provides that Mexicans by birth or by naturalization have capacity to obtain concessions for the exploitation of waters.

128. *Ley de vías generales de comunicación,* 1940 (D.O., Feb. 19, 1940), art. 8, as amended by decree of Mar. 29, 1941 (D.O., Aug. 20, 1941).

129. Ibid., art. 1.

130. Ibid., arts. 152 § I, 166, as amended by decree of Dec. 31, 1947 (D.O., Jan. 9, 1948).

131. Ibid., art. 313.

132. *Ley de navegación y comercio marítimos,* 1963 (D.O., Nov. 21, 1963).

133. *Ley federal de radio y televisión,* 1960 (D.O., Jan. 19, 1960), art. 4. Art. 1 of the law recites that "there belongs to the nation the direct dominion of its territorial space and, consequently, of the medium in which electromagnetic waves are transmitted. Said dominion is inalienable and imprescriptible."

134. Ibid., arts. 13, 14, 25.

135. Ibid., arts. 24, 31 § IV.

136. Ibid., arts. 23, 26, 27, 31 § IV, 33.

137. Constitution, art. 27, 6th para., as amended by decree of Jan. 6, 1960 (D.O., Jan. 20, 1960), and decree of Dec. 23, 1960 (D.O., Dec. 29, 1960). The acquisition of the electric utilities is discussed in Chapter II, beginning at p. 80.

138. *Ley de la industria eléctrica,* 1939 (D.O., Feb. 11, 1939), art. 6.

139. *Ley general de instituciones de crédito y organizaciones auxiliares,* 1941 (D.O., May 31, 1941).

140. Ibid., arts. 2, 8.

141. Ibid., arts. 5, 147.

142. Ibid., arts. 3, 47.

143. Ibid., arts. 6, 7.

144. *Ley de sociedades de inversión,* 1955 (D.O., Dec. 31, 1955).

145. Ibid., arts. 2, 3.

146. *Ley federal de instituciones de fianzas,* 1950 (D.O., Dec. 29, 1950), arts. 1, 3.

147. *Ley general de instituciones de seguros,* 1935 (D.O., Aug. 26, 1935), art. 1.

148. Ibid., art. 7.

149. Ibid., art. 5.

150. Ibid., art. 3.

151. The amendments were published in the *Diario Oficial* of Dec. 30, 1965, and became effective the following day. The articles amended or added are: *Ley general de instituciones de crédito* (above, n. 139), arts. 8 § II bis, 100 § III, 153 bis 2; *Ley de sociedades de inversión* (above, n. 144), arts. 2 § II bis, 17 § II bis, 19; *Ley federal de instituciones de fianzas* (above, n. 146), arts. 3, 104 § II, 111 bis; *Ley general de instituciones de seguros* (above, n. 147), arts. 13 § XII, 17 § I, 139 bis.

152. It does not seem that both penalties may be imposed for a single violation. The chapter on sanctions of each of the laws was amended to provide for forfeiture of the interest concerned to the federal government *or* revocation of the company's concession or authorization, "in the judgment of the Ministry of Finance and Public Credit, and according to the gravity of the case."

153. *Excelsior,* Dec. 11, 1965, p. 1; see *Wall Street Journal,* Dec. 13, 1965, p. 4. Although foreign investment in banking and investment and bonding companies is small, private Mexican insurance men charged that foreign insurance companies had in recent years acquired a majority of the shares of some

Mexican companies, using strawmen and taking advantage of special or difficult situations of those companies. *Excelsior,* Dec. 17, 1965, p. 1.

154. This was also suggested by the president of the Mexican bankers association. *Excelsior,* Dec. 12, 1965, p. 1.

155. Decree of June 30, 1970 (D.O., July 2, 1970).

CHAPTER IV

1. The views of CONCANACO during this period are found in its publication, *Problemas derivados de la intervención del estado en la economía* (Mexico, D.F., 1946). The best description of the evolving ideologies of the Mexican business community as expressed through the major trade associations is Raymond Vernon, *The Dilemma of Mexico's Development* (Cambridge, Mass.: Harvard University Press, 1963), pp. 163-75.

2. For CNIT's position in the words of its principal spokesman, see José Domingo Lavín, *Inversiones extranjeras* (Mexico, D.F.: Edición y Distribución Ibero Americano de Publicaciones, 1954).

3. See Vernon (above, n. 1), pp. 113-15, 144-45, 148.

4. With respect to the argument that foreign investment has been bad for the Mexican balance of payments because the annual flow of dividends, interest, and royalty payments to foreign investors has usually outweighed the annual flow of new capital into Mexico, Raymond Vernon, for one, has pointed out that the full balance-of-payments effects of foreign investments have been much more complicated and that these investments have contributed to import replacement and to the increase in exports of Mexican manufactured products. See his "An Interpretation of the Mexican View," in Raymond Vernon, ed., *How Latin America Views the U.S. Investor* (New York: Frederick A. Praeger, published in co-operation with the Harvard University Graduate School of Business Administration, 1966), pp. 110-11.

5. See CONCANACO, *Carta semanal,* Sept. 24, 1955, p. 7.

6. One of the conclusions adopted at the Fifth National Congress of Industrialists, sponsored by CONCAMIN, Feb. 19-21, 1964, was: "Foreign capital should be complementary of domestic capital and can be accepted, including in association with Mexican capital, without privileges or discriminations provided it is investment which tends effectively to join with our interests and to contribute to the economic development of the country." Although CNIT took vigorous issue with some of the congress' conclusions, its only comment on that conclusion was that it reflected a position which, in part, coincided with its own earlier position. See Cámara Nacional de la Industria de Transformación, *La CNIT frente a la problemática del desarrollo económico de México,* 2d ed. (Mexico, D.F.: CNIT, 1966), pp. 32, 94. See also for the CNIT position during this period, José Domingo Lavín, "Revisión del problema de las inversiones extranjeras directas," *Ciencias Políticas y Sociales,* Oct.-Dec. 1959, pp. 545-64. In the early 1960's José Domingo Lavín lost some of his effectiveness as the main spokesman for CNIT by selling a major interest in his Mexican chemical company to Dow Chemical Company.

7. See the discussion of the emergency decree of June 29, 1944, in Chapter III, p. 101. As pointed out there, these industries were removed from the restricted list in 1965 and 1966.

8. See the discussion of import controls in Chapter V, p. 164.

9. The industrial integration policy is discussed in Chapter V, p. 170.

10. In June, 1965, Minister of Industry and Commerce Octaviano Campos

Salas stated in an interview: "The preparation of a detailed statute on foreign investments has not been considered. The approval of investments on which there does not exist a specific legal provision is subject to general guidelines, but the cases are so diverse that the solutions must be casuistic within those guidelines." Octaviano Campos Salas, *El sentido dinámico de el México económico de nuestros días (1965)* (Mexico, D.F.: Selección de Estudios Latinoamericanos, 1965), p. 39. For a recent statement of the government's policy that foreign investors should associate with Mexican capital, see Octaviano Campos Salas, *El sentido dinámico de el México económico de nuestros días (1968)* (Mexico, D.F.: Selección de Estudios Latinoamericanos, 1968), pp. 76-77.

11. See the discussion of the border industrialization program in Chapter V, p. 191.

12. See Chapter III under The Emergency Decree of June 29, 1944, p. 104.

13. John C. Shearer, *High-Level Manpower in Overseas Subsidiaries* (Princeton, N.J.: Industrial Relations Section, Princeton University, 1960), pp. 129-30, 133, found that foreign companies in Mexico and Brazil that used nationals for their managerial positions were doing much better than firms that were fully manned from abroad.

14. In an interview in October, 1967, Minister of Industry and Commerce Campos Salas stated that he had not been informed of a single case in which a foreign enterprise failed to enter the country because it did not find a Mexican group with which to associate. See Campos Salas, *México económico (1968)* (above, n. 10), pp. 90-91.

CHAPTER V

1. An excellent study of import policy, upon which this section relies heavily, is Rafael Izquierdo, "Protectionism in Mexico," in Raymond Vernon, ed., *Public Policy and Private Enterprise in Mexico* (Cambridge, Mass.: Harvard University Press, 1964), pp. 241-89. For an earlier discussion of protectionism, see Sanford A. Mosk, *Industrial Revolution in Mexico* (Berkeley: University of California Press, 1954), pp. 67-83.

2. An important exception is made for plants established on the northern border under the border industrialization program, discussed below in this chapter p. 191. Since about 1966, the government has also occasionally permitted the establishment of plants for the production of goods exclusively for export from imported raw materials and semimanufactures where the finished products would not be internationally competitive in price if domestic materials were used.

3. Constitution, art. 131, as amended by decree of Dec. 30, 1950 (D.O., Mar. 28, 1951).

4. *Ley reglamentaria del párrafo segundo del artículo 131 de la constitución política de los Estados Unidos Mexicanos,* 1961 (D.O., Jan. 5, 1961).

5. *Ley sobre atribuciones del ejecutivo federal en materia económica,* 1950 (D.O., Dec. 30, 1950), art. 9. This law is discussed later in this chapter under Price Control, p. 176.

6. *Ley de secretarías y departamentos de estado,* 1958 (D.O., Dec. 24, 1958), art. 8 § III.

7. Decree of Mar. 22, 1948 (D.O., Apr. 26, 1948).

8. *Tarifa del impuesto general de importación,* 1964 (D.O., Nov. 10, 1964). The tariff is published privately with a loose-leaf service by Información Aduanera de México, S.A.

9. See, e.g., the revenue law for 1969, *Ley de ingresos de la federación para el*

ejercicio fiscal de 1969, 1968 (D.O., Dec. 31, 1968), art. 1 § X(4). Under that law the additional duty applied to over 2,100 product classifications, listed in art. 17. Imports from members of LAFTA were exempt.

10. This is discussed below under Tax Exemptions, p. 181. A subsidy of 50 or 75 percent of the duties may also be granted for the importation of machinery and equipment under rule 14 of the general rules of the general import tariff.

11. The import-licensing system was adopted in 1944 but was first applied in July, 1947. See Izquierdo (above, n. 1), pp. 263-65.

12. *Reglamento para la expedición de permisos de importación de mercancías sujetas a restricciones,* 1956 (D.O., Nov. 28, 1956).

13. Izquierdo (above, n. 1), p. 257, states that committee recommendations were apparently adopted on very few occasions during the 1955-58 period. In 1967, however, the writer was informed by an official of the Ministry of Industry and Commerce that 90 percent of the committee recommendations were being followed.

14. For a discussion of the evolution of Mexico's import policy, pointing out the need to extend import replacement to intermediate products, see Izquierdo (above, n. 1), esp. pp. 261-76, 286-89.

15. See ibid., pp. 271-73.

16. Decree of Aug. 23, 1962 (D.O., Aug. 25, 1962).

17. The companies were General Motors, Ford, Chrysler-affiliate Fábricas Automex, S.A., Volkswagen, government-controlled Diesel Nacional, S.A. (making Renaults), Vehículos Automotores Mexicanos, S.A. (making Jeeps and Ramblers), Auto Union DKW, and Fábrica Nacional de Automóviles, S.A. (making Borgwards). Subsequently, Auto Union DKW withdrew, and the Japanese company, Nissan, was admitted to make Datsuns.

18. See Edgar Molina, "Automotive Industry Integration under Government Decree," in American Management Association, International Management Division, *Doing Business in Mexico: Prospects in a Growing Market* (Management Bulletin 57, 1964), p. 20.

19. This law is discussed below under Tax Exemptions, p. 181.

20. *Ley sobre atribuciones del ejecutivo federal en materia económica,* 1950 (D.O., Dec. 30, 1950), as amended by decree of Feb. 10, 1959 (D.O., Mar. 6, 1959), hereafter in this chapter cited as law on economic powers. The regulations to the law are the *Reglamento de los artículos 2, 3, 4, 8, 11, 13, 14, 16 a 20 de la ley sobre atribuciones al ejecutivo federal en materia económica,* 1951 (D.O., Jan. 10, 1951), as amended by decree of Feb. 27, 1951 (D.O., Mar. 2, 1951), hereafter in this chapter cited as regulations to law on economic powers. The law, regulations, and most decrees issued under it are collected in Manuel Andrade, comp., *Constitución política mexicana* (Mexico, D.F.: Ediciones Andrade, looseleaf), pp. 198 bis 33a to 198 bis 51.

21. Andrés Serra Rojas, *Derecho administrativo,* 3d ed. (Mexico, D.F.: Librería de Manuel Porrúa, 1965), p. 941.

22. The preamble sets out the purposes of the law at some length. It has been claimed that there was a political motive as well, to demonstrate government concern for the rising cost of living and to place responsibility for it on existing world economic conditions beyond the government's control. See Gustavo R. Velasco, *Libertad y abundancia* (Mexico, D.F.: Editorial Porrúa, 1958), p. 214.

23. Law on economic powers, art. 1.

24. Ibid., arts. 8, 12. The broad authority under the law to require production of certain goods is somewhat restricted by the regulations; the product must be one that is ordinarily manufactured by the enterprise and it must be scarce, not

produced in sufficient quantity, or not possible to import in necessary amounts. Regulations to law on economic powers, art. 10.

25. Law on economic powers, arts. 18, 19. Under art. 18, authority to fix prices was originally exercisable only by the president, and the Supreme Court has established binding precedent that maximum prices established by the director of prices of the Ministry of Industry and Commerce under a 1951 delegation of authority by the minister are invalid. *Informe rendido a la Suprema Corte de Justicia de la Nación . . . 1963* (Mexico, D.F.: Antigua Imprenta de Murguía, 1963), Anexo . . . de la Segunda Sala, p. 19. The 1959 amendments to the law changed art. 18 to give price-control authority also to the minister of industry and commerce (then minister of economy). The *Ley de secretarías y departamentos de estado* (law of state ministries and departments), 1958 (D.O., Dec. 24, 1958), art. 8 § IV, also gives price-fixing authority to the Ministry of Industry and Commerce.

26. Law on economic powers, art. 13.

27. The original decree is the decree of Jan. 2, 1951 (D.O., Jan. 4, 1951); this was amended or supplemented by decrees of Feb. 13, 1951 (D.O., Feb. 14, 1951), Mar. 27, 1951 (D.O., Apr. 5, 1951), Sept. 11, 1951 (D.O., Sept. 13, 1951), Dec. 19, 1951 (D.O., Jan. 10, 1952), Mar. 25, 1965 (D.O., Apr. 22, 1965), June 17, 1965 (D.O., June 19, 1965), Oct. 11, 1966 (D.O., Oct. 22, 1966), Dec. 5, 1967 (D.O., Dec. 27, 1967).

28. See regulations to law on economic powers, arts. 1-5.

29. Regulations to law on economic powers, arts. 17-20 (national price commission), art. 21 (special committees), art. 22 (local price and distribution committees). Regulations for the two types of committees were issued by the ministry in 1951: *Reglamento para los comités especiales a que se refiere el artículo 21 del reglamento de la ley sobre atribuciones del ejecutivo federal en materia económica,* 1951 (D.O., Jan. 26, 1951); *Reglamento de los comités de precios y distribución, a que se refiere el artículo 22 del reglamento de la ley sobre atribuciones del ejecutivo federal en materia económica,* 1951 (D.O., Feb. 21, 1951).

30. Velasco (above, n. 22), p. 120.

31. See ibid., pp. 121-23; Fernando Cervantes Conde, *La libre concurrencia y el control de precios en el régimen constitucional mexicano* (Thesis for Licenciado en Derecho, Escuela Libre de Derecho, 1966), pp. 123-25.

32. The more important decisions are collected in Francisco Barrutieta Mayo, *Jurisprudencia y tésis sobresalientes de la Suprema Corte de Justicia de la Nación, 1955-1963, sustentadas por la sala administrativa* (Mexico, D.F.: Mayo Ediciones, 1965), pp. 714-19. See also *Cía. Embotelladora Nacional, S.A.,* 38 S.J.F. (6th) 88 (3d pt.) (1960).

33. *Ley de fomento de industrias nuevas y necesarias,* 1954 (D.O., Jan. 4, 1955), hereafter in this chapter cited as new industries law. Implementing regulations are the *Reglamento de la ley de fomento de industrias nuevas y necesarias,* 1955 (D.O., Dec. 2, 1955), hereafter in this chapter cited as regulations to new industries law. The most complete study of this law, containing English translations of the law and regulations and instructions for applications, is Stanford G. Ross and John B. Christensen, *Tax Incentives for Industry in Mexico* (Cambridge, Mass.: Law School of Harvard University, International Program in Taxation, 1959). For a general study of tax incentives, see Jack Heller and Kenneth M. Kauffman, *Tax Incentives for Industry in Less Developed Countries* (Cambridge, Mass.: Law School of Harvard University, 1963).

34. New industries law, art. 1.

35. Ibid., art. 2.

36. Ibid., art. 3.

37. Regulations to new industries law, art 9.

38. New industries law, arts. 4, 5 § I; regulations to new industries law, arts. 11, 12.

39. New industries law, art. 6 § II.

40. Regulations to new industries law, art. 10.

41. New industries law, arts. 3, 5 § II, § III, § IV, § V.

42. Regulations to new industries law, art. 14.

43. New industries law, art. 14. Federal taxes are discussed in Chapter VIII.

44. The types of articles that may be imported free of duty are listed in regulations to new industries law, art. 28.

45. New industries law, art. 11.

46. Ibid., art. 7.

47. Ibid., art. 8; regulations to new industries law, art. 15.

48. Regulations to new industries law, art. 16.

49. New industries law, art. 15; regulations to new industries law, art. 37.

50. New industries law, art. 9; regulations to new industries law, art. 18.

51. New industries law, art. 15; regulations to new industries law, art. 37.

52. New industries law, arts. 10, 15.

53. Ibid., art. 15.

54. Ibid., art. 17.

55. Ibid., arts. 28, 29, 30.

56. A list and examples of state tax exemption laws then in effect were published by Nacional Financiera in 25 *El Mercado de Valores* 459 (1965).

57. For a study of the effect of tax exemption in the Federal District, from which it was concluded that local tax exemption had little influence in decisions of companies to locate there, see Gustavo Romero Kolbeck and Victor L. Urquidi, *La exención fiscal en el Distrito Federal como instrumento de atracción de industrias* (Mexico, D.F., 1952).

58. *Ley orgánica del artículo 28 constitucional en materia de monopolios,* 1934 (D.O., Aug. 31, 1934), as amended by decree of Dec. 29, 1941 (D.O., Jan. 10, 1942), and decree of Dec. 30, 1952 (D.O., Dec. 31, 1952), hereafter in this chapter cited as monopolies law.

59. *Reglamento de la ley orgánica del artículo 28 constitucional,* 1931 (D.O., Dec. 19, 1931), hereafter in this chapter cited as regulations to monopolies law.

60. See monopolies law, statement of purposes.

61. See regulations to monopolies law, arts. 29, 30.

62. Monopolies law, art. 6.

63. Decree of Nov. 23, 1935 (D.O., Feb. 1, 1936).

64. *Reglamento de las fracciones IV y V del artículo 5º de la ley orgánica del artículo 28 constitucional,* 1938 (D.O., Aug. 12, 1938).

65. Monopolies law, arts. 7, 8.

66. *Reglamento sobre artículos de consumo necesario,* 1941 (D.O., Dec. 23, 1941), as amended; see also decree of Aug. 10, 1942 (D.O., Aug. 15, 1942).

67. Monopolies law, arts. 11, 12.

68. See Mosk (above, n. 1), p. 98, stating that, at least with respect to matches, flour milling, and cigarettes, "There is absolutely no evidence that the government made careful studies of the structure of any of these industries before acting to close them against new firms." The original control of the flour milling industry was partially lifted in 1947 but was re-established by decree of Mar. 14, 1963 (D.O., Mar. 22, 1963), which recited that the industry was overcapitalized and had an installed capacity much greater than market requirements.

69. Monopolies law, arts. 13, 14.

70. Ibid., arts. 19-23.

71. See Izquierdo (above, n. 1), p. 249. Estimates of the annual volume of smuggling have varied from $250 million to $400 million. See *Wall Street Journal,* Apr. 3, 1967, p. 1; *The News,* Nov. 26, 1967, p. 17.

72. National per capita income was estimated in 1966 to be $454, as compared to $635 for the border. See Arthur D. Little, Inc., *Current Trends in Mexican Industrial Development* (n.p., 1966), p. 9. Of the more than $800 million a year of tourist expenditures in Mexico, 75 percent is spent in the border area. See Banco Nacional de Comercio Exterior, *Comercio Exterior* (May, 1966), p. 367.

73. See Robert C. McElroy and Earle E. Gavett, *Termination of the Bracero Program* (U.S. Dep't. of Agriculture, Agr. Econ. Rept. 77, June, 1965); see also Hirsh, *Effects of Changes in Use of Seasonal Workers on U.S. Mexican Agriculture and Balance of Payments* (U.S. Dep't of Agriculture, Aug., 1967).

74. Minister of Industry and Commerce Octaviano Campos Salas estimated in 1965 that there were 300,000 unemployed workers in the border area, *Excelsior,* May 24, 1965, p. 1.

75. Proposed investment under PRONAF is $20 million per year for fifteen years (1963-77). A good description of the program is found in María Ventura Campos Salas, *El rico mercado fronterizo: Un análisis de sus posibilidades comerciales* (Thesis for Licenciado en Economía, Universidad Nacional Autónoma de México, 1964), pp. 25-55.

Freight and tax benefits are granted by the Ministry of Finance with the approval of the office of the national border program, and manufacturers must be registered with the program to qualify. The benefits may be refused if they result in unfair competition, the goods do not replace imports, there is no price reduction as a result of the benefits, the goods are already selling at a lower price than imported products, or wholesale prices fixed by manufacturers to buyers in the border zones are higher than prices to foreign wholesalers.

76. See Harold O. Walker, Jr., "Border Industries with a Mexican Accent," 4 *Columbia Journal of World Business* 27 (1969). *Comerico Exterior* (above, n. 72), p. 367, reported that border sales quadrupled between 1961 and 1965, but it was not possible to distinguish between U.S. and Mexican purchases.

77. See, e.g., speeches of Octaviano Campos Salas, reported in *Excelsior,* Mar. 20, 1966, p. 1, and May 8, 1968, p. 1.

78. See *Excelsior,* May 24, 1965, p. 1; *New York Times,* May 30, 1965, § III, p. 1. Reference to the program was made by President Díaz Ordaz in both his first and second annual reports to Congress, Sept. 1, 1965, and Sept. 1, 1966. In the first, he described it as a "far-reaching program for the industrialization of the northern border area."

79. Restrictions on foreign investment and ownership of land are described in Chapter III.

80. See *Excelsior,* Apr. 26, 1968, p. 1; *Wall Street Journal,* Feb. 21, 1969, p. 1.

81. A partial list of companies operating within the program can be found in *Business Abroad,* Dec. 11, 1967, p. 20, and *Mexican-American Review,* Feb. 1968, p. 15. It is reported that most companies consider their operations successful and have found Mexican workers easily trainable, dependable, and productive. See, e.g., Walker (above, n. 76), p. 28. But some commentators have questioned the productivity of Mexican workers and have incorrectly reported that border plants are required by law to pay wages 50 percent in excess of the minimum wage for the area: Anna-Stiner L. Ericson, "Economic Development in the Mexican Border Areas," U.S. Department of Labor, *Labor Developments Abroad,* June, 1967;

Benjamin J. Taylor and M. E. Bond, "Mexican Border Industrialization," 16 *MSU Business Topics* 33 (Spring, 1968).

United States tariff regulations seem to make the program unattractive for other than assembly activities. Section 807 of the U.S. Tariff Code applies to "articles assembled abroad in whole or in part of fabricated components, the product of the United States, which (a) were exported in condition ready for assembly without further fabrication, (b) have not lost their physical identity in such articles by change in form, shape, or otherwise, and (c) have not been advanced in value or improved in condition abroad except by being assembled and except by operations incidental to the assembly process such as cleaning, lubricating, and painting." On those articles there is a duty upon the full value of the imported article, less the cost or value of the component United States products. 19 United States Code § 807 (1963). However, if a foreign-produced item is imported, it is subject to duty on its full value.

82. It has been estimated that as much as 60 percent of the retail sales of neighboring U.S. cities are made to Mexican purchasers. See *Comercio Exterior* (above, n. 72), p. 395; *Business Week*, Dec. 2, 1967, p. 121; *Wall Street Journal*, Dec. 12, 1967, p. 1.

83. Organized U.S. labor has argued that U.S. labor standards should be applied to the border plants on the theory that they operate within the U.S. economy. See *Wall Street Journal*, Dec. 12, 1967, p. 1. In February, 1969, it was reported that the AFL-CIO executive council was planning to seek an increase in U.S. tariffs on imports from border plants, to seek a requirement that their products be labelled as to origin, to help Mexican unions organize the plants and increase wages, and was considering boycotts and picketing of stores that sell Mexican-made goods. See *Wall Street Journal*, Feb. 21, 1969, p. 1.

84. One of the few speeches in the U.S. by a Mexican government official is Rodolfo Villarreal Cárdenas, "Industrialization of Mexico's Northern Border and the United States Investor," *Arizona Review*, Jan., 1968, p. 6.

CHAPTER VI

1. *Ley general de población*, 1947 (D.O., Dec. 27, 1947), as amended by decree of Dec. 24, 1949 (D.O., Dec. 27, 1949), and decree of Dec. 29, 1960 (D.O., Dec. 30, 1960), hereinafter cited as population law; *Reglamento de la ley general de población*, 1962 (D.O., May 3, 1962), hereinafter cited as regulations to population law. Fees for entry permits are covered by the *Ley de impuestos de migración*, 1960 (D.O., Dec. 30, 1960). There are special laws on tourism and its promotion, e.g., *Ley federal de turismo*, 1961 (D.O., Mar. 1, 1961); and *Reglamento de guías de turistas, guías-choferes y similares*, 1967 (D.O., Aug. 14, 1967).

2. Population law, art. 51.

3. Population law, art. 52; regulations to population law, art. 78. Persons admitted as nonimmigrant transients are excepted and may not change their status.

4. Population law, arts. 56, 14.

5. Ibid., art. 60(d). Under that article the ministry may also deny entry to aliens when there does not exist international reciprocity, when the "equilibrium of demographic exchange" so requires, when quotas authorized by the law are filled, when the alien's conduct in the country has not been above reproach, when he has violated the law or regulations, or for similar reasons. Article 58 of the law authorizes the ministry to establish annual quotas, either by nationalities, by types of entry permits, or by activities, but the only year for which quotas have been established was 1947 (D.O., Dec. 13, 1946).

6. Regulations to population law, art. 27.

7. The provisions for the entry of immigrants are found in population law, arts. 43-49, and regulations to population law, arts. 44-64. Special immigration privileges are given to aliens who are married to Mexicans by birth and those who have children born in Mexico. Population law, art. 49; regulations to population law, art. 62.

8. Confidential employees are covered by population law, art. 48 § V, and regulations to population law, art. 59.

9. Population law, art. 48 § VI; regulations to population law, art. 60.

10. Population law, art. 48 § I; regulations to population law, art. 55.

11. Population law, art. 48 § II; regulations to population law, art. 56.

12. The various forms of Mexican business associations are discussed in Chapter VII.

13. Population law, art. 48 § III; regulations to population law, art. 57.

14. Population law, art. 48 § IV; regulations to population law, art. 58. These provisions are inconsistent with the law of professions, which, as discussed in the next section under Rights and Obligations of Aliens, p. 205, expressly prohibits the practice of a profession by aliens in the Federal District and territories. That prohibition has, however, been held unconstitutional in several decisions.

15. Population law, arts. 24-27; regulations to population law, arts. 87-92.

16. Population law, art. 46; regulations to population law, art. 50.

17. Population law, art. 45; regulations to population law, art. 52.

18. *Inmigrados* are covered by arts. 64-68 of the population law and arts. 65-67 of its regulations.

19. The entry of nonimmigrants is governed by population law, art. 50, and regulations to population law, arts. 68-78.

20. This distinction is clearer in practice than in the population law, which merely defines nonimmigrant visitors as aliens who enter the country "to engage in the exercise of some activity lucrative or not." The *Ley de impuestos de migración* (above, n. 1), art. 2(f) and (g), clearly differentiates between them, establishing an entry free of 62.50 pesos for unremunerated visitors and 518.75 pesos for remunerated visitors. Visitors are covered by population law, art. 50 § III, and regulations to population law, art. 71.

21. Population law, art. 50 § I; regulations to population law, art. 69.

22. For a full treatment of individual guarantees, see Ignacio Burgoa, *Las garantías individuales,* 4th ed. (Mexico, D.F.: Editorial Porrúa, 1965).

23. D.O., Aug. 20, 1931.

24. *Ley reglamentaria de los artículos 4°. y 5°. constitucionales relativos al ejercicio de las profesiones en el distrito y territorios federales,* 1944 (D.O., May 26, 1945), arts. 15, 25 § I.

25. E.g., *Faustino Ballvé Pallisé y coags.,* 97 S.J.F. (5th) 1666 (1948); *Nollau Dore Zurhellen,* 109 S.J.F. (5th) 1303 (1951); *Rafael De Piña Vara,* 114 S.J.F. (5th) 477 (1952); *Karl Cornelius Lairtus Amorós,* 116 S.J.F. (5th) 677 (1953); *Alma Paredes Delgado,* 119 S.J.F. (5th) 3597 (1954); *Higinio Nieves Díaz,* 35 S.J.F. (6th) 141 (1st pt.) (1960).

26. Decisions in *amparo* suits are binding only with respect to the case in which they are rendered and protect only the individual complainant in that case. The *amparo* suit is discussed in Chapter I under Judicial Protection against Governmental Acts—The *Amparo,* p. 28.

27. Constitution, arts. 32, 130. The prohibition against engaging in religious ministry is not strictly enforced.

28. The application of this article is delegated to the Ministry of Internal

Affairs by the *Ley de secretarías y departamentos de estado,* 1958 (DO., Dec. 24, 1958), art. 2 § VI.

29. *Mario Bergeron,* 15 S.J.F. (5th) 25 (1924); *Vicente González,* 15 S.J.F. (5th) 890 (1924); *J. Domingo Chong Bing,* 16 S.J.F. (5th) 59 (1925).

30. *Ley de nacionalidad y naturalización,* 1934 (D.O., Jan. 20, 1934), art. 32. See the discussion under The Calvo Clause in Chapter III, p. 100.

31. Ibid., art. 31.

32. Civil Code for the Federal District and Territories, art. 12, hereinafter cited as Civil Code. This code, though applicable primarily in the Federal District and federal territories, applies nationally insofar as it relates to civil rights of aliens. *Ley de nacionalidad* (above, n. 30), art. 50.

33. Commercial Code, art. 13. Acts of commerce are defined in art. 75 of the code. See the discussion under The Commercial Code in Chapter I, p. 43.

34. Population law, arts. 44, 51; regulations to population law, arts. 48, 53. The ministry may also establish conditions on aliens' places of residence. Population law, art. 56.

35. The ministry establishes the activities in which a political refugee may engage. Regulations to population law, art. 72(B) § I. Students may do work for professional practice or social service with the ministry's permission. Ibid., art. 73 § VIII.

36. Population law, art. 50 § I.

37. Regulations to population law, arts. 55 § IV *(rentiers),* 56 § I (investors in industry, agriculture, livestock, or export trade), 57 § I (investors in securities).

38. Population law, art. 66; regulations to population law, art. 67.

39. Population law, art. 63; regulations to population law, art. 51.

40. Population law, art. 57.

41. Population law, art. 71; regulations to population law, art. 14(B). Under art. 70 of the law authorization of the ministry is even required for an alien to marry a Mexican.

42. See Rafael Rojina Villegas, *Derecho civil mexicano* 6 vols. (Mexico, D.F.: Antigua Librería Robredo), 1:340-44, 423-27 (3d ed., 1959); 5(1): 484-89 (2d ed., 1960).

43. The provisions of the Civil Code on capacity are applicable also to commercial acts, including commercial contracts. Commercial Code, arts. 2, 81.

44. The commercial companies law, discussed in detail in Chapter VII, requires that shareholders meetings be held at the corporate domicile but contains no provision relating to the place of board of directors meetings. In the opinion of some Mexican lawyers, the board of a Mexican company may meet outside Mexico, in which case an alien director would not have to enter the country and thus would not be subject to the permit requirement.

45. Civil Code, arts. 1799, 2230.

46. Civil Code, art. 2239.

47. Population law, art. 109.

48. Ibid., art. 95 § V.

49. Ibid., art. 71. Restrictions on ownership of real property are discussed in Chapter III, p. 113.

50. The provisions for foreign civil companies are contained in arts. 2736-38 of the Civil Code; civil companies are defined in art. 2688. The dichotomy between civil law and commercial law is discussed in Chapter I under The Civil Codes, p. 41.

51. The commercial companies law is discussed in detail in Chapter VII.

52. See José Luis Siqueiros P., *Las sociedades extranjeras en México* (Mexico, D.F.: Imprenta Universitaria, 1953), pp. 81, 82-85, 113; Julio C. Treviño, "The

Concept of Doing Business in Mexico by Foreign Enterprises," in Harry K. Wright, ed., *Commercial Law of Mexico and the United States* (Austin: University of Texas School of Law, 1966), p. 11. Acts that are considered commercial are listed in art. 75 of the Commercial Code and include virtually any activity for profit, such as retail and wholesale trade, manufacturing, and construction.

53. *Koppel Industrial Car & Equipment Co.*, 26 S.J.F. (5th) 1171 (1929).

54. E.g., Siqueiros (above, n. 52), pp. 82-85.

55. E.g., *Stetten & Co. vs. Gross*, 37 S.J.F. (4th) (1908), in which a French company that had made a contract of sale by mail with a Mexican purchaser was held to have standing to sue on the contract without being registered, the Court stating that the registration requirement was applicable only to "companies established in the Republic or having the intention of becoming established therein, but not to companies established abroad."

56. *The Palmolive Company*, 27 S.J.F. (5th) 1294 (1929). Similar decisions were reached in *Zardaín Hermanos y coags.*, 27 S.J.F. (5th) 387 (1929); *Cía. del Ferrocarril Inter-California*, 27 S.J.F. (5th) 1781 (1929); and *The Salinas of Mexico Limited*, 29 S.J.F. (5th) 1107 (1930). In one case decided during this period, however, the criminal chamber of the Court followed the pre-1929 line of decisions and held that the filing of an *amparo* suit was not a commercial act for which a foreign company was required to be registered and that an unregistered company did have capacity to bring such a suit. *Chickering and Sons*, 29 S.J.F. (5th) 16 (1930). These and other decisions referred to in this section are discussed in Siqueiros (above, n. 52), pp. 72-78, 88-93; see also Edward Schuster, "The Judicial Status of Non-Registered Foreign Corporations in Latin America—Mexico," 7 *Tulane Law Review* 353 (1933).

57. *Guillermo C. de Wit*, 44 S.J.F. (5th) 2152 (1935); *Utah Tropical Fruit Co.*, 49 S.J.F. (5th) 1207 (1936); *American International Fuel & Petroleum Co.*, 57 S.J.F. (5th) 856 (1938); *Gabino Camino*, 79 S.J.F. (5th) 3066 (1944); *Julio Weill y coags.*, 99 S.J.F. (5th) 969 (1949); *Josefina Herrera y coags.*, 102 S.J.F. (5th) 118 (1949); *United States Land and Lumber Co.*, 7 S.J.F. (6th) 303 (4th pt.) (1958).

58. *Ayuntamiento de Saltillo, Coah.*, 76 S.J.F. (5th) 2077 (1943).

59. The most recent official collection of jurisprudence states that the binding precedent established by the earlier decisions under the Commercial Code has been replaced by later decisions under the commercial companies law. *Jurisprudencia de la Suprema Corte de Justicia de la Nación de los fallos pronunciados en los años de 1917 a 1965*, 6 vols. (Mexico, D.F.: Imprenta Murguía, 1965), 4:1025-27.

60. *Ley del notariado para el Distrito Federal y territorios*, 1945 (D.O., Feb. 23, 1946), art. 76. Before judicial authorization is granted, the documents are examined for completeness and proper form by the public attorney's office.

61. See Siqueiros (above, n. 52), pp. 109-12. See The Calvo Clause section in Chapter III, p. 97.

62. Roberto L. Mantilla Molina, *Derecho mercantil*, 5th ed. (Mexico, D.F.: Editorial Porrúa, 1961), p. 461, also stating that registration should not be denied merely because the laws of the country of incorporation do not afford the same protections to minority shareholders as are granted under Mexican law.

63. Treviño (above, n. 52), p. 8.

64. Mantilla Molina (above, n. 62), p. 463; Siqueiros (above, n. 52), pp. 56, 101, 108.

65. Siqueiros (above, n. 52), pp. 85-88.

66. Decree of Dec. 31, 1942 (D.O., Feb. 2, 1943).

CHAPTER VII

1. *Ley general de sociedades mercantiles,* 1934 (D.O., Aug. 4, 1934), hereinafter cited as commercial companies law. As pointed out in Chapter I, the Mexican civil codes also contain provisions for companies, but a civil company may engage in only nonprofit activities. See, e.g., Civil Code for the Federal District and Territories, arts. 2688-2735. Any company, whatever its purpose, constituted in the form of a commercial company is governed by the commercial law. Commercial companies law, art. 4; Civil Code for the Federal District and Territories, art. 2695.

2. Commercial companies law, arts. 25-50.

3. Ibid., arts. 51-57.

4. Ibid., arts. 207-11.

5. The provisions relating to limited liability companies are found in arts. 58-66 of the commercial companies law.

6. Ibid., art. 2.

7. The traditional concept that the legal personality of a company arises from the contract of association has been modified somewhat in the law. Although there is no grant of authority from the state, art. 2 of the law provides that companies recorded in the public commercial register and unrecorded companies that have been held out to third parties as companies, whether or not a contract of association has been executed, have juridical personality. The permit from the Ministry of Foreign Relations required by the emergency decree of 1944, discussed in Chapter III and referred to below under Formation, p. 221, for the constitution of a company is not a grant of charter within the concept of Anglo-American law.

8. The provisions on incorporation are contained in arts. 5-8 and 89-110 of the commercial companies law.

9. The law does not impose any restriction on the life of a corporation and in theory it may be for an unlimited period, but on occasion recordation has been refused where an indefinite duration is stated, and the Supreme Court has upheld this. See Roberto L. Mantilla Molina, *Derecho mercantil,* 11th ed. (Mexico, D.F.: Editorial Porrúa, 1970), p. 218 and authorities cited.

10. On the entry and status of aliens and foreign companies, see Chapter VI.

11. The Ministry of Foreign Relations is of the opinion that this requirement applies to the transfer to a foreigner of any number of shares. See the discussion under The Emergency Decree of June 29, 1944 in Chapter III, p. 108.

12. See Chapter III under The Emergency Decree of June 29, 1944, p. 110.

13. Commercial companies law, arts. 260-64.

14. The federal register of taxpapers is discussed in Chapter VIII, p. 248.

15. The social security system is discussed in Chapter IX, p. 310.

16. Commercial companies law, art. 89 §§ II-IV. Although 25,000 pesos is the minimum capital for incorporation, a company that wishes to obtain authorization for the entry of foreign personnel must have substantially greater capital. See Chapter VI, p. 198.

17. Commercial companies law, art. 141.

18. Ibid., art. 12.

19. Ibid., arts. 118-21.

20. Ibid., art. 117.

21. Ibid.

22. Ibid., arts. 104-10.

23. Ibid., art. 114 and statement of purposes. Labor unions have showed no

interest in these special shares and they have been little used. The constitutional requirement of profit sharing was implemented by law in 1963, discussed in Chapter IX, p. 293.

24. Ibid., art. 115.

25. Ibid., art. 125 § IV.

26. Ibid., arts. 134, 138-39.

27. Ibid., arts. 16-22. Directors who have paid illegal dividends and shareholders who have received them are liable for the amount thereof. Either the corporation or its creditors may bring suit. Ibid., arts. 19, 22.

28. Ibid., art. 123. As pointed out in Chapter VIII at p. 259, payments of interest under this provision are not deductible by the corporation for income tax purposes but are treated as dividends.

29. Commercial companies law, arts. 112-13.

30. Ibid., arts. 111, 117.

31. Ibid., arts. 128-29, 131.

32. Ibid., arts. 117, 124.

33. On limitations on foreign investment, see Chapter III.

34. Commercial companies law, arts. 124-27.

35. Ibid., art. 130.

36. On amendments to the articles of incorporation, see ibid., arts. 5, 182, 260-64. The permit requirement is discussed in Chapter III under The Emergency Decree of June 29, 1944, pp. 102, 107.

37. The provisions on capital increase are contained in the commercial companies law, arts. 9, 132-33. If all the shareholders are present at the meeting at which the capital increase is resolved, the generally accepted view is that the pre-emptive right must be exercised within fifteen days of the date of the meeting.

38. The provisions on reduction of capital are contained in the commercial companies law, arts. 9, 135-37.

39. Variable capital companies are provided for in the commercial companies law, arts. 213-21.

40. See Chapter III on The Emergency Decree of June 29, 1944, p. 107. Another advantage is lower cost of incorporation. Since notarial fees are based on the amount of capital stated in the articles of incorporation or an amendment to increase capital, expenses of incorporation may be reduced by using a variable capital company with the legal minimum capital.

41. Commercial companies law, art. 194.

42. The provisions on management are contained in the commercial companies law, arts. 142-63. Shareholders meetings are discussed below under Rights and Protections of Shareholders, p. 233.

43. Ibid., art. 178. Art. 91 § VI of the law states that the articles of incorporation should provide for the powers of the general shareholders assembly. However, in view of the broad language of art. 178, it is doubtful that an attempt to restrict the shareholders' powers would be effective.

44. Shareholder action on dividends is required by art. 181 § I of the commercial companies law, which provides that the annual meeting shall "discuss, approve or modify the balance sheet . . . and take the measures that it deems appropriate. . . ."

45. Certain obligations are expressly imposed on the directors by art. 158 of the commercial companies law, but these are related to their general power of management.

46. Commercial Code, art. 21 § VII; commercial companies law, art. 153.

47. Commercial companies law, art. 151.

48. See Chapter VI on the entry and status of aliens.

49. See, e.g., Joaquín Rodríguez Rodríguez, *Tratado de sociedades mercantiles*, 2d ed., 2 vols. (Mexico, D.F.: Editorial Porrúa, 1959), 2:95, and authorities cited.

50. *Editorial Cima, S.A.*, 79 S.J.F. (5th) 6603 (1944).

51. See Ignacio Galindo Garfias, *Sociedad anónima: Responsabilidad civil de los administradores* (Mexico, D.F., 1957), p. 99.

52. See J. M. Cormack and F. F. Barker, "The Mexican Law of Business Organizations," 6 *Southern California Law Review* 181, at 228 (1933), suggesting as a general principal that "provisions of the law made in interests of the public treasury, creditors of the organization, public policy, or the community at large" may not be modified.

53. Commercial companies law, arts. 87, 116.

54. Ibid., art. 23.

55. Mantilla Molina (above, n. 9), p. 208.

56. The provisions on shareholders meetings are contained in the commercial companies law, arts. 178-206.

57. Ibid., art. 168.

58. It has also been suggested that the articles should require the presence of the foreign minority shareholder at the first roll call to constitute a quorum. Michael Roy Sonnenreich, "Protecting the United States Minority Shareholder in Joint International Business Ventures in Latin America," 5 *Virginia Journal of International Law* 6 (1964).

59. *Sol J. Arouesty*, 115 S.J.F. (5th) 437 (1953).

60. Commercial companies law, art. 206.

61. Ibid., art. 113.

62. See Mantilla Molina (above, n. 9), p. 383. Zafra Meléndez, however, believes that such shareholder agreements are valid despite art. 198, *La protección de las minorías en la sociedad anónima* (Mexico, D.F., 1957), p. 41.

63. See Mantilla Molina (above, n. 62), p. 394.

64. Commercial companies law, art. 144.

65. Ibid.

66. The *reporto* contract is provided for in the *Ley general de títulos y operaciones de crédito*, 1932 (D.O., Aug. 27, 1932), arts. 259-66. See also H. P. Crawford, "Use of Mexican Corporate Shares," 4 *Tulane Law Review* 383 (1953).

67. Commercial companies law, art. 190.

68. Sonnenreich warns of this risk (above, n. 58), p. 15.

69. Commercial companies law, art. 186.

70. Provisions on *comisarios* are contained in ibid., arts. 164-71. The word *comisario* is often translated as "inspector," "auditor," or "examiner," but there is no generally accepted English equivalent.

71. Ibid., art. 162.

72. Ibid., art. 202.

73. *Donato Ramos Farías*, 6 *Boletín de Información Judicial* 17 (1953).

74. *José Manuel Chavarri*, 49 S.J.F. (6th) 145 (4th pt.) (1961); *Sol J. Arouesty*, 115 S.J.F. (5th) 437 (1953).

75. The provisions on merger are contained in the commercial companies law, arts. 222-26. Art. 222 provides that a merger must be resolved in the form and terms required according to the type of company concerned. In the case of a corporation, art. 182 § VI and § VII require that merger and transformation be

decided by an extraordinary shareholders meeting. Mexican law does not distinguish, as does United States law, between merger, meaning the absorption of one corporation by another, and consolidation, meaning a combination of two or more corporations that results in the creation of a new corporation. The Spanish term "fusión," as used in the law, and the term "merger," as used in this section, denote both merger and consolidation.

76. The provisions on transformation are contained in the commercial companies law, arts. 227-28.

77. The provisions on dissolution are contained in the commercial companies law, arts. 229-33.

78. The provisions on liquidation are contained in the commercial companies law, arts. 234-49.

CHAPTER VIII

1. For a thorough recent study of the real property tax and other taxes and charges on urban land, as well as land use, housing, and urban planning, in the Federal District, see Oliver Oldman et al., *Financing Urban Development in Mexico City* (Cambridge, Mass.: Harvard University Press, 1967).

2. *J. Jesús Delgado,* 89 S.J.F. (5th) 2072 (1946); see Constitution, art. 115 § II.

3. The federal Congress has the express function to prevent restrictions on interstate commerce. Constitution, art. 73 § IX.

4. Constitution, art. 73 § XXIX, provides for the participation of the states in the special federal taxes listed in that section to the extent determined by federal law. All federal laws on transactions taxes, except for taxes in areas that are exclusively within federal jurisdiction or which are set aside for specific purposes, provide for state participation, usually on the condition that the state renounce its right of taxation with respect to the products, services, or other activities covered by the federal tax.

5. *Código fiscal de la federación,* 1966 (D.O., Jan. 19, 1967), hereinafter cited as Fiscal Code. The basic rules of the Fiscal Code apply to all federal taxes unless they are modified by particular laws.

6. *Ley orgánica del Tribunal Fiscal,* 1966 (D.O., Jan. 19, 1967), art. 1. Composition and jurisdiction of the tax court are covered by this law. Proceedings before the tax court are covered by Fiscal Code, arts. 169-233, and are described in Henry J. Gumpel and Hugo B. Margain, *Taxation in Mexico,* World Tax Series, Harvard Law School (Boston: Little, Brown and Company, 1957), pp. 298-304. This exhaustive study of the Mexican tax system, although written before the adoption of the current income tax law, is still extremely useful.

7. The *amparo* suit is discussed in Chapter I, p. 28.

8. Review and appeals of tax court decisions are provided for in Fiscal Code, arts. 240-244.

9. *Ley del impuesto sobre la renta,* 1964 (D.O., Dec. 31, 1964), hereafter cited as income tax law. An English version of the law, together with the Spanish text, is found in *Mexican Income and Commercial Receipts Tax Laws as of January 1, 1968* (Chicago: Commerce Clearing House, 1968).

10. Decree of Dec. 29, 1965 (D.O., Dec. 31, 1965); decree of Dec. 28, 1966 (D.O., Dec. 31, 1966); decree of Dec. 28, 1967 (D.O., Dec. 29, 1967); *Ley que establece, reforma y adiciona las disposiciones relativas a diversos impuestos,* 1968 (D.O., Dec. 31, 1968), hereinafter cited as 1968 amendments.

11. Income tax law, trans. art. 2. The regulations are *Reglamento de la ley del impuesto sobre la renta,* 1954 (D.O., Feb. 10, 1954), as amended by decree of Jan. 31, 1956 (D.O., Feb. 4, 1956), hereafter cited as regulations to income tax law. There has been no official indication of which articles of the regulations are still in effect. A useful annotated edition of the law with cross references to relevant provisions of the regulations is Pedro L. Latre, comp., *Impuesto sobre la renta: Ley y reglamento 1968,* 3d ed., Biblioteca Sistema, vol. F-1 (Mexico, D.F.: Editorial Sistema, 1968).

12. Income tax law, art. 3.

13. Ibid., art. 19 § III.

14. See Gumpel and Margain (above, n. 6), pp. 239-46. Isolated commercial acts performed in Mexico by nonresident foreigners are taxed individually as in the case of Mexican residents.

15. Income tax law, arts. 3 § II, 31 § I.

16. Ibid., arts. 5, 25.

17. Ibid., arts. 16, 17. Commercial, industrial, agricultural, livestock raising, and fishing activities are defined in art. 16.

18. Ibid., arts. 16 § I, 19 § I; Commercial Code, art. 3 § II. The commercial companies law is discussed in Chapter VII.

19. Income tax law, arts. 3 § III, 16, 17, 89.

20. Ibid., arts. 17, 19 § II; Fiscal Code, art. 13.

21. The rules for taxation of income of individuals are contained in income tax law, arts. 48-88.

22. Fiscal Code, arts. 13, 93; *Reglamento para el Registro Federal de Causantes,* 1962 (D.O., Dec. 13, 1962).

23. Secretaría de Hacienda y Crédito Público, Subsecretario de Ingresos, Oficio 321, RFC-39, Oct. 30, 1965 (D.O., Nov. 10, 1965). Generally, individuals who receive tax-exempt income from personal services, domestic servants, and ministers of religious faiths are also exempt from the registration requirement. Secretaría de Hacienda y Crédito Público, Subsecretario de Egresos, Oficio 318, RFC-15, Jan. 16, 1963 (D.O., Jan. 28, 1963).

24. Income tax law, art. 26 § IV.

25. Ibid., arts. 17, 43-47.

26. Ibid., art. 18.

27. Ibid., arts. 1, 2.

28. Ibid., art. 19 § IV, § V, as amended by 1968 amendments.

29. Ibid., art. 19 § VI (b), (c).

30. Ibid., art. 19 § VI (e).

31. Ibid., art. 22.

32. Ibid., art. 19 § VI (g).

33. Ibid., art. 30.

34. Regulations to income tax law, art. 27. Commercial acts are listed in Commercial Code, art. 75.

35. Income tax law, arts. 32, 33. The rules for determination of gross income by estimate of "minor" taxpayers are found in ibid., art. 44.

36. The general requirements for deductions are contained in ibid., art. 26.

37. Ibid., art. 26 § III.

38. Ibid., arts. 7, 31, 41, 49 § I, 56, 67.

39. Ibid., art. 26 § IV.

40. Ibid., art. 26 § V.

41. Ibid., arts. 59, 60 § I, 65, 72. Entities subject to the tax on enterprises are

not required to pay income tax through revenue stamps, with the exception of tax-payers engaged in livestock raising. Ibid., arts. 35, 45.

42. Regulations to income tax law, arts. 41, 42, 44, 85-86.

43. Income tax law, art. 20 § II.

44. Regulations to income tax law, art. 43; determination of income by estimate is provided for in income tax law, art. 32.

45. Regulations to income tax law, art. 46.

46. Ibid., art. 82.

47. Ibid., art. 83. Manufacturing and extractive enterprises may be permitted by the Ministry of Finance to value finished products at sale price less selling expenses (cash realizable value) if the characteristics and the custom of the industry recommend this method of valuation. Ibid., arts. 81 § V, 83.

48. Ibid., arts. 109, 110.

49. The rules on depreciation and amortization are found in income tax law, arts. 21, 26 § VI.

50. Ibid., art. 27 § IX.

51. Ibid., art. 21 § III. The requirements for applications for increased depreciation and amortization rates are set out in regulations to income tax law, art. 92 § III.

52. Income tax law, art. 22, trans. art. 9.

53. Casualty losses are covered by ibid., art. 23, and regulations to income tax law, arts. 51-52.

54. Bad debt losses are covered by income tax law, art. 24.

55. Ibid., trans. art. 10; Secretaría de Hacienda y Crédito Público, Oficio 311-15521, Mar. 16, 1966, quoted in Latre (above, n. 11), pp. 359-60.

56. Contributions to pension and retirement plans are covered by income tax law, art. 25.

57. Ibid., art. 26 § XIII, as amended by 1968 amendments.

58. Ibid., art. 26 § IX.

59. Ibid., art. 26 § VII, § VIII; regulations to income tax law, art. 48.

60. Income tax law, art. 26 § VIII; see communication from the Dirección General del Impuesto sobre la Renta, transcribed as Criterio No. 30, in Latre (above, n. 11), pp. 377-78.

61. Income tax law, art. 26 § VIII.

62. Ibid., art. 26 § X.

63. Ibid., art. 26 § XI; regulations to income tax law, art. 49; see communication of the Dirección General del Impuesto sobre la Renta, transcribed as Criterio No. 36, in Latre (above, n. 11), pp. 387-88.

64. Income tax law, art. 29; regulations to income tax law, arts. 97, 100, 102.

65. Income tax law, art. 27.

66. Under the commercial companies law, a corporation is permitted to pay interest on its shares for a maximum period of three years from the date of issue. See Chapter VII, p. 225.

67. Income tax law, arts. 18, 34, as amended by 1968 amendments. Special rules are established in the law for computation of the tax by taxpayers whose fiscal year includes parts of two calendar years for which different tax rates apply, and for fiscal periods of less than twelve months. Ibid., arts. 38, 39.

68. Ibid., art. 34, as amended by 1968 amendments.

69. Ibid., art. 41; see ibid., art. 7.

70. Ibid., arts. 30, 41.

71. Ibid., arts. 31 § II, 41 § I.

72. Ibid., art. 3.

73. Ibid., art. 35; see also ibid., arts. 36, 37.

74. Ibid., arts. 6, 7, 10, 42 § IV. Credit institutions and insurance and bonding companies must file annual returns and pay any deficiency in the tax due within thirty days after their balance sheets have been approved by the appropriate supervising authorities. Ibid., arts. 35, 42 § IV. Amended returns are provided for in ibid., art. 9.

75. Ibid., art. 6.

76. Ibid., arts. 7, 11.

77. Ibid., art. 7. Under current administrative practice, when payment is made after collection proceedings have been initiated, the penalty is 3 percent if payment is made within one month after the due date and increases by 1 percent per month for each additional month's delay; if payment is made five months or more late, the penalty is 8 percent per month but may not exceed a total of 300 percent of the deficiency. Secretaría de Hacienda y Crédito Público, Subsecretaría de Ingresos, Circular 102-A-1-24 (D.O., Apr. 14, 1965). If payment is made before collection proceedings are initiated, the penalty is 2 percent per month.

78. Income tax law, art. 43. The percentages of gross income that are taken as net taxable income are set out in ibid., art. 33.

79. Ibid., arts. 42, 43.

80. Ibid., art. 46. This article also contains rules covering "minor" taxpayers whose gross income exceeds 150,000 pesos in a taxable year.

81. Ibid., arts. 45, 47.

82. Ibid., art. 49.

83. Ibid., arts. 48, 50 § II (g).

84. Ibid., art. 49 § II.

85. Ibid., art. 53.

86. Ibid., art. 50 § II. Rules for the computation of the tax on profit participations of workers who receive only the general minimum wage for the economic zone concerned are contained in Secretaría de Hacienda y Crédito Público, Dirección General del Impuesto sobre la Renta, Oficio 311-17209, Mar. 29, 1966 (D.O., Apr. 1, 1966).

87. Income tax law, art. 50 § I. Foreign technicians contracted by Mexico are exempt only if the exemption is provided for in an agreement with the foreigner's home country. Ibid., art. 50 § I (g).

88. The authorized deductions and requirements for deductions are set out in ibid., art. 51.

89. Ibid., arts. 51, 53.

90. Ibid., art. 52.

91. Ibid., art. 54. Rules for computation of the tax on personal-service income by taxpayers who work less than a year and on separation, retirement, and similar pay are established in ibid., art. 55.

92. Ibid., arts. 56, 88 § I (c), (e).

93. Ibid., arts. 58, 87 § I (b) (3).

94. Ibid., arts. 57, 87 § I (b) (1), (2).

95. Ibid., arts. 59, 87 § I (a), (c).

96. Ibid., art. 88 § II.

97. Ibid., art. 87.

98. Ibid., art. 60 § I (i).

99. Ibid., art. 60 § I (a), § II.

100. Ibid., art. 62 § I, § II, § III, § V, § VII.

101. Ibid., art. 63.

102. Ibid., art. 65.

103. Ibid., arts. 65, 87 § II.

104. Ibid., art. 66.

105. Ibid., art. 67.
106. Ibid., arts. 60 § V, 73.
107. Ibid., art. 60 § VI, § VIII.
108. Ibid., arts. 60 § V, 73 § II.
109. Ibid., art. 74.
110. Ibid., art. 60 § IV.
111. Ibid., art. 72.
112. Ibid., art. 60 § III.
113. The exemption for 1968 was contained in *Ley de ingresos de la federación para el ejercicio fiscal de 1968,* 1967 (D.O., Dec. 31, 1967), art. 4, and was repeated in the revenue law for 1969. This exemption does not apply to gains of enterprises.
114. Income tax law, art. 68. The method of computing the taxpayer's basis in property acquired by gift or inheritance is also established in that article.
115. Ibid., art. 69.
116. Ibid., art. 70.
117. Ibid., art. 71. In practice, the notary before whom the deed is executed customarily requests evidence of payment of the tax.
118. Ibid., arts. 60 § I (h), 62 § IV.
119. Ibid., arts. 65, 87 § II.
120. Ibid., art. 60 § I (d)-(g).
121. Ibid., art. 64.
122. Ibid., arts. 76, 77, 79.
123. Ibid., art. 80.
124. The exclusion for 1968 was contained in *Ley de ingresos* (above, n. 113), art. 4, and was repeated in the revenue law for 1969.
125. Income tax law, arts. 81, 83 § II.
126. Authorized deductions are listed in ibid., art. 82; requirements for and limitations on deductions are contained in ibid., art. 83.
127. Ibid., art. 84.
128. Ibid., arts. 85, 86.
129. Ibid., art. 85.
130. Ibid., art. 87 § III.
131. *Ley federal del impuesto sobre ingresos mercantiles,* 1951 (D.O., Dec. 31, 1951), as amended by decrees of Dec. 21, 1953 (D.O., Dec. 26, 1953); Dec. 27, 1954 (D.O., Dec. 31, 1954); Dec. 26, 1956 (D.O., Dec. 31, 1956); Dec. 30, 1960 (D.O., Dec. 31, 1960); Dec. 30, 1966 (D.O., Dec. 31, 1966), art. 15; and Dec. 28, 1967 (D.O., Dec. 29, 1967), art. 17. The law is hereinafter cited as commercial receipts tax law. An English version and the Spanish text of the law as amended through 1967 are found in *Mexican Income* (above, n. 9).
132. Commercial receipts tax law, art. 15, provides that the additional rate in participating states may not exceed 1.2 percent, and that rate has been fixed in all participating states. The taxes that may be retained by a participating state under its agreement with the federal government are listed in ibid., art. 81.
133. Ibid., arts. 10, 11.
134. Ibid., art. 10. This provision does not apply to hotels, guest houses, restaurants, tourist camps, or similar businesses authorized to operate under the federal tourism law.
135. Ibid., arts. 1, 4-7.
136. Ibid., arts. 2, 3.
137. Ibid., arts. 8, 23. Receipts of persons who receive commissions or brokerage as a form of salary or additional compensation subject to income tax are exempt from the commercial receipts tax. Ibid., art. 18 § XXVI.

138. Ibid., art. 9.

139. Ibid., arts. 21, 22.

140. Exempt receipts are listed in ibid., art. 18. See Gumpel and Margain (above, n. 6), pp. 85-86, 346-49.

141. This exemption does not apply to rentals from leases of furnished houses or apartments or to the receipts of hotels. Commercial receipts tax law, art. 18 § XI.

142. Ibid., arts. 14, 15.

143. Ibid., art. 16.

144. Ibid., art. 17, which imposed the tax on half the receipts listed, was repealed by decree of Dec. 28, 1967 (D.O., Dec. 29, 1967), art. 17, effective Jan. 1, 1968. At the same time, certain types of receipts included in art. 17 were added to the list of tax-exempt receipts in art. 18.

145. Provisions for filing of returns and payment of the tax are contained in ibid., arts. 12, 38-45; see alo arts. 24-25 (correction of errors in returns), 63 (examination of returns), 65-70 (penalties for failure to file).

146. Ibid., art. 31.

147. Ibid., art. 32. The law for the promotion of new and necessary industries is discussed in Chapter V under Tax Exemptions, p. 181.

148. Commercial receipts tax law, arts. 19, 48, 49.

149. Ibid., arts. 82, 83.

150. Ibid., art. 52.

151. Ibid., arts. 53-57.

152. Ibid., arts. 27, 28. The date of commencement of operations is the date on which the business is opened or on which taxable receipts are first collected. Ibid., art. 29. The penalty for failure to register is established in art. 64.

153. Ibid., arts. 30, 33, 34; see also arts. 35-37.

154. Ibid., art. 31.

155. Ibid., art. 46 § III, § IV, § V. Book entries must be made within sixty days from the date of the transaction, and receipts must be recorded within the first twenty days of the following month. Books and supporting documents must be preserved for five years. Ibid., art. 46 § VI, § XI. Penalties for failure to keep proper books and records are established in art. 71.

CHAPTER IX

1. See Mario de la Cueva, "Síntesis del derecho del trabajo," in *Panorama del derecho mexicano,* 2 vols. (Mexico, D.F.: Instituto de Derecho Comparado, Universidad Nacional Autónoma de México, 1965), 1:229. This is a useful, though somewhat theoretical, summary treatment of the 1931 labor law. For a thorough study see the two volume work by the same author, *Derecho mexicano del trabajo,* 8th ed. (Mexico, D.F.: Editorial Porrúa, 1964). A useful guide to article 123 of the Constitution and its amendments, including those adopted in 1962, is Alberto Trueba Urbina, *El nuevo artículo 123* (Mexico, D.F.: Editorial Porrúa, 1962).

2. *Ley federal del trabajo,* 1931 (D.O., Aug. 28, 1931), hereinafter cited as labor law of 1931.

3. D.O., Dec. 31, 1962.

4. *Ley federal del trabajo,* 1969 (D.O., Apr. 1, 1970), hereinafter cited as labor law.

5. *Ley federal de los trabajadores al servicio del estado,* 1963 (D.O., Dec. 28, 1963).

6. Labor law, art. 9. The special provisions on confidential workers, called confidential employees in the 1931 law, are contained in labor law, arts. 182-86.

7. Labor law, arts. 8, 20.

8. E.g., *Gómez Ochoa y Cía.*, 44 S.J.F. (5th ser.) 3309 (1935).

9. Labor law, art. 16.

10. Labor law, arts. 20, 21, 26.

11. Individual labor contracts are covered generally in arts. 20-34 of the labor law.

12. Labor law, art. 47 § XI. See, e.g., *Alfredo Jiménez Torres* (1964), cited in Juan B. Climent Beltrán, *Ley federal del trabajo y otras leyes laborales* (Mexico, D.F.: Editorial Esfinge, 1967), p. 141. If the contract fails to specify the services, the worker is obligated to do only such work as is compatible with his strength, ability, and condition, and consistent with the purpose of the employer's business. Labor law, art. 27.

13. Provisions on the duration of individual labor contracts are contained in arts. 35-41 of the labor law.

14. Labor law, art. 47 § I.

15. Labor law of 1931, art. 122 § I. See De la Cueva, *Derecho mexicano* (above, n. 1), 1:768-69.

16. Labor law, art. 159.

17. Labor law, art. 7. All employed medical doctors, seamen, aircraft crews, and railroad workers must be Mexicans. Labor law, arts. 7, 189, 216, 246.

18. Closed shop is authorized by labor law, art. 395.

19. Preference in hiring and promotions are provided for in arts. 154-61 of the labor law.

20. Employment of women and minors is covered by labor law, arts. 5 § I, § IV, § XII, 22-23, 164-80. Prohibitions against discrimination are found in arts. 3, 5 § XI, 56.

21. Hours of work are covered by labor law, arts. 58-68.

22. Rest days are covered by labor law, arts. 69-75.

23. Labor law, art. 71. This requirement, an innovation of the 1969 law, was effective July 1, 1970. Labor law, trans. art. 1.

24. Vacations are covered by labor law, arts. 76-81. The vacation bonus requirement was effective Sept. 1, 1970. Labor law, trans. art. 1.

25. Labor law, arts. 166, 168-70, 177-79.

26. Provisions on wages are contained in labor law, arts. 5 §§ V-VIII, § XI, 57, 82-89.

27. Labor law, arts. 90-97.

28. The composition and duties of the minimum wage commissions and the procedure for establishing minimum wages are provided for in labor law, arts. 551-74. As an indication of the dominant role of the national commission, the regional commissions in some 20 zones failed to agree on recommended wage rates for 1968-69.

29. Labor law, art. 90. However, the technical bureau of the national commission is called on to make investigations and studies necessary to determine economic conditions in the country and the zones, cost of living, minimum budget to satisfy designated needs of a family, and the economic conditions of the consumer markets. Labor law, art. 562 § I.

30. Minimum wage rates for each biennium are published in the *Diario Oficial*, usually Dec. 30 or 31 of the year immediately preceding the biennium, and also in booklet form by the Comisión Nacional de los Salarios Mínimos.

31. Labor law, art 87. This requirement was effective July 1, 1970. Labor law, trans. art. 1.

32. Labor law, arts. 5 § VIII, 88, 101, 108.

33. Provisions on protection of wages are contained in arts. 98-116 of the labor law.

34. *Ley del seguro social,* 1942 (D.O., Jan. 19, 1943), art. 30.

35. Constitution, art. 123 § A VI, § A IX.

36. E.g., *Cervecería Moctezuma, S.A.,* 12 S.J.F. (5th ser.) 753 (1923); *Antonio Maldonado,* 71 S.J.F. (5th ser.) 3265 (1942); *Alberto Martínez,* 92 S.J.F. (5th ser.) 229 (1947). See Alfonso Alvírez Friscione, *La participación de utilidades* (Mexico, D.F.: Editorial Porrúa, 1966), pp. 231-35.

37. Constitution, art. 123 § A IX, was amended by decree of Nov. 20, 1962 (D.O., Nov. 21, 1962). The 1931 labor law was amended by decree of Dec. 29, 1962 (D.O., Dec. 31, 1962), which added a new Chapter V-bis, arts. 100 G-100 U, and a new Chapter IX-3, arts. 428 I-428 Y.

38. *Resolución de la Comisión Nacional para la Participación de los Trabajadores en las Utilidades de las Empresas,* 1963 (D.O., Dec. 13, 1963). For a thorough study of profit sharing in Mexico, with the text of the resolution, see Alvírez Friscione (above, n. 36), pp. 203-377. A useful practical guide is the Confederación Patronal's publication, *Manual para la aplicación del reparto de utilidades en México* (Mexico, D.F., n.d.).

39. The provisions on profit sharing are contained in arts. 117-31 of the labor law; the organization and operation of the national profit-sharing commission are provided for in arts. 575-90.

40. Labor law, art. 126, which lists the exempt employers, provides in § VI for an exemption for "enterprises that have a capital of less than that fixed by the Ministry of Labor and Social Welfare, by branches of industry, after consultation with the Ministry of Industry and Commerce." The labor ministry established the exemptions for small businesses stated in the text by resolution of Mar. 18, 1963. See *Resolución* (above, n. 38), preamble para. 7.

41. Constitution, art. 123 § A IX (b), as amended.

42. Decree of Dec. 29, 1962 (D.O., Dec. 31, 1962), trans. art. 7, as amended by decree of Jan. 3, 1964 (D.O., Mar. 5, 1964).

43. Income tax law, art. 26 § II.

44. Labor law, arts. 587-89.

45. Labor law, trans. art. 7.

46. Labor law, arts. 136-53.

47. Constitution, art. 123 § A XII.

48. *Reglamento de la fracción III del artículo 111 de la ley federal del trabajo,* 1941 (D.O., Dec. 31, 1941) (covering enterprises under federal jurisdiction); *Reglamento de la fracción III del artículo 111 de la ley federal del trabajo, para empresas que no sean de jurisdicción federal,* 1942 (D.O., Feb. 6, 1942).

49. Labor law, art. 162. The rules for payment of the bonus to those who are employed on the effective date of the law are contained in trans. art. 5: workers with less than ten years of service who voluntarily resign their job within one year following the effective date of the law are entitled to twelve days' wages; those with more than ten and less than twenty years of service who voluntarily resign within two years of the effective date of the law are entitled to twenty-four days' wages; those with more than twenty years of service who voluntarily resign within three years of the effective date of the law are entitled to thirty-six days' wages; workers who resign after those periods are entitled to the full bonus provided for in art. 162; workers who are discharged or who resign for cause within one year from the effective date of the law are entitled to twelve days' wages, and after that period, to the full bonus.

50. Labor law, art. 132 § XIII.

51. Labor law, art. 132 § XV.

52. Labor law, art. 132 § XIV.
53. Labor law, art. 132 § XII.
54. *Ley orgánica de la educación pública*, 1942 (D.O., Jan. 23, 1942), arts. 67-71; *Reglamento del capítulo IX de las escuelas primarias artículo 123 constitucional, de la ley orgánica de la educación pública*, 1957 (D.O., Jan. 2, 1958).
55. Labor law, art. 132 § XXV.
56. Constitution, art. 123 § A XXII, as amended; labor law, art. 46.
57. Labor law, arts. 35-37.
58. Rescission of employment contracts by the employer is covered by arts. 46-50 of the labor law.
59. Labor law, arts. 185-86.
60. *Oscar Cué*, 67 S.J.F. (5th ser.) 2044 (1941). For an analysis and criticism of this decision, see De la Cueva, *Derecho mexicano* (above, n. 1), 1:819-27; see also Joseph M. Cormack, "Operation of the Mexican Labor Law," 7 *Southwestern Law Journal* 316-21 (1953).
61. Rescission by the worker is covered by arts. 51-52 of the labor law.
62. Termination of individual contracts is provided for in arts. 53-55 of the labor law; collective termination of labor relations, in arts. 433-39.
63. Suspension of individual labor relations is provided for in arts. 42-45 of the labor law; collective suspension, in arts. 427-32.
64. Labor law, art. 41.
65. See Climent Beltrán (above. n. 12), pp. 64-65 and authorities cited.
66. Unions are provided for in arts. 354-85 of the labor law.
67. Labor law, arts. 11, 183, 363.
68. Collective contracts are provided for in arts. 386-403 of the labor law.
69. Labor law, arts. 184, 396.
70. Provisions on the contract-law are contained in arts. 404-21 of the labor law.
71. Federal boards of conciliation are covered in arts. 591-600 of the labor law; local boards of conciliation in arts. 601-3; the federal board of conciliation and arbitration in arts. 604-20; and local boards of conciliation and arbitration in arts. 621-24.
72. Labor law, arts. 527-29.
73. Procedural rules are contained in labor law, arts. 745-50 (boards of conciliation), arts. 751-81 (individual disputes and collective disputes of a legal nature), and arts. 789-815 (collective disputes of an economic nature).
74. Constitution, art. 123 § A XVII, § A XVIII. Strikes are covered by arts. 440-71 of the labor law.
75. See, e.g., Alberto Trueba Urbina, *Evolución de la huelga* (Mexico, D.F.: Editorial Porrúa, 1950), p. 262.
76. See, e.g., *Cía. de Electricidad Mérida, S.A.*, cited in De la Cueva, *Derecho mexicano* (above, n. 1), 2:810.
77. Labor law, arts. 4 § II, 467-68.
78. Provisions on occupational accidents and illnesses are contained in arts. 472-515 of the labor law.
79. Labor law, trans. art. 8.
80. Constitution, art. 123 § A XXIX.
81. D.O., Sept. 6, 1929. For the history and background of social security legislation in Mexico see Gustavo Arce Cano, *Los seguros sociales en México* (Mexico, D.F.: Ediciones Botas, 1944); Miguel García Cruz, *La seguridad social: Bases, evolución, importancia económica, social y política* (Mexico, D.F., 1955); De la Cueva, *Derecho mexicano* (above, n. 1), 2:187-90; Alfonso Herrera Gutiérrez, *La ley mexicana del seguro social* (Mexico, D.F., 1943).

82. *Ley del seguro social,* 1942 (D.O., Jan. 19, 1943), hereinafter cited as social security law. Many amendments have been made to the law and there are numerous supplementary regulations covering such matters as registration of employers and workers, payment of contributions, classification of enterprises and grades of risks for purposes of occupational injury insurance, penalties for violations of the law, and functioning of the social security institute. A compilation of the law as amended and the regulations may be found in Manuel Andrade, comp., *Legislación sobre trabajo* (Mexico, D.F.: Ediciones Andrade, loose-leaf), pp. 1013 *et seq.*

Federal and Federal District government workers are provided similar benefits under a separate law, *Ley del Instituto de Seguridad y Servicios Sociales de los Trabajadores del Estado,* 1959 (D.O., Dec. 30, 1959).

83. Social security law, art. 6.

84. The functions and organization of the IMSS are covered by social security law, arts. 107-23. See also *Reglamento de la ley del seguro social,* 1943 (D.O., May 14, 1943), arts. 20-22 (director general), and arts. 23-25 (technical board); *Reglamento de la asamblea general del Instituto Mexicano del Seguro Social,* 1945 (D.O., Feb. 12, 1945) (general assembly).

85. Social security law, arts. 4, 5.

86. Occupational accident and illness insurance is covered by social security law, arts. 35-50.

87. *Reglamento de clasificación de empresas y grados de riesgos para el seguro de accidentes del trabajo y enfermedades profesionales,* 1964 (D.O., Jan. 29, 1964). Although the social security law, art. 45, calls for the revision of the classification and rate schedule at least every three years, the 1964 regulations were still in effect as of May, 1970. The employer's and worker's contributions for all three types of insurance are contained in *Reglamento para el pago de cuotas y contribuciones del régimen del seguro social,* Instituto Mexicano del Seguro Social, *Leyes, reglamentos e instructivos* (Mexico, D.F., 1969), pp. 163-64.

88. Social security law, art. 16; *Francisca Rodríguez Vda. de Silva,* 126 S.J.F. (5th ser.) 401 (1955).

89. Nonoccupational illness and maternity insurance is covered by social security law, arts. 51-66.

90. Social security law, arts. 67-95.

91. Social security law, art. 90.

CHAPTER X

1. See the section of Chapter III on Real Property, p. 121.

2. The applicable provisions of the Civil Code for the Federal District and Territories are contained in arts. 2893-2943. The references and citations in this chapter to the Civil Code are to this code. For a comprehensive treatment of Mexican mortgage law, see Rafael Rojina Villegas, *Derecho civil mexicano,* 6 vols. (Mexico, D.F.: Antigua Librería Robredo, 1960), 6(3):9-355.

3. Civil Code, arts. 2895, 2896.

4. Civil Code, art. 2917, as amended by *Ley del notariado para el Distrito Federal y territorios,* 1945 (D.O., Feb. 23, 1946), art. 54.

5. Civil Code, arts. 2919, 3003. Mortgages on property located in the Federal District are recorded in the public register of property of the Federal District, which is governed by the *Reglamento del Registro Público de la Propiedad del Distrito Federal,* 1940 (D.O., July 13, 1940).

6. This conclusion seems to follow from Civil Code, art. 751, which provides that movable property that has been considered an immovable reassumes the

character of a movable when the owner separates it from the building, unless it has been included in the value of the building for purposes of the creation of a real right in favor of a third person.

7. This conclusion is based on Civil Code, art. 750 § VI, which defines as immovable property "machines, receptacles, instruments, or utensils destined by the owner of the land directly and exclusively to the industry or exploitation thereof." Rojina Villegas, however, does not agree with this statement. Art. 2898 § II of the code provides that "movable objects permanently placed in buildings either for their adornment or comfort or for the service of an industry" may not be mortgaged except with the building in which they are located, and from this provision he concludes that chattels that are immovables by destination are not covered by a mortgage on the land in the absence of an express provision. Rojina Villegas (above, n. 2), pp. 49-50. It would seem, however, that the intent of art. 2898 § II is merely to prohibit a mortgage of such property independently of the mortgage on the building in which it is located.

8. Civil Code, art. 3002 lists all transactions susceptible of recordation but does not mention the mortgage of movable property.

9. *Ley de navegación y comercio marítimos*, 1963 (D.O., Nov. 21, 1963), arts. 121-26; *Ley de vías generales de comunicación*, 1940 (D.O., Feb. 19, 1940), arts. 362-66.

10. *Ley general de instituciones de crédito y organizaciones auxiliares*, 1941 (D.O., May 31, 1941), arts. 26 § X, 28 § VIII, 124.

11. The provisions of the Civil Code are contained in arts. 2856-92. See Rojina Villegas (above, n. 2), pp. 355-486. The commercial pledge is governed by *Ley general de títulos y operacions de crédito*, 1932 (D.O., Aug. 27, 1932), arts. 334-45, as amended (D.O., Aug. 31, 1933), hereafter in this chapter cited as credit instruments law.

12. Credit instruments law, art. 1.

13. Commercial Code, art. 358.

14. Credit instruments law, art. 334, provides in part, "In commercial matters, the pledge is constituted: I. By the delivery to the creditor of the goods. . . ." Thus, the theory of the law is that the delivery itself creates the pledge, and without delivery there can be no pledge.

15. *Banco Comercial Mexicano*, 11 *Boletín de Información Judicial* 671 (1956); *Oscar Torres*, 113 S.J.F. (5th) 943 (1952).

16. Credit instruments law, art. 334 § V.

17. Ibid., art. 335.

18. Ibid., art. 334 § IV.

19. Ibid., art. 334 §§ I-IV.

20. Ibid., art. 36.

21. *Ley sobre el contrato de seguro*, 1935 (D.O., Aug. 31, 1935), art. 109.

22. Ibid., art. 110.

23. Civil Code, art. 2880.

24. Credit instruments law, art. 338, as amended (D.O., Aug. 31, 1933), art. 12.

25. There is no usury statute in Mexico; however, art. 2395 of the Civil Code provides that the legal interest is 9 percent but permits the parties to agree to a higher or lower interest rate. It further provides that when the interest is so disproportionate that it gives good grounds for belief that there has been an abuse by reason of the pecuniary straits or the inexperience or ignorance of the borrower, the judge may make an equitable reduction to the legal rate.

26. Penal Code for the Federal District and Territories, art. 387 § VIII.

27. Credit instruments law, art. 343.

28. The various opinions are discussed in Roberto L. Mantilla Molina, *Derecho mercantil,* 11th ed. (Mexico, D.F.: Editorial Porrúa, 1970), p. 357.

29. *Ley general de sociedades mercantiles,* art. 198. See the discussion of shareholder voting agreements in Chapter VII, p. 236.

30. Credit instruments law, art. 344: "The pledge creditor may not become owner of the goods or instruments pledged without the express consent of the debtor, given in writing and after the constitution of the pledge." Civil Code, art. 2883: "The debtor . . . may agree with the creditor that the latter shall keep the pledged property at the price fixed for it upon the maturity of the debt, but not at the time the contract is executed. . . ."

31. Civil Code, arts. 2881, 2884.

32. *Ley general de instituciones de crédito* (above, n. 10), art. 111.

33. Credit instruments law, art. 341.

34. Ibid.

35. *Ley de quiebras y de suspensión de pagos,* 1942 (D.O., Apr. 20, 1943), art. 270, hereafter cited as bankruptcy law.

36. Ibid., art. 159 § VI (d). Under this provision the trustee in bankruptcy may, with judicial authorization, prevent the separation by paying the total amount of the debt secured by the pledge.

37. *Ley federal del trabajo,* 1969 (D.O., Apr. 1, 1970), art. 113; bankruptcy law, arts. 261, 262 § III.

38. Bankruptcy law, art. 159 § VI (d).

39. There are numerous decisions to this effect. One of the most recent is *Benita Gómez Vda. de Mancera,* 48 S.J.F. (6th) 178 (4th pt.) (1961). See also Rafael Rojina Villegas, *Compendio de derecho civil,* 4 vols. (Mexico, D.F.: Antigua Librería Robredo, 1962), 4:463.

40. These types of loan are provided for only in the commercial law, credit instruments law, arts. 321-333, and are not recognized in the civil law. There is no satisfactory English equivalent for *habilitación o avío,* though it is sometimes translated "equipment or operating credit."

41. Credit instruments law, art. 321.

42. Ibid., art. 322.

43. Ibid., art. 323.

44. Ibid., art. 324.

45. Ibid., art. 326 § II.

46. Ibid., art. 327.

47. Ibid., art. 330.

48. Ibid., art. 326 § IV.

49. Apart from art. 387 § XIV of the Penal Code for the Federal District and Territories, which imposes criminal sanctions on persons who "sell or transfer a business without authorization of the creditors thereof, or without the new acquirer's undertaking to respond for the debts, provided such debts are not paid."

50. Credit instruments law, art. 328.

51. Ibid.

52. Ibid., art. 333.

53. Ibid., art. 325.

54. Civil Code, art. 2926.

55. Civil Code, art. 2887. However, the debtor may agree to sell the pledged property to the creditor at a price established at the maturity of the debt but not at the time of execution of the contract. Civil Code, art. 2883.

56. Credit instruments law, art. 344.

57. One of the most recent cases to this effect is *Ignacia Hernández de Cortés*

Foreign Enterprise in Mexico

y coag., 55 S.J.F. (6th) 57 (4th pt.) (1962). The provisions on "simulation" are contained in Civil Code, arts. 2180-84.

58. A sale for the purpose of securing a debt was upheld in *Hermenegildo Moreno González*, 38 S.J.F. (6th) 177 (4th pt.) (1960), and again in *José López Sierra*, 16 *Boletín de Información Judicial* 735 (1961).

59. The original trust statute was the *Ley de bancos de fideicomiso*, 1926 (D.O., July 17, 1926). The provisions of the credit instruments law on the trust are contained in arts. 346-59. There are no provisions on trusts in the Civil Code. For a full treatment of the Mexican trust law see the excellent study by Rodolfo Batiza, *El fideicomiso: Teoría y práctica* (Mexico, D.F.: Librería de Manuel Porrúa, 1958).

60. *Ley general de instituciones de crédito* (above, n. 10), arts. 44-46, 135-38, governs the operations and duties of trust institutions.

61. Credit instruments law, art. 348, as amended by decree of Aug. 30, 1933 (D.O., Aug. 31, 1933).

62. See the section of Chapter III on Real Property, p. 118.

63. Credit instruments law, art. 352.

64. Ibid., art. 350; *Ley general de instituciones de crédito* (above, n. 10), art. 2, as amended by decree of Dec. 29, 1962 (D.O., Dec. 31, 1962).

65. Credit instruments law, arts. 353, 354.

66. *Mexicana de Fideicomisos, S.A.*, 103 S.J.F. (5th) 1768 (1950), is the leading case. The earlier attitude is reflected in *Financiera de Industria y Comercio, S.A. de C. V.*, 99 S.J.F. (5th) 1649 (1949) (dictum). The decisions are discussed in Rodolfo Batiza, "The Evolution of the Fideicomiso (Trust) Concept under Mexican Law," in *Mexico: A Symposium on Law and Government*, University of Miami School of Law, Interamerican Legal Studies, No. 3 (Coral Gables, Florida: University of Miami Press, 1958), pp. 71-74.

67. E.g., *Efraín Sosa García*, 108 S.J.F. (5th) 1328 (1951).

68. Civil Code, arts. 2310 (installment sale subject to rescission) and 2312 (title retention sale). Conditional sale contracts, as other types of contracts, may be commercial or civil in nature. However, the commercial law does not contain specific provisions on these contracts, and the Civil Code is therefore applicable under Commercial Code, art. 2. See Chapter I, p. 43. For a discussion of the conditional sale contract as used in retail installment sales, including the problem of classification as civil or commercial, see William D. Warren, "Mexican Retail Instalment Sales Law: A Comparative Study," 10 *UCLA Law Review* 15 (1962).

69. Civil Code, arts. 2310, 2312. *Reglamento del Registro Público de la Propiedad del Distrito Federal*, 1940 (DO., July 13, 1940), art. 70, provides that recordation of chattels in the public register shall contain model number, series, manufacturer's number, type, manufacturer's name, motor number, and any other marks that serve to identify them in an "indubitable manner."

70. Civil Code, arts. 2310 § III, 2312.

71. *Código de procedimientos civiles para el distrito y territorios federales*, 1932 (D.O., Sept. 1-21, 1932), arts. 430 § XII, 465-67.

72. Civil Code, art. 2311; *Código de procedimientos civiles* (above, n. 71), arts. 465, 466.

73. *Código de procedimientos civiles* (above, n. 71), arts. 465, 466.

74. E.g., *Cooperativa de Auto Transportes "Díaz Ordaz," S.C.L.*, 45 S.J.F. (6th) 15 (4th pt.) (1961). See Civil Code, art. 2311. For older cases, see *Luis Ramón*, 100 S.J.F. (5th) 1061 (1949); *Cooperativa Industrial Carbonífera "La Conquista," S.C.L.*, 7 S.J.F. (6th) 106 (4th pt.) (1958); *Ignacio Navarro Padilla*, 21 S.J.F. (6th) 63 (4th pt.) (1959).

75. Civil Code, art. 1840: "The contracting parties may stipulate a certain payment as a penalty in the event the obligation is not fulfilled or is not fulfilled in the manner agreed."

76. Bankruptcy law, arts. 159 § I & § IV, 161.

77. *Ley federal del trabajo* (above, n. 37), arts. 830-35; *Código fiscal de la federación*, 1966 (D.O., Jan. 19, 1967), art. 111. See also Rafael Rojina Villegas, *Derecho civil mexicano*, 3d ed. (Mexico, D.F.: Antigua Librería Robredo, 1961), pp. 437-38.

78. *Compañía de Terrenos Algarín, S.A.*, 74 S.J.F. (5th) 226 (1942) (land taxes); *Abelardo García Arce*, 115 S.J.F. (5th) 25 (1953) (automobile).

79. Civil Code, art. 2315.

80. Civil Code, art. 2468.

81. See Civil Code, arts. 2412 § IV (lessor's warranty of peaceful use and enjoyment), 2283 § III (seller's warranty against eviction), 2144-49 (buyer's right to rescind for hidden defects), 2421 (lessee's right to rescind for hidden defects).

82. *Miguel Zaldívar*, 117 S.J.F. (5th) 1059 (1953); see also *Impulsora Automotriz, S.A.*, 109 S.J.F. (5th) 1695 (1951); *Rómulo Orozco*, 98 S.J.F. (5th) 193 (1948).

83. *Carlos Vales Cámara*, 38 S.J.F. (6th) 69 (4th pt.) (1960).

84. *Fraccionadora Morelense, S.A.*, 40 S.J.F. (6th) 92 (4th pt.) (1960).

85. Civil Code, arts. 1833, 2232.

86. *La Compañía de Terrenos Mexicanos, S.A.*, 43 S.J.F. (5th) 3462 (1953). These cases appear to be incorrectly decided. If there has been partial performance of a contract defective in form, the defect is considered cured under Civil Code, art. 2234. The Supreme Court recognized this in *Compañía de Terrenos Mexicanos*, 114 S.J.F. (5th) 332 (1952).

87. Civil Code, arts. 2243-47, govern the precontract or preparatory contract. Civil Code, arts. 2248-2326, cover the contract of sale.

88. *Código de procedimientos civiles* (above, n. 71), art. 517 § III.

89. This rule is contained in the following theses of binding jurisprudence: Thesis 244 of the 1954 appendix to the *Seminario Judicial de la Federación*, which appeared as thesis 241 of the appendix to vol. 97 of the S.J.F.; thesis 1121 of the 1954 appendix, which repeats thesis 1113 of the appendix to vol. 97; and thesis 599 of the 1955-1963 appendix. For a recent case confirming the continued vigor of this rule, see *Delfina Guadarrama*, 48 S.J.F. (6th) 120 (4th pt.) (1961).

90. This explanation was given in *Reynaldo Cantú*, 6 *Boletín de Información Judicial* 123 (thesis 558) (1950).

CHAPTER XI

1. *Ley de la propiedad industrial*, 1942 (D.O., Dec. 31, 1942), as amended by decree of Dec. 29, 1949 (D.O., Dec. 31, 1949), decree of Dec. 31, 1953 (D.O., Jan. 6, 1954), and decree of Nov. 21, 1966 (D.O., Dec. 16, 1966), hereinafter in this chapter cited as industrial property law; *Reglamento de la ley de la propiedad industrial*, 1942 (D.O., Dec. 31, 1942), hereinafter cited as regulations to industrial property law.

2. Industrial property law, arts. 4-6.

3. The problem of chemical products is discussed in César Sepúlveda, *El sistema mexicano de propiedad industrial* (Mexico, D.F.: Impresiones Modernas, 1955), pp. 28-34.

4. Industrial property law, arts. 11, 12.

5. Ibid., art. 13 § I, § III; regulations to industrial property law, art. 54.

6. Industrial property law, art. 93.

7. Ibid., arts. 75-83; regulations to industrial property law, arts. 61-62. An extraordinary examination may also be requested to determine if an invention has been patented in Mexico, either for the purpose of determining if its exploitation would invade existing patent rights or to determine if it is patentable as a new invention.

8. Industrial property law, arts. 13 § IV, 39.

9. Ibid., art. 13 § II.

10. Applications are covered by industrial property law, arts. 14-37, and regulations to industrial property law, arts. 1-54. Fees are established in the *Decreto que establece la tarifa para el cobro de derechos relativos a la propiedad industrial,* 1961 (D.O., Feb. 9, 1962).

11. A patent issued on more than one invention is void. Industrial property law, art. 93 § IV.

12. Patent terms and fees are covered by industrial property law, arts. 38-52.

13. Ibid., art. 7.

14. Ibid., art. 8.

15. Infringement of patents is covered by arts. 84-92, administrative procedure by arts. 229-35, and criminal penalties and civil damage liability by arts. 240-50 of the industrial property law. Under certain circumstances the owner of an infringed patent may have the infringing products and instruments impounded and the use of patented processes restrained pending final judgment.

16. Industrial property law, arts. 53-71.

17. Assignments are covered by industrial property law, arts. 72-74, and regulations to industrial property law, arts. 55-60.

18. Industrial property law, arts. 96, 97. Penalties are provided for in arts. 251-54, 259-60.

19. Ibid., art. 105.

20. Art. 6 sexies of the Paris Union Convention, as revised in Lisbon, provides that Union countries undertake to protect service marks but expressly does not require them to provide for their registration.

21. Registration applications, terms, renewals, and fees are covered by industrial property law, arts. 113-39.

22. The *amparo* suit is discussed in Chapter I, p. 28.

23. Industrial property law, arts. 156-57, 171, 204.

24. Ibid., arts. 206-8, 229-35.

25. The leading case is *Isaías Broussi,* amp. en rev. no. 49/59, involving the trademark "McGREGOR," discussed and quoted from at length in Salvador González Alfaro, *El uso de las marcas* (Thesis for Licenciado en Derecho, Universidad Nacional Autónoma de México, 1963), pp. 56-58, 60-65. This interpretation is criticized in César Sepúlveda, "Peculiaridades de las licencias de uso de marcas en el derecho mexicano," 42 *Boletín del Instituto de Derecho Comparado* 640 (1961). For a subsequent administrative resolution following the Court's decision, see Resolution No. 153 of Jan. 2, 1961, *Gaceta de la Propiedad Industrial,* Jan. 1961, pp. 48, 57.

26. Industrial property law, arts. 98, 155.

27. The decrees are collected in Manuel Andrade, comp., *Legislación e impuestos sobre propiedad industrial* (Mexico, D.F.: Ediciones Andrade, loose-leaf), pp. 143 to 152-6-3.

28. Use of trademarks is covered by industrial property law, arts. 140-57.

29. Ibid., arts. 105 § XIV (c), 128.

30. Ibid., arts. 200 § V, 201 § VI.

31. Ibid., arts. 105 § XIV, 106.

32. See César Sepúlveda, *A Monography on the So-Called Famous or Well-*

Known Trademarks, trans. Louis G. Kaufer (Mexico, D.F., no date), p. 21, citing the denial of "LUCKY STRIKE" for perfumes, "DUNHILL" for perfumes, "YARDLEY" for shoes, "FRAM" for automobile parts, "EVERSHARP" for cigarette lighters, and others.

33. The leading case involved the trademark "IPANA," in which cancellation of an identical registration covering chewing gum was granted by the bureau and upheld by the Supreme Court. *Gaceta de la Propiedad Industrial,* Feb. 1943, pp. 143-44. For similar decisions see ibid., Mar. 1948, pp. 293-94 ("EVER-SHARP"); ibid., Jan. 1944, pp. 154-55 ("GE"); ibid., Jan. 1955, pp. 149-50 ("REVLON"). These and other cases are discussed in Sepúlveda (above, n. 32), pp. 22-27.

34. Industrial property law, arts. 99, 100, 200 § II, § III.

35. Ibid., arts. 255-57.

36. Ibid., art. 163.

37. Ibid., arts. 265-68.

38. For licensee user requirements, see ibid., arts. 158-67.

39. Ibid., arts. 172-83.

40. Ibid., arts. 209-13.

41. Ibid., arts. 214-28.

42. The income tax and commercial receipts tax are discussed in Chapter VIII.

43. The law for the promotion of new and necessary industries is discussed in Chapter V under Tax Exemptions, p. 181.

Index